Covenant & Commonwealth

DANIEL J. ELAZAR

Covenant & Commonwealth

From Christian Separation through the Protestant Reformation
The Covenant Tradition in Politics
Volume II

Transaction Publishers
New Brunswick (U.S.A.) and London (U.K.)

Preparation of this book for publication was made possible through the Milken Library of Jewish Public Affairs, funded by the Foundations of the Milken Families.

Library of Congress Catalog Number: 95-18560
ISBN: 1-56000-208-5
Printed in the United States of America

Library of Congress Cataloging-in-Publication Data

Elazar, Daniel Judah.
    Covenant and commonwealth : Europe from Christian separation through the Protestant Reformation / Daniel J. Elazar.
        p. cm. — (The covenant tradition in politics ; v. 2)
    Includes bibliographical references and index.
    ISBN 1-56000-208-5
    1. Covenants—Religious aspects—Christianity—History of doctrines. I. Title. II. Series: Elazar, Daniel Judah. Covenant tradition in politics ; v. 2.
BL65.P7E43   1995
[BT155]
320'.01'1 s—dc20   95-18560
                                                                      CIP

For Gilad, on his first birthday

Contents

Part III—Reformation Federalism

Preface

This book is the second in a series of volumes exploring the covenantal tradition in Western politics. The first, *Covenant and Polity in Biblical Israel,* consisted of an in-depth, if necessarily selective, exploration of the biblical sources of the covenant tradition, its development in Scripture, and subsequently in Jewish history and thought. It dealt with the biblical idea of covenant as it appeared on the world scene and the political culture, tradition, and behavior to which it gave birth. It analyzed how the Bible set forth the idea of covenant within the context of ancient Israel and in the Jewish political tradition that emerged from the Bible.

This book takes those themes a step further to examine covenant as a political idea and its related political tradition with the culture and behavior that they produced, to focus on the struggle in Europe to produce a Christian covenantal commonwealth constituted on a similar religious basis that reached its climax in the Reformed Protestantism of the Protestant Reformation in the sixteenth and seventeenth centuries. This Christian adaptation of the biblical tradition, the integration of that adaptation with the traditions of the tribal oath societies of Northern Europe, the perforce limited medieval expressions of that synthesis, and the revival of covenant as the architectonic principle of the Protestant Reformation is an intricate and fascinating story. The book also briefly examines covenant and hierarchy in Islam and other premodern polities.

The third and fourth volumes, *Covenant and Constitution: The Great Frontier and the Matrix of Federal Democracy* and *Covenant and Civil Society: The Constitutional Matrix of Modern Democracy,* will examine the progressive secularization of the covenant idea in the seventeenth and eighteenth centuries and its application through principles of constitutionalism and federalism to both the building of new societies in the New World and the efforts to reconstitute old societies in Europe, and will conclude with a general analysis of the dynamics of covenant and the possible future role of the covenant tradition in the postmodern world.

The four books, despite their combined scope, cannot trace all the human connections that show the transmission of covenant ideas and ways. Consequently, they seek to highlight those critical elements that shaped history and civilization, particularly in the Western world. In a sense it is also a history of, first, the *westering* (an American pioneer term for moving westward until the frontier) of covenant from West Asia to the Pacific Ocean, and then its universalization in the politics of constitutional democratic republicanism.

Ideally, it is the aim of these books not only to trace the interconnections between ideas, culture, and behavior, but between peoples and generations as well, to follow the path of the covenant idea and covenantal cultures and behavior in time and space. This is a daunting task, requiring dozens of monographic studies not yet undertaken, and probably can never be done because of the great gaps in the historical data available. For example, in the history of ancient Southwest Asia and adjacent regions, by far the most substantial record we have is the Bible, much of which is not corroborated by any other source in regard to the matters under discussion here.

The scriptural account, while full of fascinating behavioral details that give us great insight into covenantal ideas, culture, and behavior, useful in fostering our understanding of other covenantal situations in other times and climes, is not comprehensive history, but rather a series of moral case studies designed for purposes other than illustrating the issues under consideration here. We also can benefit from the documents from other ancient West Asian civilizations discovered since the last century.[1] In recent years archeologists have discovered records from various ancient Southwest Asian archives that testify to the existence of vassal treaties in one form or another and modified covenantal elements among peoples adjacent to ancient Israel, but the only record we have of a fully covenantal civilization is that of ancient Israel as portrayed in Scripture.

The European history of the West in the more conventional sense begins with the Greeks, more or less at the time the First Jewish Commonwealth was destroyed in the fifth and sixth centuries B.C.E. Greek histories focus on heroic actions and events. They gave us the political and military histories of the Greek Leagues, the most important of which were in Asia Minor, also a part of Southwest Asia—a point often ignored or forgotten. But again, their purpose is not to trace connections. There, too, we have only those limited written records. Documentation is lacking and not likely to be found. Not only that, but the survival of Greek philosophic works, which are emphatically noncovenantal, has strongly influenced and distorted our understanding of Greek political life.[2]

There is a greater variety of sources from the Hellenistic and Roman periods, where a particular brand of political compacting was developed. Careful study of those materials in light of the prior Greek and biblical sources helps to reveal which cultures were more covenantally oriented and which were not, and helps us begin to trace the macro connections; but we are still at a loss when it comes to the micro connections. We can continue that macro kind of tracing through medieval Europe. The situation improves considerably with the coming of the Renaissance and the Reformation, which created more awareness of issues of ideas, culture, and behavior. Indeed, this was one of their great contributions to the forging of the modern epoch. They also opened an era of better and more comprehensive record keeping. Indeed, it can be said that those two great historical events brought a sea change to historiography, for the first time making it possible to trace historical connections in a more comprehensive manner.

This book seeks to identify the emergence of the covenantal idea of commonwealth out of the biblical religious tradition in Christian Europe. Christendom was a recognized phenomenon throughout most of the period and covenant and its political manifestations were used by the Reformed Protestant federalists in an effort to transform it into what were then political as well as theological terms. Those who began with theology developed a theo-political doctrine of resistance to tyranny and brought the whole to a climax in the English Civil War and, in the sixteenth and first half of the seventeenth centuries, in a striving for political commonwealth based on covenantal forms among those peoples and countries where covenant found its major expression. The pursuit of commonwealth was integrally linked to their federal theology, through which covenant was to inform every aspect of a religiously grounded and politically integrated polity in which individuals would find self-expression through an elemental common unity.

It was a moment of struggle and glory that failed as Europe underwent a radical change in practically every respect. Politically, its major residue was the Protestant federalist effort that would be transformed by modernity into constitutionalism and federalism. In the process of seeking appropriate modern uses for that Reformation heritage, the very political concepts of Reform Protestantism were relegated to history or to the constricted realm of the historian. It was not that the modern world was unaware of Reformed Protestantism and its contribution, but they lost their understanding of its covenantal character in their pursuit of other lines of thought. This in turn served to block attempts to reconstruct that covenantal character and the relationship of covenant to the pursuit of the idea of commonwealth, which in time became the idea of modern constitutional democratic republicanism.

From that point on, the problem is increasingly one of information overload, replacing the fragmented nature of available information in earlier epochs. So, for example, we can trace lines of intellectual influence in the Reformation—that is to say, who studied with whom and where—a very important addition to understanding the flow of ideas and even culture, but more limited on the behavioral side. It has been too easy for historians to treat the great chain of thought as if it were equally a chain of action. That is a pitfall that must be avoided.

Thus, for example, the seventeenth-century European political philosophers were given much more credit for shaping the British colonies in North America and subsequently the United States of America, than they deserved. We now know that, having explored the less philosophically glitzy manifestations of Reformed Protestant (especially Puritan) patterns of thought and behavior as manifested in British North America, most especially as a result of the Puritan Great Awakening in England of 1610 to 1640. The recovery of the true character of that line of development over the last forty years or so has not only much enriched our understanding of American beginnings, but has also demonstrated what it is possible to do when the records are available for study. But what has been done for American history has not been done for any other.[3]

Covenant theory and practice entered Europe through religious conflict and political stealth. It took Europeans until the very last generations of the Middle Ages—nearly three millennia after European civilization emerged as an articulated reality—to achieve the covenanted commonwealth in theory and practice, even in Europe's most advanced parts. Prior to that, some Europeans knew the theory of covenant and still others had practices that were essentially covenantal, but there was little or no linkage between the two. The separation of theory and practice was a notable dimension of medieval life for 1200 years, no doubt stimulated by the utopian or messianic theories of

Christianity and the all-too-real cruel and authoritarian practices of so much of medieval Europe.

Theory and practice were successfully if unintentionally separated at the very beginning of the Middle Ages, seemingly in every sphere. Even as new theories or original developments of old theories came to project a world overflowing with Christian justice, new hierarchies, civil and religious, were gaining power and ruling in as forceful a manner as they could, modified only by the stronger force of circumstances. Fortunately, the latter was strong throughout much of Europe and very strong in some places, so covenantal systems survived in practice as well as theory throughout the period, sometimes in ways even counter to the theories, as for example in Scandinavia, or at the very least, through modifications of them as in the Swiss republics. To some extent these eventually led to new theories, perhaps built upon older ones, perhaps not. They, in turn, ultimately led to the Protestant Reformation and Reformed Protestantism that brought with it a new emphasis on covenanted commonwealths, both in theory and practice.

In a sense, one can view medieval Europe as the successive emergence of feudal hierarchies, organic urban corporations, and finally covenanted commonwealths, almost repeating the phenomenon described in the Bible as a movement from hierarchy to covenant. The imperial Romans introduced hierarchy wherever they trod, but Christianity, following in the Roman wake, brought with it a measure of covenantalism, even though it had been considerably transformed from its Hebrew origins under the impact of the early Church. In a sense, this was a repetition of the biblical record of human history from Adam to Noah—hierarchical, but with a hierarchically inspired covenantal intervention.

The combination of necessity and the human drive for greater freedom and self-government led to the emergence of medieval corporations within feudal hierarchical systems. In the course of time, the network of medieval corporations—from Italian cities where civic republicanism flourished to the guilds and the guild-based cities of German-speaking Europe, to the various religious-based corporations within Christendom or without—became the dominant phenomena of medieval Europe, the cutting edge for ideas and technological, social, economic, and political progress. While these medieval corporations were usually based on some combination of contractual and organic relationships, they offered a means whereby covenantal ideas could enter, if only through the back door. The institutions and behavior they produced often reflected dimensions that approximated those of covenantal systems.

Covenantalism never entirely disappeared from Europe, surviving not only as an undercurrent in medieval corporatism or on the peripheries of European Christendom in the oath societies of Scandinavia, but also as a minor note within the Church itself, in the monastic orders as distinct from the Roman hierarchy. Indeed, in the early Middle Ages the two were even competitive as to who would gain dominance in the Church. It appears there were also pockets of covenantal cultural survival scattered throughout Europe—in the chain of mountains running from the Pyrenees through the Alps and on into the Carpathians, dividing Europe north and south, where peoples seeking to be free fled from the tyrannies of feudalism along borderlands where different cultures clashed and had of necessity to find means of cohabitation, in the piedmont areas of the Iberian peninsula, and among the Alemannian Germans on a more mixed basis. Periodically throughout the Middle Ages these covenantal pockets manifested themselves in history and politics. Thus Andorra in the Pyrenees and the Helvetic Confederation in the Alps both date back to the thirteenth century; Iceland dates back even earlier, to the tenth century. Other less formal manifestations punctuated those in other centuries.

The Reformation burst on Europe in the sixteenth century, in the wake of the failure of the Conciliar movement within the Catholic Church, in a movement of covenantal renewal and swept forward, not only adapting to the cultures among the peoples it reached, but spreading beyond. Those groups in the Reformation that emerged out of covenantal backgrounds moved their covenantalism from being a matter of political culture, with appropriate accompanying institutions and behavior, into the realm of ideas, developing extensive theologies and related political theories of covenant and transforming those into ideologies accessible to larger publics. Backed by these, their institutions became more comprehensive and gained theological justification, the most potent kind at that time. Larger covenantal commonwealths emerged, mostly along the same geographic and cultural fault lines that had preserved covenantalism throughout the long years of relative darkness.

The religious covenants of Reformed Protestantism gave birth to covenanted commonwealths, the political expressions of those ideas, from Switzerland to Scotland and then in British North America and Puritan England. These commonwealths preserved the old medieval unities of religion, state, and society, but in a new republican ideational, institutional, and behavioral framework. Their lives were to be relatively brief as they encountered the new ideas of modernity, but enormously important in fertilizing modern philosophy, political society, and politics.

Great transformations rest on great ideas, great movements, and great actions, and occur when all three come together. Thus, at the very beginning of the history of covenant there was the great idea of biblical covenantal monotheism whereby humans were envisaged as entering into a morally grounded and informal pact with God, out of which came the people Israel formed through the Exodus from Egypt and the Sinai experience. In the sixteenth century, through the Protestant Reformation, a new theology of covenant gave rise to Reformed Protestantism and the theo-political transformation that followed in countries such as Switzerland, the Netherlands, Scotland, and England.

What a combination of covenant theology, religious reformation, and local or national political transformation did for the sixteenth century, a revolution in political philosophy and a series of more or less radical movements culminating in the British Isles and British North America as Whiggism, which led to the Glorious Revolution of 1688-89 and the formation of the American colonies as they were during that same period across the Atlantic, did the same for the seventeenth century. In the eighteenth century the great wave of ideas derived from the Enlightenment brought about the two great revolutions of the modern epoch—the American and the French—and the invention of Federalist and Jacobin democracy, modern constitutionalism, the United States of America, and modern democratic republicanism on both sides of the ocean.

*   *   *

Sometime during the period when I was completing high school and beginning university I discovered the covenantal basis of Judaism and the Jewish people, perhaps the best kept secret of my otherwise rather good Jewish education. During the next several years, my university studies of history brought me face to face with the covenantal basis of Reformed Protestant Christianity and its derivation from the same biblical tradition. It was also at that time that my study of American government led me to understand how the American polity was founded on that Reformed Protestant covenantal tradition in its Puritan expression and in its secularized Lockean form.

By the end of the 1950s, the convergence of these various lines of exploration brought me to a recognition that covenant was a truly seminal concept in Western civilization and stimulated me to begin what has been a decades-long exploration of the covenant tradition in the Western world, especially in its political dimensions. In the interim I have published several books and numerous articles on the subject, have organized two continuing research workshops, in Israel and the United States, and quite a few conferences and seminars in both countries to further the exploration and to learn from others, as I have, to my immense benefit. After two decades of systematic exploration I felt the need for a more comprehensive study of the covenant tradition in Western politics than any I had found.

While I felt, and still feel, inadequate to the task, a decade ago I resolved to begin it. This work is the result. After devoting so many years to it I feel no less inadequate with the product in hand. I am confident that a better scholar could have produced a better result, and that my poor effort is unworthy of the subject it treats. Nevertheless, I submit it to the reading public for what it is.

It goes without saying that the end product is entirely my own. At the same time I wish to express my gratitude to all those who assisted me in this project. My initial education came from a group of Jewish scholar-theologians whose work in the 1950s restored covenant to its rightful place in Jewish thought: Eugene B. Borowitz, Monford Harris, Jacob J. Petuchovoski and Arnold Jacob Wolf. While I learned from them initially through their writings, all of them subsequently became friends as well as teachers.

I was not so privileged with regard to Andrew J. McLaughlin, whose writings introduced me to the connections between the covenant tradition and the American founding. While I did study at the University of Chicago, the institution at which he taught for so many years, I did so many years after he had passed on. Nevertheless, I consider him my premier mentor in this sphere. Later I discovered that I was indeed following in his tradition of political science, and am pleased to acknowledge that fact, since by now I am convinced that our common rootedness in the covenantal view of politics makes that so.

I am equally grateful to my good friend Harold Fisch, whose writings brought me to see from whence emerged these two great expressions of covenant. Professor Fisch also was of great assistance through the Kotler Institute for Judaism and Contemporary Thought, which he founded at Bar-Ilan and which he put at my disposal for the organization of an initial conference on the subject.

As my exploration into covenant expanded, the inadequacy of my knowledge became increasingly apparent to me. In an effort to overcome those inadequacies I organized the Workshop in the Covenant Idea and the Jewish Political Tradition at Bar-Ilan University in 1975 through the Senator N.M. Paterson Chair in Intergovernmental Relations in the Department of Political Studies and the Center for Jewish Community Studies, which is now part of the Jerusalem Center for Public Affairs. Funding for that Workshop came principally from Bar-Ilan University sources, for which I am duly grateful, and from funds provided by the President of the University, Professor Emanuel Rackman, who was also a participant in the Workshop. I owe a special debt to Meir Kassirer, coordinator of the Workshop, who has been of great assistance over the years and whom I count among my friends.

I am indebted to all my colleagues who participated in and contributed to these workshops, most especially Ella Belfer, Lawrence V. Berman, Gerald Blidstein, Gershon Cohen, Stuart A. Cohen, Yoel Cohen, Eliezer Don-Yehiya, Menachem Elon, Harold Fisch, Gordon M. Freeman, Mark Galanter, Ruth Gil, Shlomo Dov Goitein, Steven Goldstein, Moshe Greenberg, Ilan Greilsammer, David Hartman, Yosef Lanier, Sam Lehman-Wilzig, Charles S. Liebman, Leah Bornstein Makovsky, Peter Y. Medding, Avraham Melamed, Meir Nitzan, Emanuel Rackman, Yaakov Reuveny, Neal Riemer, Yechiel Rosen, Pinchas Rosenblit, Mordechai Rotenberg, Shmuel Sandler, Eliezer Schweid, Dan V. Segre, Martin Sicker, Bernard Susser, Moshe Weinfeld, and Aaron Wildavsky

A year later I organized a similar workshop in covenant and politics through the Center for the Study of Federalism at Temple University in the United States. That workshop received its principal support from the National Endowment for the Humanities and also from the United Church of Christ. It brought together several dozen leading scholars in the United States and abroad and had over 200 corresponding scholars on its list. I owe much to the participants in workshop meetings and conferences, particularly to my close colleague and friend Vincent

Ostrom, who built a bridge between my historically oriented investigations and the more rigorous methodologies of contemporary political theory. Other scholars to whom I owe a debt of gratitude include J. Wayne Baker, James D. Bratt, Harold Fisch, Gordon M. Freeman, Vernon L. Greene, J. David Greenstone, Charles Hyneman, John Kincaid, Donald S. Lutz, Alexandre Marc, Charles S. McCoy, Stuart D. McLean, John Peacock, W. Stanford Reid, Neil Reimer, Rozann Rothman, Filippo Sabetti, Stephen L. Schechter, Mary Lyndon Shanley, Rowland A. Sherrill, James W. Skillen, John F.A. Taylor, and James B. Torrance.

The Fellows of the Center for the Study of Federalism were also very helpful in this effort, as in all my others of similar character: John Kincaid, first my student, then my colleague and always my friend, undertook responsibility first as coordinator and then as co-director of the Philadelphia Covenant Workshop. The workshop brought me into contact with Donald Lutz, who has taught me so much about the American experience. Stephen L. Schechter and Ellis Katz were active members of the workshop inner circle, while Benjamin Schuster, program director of the center at the initial stages of the work, was of invaluable assistance.

My seemingly interminable effort to produce this book has been supported from the beginning by the Earhart Foundation of Ann Arbor, Michigan. I owe them an immeasurable debt of gratitude for enabling me to carry on this work, which has brought me in contact with civilizations and new societies across the length and breadth of the globe and the ideas and actions spawned within them. I am especially grateful to the foundation's former president, Richard Ware; its current president, David Kennedy; and its secretary and director of program, Dr. Antony Sullivan.

In the course of my work I have been assisted by a string of excellent research assistants in Israel, including Ruth Gil, Ellen Friedlander, Kirk Preuss, and Rina Edelstein; and in the United States, including Alexis Samryk, Gail Charette, Joseph Marbach, Rasheeda Didi, Steven D'Agguano, and Paul Neal.

Special thanks are due to Clara Feldman, who shared responsibility for the functioning of the Bar-Ilan Workshop, and Sarah Mayer, who worked with me for several years on this project and stimulated me enormously. Mark Ami-El has done yeoman work in making the manuscript of this book ready for publication.

A project of the magnitude of this one requires considerable support from many sources, but no support is more extensive or more critical than that provided by one's own family. My wife Harriet and my children were everything that one could possibly expect in this connection and even more, making it possible for me to live and work in a way most conducive to beginning this undertaking, staying with it, and finally bringing it to a proper conclusion. My love for them is inexpressible as is my gratitude.

Daniel J. Elazar,
Jerusalem
Tammuz 5754—June 1994

Notes

1. Chaim I. Bermant, *Ebla: A Revelation in Archaeology* (New York: Times Books, 1979); Herbert B. Huffmon, "Prophecy in the Mari Latters," and Anson F. Rainey, "The Kingdom of Ugarit," in Edward F. Campbell, Jr. and David Noel Friedman, eds., *The Biblical Archaeologist Reader,* vol. 3 (New York: Doubleday, 1970); Harry M. Orlinsky, *Understanding the Bible Through History and Archaeology* (New York: Ktav, 1972).
2. Leo Strauss and Joseph Cropsey, eds., *History of Political Philosophy* (Chicago: University of Chicago Press, 1987).
3. Andrew McLaughlin, *The Foundations of American Constitutionalism* (Greenwich, Conn.: Fawcett, 1961); Perry Miller, ed., *The American Puritans* (New York: Doubleday Anchor Books, 1956), and *The New England Mind: The Seventeenth Century* (Cambridge: Harvard University Press, 1963); Donald Lutz, "From Covenant to Constitution," *Publius* 10, no. 4 (Fall 1980), and "The Theory of Consent in the Early State Constitutions," *Publius* 9, no. 2 (Spring 1979).

Introduction:
Covenant and the Three Separations

I

No one seriously immersed in the Jewish and Christian traditions has escaped the theological impact of the covenant idea. Covenant was once the subject of so many theological treatises that at times it seems as if there is little new to be said about it. On the other hand, covenant is less a theological concept than a theo-political one. The word itself is used so frequently in the English language that it has become a mere commonplace term; if not quite like freedom and democracy, then certainly like republic and constitution. Even so, far too little has been written about covenant as a factor in political affairs.

Politically, a covenant involves a coming together (con-gregation) of basically equal humans who consent with one another through a morally binding pact supported by a transcendent power, establishing with the partners a new framework or setting them on the road to a new task, and which can be dissolved only by mutual agreement of all the parties to it.

Covenant, Compact, and Contract

Covenant is tied in an ambiguous relationship to two related terms, compact and contract. On one hand, both compacts and contracts are related to, and even may be derived from, covenant, and sometimes the terms are even used interchangeably. On the other hand, there are very real differences between the three that need clarification.

Both *covenants* and *compacts* differ from *contracts* in that the first two are constitutional or public, and the last private in character. As such, covenantal or compactual obligation is broadly reciprocal. Those bound by one or the other are obligated to respond to each other beyond the letter of the law rather than to limit their obligations to the narrowest contractual requirements. Hence, covenants and compacts are inherently designed to be flexible in certain respects as well as firm in others. As expressions of private law, contracts tend to be interpreted as narrowly as possible so as to limit the obligation of the contracting parties to what is explicitly mandated by the contract itself. Contracts normally contain provisions for unilateral abrogation by one party or another under certain conditions (and with penalties where appropriate); compacts and covenants generally require mutual consent to be abrogated, designed as they are to be perpetual or of unlimited duration.

A covenant differs from a compact in that its morally binding dimension takes precedence over its legal dimension. In its heart of hearts, a covenant is an agreement in which a higher moral force, traditionally God, is either a direct party to, or guarantor of, the particular relationship. Whereas, when the term *compact* is used, moral force is only indirectly involved. A compact, based as it is on mutual pledges rather than guarantees by or before a higher authority, rests more heavily on a legal though still ethical grounding for its politics. In other words, compact is a secular phenomenon.

This is historically verifiable by examining the shift in terminology that took place in the seventeenth and eighteenth centuries, reaching a climax in the American and French revolutions and their respective aftermaths. In the United States, the terms *covenant* and *compact* were used almost interchangeably until after 1791. In the British North American colonies the accepted term in the seventeenth century was *covenant*. Compact was introduced in the mid-eighteenth century as part of the spread of Enlightenment secular thought during the Revolutionary era. Those who saw the hand of God in political affairs in the United States continued to use the term *covenant,* while those who sought a secular grounding for politics turned to the term *compact*. While the distinction is not always used with strict clarity, it does appear consistently.[1]

The issue was further complicated by Rousseau and his followers, who talk about the social contract, a highly secularized concept, which, even when applied for public purposes, never develops the same level of moral obligation as either covenant or compact. The Rousseaunian formulation had limited popularity in the United States but became the dominant terminology in revolutionary France, although it did share the field with the other two terms, particularly compact, especially in the early years of the Revolution. With the triumph of Jacobin ideas, which themselves are an outgrowth of Rousseaunian thought, the term *contrat social* swept the field.[2]

Covenant, then, is the oldest of several terms that deal with the formation of the political order through consent as manifested in a pact or an appropriate level of mutual binding. In the following chapter we will examine this idea of pact and consent in light of the other theories of political order.

The covenants of the Bible are the founding covenants of Western civilization. Perforce, they have to do with God. They have their beginnings in the need to establish clear and binding relationships between God and humans and among humans, relationships which must be understood as being political far more than theological in character, designed to establish lines of authority, distributions of power, bodies politic, and systems of law. It is indeed the genius of the idea and its biblical source that it seeks to both legitimize political life and to direct it into the right paths; to use theo-political relationships to build a bridge between heaven and earth—and there is nothing more earthly than politics even in its highest form—without letting either swallow up the other.

The covenant idea has within it the seeds of modern constitutionalism in that it emphasizes the mutually accepted limitations on the power of all parties to it, a limitation not inherent in nature but involving willed concessions. This idea of limiting power is, as the Puritans discussed in this book well understood, of first importance in the biblical worldview and for humanity as a whole since it helps explain why an omnipotent God does not exercise His omnipotence in the affairs of humans. In covenanting with humans, God at least partially withdraws from controlling their lives. He offers humans freedom under the terms of the covenant, retaining the covenantal authority to reward or punish the consequences of that freedom at some future date. By the same token, the humans who bind themselves through the covenant accept its limits in Puritan terms, abandoning natural for federal liberty—to live up to the terms of their covenants. Beyond that, the leaders of the people are limited in their governmental powers to serving the people under the terms of the covenant. Thus, the idea of constitutional or limited government is derived from the idea of covenant.

Covenant as a theo-political concept is characterized by a very strong measure of realism. This recognition of the need to limit the exercise of power is one example of this realism. It also recognizes the distinction between those who are bound by the covenant and those who are not. At the same time it makes provisions for appropriate linkages between those so bound and others, granted of a different order, but designed to keep the peace in the world in the face of the realities of conflicting human interests, needs, and demands. In this book we are concerned with the political use of the idea of covenant, the tradition that has adhered to that idea, and the political arrangements that flow from it.

In more secular terms, the task of politics is not simply to construct civil societies compatible with human nature, but to help people make the most of their potential by creating conditions and opportunities for leading the best possible lives. As Aristotle observed: people form political associations, not only to maintain life, but to achieve the good life.

II

Politics has two faces. One is the face of *power*; the other is the face of *justice*. Politics, as the pursuit and organization of power, is concerned (in the words of Harold Lasswell) with "who gets what, when and how." However, politics is equally a matter of justice, or the determination of who *should* get what, when, and how—and why. Power is the means by which people organize themselves and shape their environment in order to live. Justice offers the guidelines for using power in order to live well.

Politics cannot be understood without reference to both faces. Without understanding a polity's conception of justice, or who should have power, one cannot understand clearly why certain people or groups get certain rewards, at certain times, in certain ways. On the other hand, one cannot focus properly on the pursuit of justice without also understanding the realities of the distribution of power. Both elements are present in all political questions, mutually influencing each other.

The need to pursue justice through a politics set on the right path is as real in a secular age as in a religious one. The true essence of *realpolitik* is the understanding that just as politics cannot avoid the realities of human relationships and power, it cannot be detached from the pursuit of justice and the paths of morality either. Machiavellian methods are effective only in the short run simply because in the long run, everyone involved in political affairs comes to understand the use of those methods. Those who cannot use them leave the political arena, turning it over to those who can, who then proceed to transform that arena into a jungle, in which every man's hand is raised against every other man's as each tries to use the political methods that the master suggested to his prince—returning to what seventeenth- and eighteenth-century political theorists referred to as the state of nature with the chaos and insecurity that it entails. Realistically, Machiavellian methods work best in situations where they are unexpected; that is to say, where there already exists a connection between politics and a sense of morally obligatory limitations on political behavior, which, of course, those methods then subvert.

The collapse of a shared moral understanding inevitably leads to a collapse of the rules of the game. We are witness to just such a collapse in many polities in our time, for precisely that reason, a collapse which has brought in its train the present crisis of humankind. It is the discovery of a proper moral base or foundation, and its pursuit in such a way that recognizes the realities of power essential for a good politics. That is what the conceptual system rooted in covenant is all about. The rules of the game for some may have emerged originally through an evolutionary process, to be accepted by those bound by them as a matter of course. Once disrupted, however, they can only be restored by consent; that is to say, through covenanting.

Through covenant, the two faces of politics, power and justice, are linked to become effective both morally and operationally. In the course of this book, I will suggest that covenant is by far the best source for developing a proper moral understanding and proper moral path in politics; that it is, indeed, the way to achieve a general public commitment to the political institutions required for the good life and to emerge from the Machiavellian jungle as free, morally responsible people. Perhaps such covenants may be civil rather than theo-political in character; that is still a question facing humanity. The idea of a civil covenant is one of the most important contributions of the last previous great revival of the covenant idea, the period from the sixteenth through the eighteenth centuries, the crucible that led to the emergence of modern democracy. The range of its possibilities was tested in the modern epoch and, by itself, found very useful but wanting. So, too, with the theo-political covenants of the past.

The genius of the covenant idea does not rest upon its philosophic explication, although such explication has much to contribute for a finer understanding of it. While ideas have their own subtle influence on people, their influence grows exponentially if they are embodied in a tradition—in the case of the covenant idea, a political tradition that continues from generation to generation. Such a tradition has both visible and invisible, conscious and subconscious manifestations. Its visible ones are easily traced, but the greatest part of its impact is in its invisible manifestations, those that are part of the substructure of the society, that constitute its culture, in this case political culture. To the extent that the covenant idea is mediated through certain political traditions to become part of the political culture, it has become second nature to those peoples influenced by it.

III

What are the components of a political tradition? First of all, it is a mode of thinking and body of thoughts shared by members of a particular body politic, especially those in any way involved in politics. In order to think about political things, they must have a political vocabulary—a set of terms that, individually and in relation to one another, offer ways to delineate and express political meaning. Such terms constitute a political vocabulary that represents the "program" through which people consider political things. The key words in any political vocabulary are what Kadushin has referred to as value concepts, that is to say, terms whose precise definition may be difficult or well nigh impossible, but which are understood to have a common core meaning within a particular culture.[3]

A political tradition begins with the founding of the body politic and revolves around certain fundamental principles and the relations—including the tensions—between them, which already are part of the founding. Every body politic is founded on its own principles of organization, power and authority relationships, and fundamental tensions, explicit or implicit. The latter are those that are "present at the creation" of the body politic and that have to be bridged in order for the body politic to come into existence. Because they are only bridged but not resolved, they are built into the very fabric of the body politic, which must reconcile them anew in every generation as long as the body politic exists in the same form. It is a task of the political tradition to keep those principles, relationships, and tensions alive and operational as the body politic confronts changing situations and circumstances.

The political tradition is kept alive by the chain of political leaders and thinkers who utilize that vocabulary to undertake or explain the political acts that shape and direct the body politic. In the course of time, a tradition becomes embodied in certain basic texts that reflect the political ideas of a particular body politic its political vocabulary, and celebrate the figures, events, and concepts that most embody the tradition. In that sense, the visible dimensions of a tradition sooner or later come to involve the interaction of texts and behavior in dealing with the internal and external influences on the body politic.

In sum, a tradition is a major integrative force within the body politic. Some polities rely on tradition more than others for integration. Covenanted polities are particularly in need of an appropriate political tradition for their integration. In every case they are covenanted polities because their political tradition rests upon the covenant idea and a covenantal political culture.

This book is an exploration of the covenant tradition as it was manifested and explicated in medieval and Reformation Europe, examining the ways in which that idea and its derivatives penetrated and permeated, shaped, or gave rise to particular political systems, institutions, and behavior. These indeed are the elements of politics that count, through which ideas are made meaningful and real. Thus, it is simultaneously the statement of a thesis, its documentation through case studies, and something of a guide for those who would learn how to conduct political life according to the covenant tradition.

More than anything else, cultures, systems, and humans informed by the covenantal perspective are committed to a way of thinking and conduct that enables them to live free while being bound together in appropriate relationships, to preserve their own integrities while sharing in a common whole, and to pursue both the necessities of human existence and the desiderata of moral response in some reasonable balance. There is a dialectic tension between each of these dualities, which adds the requisite dynamic dimension to covenant-based societies, one that makes such societies covenant-*informed* as well as covenant-based. This dialectic tension is an integral element in covenantal systems, one which provides such systems with the necessary self-corrective mechanisms to keep them in reasonable balance over the long haul, at least so long as covenantal principles continue to inform and shape the polities concerned.

This is not to suggest that all of human life is informed by covenant. As discussed in *Covenant and Polity in Biblical Israel* and below, there are hierarchical and organic ideas and systems that compete with covenantal ones and which have shaped very substantial segments of the human race. Presumably, they too can be penetrated to achieve better understanding of human behavior. At the same time, the extent to which covenantal relationships are spread among humans is an open question. It is possible to understand covenantal relationships as the property of a rather exclusive segment of the human race, those who have achieved that level of equality and social cooperation through some measure of conscious understanding and semi or subconscious behavior. It is also possible to see covenantal behavior as a human psychological necessity and, hence, extremely widespread, even within otherwise hierarchical and organic systems, at least in certain respects. Of course, there are positions between these two extremes.

We must approach the subject aware of two realities: (1) that partisans of each worldview, such as the Bible in the matter of covenant or Greek philosophy in the matter of organic development, will claim that theirs is the most natural and that where it does not exist, it is being artificially prevented from being; and (2) reality suggests that there are hierarchical, organic, and covenantal sociopolitical arrangements in the world, and combinations of the three. This writer takes a moderate position, holding that there is a somewhat exclusive "club" of those peoples and polities consisting of that segment of the human race that is truly immersed in the covenantal way of life, but that in some ways all human beings have some psychological propensity for contractual relationships, that is to say, transactional ones based upon mutual agreement, which can include a covenantal dimension, and that there are gradations of covenantalism to be found in between.

IV

Since covenants are grounded in moral commitment, they also provide a basis and a means for placing all of us under judgment. That is to say, a proper covenant not only offers humans the right path or way but provides means for the self-same humans to judge and be judged as to how well they stay on that path or maintain that way. Given human propensities to stray from the right path, no human system—and espe-

it may, the interaction between the two streams produced the American Revolution, the Declaration of Independence, the Federal Constitution, and the United States of America with all its subsequent impact on world affairs. So, too, in the twentieth century did the interaction produce the most successful efforts to date at world organization. If the League of Nations could not be sustained, the United Nations could combine a general charter with specific covenants to become, at the very least, a useful device in the post-World War II world, and perhaps even an essential one.[16]

Thus, in order to understand the influence of covenant in the Western political tradition, it is necessary to understand the three separations, the four streams of covenantal tradition, and their interaction. We have already examined the Jewish covenantal tradition. In chapter 1 we shall explore and outline the overall Christian, Reformed Christian, and secular compact traditions in general terms so that in subsequent chapters we may look at them in the specific contexts of the polities they inform singly, or more frequently, in tandem.

Notes

1. Cf. Donald Lutz, *From Covenant to Constitution in American Political Thought* (Philadelphia: Center for the Study of Federalism, Temple University, 1980).
2. Simon Schama, *Citizens: A Chronicle of the French Revolution* (New York: Knopf, 1989); Alexis de Tocqueville, *Ancien Regime et la Revolution,* trans. Stuart Gilbert (New York: Doubleday, 1955). See also Jean Jacques Rousseau, *Du Contrat Social* (Paris: Le Livre de Poche, 1978).
3. Max Kadushin, *Organic Thinking* (New York: Jewish Theological Seminary, 1938) and *The Rabbinic Mind* (New York: Jewish Theological Seminary, 1952).
4. Cf., inter alia, Moshe Weinfeld, "Covenant Terminology in the Ancient Near East and its Influence on the West," *Journal of the American Oriental Society* 93 (1973): 190-99.
5. On covenant as a binding, see Delbert Hillers, *Covenant: The History of the Biblical Idea* (Baltimore: Johns Hopkins University Press, 1969); George F. Mendenhall, *Law and Covenant in Israel and the Ancient Near East* (Pittsburgh: University of Pittsburgh, 1955); and Moshe Weinfeld, "Covenant" in *Encyclopedia Judaica* 5 (Jerusalem: Keter Books, 1973): 1012-22.
6. A. Cohen, *The Parting of the Ways: Judaism and the Rise of Christianity* (London: Lincolns-Praeger, 1954); Leo Baeck, *Judaism and Christianity: Essays,* trans. Walter Kaufmann (New York: Atheneum, 1970); Hans Joachim Schoeps, *The Jewish-Christian Argument: A History of Theologies in Conflict,* trans. David E. Green (London: Faber and Faber, 1963); Solomon Grayzel, *The Church and the Jews in the XIIIth Century: A Study of Their Relations During the Years 1198-1254, Based on the Papal Letters and the Conciliar Decrees of the Period* (Philadel-

phia: Dropsie College, 1933); Herbert Danberg, *The Jew and Christianity: Phases, Ancient and Modern, of the Jewish Attitude Towards Christianity* (London: Society for Promoting Christian Knowledge, 1941); Frederick Clifton Grant, *Ancient Judaism and the New Testament* (Westport: Greenwood Press, 1978); Marcel Simon, *Recherches D'Histoire Judeo-Chretienne* (Paris: Mouton, 1962); James William Parks, *Judaism and Christianity* (London: V. Gollancz, 1948); Samuel Sandmel, *Judaism and Christian Beginnings* (New York: Oxford University Press, 1978); Adolf Hilgenfeld, *Judenthum und Judenchristenthum* (Leipzig: Fues, 1886); Albrecht Oepke, *Das Neue Weltgestaltung* (Guetersloh: C. Bertelsmann, 1950); David Flusser, *Judaism and the Origins of Christianity* (Jerusalem: Magnes, 1988); E. P. Sanders, ed., *Jewish and Christian Self-Definition* (London: SCM Press, 1981); William David Davies, *Christian Origins and Judaism* (Philadelphia: Westminster Press, 1962); S. H. Hooke, Robert Loewe, E. O. James, and W. O. E. Oesterley, *Judaism and Christianity* (London: Sheldon Press, 1937); *Judaism and the Beginnings of Christianity,* A Series of Lectures Delivered in 1923 at Jews' College, London, under the auspices of the Union of Jewish Literary Societies (London: G. Routledge, 1923).

7. Emile G. Leonard, *A History of Protestantism,* ed. H. H. Rowley (London: Nelson, 1965); Paul Tillich, *The Protestant Era,* trans. James Luther Adams (Chicago: University of Chicago Press, 1957); Thomas Sanders, *Protestant Concepts of Church and State* (New York: Holt, Rinehart and Winston, 1964); John Dillenberger and Claude Welch, *Protestant Christianity, Interpreted Through Its Development* (New York: C. Scribner's Sons, 1964); Lewis William Spitz, *The Protestant Reformation, 1517–1559* (New York: Harper and Row, 1985); Hans Joachim Hillerbrand, ed., *The Protestant Reformation* (New York: Harper and Row, 1968); Henry Daniel-Rops, *The Protestant Reformation* (London: J. M. Dent, 1961); D. J. Callahan, H. A. Oberman, and D.J. O'Hanlon, eds., *Christianity Divided: Protestant and Roman Catholic Theological Issues* (London: Sheed and Ward, 1962); John Sheldon Whale, *The Protestant Tradition: An Essay in Interpretation* (Cambridge: Cambridge University Press, 1955); Henri Hauser, *La Naissance du Protestantisme,* 2nd ed. (Paris: Presses Universitaires de France, 1962); J. Wayne Baker, *Heinrich J. Bullinger and the Covenant* (Athens, Ohio: University of Ohio Press, 1981).

8. Leo Strauss and Joseph Cropsey, eds., *History of Political Philosophy* (Chicago: Rand McNally, 1963); Jacob Ben-Amittay, *The History of Political Thought From Ancient to Present Times* (New York: Philosophical Library, 1972); William R. Hutchinson, *The Modernist Impulse in American Protestantism* (Cambridge, Massachusetts: Harvard University Press, 1976); Otto Gierke, *The Development of Political Theory* (New York: Norton, 1939); Bernard Bailyn, *Ideological Origins of the American Revolution* (Cambridge, Mass.: Belknap Press of Harvard University Press, 1967); Morton Frisch and Richard Stevens, *The Political Thought of American Statesmen* (Itasca, Ill.: F. E. Peacock, 1973); Ralph Henry Gabriel, *The Course of American Democratic Thought,* 2nd ed. (New York: Ronald Press, 1956).

9. Robert Bellah, *The Broken Covenant: American Civil Religion in Time of Trial* (New York: Seabury Press, 1975); Charles McCoy, *Covenant and Community in the Thought of Heinrich Bullinger* (Philadelphia: Center for the Study of Federalism, 1980); William Johnson Everett, *God's Federal Republic* (New York/Mahwah: Paulist Press, 1988); Daniel J. Elazar and John Kincaid, eds., *Covenant, Polity and Constitutionalism* (Lanham, Md.: University Press of America, 1983).

10. On Judeo-Christian corporative relations, see James William Parkes, *Judaism and Christianity* (Chicago: University of Chicago Press, 1948); *Prelude to Dialogue: Jewish Christian Relationships* (London: Vallentine, Mitchell, 1969); *Jews, Christians and the World of Tomorrow* (Southhampton: Parkes Library, 1969); Richard Rousseau, ed., *Christianity and Judaism: The Deepening Dialogue* (Montrose, Pa.: Ridge Row Press, 1983); and Norman Soloman, *The Jewish-Christian Dialogue and Peace* (Oxford: Oxford Project for Peace Studies, 1988).

11. Will Herberg, *Protestant-Catholic-Jew* (Garden City, N.Y.: Doubleday, 1960); other ecumenical works include the following by Franklin H. Littell: *From State Church to Pluralism* (Chicago: Aldine Publishing Co., 1962) and *The Crucifixion of the Jews* (New York: Harper and Row, 1975).

12. On postwar intra-Christian ecumenicism, see Robert M. Brown, *An American Dialogue: A Protestant Looks at Catholicism and a Catholic Looks at Protestantism* (Garden City, N.Y.: Doubleday, 1960); S. M. Cavert, *Church Cooperation and Unity in America, 1900–1970* (New York: Association Press, 1970); J. O'Hanlon, ed., *Christianity Divided: Protestant and Roman Catholic Theological Issues* (London: Sheed and Ward, 1962); and Willem Hendrik van de Pol, *The Christian Dilemma* (London: J. M. Dent, 1952).

13. Cf. op. cit. Brown and op. cit. Cavert.

14. Leo Strauss, *Natural Right and History* (Chicago: University of Chicago Press, 1953); Otto Gierke, *Natural Law and the Theory of Society,* trans. Ernest Barker (Cambridge: Cambridge University Press, 1934); Robert Horowitz, *The Moral Foundations of the American Republic* (Charlottesville: University Press of Virginia, 1979).

15. Andrew C. McLaughlin, *The Foundations of American Constitutionalism,* introduction by Henry Steele Commager (Gloucester, Mass.: Peter Smith, 1972); Bernard Bailyn, *Ideological Origins of the American Revolution* (Cambridge, Mass.: Belknap Press of Harvard University Press, 1967); Bernard Bailyn, *The Origins of American Politics* (New York: Knopf, 1968); Gordon Wood, *The Creation of the American Republic, 1776–1787* (Chapel Hill: University of North Carolina Press, 1969); Henry Adams, ed., *Documents Relating to New England Federalism, 1800–1815* (Boston: Little, Brown, 1905); Ralph Henry Gabriel, *The Course of American Democratic Thought,* 2nd ed. (New York: Ronald Press, 1956); Andrew C. McLaughlin, *The Confederation and the Constitution, 1783–1789* (New York: Collier Books, 1962); Andrew C. McLaughlin, *A Constitutional History of the United States* (New York: Appleton-Century-Crofts, 1963); Donald S. Lutz, *Popular Consent and Popular Control: Whig Political Theory in the Early State Constitutions* (Baton Rouge: Louisiana State University Press, 1980); Donald S. Lutz, "The Purposes of American State Constitutions," *Publius* 12, no. 1 (1982): 27–44.

16. On the League of Nations and United Nations, see Philip E. Jacob, *The Dynamics of International Organization* (Homewood, Ill.: Dorsey Press, 1972).

Part I

Beginnings and Separations

1

Covenant Traditions in the West

West Asian Oaths, Contracts, and Treaties

While full-fledged covenantalism in the ancient world was confined to the Jewish polity, the very fact that pact is one of the three original bases for political organization made it inevitable that other political societies would also exist that in some way or another drew upon the tradition, practice, and sometimes even theory of agreement and consent for the construction of their political organizations. In practical terms, this practice was manifested in three ways: through mutually binding oaths, through contracts, or through treaties. What was characteristic of all of these was their almost exclusive reliance on the self-interest of the parties involved. Even when the gods were invoked, the arrangements established survived only so long as the parties were interested in having them survive or too weak to do anything about it.

Thus, the ancient West Asian vassal treaties barely lasted from one revolt to another, not to speak of the frequent changes at the imperial level that required reestablishment of the treaties with the new imperial rulers. There was no moral commitment here, only the realities of naked power, usually military at that. In other words, these treaties were in the category of feudal arrangements whereby oaths and contracts via treaty could temper the reality of conquest by brute force.[1]

No doubt those vassal treaties rested on an earlier structure of contractualism, since they emerged in Western Asia, but not to the east or south where organic or hierarchical forms or some combination of the two prevailed. Thus, except when conquered by foreign powers with oath or treaty cultures, Egypt has never known anything but hierarchical rule.

The situation in Mesopotamia was quite different, especially after the Sumerians were replaced by the Semites in the first half of the third millennium B.C.E. The Sumerians, who had settled in southern Mesopotamia between 3200 and 2800 B.C.E., had created city-states in the organic model that established a kind of state socialism under priestly rule. The Semites discontinued the state socialism and reduced the power of the temples and priests, establishing the palace along with the temple as a separate center of power.[2]

The oldest historical document that we have comes from the city of Lagash, during the second half of the third millennium. There, after a series of dynastic wars, Urukagina, who had usurped the throne, introduced social reforms through a contract with Ningirsu, the local deity, through which the income of the priests was cut and protections were instituted for widows and orphans. All this is recorded on the stele of vultures. Thus, the very first historical document available to us is not only a political contract, but one with a social as well as political purpose.

Unfortunately, this contract apparently did not last long since the local priests combined with Lugalzaggisi (King of the Lands) of Umma, the last of the Sumerian rulers, who conquered Lagash with their help. Lugalzaggisi briefly succeeded in conquering the other major cities of the lower valley, even advancing to the Mediterranean, but in doing so he evoked the opposition of the Akkadian Empire to the northwest, which conquered him in turn. The Akkadians introduced a typical imperial hierarchy, transforming the ruler into a god, the rulers of the formerly independent cities into subordinate governors, and introducing a bureaucracy to maintain imperial control.

Shortly thereafter, Western Asia entered into an era of vassal treaties. These treaties, in turn, became the basis for what was to become a feature of West Asian imperialism, namely, the maintenance of the local autonomy of conquered peoples within the great imperial systems. That policy became fully articulated with the rise of the Persian Empire in the sixth century B.C.E. Except for the Neo-Assyrian Empire, which dominated the region from the beginning of the ninth to the beginning of the seventh centuries B.C.E. with its policy of population transfers in an effort to increase the military dominance of the imperial center, it was at least the de facto policy for every successive imperial regime. Thus, very early on in West Asia it became established that peoples were more enduring than states, a principle that remains as true today as it ever did.

No doubt Western Asia was also the locus of confederacies of nomadic tribes throughout this period. Echoes of the existence of some such confederacies are to be found in the Bible. Unfortunately, there are no other records except for scattered references in recovered texts to tell us who, what, when, where, and how. While ancient Israel soon transcended that kind of kinship-based confederacy, echoes of it are to be found in the Israelite tribal federation. If the pattern was anything like the pattern among Bedouin today, it seems that what was most characteristic of the nomadic tribes was the sense of being bound by a common kinship. Hence, confederal arrangements emerged through the identification of a putative common ancestor, which then made the confederates kin. This is reflected in the use of the term *Beni* (sons of) to identify such confederations among the Bedouin. There may be a carryover of this in the Hebrew *bnai brit* to describe those who are federated through covenant. The kinship principle of "sons of" is carried over into the terminology, but the fact that they are sons of a covenant rather than a common ancestor shows the great difference.[3]

Canaan seems to have been a point of transition or merging of tribal kinship federalism and a more articulated federalism of settled peoples even before and including the Israelites. Permanent alliances of Canaanite city-states are evident from the archaeological evidence.[4] The Sea Peoples who came from Crete and the other Greek islands, who became known as the Philistines, established a pentocracy, a five-city confederation, which was apparently a typically Greek league of cities.[5] This characteristic of that land was to persist not only in connection with the Israelites but in later Hellenistic and Roman times as well, through such political associations as Decapolis, the confederation of ten cities established by Rome in 62 B.C.E. Similar political associations could be found in Phoenicia, today's Lebanon. Each city-state was politically autonomous, governed by families of notables united under a common king with limited powers.

The Hellenic-Ionian Leagues

While the idea of covenant was a minor theme at best in Greek and Roman political thought, the application of federal devices in the real world was more widespread. In the fourth century B.C.E., the growing power of the Macedonian kingdom put an end to the independence of these Greek city-states, bringing them under Macedonian imperial rule. As John Ferguson states in *The Heritage of Hellenism*, "Cosmopolis did not destroy the *polis*."[6] The Macedonians were, after all, Greeks and had certain Greek sensibilities. Thus, they developed an imperial style, which the Romans were shortly to copy, that strongly resembled imperial federalism, albeit without its democratic elements, at least on the imperial plane.

Indeed, in theory, Alexander the Great established his world empire as president of a league of Greek states—the Corinthian League. In 311, Antigonus, his successor, negotiated a treaty with his rivals, recorded on a marble column, which stated: "We have declared in our treaty that all Greeks shall bind themselves by oath to the mutual defense of their freedom and autonomy." This treaty became the basis for the post-Alexandrian empire in Ionia and Asia Minor, whereby the empire formally continued to be a league of cities, now with one imperial ruler, while the cities kept their local autonomy and their right to create regional confederations within the imperial domain. This and other treaties essentially relied upon the traditional communal liberties of each city to determine its precise status within the overall *imperium*.[7] In a sense, this represented a merger of the Canaanite-Phoenician city-state culture with the Hellenic polis culture to form the local basis of the Hellenistic polity.

This pattern of imperial quasi federalism persisted through the Hellenistic period and well into the Roman Empire. The Seleucid rulers were particularly notable for the freedom they allowed the cities within their empire, albeit requiring each of them to have a Greek constitution. For example, the Hasmonean revolt began when the Seleucids intervened to force the small province of Judea to reconstitute itself as a Greek *polis*.

The anchor of these local liberties was to be found in the principle of respect for the ancestral laws of each city, but it was extended beyond this because the age was one of the foundation of new cities for which constitutions were written and which were given the same autonomy as the old, established ones, much in the way that those American states admitted to the union after the adoption of the federal Constitution were deemed the equals of those which had established the federal republic in the first place. To the extent that cities were founded and refounded, they acquired constitutions and had contractual elements in them, but no theory of political compact developed as a result. The form of government was some combination of democracy and oligarchy, whereby all adult male citizens had full political rights, including the eligibility for office, but in fact the offices tended to be in the hands of the wealthy more often than not.

Within the context of these empires, cities were encouraged to form confederacies. As indicated above, the empire itself grew out of the League of Corinth, of which Philip of Macedonia served as *hegemon*, or president, and which comprised all the states of Greece except Sparta.[8] Alexander followed this form and the league was reorganized in 302 and continued formally as the linking vehicle for the empire. Foreign and military policy was concentrated in the hands of the *hegemon*, although there was no common citizenship. On the other hand, in the League of the Islanders, built around a religious center on Delos, common citizenship was introduced.

The third century B.C.E. became a century of confederacies, including the Ionian League; the Boetian League, dominated by Thebes; the Aetolian League, which had a strong primary assembly for the entire confederacy and involved three arenas: cities, tribal districts, and the confederacy as a whole; in effect, a federal constitution. Such, too, was the Acheanian League.[9] When not fighting one another, the two confederacies established a common superleague.

Perhaps the most federal of all was the Lycian League. Located in the mountains of Asia Minor, the Lycians were not Greeks. Under Greek influence they developed a federal constitution that developed to the point where the federal assembly was a representative body whose seats were distributed approximately in proportion to the population of each member city. On a circumscribed basis it survived well into the period of Roman rule.

The closest to a prefiguring of the federal principle as vital for freedom came in the history of the second Achaean League.[10] The first Achaean League had been established in the fourth century B.C.E., but collapsed shortly after 300 B.C.E. It was revived in 281 to 280 B.C.E. and rapidly consolidated its power vis-à-vis Macedonia and the city-states surrounding it.

A generation later, in 251, Aratus led the citizens of Sicyon, his native city, in their successful effort to overthrow its dictator, and brought the city into the Achaean League. Perhaps because Sicyon was not an Achean city, Aratus had wider ambitions than the older members of the confederacy. Loathing dictators and Macedonian rule, he saw the league's task as that of liberating Hellas from both by instituting federal democracy. In 245 B.C.E. he was elected the general of the league's armies and became its dominant figure. His first great victory was in 243, when he liberated Corinth. The league then expanded for a while, but by the end of the decade Aratus had reached the limits of his powers and the league had failed to absorb either Athens or Sparta. Clemonomes of Sparta took the lead in opposing Aratus and became his *bête-noire*.

Aratus, who has been described by Ferguson as being "incorruptible, adventurous, persuasive, skilled in diplomacy, passionately attached to freedom, and implacably ambitious," was the partisan of federalism, but opposed social revolution. Clemonomes was not only a Spartan nationalist, but a social revolutionary. In a sense, their struggle was a prefiguring of the struggle between the federalists and the Jacobins in determining the course of the democratic world two millennia later.

In the end, in order to preserve the federation, Aratus had to invite the hated Macedonians to intervene and Clemonomes was defeated in 222 B.C.E. While the Achaean League was allowed to retain limited local liberty, it was restored firmly to Macedonian suzerainty. It survived until 146 B.C.E.

The Achaean League was governed by a primary assembly of all male citizens over the age of thirty, which met to deal with major constitutional issues, and an elected council of several hundred, which met regularly and elected the magistrates. The league adopted common gods and at its greatest extent controlled the whole of the Peloponnesus.

Roman Foederatii

In the Battle of Pydna in 168 B.C.E., the Romans triumphed over the allied Greek cities. In its wake the walls of the conquered cities were razed and the Greek confederacies were dissolved. Thus, the history of classical Greece came to an end just as the Jews of Judea launched their successful revolt against the Seleucid extension of Aexandrian Greece in western Asia.

Nevertheless, the rise of Rome did not alter the Greek emphasis on the *polis* and confederations of like *politea*. The Romans, like their Greek predecessors, were colonizers, planting cities wherever their armies trod. Under them the *polis* became the *municipium*. Citizens of the *municipium* had a double loyalty, to their city and to Rome. It has been stated that "Rome conquered by force, but ruled by consent."[11] Indeed, the Roman

Empire was originally constructed out of a network of treaties, presumably among equals, between Rome and her allies, the *foederatii*, which further encouraged this duality.[12]

The Roman *municipium* became part of a political-juridical constitutional order based upon a public social contract. As Walter Lippman put it: "In this way, freedom emanating from a constitutional order has been advocated, explained, and made real to the imagination and the conscience of Western men; by establishing the presumption that civilized society is founded on a public social contract."[13] Lippman's rather optimistic analysis of the Roman public philosophy of contract reflects what has earlier been stated in this book, namely, that "a contract is an agreement reached voluntarily, *quid pro quo*," namely, it has that narrowness that distinguishes it from covenant in its practical rather than moral foundations and its *quid pro quo* character. Still, as Lippman suggests, it helped to advance the idea that "the first principle of the civilized state is that power is legitimate only when it is under contract."

The reality of municipal liberty, federal treaties, and the contractual public philosophy disappeared in the Roman Empire to be replaced by a European version of Oriental despotism. At most, echoes of the theory lived on. As we have seen, while the Church may have tried to absorb a version of covenantal thinking into its theology, when it came to matters of governance it followed the Roman imperial model and built a hierarchy.

The idea of Christian republicanism was preserved by a chain of Christian political theorists throughout the Middle Ages. While their theories had some covenantal overtones, it would be hard to describe them as covenantal per se. Nevertheless, with the demise of the Roman Empire, the way was open to new arrangements that combined the Roman experience with hierarchy with others derived from covenant and contract. This is reflected in the continuing use of the terms *foedus*, *foedere*, and *foederatii* in medieval Latin to describe covenantal and oath-based linkages among individuals and groups.

The Separation of the Jewish and Christian Traditions

In the last analysis, it was through the Christian reconstitution of the Jewish world that the covenant entered European civilization. After its substantial—even radical—redefinition, covenant was to appear sporadically as a political idea for the next millennium or more. In that context, some philosophers and theologians developed more systematic expressions of both the general principle and specific theories of covenant relationships. Their practice, however, was obstructed by organic and hierarchic conceptions of the universe and body politic, ecclesiastical custody of the Gospel covenant, and feudalism.[14]

Christianity, like Judaism, regards itself as being founded upon a covenant, but a fundamentally different covenant, from God in the person of Jesus, who, for Christians, is the source of human salvation.[15] Common to the Christian concept of covenant is that, rather than being a matter of agreement and partnership between God and humanity (or some segment of humanity), it was a unilaterally gracious act on the part of God, a bestowal on humanity, whose response was merely one of acknowledging (witnessing, in Christian terminology) God's grace. The orthodox Christian view of covenant was as far removed from a classic covenantal perspective as it could be and still remain within the parameters of the idea. Christian witness, rather than partnership, became the active element that must be present in any covenantal framework. Witnessing was the element of consent and so it remains to this day. A homely demonstration of this understanding of covenanting is to be found in the American revival meeting, where people come up and witness or testify for Jesus, and are thereby brought into his covenant and saved.

On the other hand, those Christian theologians whose own theological position is covenantal emphasize the New Testament as a covenantal document, suggesting that, like Deuteronomy, it is a renewal of the old covenant.[16] Their argument is that the whole New Testament has to be understood as a single treaty covenant with the gospels introducing Jesus as the new king of the church polity, followed by covenant history in the Book of Acts recording the ratification of the new covenant, with the Epistles paralleling the Old Testament prophets and wisdom and worship literature. This, however, is the interpretation of one particular wing of Christian theology that emerged in the Reformation.

Since Christianity was and is a community based upon consent rather than a primordial group based on kinship, and in that respect is a true heir of the Hebrew Bible, even carrying the biblical demand for consent to an extreme, this form of covenanting is not lightly to be dismissed, even by those who favor a more classic partnership approach.

On the other hand, neither should its problematics be ignored, namely, an extreme individualization of the covenantal experience and the reduction of humans to very weak reeds in the face of an all-powerful, but hopefully gracious, God who sent His specially begotten son to save them. Paul was the first to state the New Testament covenantal doctrine (in Romans I:19–20 and Acts 17:24–27). Paul's idea of the natural covenant under which pagans lived derived from the Jewish concept of the Noahide covenant. Over the centuries, Christian theology and practice have attempted to deal with both of these problems. The classic solution of the first was that of medieval Europe, namely, a hierarchical Church and Empire that organized, respectively, the spiritual and temporal life of Christendom. This solution also reintroduced the element of kinship by the back door, in effect making it impossible for any resident of Christendom born to a Christian family to avoid membership in the Church with its ritualized way of acknowledging Jesus Christ. The second involved the elaboration of theology so as to introduce a covenant of works parallel to the covenant of grace (or some other form of double covenant), which thereby demanded that Christians behave as if they were partners with God, even though the latter was the real source of salvation.

Christians understand their covenant as fulfilling the promise of the old covenant with Israel as presaged, in the Christian view, by such prophets as Isaiah (55:3) and Jeremiah (31:31–34). Therefore, the Christian Bible is divided into Old and New Testaments, the first being prehistory of God's church and primitive statement of the moral law designed to establish and sustain the people through whom Jesus would come to save humanity. The choice of the term "testament" (especially as used in the original Greek) was deliberate, reflecting as it did the new understanding of covenant as witnessing.

In seeking to translate "covenant," the early church faced several problems. Since the covenant tradition of Israel was seen as referring to the Mosaic law, it could not be readily transferred to the new covenantal scheme established through Jesus called Christ, which was understood to supersede the Mosaic covenant. Linguistically, moreover, in the context of the Roman Empire, covenant could be interpreted as meaning both a legal contract and an unlawful secret society.

The church fathers' problem had been presaged in the Septuagint, the Jewish translation of the Hebrew Bible into Greek two to three centuries before the rise of Christianity. The Greek word *syntheke*, suggesting covenant as compact or treaty, might have been used in that translation; but it was understood as suggesting a loose tie linking separate but equal partners in a kind of alliance as *baalei brit* rather than *bnai brit*, following the Hebrew view that implied that God and humans are equal partners in the redemption of the world. Instead, the word chosen for the Septuagint was *diatheke*, which came close to reflecting the Hebrew *edut* (witnessing), often used as a synonym for *brit* in the Pentateuch. The church fathers adopted this usage, rejecting *syntheke* and accepted *diatheke*, meaning "testament." Later, the Latin Vulgate Bible, translated by Jerome, a careful scholar, restored the original distinction by using *foedus* and *pactum* for covenant in much of the Old Testament and *testamentum* for covenant in the Psalms and New Testament.

Like a testator who makes a last will and testament to be executed by his heirs, God is seen as freely offering a last and everlasting covenant through the death and resurrection of Christ. Just as the testator and heirs are not on the same level, but exercise a kind of mutual responsibility, there is a similar mutuality in the New Testament with God remaining superior (Hebrews 9:15–20). This translation of "covenant" as "testament" permanently alters the meaning of covenant as understood in the Old Testament."[17]

Some thirty-three references to covenant (*diatheke*) appear in the New Testament, though almost half of these quote from or refer to the Old Testament (e.g., Romans 11:27; Acts 3:25). The principal reference, the covenant of the New Testament, occurs in the Last Supper:

> Now as they were eating, Jesus took bread, and blessed, and broke it, and gave it to the disciples and said, "Take, eat; this is my body." And he took a cup, and when he had given thanks, he gave it to them, saying, "Drink of it, all of you; for this is my blood of the covenant, which is poured out for many for the forgiveness of sins. (Matthew 26:26–28)

This new covenant, confirmed in blood like the Mosaic covenant (Exodus 24:8), is also referred to in other passages (Mark 14:24; Luke 22:20; I Corinthians 11:25) and alluded to in many others. The book of the New Testament that makes the most use of covenant is the Epistle to the Hebrews (seventeen references), an anonymous letter written to win back those who were about to abandon Christianity to return to the religion of Israel by convincing them of the superiority of the new covenant over the "obsolete" Mosaic covenant.

It was obviously directed to touch these former Jews conceptually and, *inter alia*, serves as evidence of the degree to which covenantal thought was important to the Jews of that period. Paul used the term elsewhere on nine occasions: four in the synoptic gospels, two in Acts, and one in the Apocalypse.

The polemics that begin this process of separation were principally written between the years 90 and 100 C.E. with the publishing of Paul's letters and the response of the Jewish sages to those letters.[18] As Paul built upon the omnipotent God's unilateral covenant of grace, whose first appearance was with the Patriarchs, the Jewish sages emphasized the reciprocal covenant of Sinai and the Torah, which was part of it, and which became the possession of the Jewish people.

In the days of the early church, *sacramentum* was a secular term referring primarily to the soldiers' oath of loyalty to the emperor—whose formula goes back to the time of the Hittites. The early church used it to refer to the Last Supper as the central covenant enactment of Christianity. Those who were parties to the reenactment of this sacramentum became the *ekklesia,* the assembly, or the Greek equivalent of the *edah*. It was the post-Apostolic church that transformed those two terms and gave them their present meaning of sacrament and church. In the theology of the church fathers, covenant concepts seem to have centered on transferring the Davidic covenant to Jesus as Messiah. This already marked the step in the direction of a hierarchical rather than a covenantal view of the church. Augustine (354–430) was the last great theologian to pay any attention to covenant until the Reformation.

The Church Fathers

While the original Christian understanding of covenant was derived from the early Christian interpretations of the Old Testament, the true foundations of that understanding were developed in the writings of the church fathers, especially those of the fourth and fifth centuries—in other words, at the same time that the Jews were completing the Talmud. The church fathers fell into two groups: those who wrote in Greek, and those who wrote in Latin. It was the works of the latter that continued to be read in Western Christendom during the Middle Ages and hence were most influential. Some of the Greek works were translated into Latin and thus made available as well, although it is not known how many were thus transmitted.[19]

The major problem of these early Christian thinkers was that of the relationship between the old covenant and the new; that is to say, between Judaism and Christianity, and between Jews and Gentiles. Basically three answers were proposed to this problem, each represented by a different group of patristic thinkers. The first group consisted of Judaizers, those who required of all believers a strict observance of biblical law. Justin, a convert from Judaism, is perhaps the foremost of the church fathers in this school as he demonstrates in his *Dialogue with Trypho,* a Jew. They rejected Pauline Christianity and saw Paul as an apostate because he rejected the Mosaic law. Their principal proof text was the Ebionite gospel of the Hebrews, a rescension of Matthew's gospel. This group was called "Nazarenes" by Jerome and apparently were still widespread in the East during his time.[20]

The Judaizers were opposed by Marcion and the Marcionites. Marcion, who came to Rome around the year 140, presented a radical antithesis suggesting that there was an absolute opposition between Christianity and Judaism, that Judaism was thoroughly evil and Christianity thoroughly good. Hence the old and new covenants were absolutely different from one another. Accepting the gnostic teachings of Cerdo, Marcion actually posited a double god—the God of the Old Testament who created the world but is himself imperfect, wrathful, and warlike, who knows nothing of grace, and Christ, the good God who overcame his evil rival and was crucified as a result. This enabled Christ to liberate the Gentiles while damning pious Jews. Marcion was for all intents and purposes an anti-Semite and his Marcionite teachings became the foundation of Christian anti-Judaism. They are presented in his *Antithesen.*[21]

The mainstream church fathers rejected both the Judaizers and Marcionites as heretics. They sought to define the relationship between the old and new covenants as part of God's plan for the progressive revelation of His presence in the world. In this respect they were Pauline, accepting the idea that even the Gentiles have a certain natural knowledge of God. Therefore, they can be redeemed by belief in Jesus as Christ without having to take on the practices of the Jews. It was in this belief that they turned to the Noahide covenant as a sign that God has covenanted with all men and established natural religion and morality within Gentiles as well as Jews. Physical circumcision, the Jewish sign of the covenant, could be replaced by spiritual circumcision since it was not the physical act of cutting that brought salvation, but acts of faith. Thus, in God's progressive plan, when Jesus established the new covenant, the old became obsolete and the old law abrogated. Jesus becomes personally identified with the new covenant in this system.[22]

The noted political scientist Carl Friedrich identified Augustine, Irenaeus, Tertullian, Lactantius, and Eusebius as the Church fathers in the covenant tradition, although he had to stretch the point somewhat to do so.[23] Irenaeus was the only one among them who even hinted at a conditional covenant. J. Wayne Baker suggests that he may have been an influence on Bullinger's later formulation.[24]

The patristic teaching on covenant emphasized three principal covenants: the Noahide or natural covenant—the primordial covenant for all humans; the Mosaic or old covenant for Jews; and the Christian or new covenant for Christians, and thus, potentially for all humans once again. Justin deals with covenant in chapter 47 of his *Dialogue with Trypho*.[25] In chapter 87 he emphasizes the Noahide covenant (360–61) and Jesus as the new covenant (p. 337). Jerome, one of the Latin Fathers, deals with covenant in his *Epistles* 112–113 (CSEL 55–56, 381). In his commentary on Zachariah, III, 9, PL, 25, 1503, Jerome emphasized God's blessing of Noah as a decree of universal salvation.

Clement of Alexandria, a Greek theologian, had his own gloss on the three-covenant theory,[26] suggesting that God established a covenant of philosophy for the Greeks, a covenant of the Mosaic law for the Jews, and a covenant of faith for the Christians. Ireneus follows a similar model in *Adversus Haereses* IV, 9, 3. The first of his three covenants (and he uses the term *diathekai* as equaling *foedera*) is that of the natural law of the philosophers and jurists; the second, the ceremonial law of the Jews; and the third, the moral law of the Christians, which is the fulfillment and perfection of the second. However, he sees the third as a real continuation of the second rather than a break with it. Augustine, on the other hand, recognized only two covenants, the old and the new, with the covenants with Noah and Abraham and the covenants at Sinai and the Plains of Moab in Deuteronomy all part of the same old law, with the old prefiguring the new.[27]

Augustine's image of the City of God was, among other things, designed to explain the unity of the old and new covenants as the only ones. withAbraham and Moses representing the old covenant, and Noah and Jesus representing the new (thus, the division into two cities—Jerusalem, the covenanted city of God, and Babylon, the secular city of man—the first established by Abel, the second by Cain). Through Jesus, Gentiles as well as Jews can enter the City of God, with the Hebrew scriptures written to foretell his coming and the new covenant.

Perhaps because the concept of covenant presented a number of practical and theological problems, in the course of establishing its orthodoxy and endeavoring to unify the Christian system the church deemphasized covenant, especially after it believed that it had successfully superseded the Mosaic covenant and transferred the authority of the Davidic covenant to Jesus. After Augustine (354–430), the Church paid little attention to covenant and, even though the Eucharist remained central to the Christian liturgy, it ceased to be a truly common meal and its covenantal dimension was overshadowed by other features and meanings attributed to the Last Supper.

At the same time, the New Testament did not readily lend itself to unambiguous political applications. This is partly reflected in the numerous debates concerning "the politics of Jesus" in which he has been construed, among other things, as a violent revolutionary (e.g., Matthew 21:12; Mark 12:15–16) and an entirely otherworldly king (e.g., John 18:36). Given the revolutionary period in which Jesus lived and preached, a time when the Jews were gripped by messianic and eschatological fevers that often found expression in revolt against the Roman rulers of Palestina, this dimension of his teaching is not to be casually dismissed. Anxious to maintain the divinity of Christ and universality of His covenant, the early Church sought to eradicate any conceptions of Jesus as an earthly ruler or political messiah, especially of Israel. Thus, early Christianity, like early Talmudic Judaism, downplayed the political dimensions of human existence for its own reasons, leaving the two great faiths of the Western world with a damaged legacy.[28]

It is not surprising, then, that the New Testament provides few specific guidelines for government or for the implementation of a Christian commonwealth. By overriding the structure of law associated with the Mosaic covenant, the church also jettisoned a body of wisdom and experience concerning the organization of civil society. Christ was to rule in the hearts of men and the Kingdom of God would be made manifest in their faith and behavior without the complex structure of institutional law associated with the accumulated traditions of the Mosaic covenant.

In this respect, Christianity was also reproaching Israel for having given, in its eyes, too legalistic and contractual a gloss to the idea of covenant.

Yet, in being so spiritual, the Christian covenantal scheme tends to neglect politics. The New Testament seems to suggest that Christians may and will live within a variety of political structures, including pagan, authoritarian, and decadent ones. While those who administer those structures will ultimately come under God's judgement, Christians must be more mindful of a revolution in faith than politics until the final coming of the Kingdom. As a result, Christians have had a propensity to withdraw from "this-worldly" affairs. Many early Christians sacrificed their lives in the manner of Christ rather than rebelling against Roman persecution. Furthermore, based as it is on a personal covenant emphasizing faith in Christ, the New Testament places a strong emphasis on personal relationships, especially those of service and humility, which are not contingent upon structures and, indeed, are presumed to transcend them and to liberate individuals from a dependence upon them.

Another possible channel of transmission of covenant ideas may have been through the Pelagiasian heresy. Pelagianism was developed in the fifth century by Pelagius (c.355–c.425), a British-born monk (that is, a layman committed to the religious life), who developed what was then considered a heretical theology because he rejected Augustinian doctrines of predestination and grace as too pessimistic. It was the source of considerable discord in the Church for more than a century. His life was a reverse journey through covenant-prone areas. He left Britain for Rome and then North Africa—where he had many Carthaginian followers—and Palestine—where he preached successfully for many years in Jerusalem until he was banished by the Church establishment. He was familiar with the Bible, the Latin classics, the Latin Church fathers, and some Greek theology in translation. He seems also to have been a law student since he has extensive familiarity with legal matters.

While both Augustine and Jerome fought Pelagius, aspects of his teaching that may have survived (for example, a semi-Pelagianism continued to be popular in the British Isles in the sixth century) may have later been combined with the covenantal aspects of Augustinian thought. Pelagius's doctrine essentially rejected the damnation of humanity via original sin, thereby reducing the importance of the Christian sacraments. Grace, to him, consisted of the development of the natural attributes in man that lead him to God: reason, free will, and understanding of the Gospel. Because Pelagianism minimized the role of Divine grace in human salvation, it gave more room to free will and opened the door to humans as God's partners rather than merely as beneficiaries of His grace.

In his theory Pelagius rejected both the Arian view diminishing the full divinity of Jesus and the Manichean mystical view that denied Jesus his full humanity. It was his attack on the latter that led him to emphasize free will and the goodness of human nature and to demand stricter good conduct by Christians. Pelagius was in the tradition of Bible-oriented Christian scholarship.

Toward Hierarchy

Early medieval Christian doctrine regarded political organization as a consequence of Adam's fall. Covenant is a response to sin. The murderer Cain (who founded the first city) and the pagan conqueror Nimrod (who founded the first empire) are its progenitors. While this teaching is potentially subversive of all political structures, and was so perceived by the Romans, it was more often interpreted by the Church in light of those passages that appear to emphasize uncritical obedience to civil authority (e.g., Matthew 22:21; Romans 13:1-7; Titus 3:1-11; I Peter 2:13-25; II Peter 2:10) while accenting the second coming, when perfected mankind will abolish all government except the Kingship of Christ. Under such circumstances, politics is well-nigh superfluous because salvation is a matter of individual faith and common sacraments to which political-legal structures can contribute nothing. There is even a strong antipolitical bias in this view since, once all souls are saved, so to speak, questions of politics will become moot.

However, upon assuming the reins of the Roman Empire in the face of the disintegration of the civilized Mediterranean world, the invasions of "barbarians," and the emergence of sectarian movements, the church confronted very real political problems in organizing itself institutionally and providing for the organization of civil society externally. In many instances, moreover, the church, once it had acquired a structure of its own, was compelled or itself desired to exercise governmental functions directly.

This task was greatly complicated by the universal application of the Christian covenant. Unlike the Mosaic covenant, which created a particular people and body politic of relatively small size, the New Testament was designed to encompass all humanity and obligated the church to evangelize the world. In practical terms, this presented as formidable a political problem as that of organizing a world government. Factions and heresies within the church, strong ideational pressures from indigenous paganisms, the absence of a mandated or accumulated tradition of Christian governance, the fluidity of political systems and allegiances, the diversity and large numbers of people to be brought within the Christian fold as well as the intergroup hostilities among them, and the scope of territory involved in the enterprise, all seemed to rule out a covenantal system of cooperative partnerships.

Even so, the acknowledged greatest theologian and philosopher of medieval Christendom, Thomas Aquinas, whose philosophic system was far removed from overt concerns with covenantal thought, nevertheless found his ideal regime in the Mosaic polity of the twelve tribes. To him, it was the best regime because it was a mixed regime. He understood it as being a kind of hierarchical federalism that squared with medieval feudalism as a constitutionalized power pyramid. Nor was he the only one to do so.[29]

The kind of federal solution to the problem of maintaining democratic republicanism in large commonwealths, which James Madison articulated for the United States, for example, could not have been fashioned by the Church because the Madisonian system depends upon the crosspressures of many factions and opinions, both secular and religious.[30] The church believed it necessary to convert and bind people to a common orthodoxy. As a result, like most salvational movements that seek to transform human consciousness organizationally along common ideational lines, the character of both church polity and civil polity moved in a more hierarchic, imperial direction. As one contemporary ecumenical advocate has put it: "From the second century of the Christian era onwards the Church as a federal society meant, at least to Western Christendom, the Church as a society with a fixed constitution and with definite laws to be obeyed, and it was not until the time of the Reformation that the truly Biblical view of the Church as God's covenant-people recaptured the minds and imaginations of men."[31]

The movement toward pyramidal governance was furthered by the tendency of church fathers to turn for guidance to noncovenantal models of political association, especially the more organic and hierarchic models of the Greeks and Romans. At the same time that the church turned away from the political applications of the Israelite covenants, it sought to elevate and legitimate its theology in relation to the intellectually influential systems of Greek and Roman philosophy. Since Rome had long lost its republicanism by the Christian era, the church inherited the example of imperialism and the fact of near anarchy. Rome became the seat of authority of Western Christendom, atop an episcopal system of ranked ecclesiastics.

Notes

1. On vassal treaties, see Henri Frankfort, *Before Philosophy: The Intellectual Adventure of Ancient Man: An Essay on Speculative Thought in the Ancient Near East* (Harmondsworth: Penguin, 1951) and Andre Parrot, *Sumer* (Paris: Gallimand, 1960). For vassal treaties in Phoenicia, Minoa, Philistia, Ancient Greece, and Assyro-Babylonia, see: Donald Benjamin Harden, *The Phoenicians* (London: Thames and Hudson, 1963); Andrew Robert Brown, *Minoans, Philistines and Greeks, B.C. 1400–900* (London: Kegan Paul, 1930); and Henri Frankfort, *Kinship and the Gods* (Chicago: University of Chicago Press, 1948).
2. On the government and politics of ancient Mesopotamia, see Frankfort, *Before Philosophy*; and Parrot, *Sumer*.
3. On tribal confederations cf. Gerald J. Obermeyer, "The Ritual and Politics of Oath in Tribal Society," in *Al-Abhath* 26 (1973–1977).
4. On Canaanite government and politics, see William F. Albright, *The Archaelogy of Palestine* (Harmondsworth: Penguin, 1963) and *Yahweh and the Gods of Canaan: A Historical Analysis of Two Contrasting Faiths* (London: University of London Press, 1968); and Kathleen Kenyon, *Amorites and Canaanites* (London: Oxford University Press, 1966).
5. On the Philistines, see H. Kennard, *Philistines and Israelites: A New Light on the World's History* (London: Chapman and Hall, 1893); Robert Macalister, *The Philistines: Their History and Civilization* (Chicago: Argonaut, 1965); and Allen H. Jones, *Bronze Age Civilization: The Philistines and the Danites* (Washington, D.C.: Public Affairs Press, 1975).
6. John Ferguson, *The Heritage of Hellenism* (New York: Science History Publications, 1973).
7. On Greek leagues, see Edward A. Freeman, *History of Federal Government in Greece and Italy,* 2nd ed. (London: Macmillan, 1893).
8. On the Corinthian League, see ibid.
9. On the Ionian, Aetolian, and first Achean Leagues, see ibid.
10. On the second Achean League, see ibid.
11. Bernard W. Henderson, *The Life and Principate of the Emperor Hadrian A.D. 76–138* (New York: Brentanos Publishers, 1923), p. 42.
12. On the Roman use of federal devices, see Edward Freeman, *Sicily, Phoenician, Greek and Roman* (London: T. Fisher Unwin, 1894); Gaston Boissier, *Tacitus and Other Roman Studies,* trans. W. G. Hutchison (London: A. Constable, 1906); and Wolfgang Kunkel, *An Introduction to Roman Legal and Constitutional History,* 2nd ed., trans. J. M. Kelley (Oxford: Clarendon Press, 1973).

pyramidal model embodied in the *Corpus Christianum* and representing a mix of imperial, paternal, ecclesiastical, and feudal governance. Although the system rarely worked in full accord with the model, and the church was, de facto, obligated to enter contractual relationships, establish concordats with civil authorities, and sanction political federations from time to time, the dominant ideal of a Holy Roman Empire remained organic rather than federal.[3]

Fellowships of Christian Believers

There was one important countervailing trend mitigating the linkage between the organic and hierarchical models. Paul referred to the fellowship of Christian believers as a *koinonia,* the Greek term that is closest to describing a federal relationship or, in other words, a confederacy of believers. In essence, *koinonia* is the Greek equivalent for the Hebrew *hever,* a term used at that time by the Pharisees to describe a similar phenomenon in Judaism.[4] Both are clearly covenantal terms. In fact, Paul's use of *koinonia* to describe a human social organization is far more covenantal in the sense used here than his discussions of covenant as a theological principle. He uses *koinonian* as a synonym for *societatem* (I Corinthians 1:9). Paul emphasized the confederacy based upon communion that unites those who partake of the wafer and the wine as a cultic feast, thereby uniting with Christ's body and blood; thus, becoming part of the Christian community or *koinonia* involved taking the sacraments. The original meaning of the term *sacramentum* itself was oath, promise, or contract.[5] This meaning appears as late as medieval times, even in such secular contexts as the Frisian Laws.[6] It may therefore be said that the very terminology of Western religion is covenantal through and through, at least in its original meanings, however much they changed in later centuries.

Later the first Christians formed their communal societies, living together and taking their meals in common, as *koinonia*. The term is also used as a synonym for *communicatione* (Acts 2:42). The development of medieval monasticism was an attempt to restore the early Christian communities and their *vita apostolica* with its ideal of holy *koinonia*. This becomes particularly important in medieval Christianity in the differences between Christian societies organized out of monastic Christianity, as in Scotland, and those organized out of a hierarchical church, as in Italy. The concept of *koinonia* reappears in medieval Latin as *foedere* and is used principally in relationship to the fellowship of the monasteries and secondarily in connection with other equivalent relationships. *Koinonia* is also translated as *communia* or *communem* in the New Testament and the patristic and medieval writings.

Other Greek terms of covenantal import are *synagogue*, the Greek word for *kahal* or congregation, and *synod*, the Greek word for a meeting with policymaking or governing power, used especially in ancient Greece for meetings of members of a confederation.[7] *Synagogue* literally means meeting, assembly, or con-gregation; *synod*, an assembly, convention, or council. The terms suggest covenantal and collegial relationships. While synagogue came to be applied exclusively to Jewish congregations, synod became a general term for policymaking conventions of equals. These Greek equivalents of *kahal* were paralleled by *ecclesia*, the equivalent of *edah*, a word carried over into Latin and adopted by the Church to describe itself. To this day the Church sees itself as an *ecclesia*, a public assembly, in the manner of the *edah*.

In the first centuries of the Church prior to its establishment as the imperial religion, synods were widely used to establish church doctrine and policy and to resolve disputes among churches. Once the emperor became the civil head of the church polity, he assumed authority to convene synods. Consequently, the bishops of Rome, on their way to becoming popes, rejected synodal decisions as interfering with their prerogatives. As they grew stronger, the use of synods diminished, to be revived in the fifteenth century through the conciliar movement and in the sixteenth as part of the Protestant Reformation.

In the end, the quasi-contractual relationships that developed during the Middle Ages were more like suzerainty treaties, which established feudal relationships, rather than covenantal ones. Conceptions of popular sovereignty, such as that of Marsilius of Padua, were both rare and narrow in scope. Other thrusts, such as the Conciliarist movement, which held that the church should be governed by the whole congregation of people as represented in a general council, made only limited headway and did not necessarily apply to civil government, though they served to revive certain covenantal ideas in limited ways. Perhaps more effective was the rise of Estates assemblies within the context of feudalism, especially in England, to check royal power. The Estates, representing deputies from sectors of society and major cities, pressed for authority to approve new taxes and then for roles in legislative, executive, and judicial affairs. The Estates, along with newly chartered municipal corporations, had begun to achieve some successes in pluralizing the body politic within some areas of Europe by the time of the Reformation.

By rejecting the compactual model of political association in pursuit of a higher natural or divine perfection, the Greeks and the Church rendered the just regime of philosopher kings highly improbable and, therefore, ironically unjust because it consigned the "weak" many to the strong wolves in public life. From the point of view of the new compactual political science that developed in the late sixteenth century, the impossibility of the classical Greek regimes—their imaginary status and their later ecclesiastical perversions under Christianity, as Machiavelli observed—left the poor, the "weak," and the "many" without effective solutions to their severe political problems. In effect, classical political science abandoned the "many" to some 1800 years of tyranny under caesars, clerics, feudal overlords, and divine-right monarchs.

Reformation and Covenant Revival: The Second Separation

The Reformation initiated by Martin Luther in 1517 continued the organic orientation of Catholic Christendom. Indeed, Luther's religious ideology led to the substitution of petty hierarchies—religious and political—for the great hierarchies of the Church and the Holy Roman Empire. Almost coincidentally, however, there arose a parallel reformation that repudiated the entire organized hierarchical system and turned once again to covenantal ideas as the basis for a new Christian church based upon principles of liberty and republicanism. This was the Reformation of what became known as Reformed Protestantism, often erroneously referred to as Calvinism, after its best-known figure, who was responsible for its major stream. It represented the second separation of covenantal tradition and was based on an appropriate theology whose political implications were wide-ranging.

Reformed theology became known as federal or covenant theology. This new theology led to the formation of Reformed churches in German-speaking Switzerland, parts of Germany, and the Netherlands—Calvinist congregations in Geneva and the Huguenot areas of France, the Presbyterian church in Scotland, and Puritan congregationalism in England and New England. In other words, it brought about a revolution in church governance as well as ideology, republicanizing and federalizing the church as an institution wherever the federal theology became dominant.

This second separation was not confined to the church. True to the spirit of covenant, the federal idea had a direct political impact in the reconstitution of the governments of the Swiss republics dominated by the Reformed Church; in the shaping of the United Provinces of the Netherlands; in the founding of the British and Dutch colonies in North America; in Scotland; and in the short-lived Puritan Commonwealth established as a result of the English Civil War. In other words, it represented a synthesis of theological renewal, reform of church governance, and political reconstitution, which was the cornerstone of modern republicanism and the precursor of modern federalism.

As such, it was both a separation and a return—a separation from the organic and hierarchical dimensions of medieval Catholic Christendom and a return to the covenantal thinking of biblical Israel. The striking parallels between the congregational forms of the European Jewish communities and those later developed by Reformed Protestants, as well as the similarities in form and language of Jewish congregational compacts and those of Reformed Protestant congregations, especially Puritan ones, suggest at least an affinity grounded in the common Scriptures of the two; and, very likely, actual links through the predominantly Reformed Christian Hebraists who studied with rabbinical authorities throughout Europe.[8]

Many of the federal theologians studied Hebrew (and Aramaic) so as to be able to read not only the Hebrew Scriptures (for them, the Old Testament) in the original, but also later Jewish texts, such as the Talmud and the Midrash, as well. More than a few availed themselves of Jewish teachers, so that they were also directly influenced by the Jewish understanding of those texts. But, of course, theirs could not be merely a return since the reformers were devout believers in the centrality of Jesus in their faith, which added a dimension far removed from the Jewish worldview, and were influenced despite themselves by a millennium and a half of Christian history.

Secularization: The Third Separation

The polities established by the Reformers were to be aristocratic republics, with the ministers and magistrates elected because of their holiness or some other sign of divine election. In fact, some, like the United Provinces and certain of the Swiss republics, became self-perpetuating oligarchies while others, like the North American settlements, took a turn toward popular government early on. Still others, particularly England, were rapidly secularized under the influence of a post-Puritan generation that borrowed heavily from the political teachings of the Puritans, Presbyterians, and Calvinists while dropping their all-embracing religious character. This led, in turn, to the third separation between the religious and secular covenantal traditions.

So all-embracing was the impact of the covenant idea that three and four generations after its reemergence, the fourth stream borrowed it lock, stock, and barrel as the basis for the modern, secular polity with its republican and democratic character. Rather than draw upon Roman or medieval contractualism, these modern theorists and practitioners embraced the covenant idea and secularized it, at first reducing divine involvement to a peripheral place, and then essentially eliminating that involvement altogether. Where the moral element of covenanting remained, it was on the basis of mutualism; hence, the shift in terminology from covenant to compact in the latter part of the seventeenth century.

Within the stream of secular political philosophy, the idea of covenant received its first full exposition in the work of Johannes Althusius, *Politica methodice digesta atque exemplis sacris et profanis illustrata,* published in 1603 in Herborn, one of the leading German centers of federal theology. Althusius himself was a devout member of the Reformed church.[9] Subsequently, the idea of covenant appeared in various secular forms, mainly as the idea of the social contract or compact, in what *Publius* later termed "the new science of politics" of Thomas Hobbes (1588–1679), James Harrington (1611–77), and John Locke (1632–1704). On the continent, it was given fully secular expression by Benedict de Spinoza (1632–77), who used the mould of the ancient Israelite polity for utterly contrary ends, as well as by Hugo Grotius (1582–1645), Samuel Pufendorf (1632–94), and Baron de Montesquieu (1689–1755), among others. Jean-Jacques Rousseau (1712–78) was to give it yet another form of expression as the *contrat social.*

For these theorists and those children of the Enlightenment who embraced their views, politics acquired a new legitimacy as the polity acquired a new importance detached from theological questions regarding its origin. Among some, politics began to be viewed as a vehicle for attaining secular salvation, a view that was to gain wide currency among the followers of Rousseau.[10]

As the idea of the compact became even more specific, the term *contract* was introduced in the eighteenth century, at which point critics of the theory began to raise their heads. If Hobbes and Locke were seventeenth-century exponents of a secularized covenant theory, and Rousseau the principal eighteenth century exponent of its contractual expression, David Hume, in 1752, ten years before the publication of Rousseau's *Du Contract Sociale* set forth what was to become the accepted critique of the secular compact tradition.[11] By the time of the French Revolution, when the contractual dimension of the theory was carried to its revolutionary extreme, Edmund Burke could seek to transcend it by referring to such contracts as mere partnerships for trade, suggesting instead that civil society was an interorganizational partnership; in other words, a covenant organicized.[12]

These theological and philosophical streams were intertwined in various ways. Many of the federal theologians concerned themselves extensively with politics, not only because of the political exigencies of the Reformation, but also because the theology of covenant led to constitutional ideas associated with social compacts and civil contracts. Likewise, most of the secular political philosophers were quite concerned with matters of religion, as is evident in Hobbes and Locke. In England, moreover, federal theology received its fullest European expressions in theory and, more especially, in practice. In turn, English political philosophers became the leading exponents of the compactual theories of the "new political science."

It seems to be more than accidental that virtually all of the proponents of federal theologies and theories of political compact were clustered within a single cultural belt and its extensions consisting of Switzerland, the Dutch Provinces, England-Scotland, western Germany, eastern France, and British North America. This geohistorical proximity facilitated frequent and varied communication and contacts among and between the theologians and philosophers. In the case of Hobbes and Locke, for example, one cannot ignore their close Puritan and Anglican connections.

It is therefore inaccurate to trace the line of development of modern constitutionalism and republicanism solely through the secular stream that flowed from the ancient Greeks and Romans through medieval contractualism and then through Machiavelli, Hobbes, Locke, and others without also taking into account the covenantal stream that ran above ground through ancient Israel and the Reformation and, perhaps, underground or semisubmerged during the Middle Ages. This covenantal stream had both a direct influence on the development of modern republicanism and an indirect influence through the "new political science." It is also inaccurate and incomplete to trace American constitutionalism and republicanism simply to Locke and Blackstone, as is done in most textbooks on American government, and to attribute American federalism simply to Montesquieu and unique environmental circumstances.[13] In this respect, Lord Bryce was somewhat more accurate in noting "that the American Government and the Constitution are based on the theology of Calvin and the philosophy of Hobbes."[14]

If it was in the United States that the secular theory took wing, it was never without being closely intertwined with Reformed Christian tradition. Thus, the history of American politics reflects the dominance of neither covenant nor compact, but the interaction between the two. Indeed, it was only when the first tradition was drastically weakened in the nineteenth century that the second also collapsed as the plumbline for American politics. If both survived subliminally until our time, they did so in tandem. Thus, the People's Bicentennial Commission, a last effort on the part of the 1960s radicals to take control of the political destiny of the United States, emphasized both the covenantal and compactual origins of the American civil society and its polity in their efforts to capture the American political tradition for their own ideas.[15]

Four Political Perspectives

Each of the four streams developed its own political expression of the covenant tradition that is reflected in the political life of those within it. We have already seen how covenant has shaped the Jewish political tradition in exile, so that even in exile, Jews have persisted in using covenant forms to organize their congregational republics or regional polities, combining covenantal foundations and republican arrangements with the aristocratic tendency of giving a special role to scholars and increasingly, in the diaspora, to those wealthy enough to support the burdens of the community when the host rulers demanded exorbitant sums from the Jews to allow them to continue to reside in their territories. This covenantal republicanism was skewed from time to time and from place to place by the intervention of the host authorities, who insisted that the Jewish community adopt governmental arrangements that suited their needs to exercise control.

At times these arrangements were theoretically quite hierarchical in character, as the ruling authorities sought to have one address for the Jewish community, and even to hold one person responsible for the behavior of the Jews. One of the most interesting chapters of Jewish political history is how Jewish communities were able to introduce covenantal republicanism on a nonhierarchical basis into such systems by binding the person or group nominally on top of the hierarchy to the noncentralized Jewish institutions. Needless to say, this did not succeed in every case, because where the host power was willing to intervene to insist upon hierarchical arrangements, there was little the Jewish community could do. However, for the most part the host power was interested in results, not in methods, and was content to allow the Jews their own arrangements, provided the results met their expectations.

What is most important, however, is that Jews continued to view politics as part and parcel of human life, a potentially efficacious device through which to pursue salvation, and a major human responsibility under humanity's covenantal partnership with God. Thus, in Jewish tradition the polity is a legitimate expression of human aspirations, one that will continue to exist in the messianic era, and not merely an unpleasant but necessary response to human sinfulness.

In the Christian tradition, as it was taken over by the Catholic and Orthodox Churches, the political dimension of the new covenant came to be understood in oligarchic or hierarchic terms. In that respect, emphasis on covenant as a matter of God's graciousness rather than mutual agreement lent itself to a more hierarchical approach to human government, especially since government itself was considered an institution that existed only because of man's sinfulness and, therefore, as a punishment of God and not as an instrument of human fulfillment. That alone would have been sufficient to justify hierarchical, and indeed autocratic, rule, which is what prevailed in most segments of Christendom prior to the Reformation. The exceptions were those regions where pre-Christian political cultures weakened the impact of Christianity in the sphere of governance. Most of medieval constitutionalism has to be examined not as a reflection of church doctrine but as a synthesis of tribal tradition and the Roman law of contract. It was only in the writings of certain of the political theorists of the age that any attempt was made to synthesize the Church's view of the polity, with Augustine and Aquinas the pillars of those efforts. These remained abstractions, however, far removed from the day-to-day realities of governance and the distribution and exercise of power.

Covenant came into its own as a political force with the Reformation and the second separation. The Reformed tradition took first the federal theology and then Calvinism and gave them full expression in the political arena in the most deliberate manner. Perhaps more than at any time before or since in the history of Western civilization, covenant was deliberately used as a basis and standard for the organization of polities and the conduct of government, with all links between the biblical concept and its theological and political dimensions made explicit and given elaborate intellectual and popular forms. People covenanted in the Swiss cities and cantons, in France among the Hugenots, in Scotland and Puritan England, and most of all in the British colonies of North America. Not merely a theoretical construct, covenant was as real a political device as it was in the days of the twelve tribes and the Kings of Israel and Judah.

The use of covenants in the Reformed Protestant tradition was accompanied by an intellectual outpouring that was not characteristic of the biblical epochs; reflecting, as it were, the continuation of the Greek philosophic traditions within biblical frameworks. While Reformed Protestants were ambivalent about the ultimate character of political life, in line with Christian traditions, like the Jews, they recognized the importance of polity in the effort to achieve the holy community. Hence they emphasized matters of both civil and church polity in their efforts at reforming Christianity.

As a result of the third separation, democratic republicanism came to be the principal feature of modern politics, so much so that even the revolutionaries of the left and the right had to pay obeisance to it in most cases. More often than not, democratic republican regimes were founded on secularized covenantal principles—in the most successful cases on actual covenants and compacts. Republican constitutionalism had become so much a matter of effectuating covenants and compacts that the latter were well-nigh forgotten in light of the allegiance and respect given the former.

The power of such constitutions was greatest where the covenant and compactual traditions were intertwined, as in the United States and Switzerland. In other countries, where the Reformed Protestant stream had been prominent, still other dimensions of covenantal politics came through. This was particularly true of those influenced by the Dutch Reformed Church, where in the late nineteenth century a new covenantal politics was inaugurated by Dutch political leader Abraham Kuyper, who became the architect of what was later to be called Dutch consociationalism, and who shaped Dutch politics for two generations on the basis of his covenantal perspective. In a very different way in the same period, the Afrikaners of South Africa created a covenantal politics that gained them dominance in their country in the face of British imperialism and a black majority. In both cases, covenant proved to be a powerful tool for the achievement of the most concrete political goals.

Perhaps the greatest political revolution of modernity was the republican revolution—the restoration of the idea that the polity was a *res publica,* a commonwealth, the possession of its citizens, and not of some single individual or group who happened to rule it. The republican revolution was born out of the revolt against the divine right of kings, in itself a heresy that grew out of the rejection of medieval constitutionalism in the middle of the previous epoch. The justification for the republican revolution was drawn directly and explicitly from the covenant idea in either its religious or secular form; that is to say, either because God, in establishing His covenant with humanity, rejected tyranny as a violation of the terms of that covenant, or because autonomous humans came together in political covenants or compacts to form civil society in order to protect themselves from the terrors of living in a state of nature and to gain the benefits of association on the basis of mutuality. In essence, covenants or compacts created the publics out of which republics could be constructed.

In a sense, this represented the ultimate triumph of the covenant idea in politics. No republic could exist without the consent of its public. Implicit in the idea of consent is some idea of covenant, compact, or contract. So, as the republican revolution swept the world—first the West during the modern epoch and then the East in the postmodern epoch—the idea of republican consent became universalized. Today every polity that claims to be modern must at least pay lip service and give symbolic expression to it.

But, of course, once an idea becomes all things to all men, it ceases to be effective as an idea. The history of modern times is as much a history of the perversion of covenant as a political idea as of its triumph, of its exploitation for covenantally illegitimate ends, its distortion to justify those ends, and usually covenantally illegitimate means to achieve them. Hence, modernity introduced much hypocrisy with regard to the covenant as the basis for polity. We must never forget, however, that hypocrisy is the tribute vice pays to virtue. While it must be understood for what it is, especially when it shapes and forms polities and thereby directly affects the lives of people, it must also be taken as testimony to the central importance of the virtue to which it pays tribute; in this case, covenantal principles and practices.

Our task in the following chapters will be to explore in greater depth the transmission of those principles and practices during the ancient and medieval epochs and their flowering in late medieval and early modern times. We will then examine the principal comprehensive expressions of those principles and practices that emerged as a result of that flowering and the distortions which, perforce, accompanied them as a result of the republican revolution.

Notes

1. R. G. Mulgan, "Lycophron and Greek Theories of Social Contract," *Journal of the History of Ideas* 40 (January-March, 1979): 121–28.
2. Cf. Glaucon's story of the ring of Gyges in Book II of *The Republic*.
3. Only in its medieval and early modern period were federalist conceptions put forth to try to save the declining empire. Cf. Heinz Eulau, "Theories of Federalism Under the Holy Roman Empire," *American Political Science Review* 25, no. 4 (1941): 633–64, and Patrick Riley, *Will and Legitimacy: A Critical Exposition of Social Contract Theory in Hobbes, Locke, Rousseau, Kant and Hegel* (Cambridge, Mass.: Harvard University Press, 1982).
4. J. Kittel points out this meaning of *koinonia* in his *Theological Dictionary* vol. 3, 804ff., linking the term with *hever*.
5. Tertulian, *Ad Martyres* 3, PL, I, 624 and Cyprian, *De Lapsis* 13, CSEL, III, 1, 246, 12; J. D. Ghellinck, ed., *Pour l'histoire de Mot* (Louvain, 1924); R. Much, *Die Germania des Tacitus* (Heidelberg, 1934), 163.
6. Cf. Walter Baetke, *De Religion der Germanen in Quellenzeugnisse* (Frankfurt-am-Main, 1944), 49–53.
7. William Johnson Everett, *God's Federal Republic* (New York/Mahwah: Paulist Press, 1988), 63.
8. On Christian Hebraism, see Charles Berlin and Aaron L. Katchen, *Christian Hebraism: The Study of Jewish Culture by Christian Scholars in Medieval and Early Modern Times* (Cambridge, Mass.: Harvard University Press, 1988) and

Aaron Katchen, *Christian Hebraists and Dutch Rabbis: Seventeenth Century Apologetics and the Study of Maimonides' Mishneh Torah* (Cambridge, Mass.: Harvard University Press, 1984).

9. Johannes Althusius, *Politica Methodice Digesta (1603)*, ed. Carl J. Friedrich (Cambridge, Mass.: Harvard University Press, 1935); Frederick Carney, trans., *Johannes Althusius' Politics* (Boston: Beacon Press, 1964); Otto Gierke, *The Development of Political Theory* (New York: Norton, 1939).

10. See Leo Strauss, *Natural Right and History*; Hobbes, *The Element of Law, Natural and Politic, Leviathan, Man and Citizen*; and Vincent Ostrom, "Hobbes as Reformation Theologian: Implications of the Free-Will Controversy," *Journal of the History of Ideas* 40 (July-September, 1979): 339–52. Locke, *Conduct of the Understanding, An Essay Concerning Human Understanding, Essays on the Law of Nature, Of Civil Government*; Grotius, *Prolegomena to the Law of War and Peace*; and E. Dumbard, *The Life and Legal Writings of Grotius* (Norman: University of Oklahoma Press, 1969).

11. David Hume, *A Treatise of Human Nature*, ed. L. A. Selby-Bigge, 2nd ed. (Oxford: Clarendon Press, 1978).

12. Edmund Burke, *Edmund Burke on Government, Politics, and Society* (Hassocks Sussex: Harvester Press, 1975).

13. See, for example, Thomas Lee Pangle, *The Spirit of Modern Republicanism: The Moral Vision of the American Founders and the Philosophy of Locke* (Chicago: University of Chicago Press, 1988).

14. James Bryce, *The American Commonwealth* I (New York: Macmillan, 1907), 306.

15. For a discussion of the People's Bicentennial Commission, see its publications: *America's Birthday: A Planning and Activity Guide for Citizens' Participation during the Bicentennial Years* (New York: Simon and Schuster, 1974); and *Voices of the American Revolution/The People's Bicentennial Commission* (New York: Bantam Books, 1975).

Part II

Medieval Expressions of Oath and Pact

3

Feudalism: Covenantal Fraud, Heresy, or Synthesis?

A Mixture of Hierarchy and Contract

Whatever the arguments about the true character of feudalism, and there are ever so many, all are agreed that the basic components of every feudal system are an admixture of hierarchical and contractual arrangements.[1] The disagreements come as to the character and meaning of the mixture. The hierarchical dimension of European feudalism had two aspects. One was the continuation of the hierarchical structure of the Roman Empire as adopted and adapted by the Catholic Church, which institutionalized it as its most fundamental constitutional principle, thereby continuing in at least a formal way the secular Imperium of Rome.

These ambiguities are reflected in medieval political thought, which first and foremost emphasizes the organic nature of the polity, more often than not anticipates its hierarchical ordering of authority and rule, yet at the same time has a sense of polities founded on consent, having a constitutional framework, and being ordered by contract. Volumes have been written on each of these points, offering different interpretations of their importance, place, and meaning in the medieval order, both in theory and in practice. It is not the intention of this volume to try to sort out all of this literature. For our purposes, the ambiguity and lack of clarity is even more suggestive.[2]

What is clear is that thought in the Middle Ages was communal rather than individualistic. Eccleshall has argued that, in England, individualism does not enter political philosophy until the 1640s.[3] Black says this may be true as far as the literate public is concerned, but the issue of individualism was debated among intellectuals in discussion of "the

55

nature of social entities" from the twelfth century onward, with the division being between holism and individualism. Black goes into some detail about these different views. For lawyers, society was a *universitas* or corporation, an understanding that ranged from a primarily collective concept to a collegial one along Conciliorist lines.

The second aspect is related to feudalism, which reputedly originated in response to the period of anarchy following the invasions of the barbarians and the fall of Rome. Strong men gained power by virtue of their ability to defend themselves and to protect others, developing hierarchical relationships through the exaction of fealty in return for protection. The reality of the first aspect in both its manifestations is far more persuasive than the second as the key factor in establishing the hierarchical character of feudalism.

The history of the emergence of feudalism out of the decline of the Roman Empire is in itself a reflection of the power of the idea of contract. We have already noted how contractualism was one of the great achievements of Roman civil society. When the Roman republic became an empire, theoretically it did so without changing its contractual basis, but over time status came to replace contract as part of the imperial system. Then, as the empire declined, urban patricians took up residence in the countryside to escape the confiscatory taxation associated with municipal life. They built great landed estates and benefitted from the excessive taxation of free farmers to force them to accept the status of *coloni,* who in time became tied to the soil by custom, and then in 332 by Roman law. As the Empire's ability to maintain the peace diminished, these estates became fortified places and their lords surrounded themselves with retainers and developed private armies, all of whom took oaths of fealty to the lord of the manor within the framework of nominal allegiance to the Emperor.

Through this judicious but extensive introduction of new contractual arrangements supported by fealty oaths, imperial society was transformed into feudalism. Long before Rome fell, these villas were virtually immune from imperial authority. They levied their own taxes, administered the laws, and, as proprietary churches developed on them, even became ecclesiastical units. All this was supported and strengthened by their control of the economy. Thus, feudalism developed in Italy and spread to much of the rest of Europe. This transformation was aided by the growing power of local military commanders as the

If we consider Switzerland the heartland of republican Europe, these city-states represented a southern extension of that tradition, parallel to its northern extension up the Rhine River Valley. These republics were built on a network of civic associations established on a contractual basis through the oaths of their members. There were mutual aid societies of all kinds—guilds, credit associations, religious confraternities, protective leagues—that could defend the city-republics against their enemies. While based on oaths and at times covenants, sharing one of the basic characteristics of covenant society, namely the reliance upon mutual trust, they were primarily civil and contractual, not animated by any vision of society but only by the need of people to protect themselves and to cooperate in pursuing their peace and prosperity. Since they were more contractual than covenantal, they were unable to galvanize their people in moralistic ways. This is not to take away from their achievement of a more secure and ordered life, greater equality for most if not all citizens, and economic development, but it does explain why they were only partially successful even in their heyday and were limited to very secular achievement.

Robert Putnam discusses the degree to which insecurity, civil strife, poverty, and social degeneration were present in these city-republics even in their best days, not to speak of their later ones. According to the thesis presented in this book, that points out rather precisely the limits between contractual societies and covenantal ones. The city-republics were civic and their successor cities and regions have remained so. Being civic is a great thing in its own right, but it has its limits.

Putnam and his colleagues have documented the difference between north and south through use of quantitative data, perhaps more than anyone has ever successfully used quantitative measures, to document the difference between covenantal and hierarchical orders.[10] The data show that in the normal measures of socioeconomic conditions within contemporary Italy, those northern and north-central regions are well ahead of the rest of the country, just as even a cursory comparison of international data suggests the same in those countries with a covenantal base as distinct from those countries without. Putnam suggests why: "A vertical network, no matter how dense and no matter how important to its participants, cannot sustain social trust and cooperation. Vertical flows of information are often less reliable than horizontal flows, in part because the subordinate husbands information as a hedge against exploitation. More important, sanctions that support norms of reciprocity against the threat of opportunism are less likely to be imposed upwards and less likely to be acceded to if imposed."[11]

The thirteenth- and fourteenth-century Italian civilians and canonists developed a corporation theory to establish and protect the sovereignty of cities within or outside of the imperial structures of their time which, while not necessarily covenantal, made a contribution to the emergence of European federalism. It was a juristic theory of government by the people. Two of the principal articulators of the corporation theory were Bartolus of Sassoferrato and Baldus de Ubaldis (d. 1400).[12]

They and their colleagues developed a theory of the sovereign self-governing city community, a public composed of citizens who govern themselves through the establishment of a civic corporation. This corporation rests upon effective rather than constitutionally active consent. As such it acquires the power of a single persona. This in turn gives it a new reality of the kind that inheres in corporations to this day, even though a corporation is a fictive person. They do not go so far as to have the corporation established by some kind of formal pact, but rather through acts such as choosing the corporation assembly, which then can act in the name of its people as a public. Corporations are a part of an imperial framework and also have a relationship to it not fully defined but which gives them a certain degree of independence. The corporation council or general assembly is the basis for its active existence and it is the council that develops the constitutional arrangements for the corporation and, where appropriate, its place in the empire.

In time these city republics were to develop and be guided by an ideology that came to be known as civic humanism. It became dominant in the Italian Renaissance and perhaps more than any single element characterized that great revival of art, learning, and civic spirit that, along with the Reformation, became one of the twin sources of modernism. The civic humanist ideology looked to the development of at least a class of leaders who would be at home in classical knowledge and political wisdom and the fine and practical arts, and who were both committed to and capable of governing their city republics in such a way as to preserve their independence and republican institutions.

Civic humanism was essentially a secular ideology of republicanism. As its elitist orientation suggests, it rested on the organic theory of the polity. The new doctrine of the Renaissance became the basis of a new secularized republicanism. It was a doctrine based on a Promethean theme. Civic liberty and self-government could best be preserved through the performance of public personages who, through their initiatives, sought the common good. A leadership that rejected resignation to fate or *fortuna* was what was needed in this republican order, rejecting the Christian self-abnegation of the Middle Ages.

Florence became the model of the new republicanism of civic humanism. Its polar representatives were Savonarola and Machiavelli. Savonarola, an austere Puritan, emphasized republican virtue in personal character as expressed through internalized Christian rule over individual passions. Every individual was to internalize Christ as the governor of his passions so that, as Everett says, "the political republic rested on a psychological monarchy" (69). Nicholo Machiavelli, on the other hand, looked to the external controls of the mixed regime, not expecting humans to be able to control their passions by themselves. He rejected Christian virtue as the vehicle for maintaining republicanism, seeking instead to harness the passions and ambitions of great men to the cause of liberty and justice. Neither of these models was covenantal in character. The closest that Italian city-states came to covenantalism was through the defensive leagues and confederations they found necessary to establish to protect themselves against external enemies.

One such league was the Chianti League of Tuscany, formed at the beginning of the fourteenth century for the administration and defense of the region. Like other leagues, it had an investiture oath to which its leaders had to swear before taking office. In Tuscan style, it began: "I promise to keep myself close to nature, to give a religious meaning to my life, to look around me with optimism and with love."

The league was far-reaching. Even the arts were mobilized on its behalf. At the same time that it was founded, the Tuscan painter Ambrogio Lorenzetti painted a set of frescoes of "good and bad government" in the Siena town hall, the first townscape and landscape paintings in the history of European art. Tuscany and its humanists established a tradition of beautiful landscapes and townscapes that remains powerful five centuries later.

The exceptions to this secular doctrine were to be found among the Jews, who brought elements of the spirit of civic humanism into their ghettos within the Italian city republics in the fifteenth and sixteenth centuries, and among a small group of humanist scholars who, in the latter part of the fifteenth and early sixteenth centuries, were drawn to a rediscovery of biblical and Jewish sources and were at least modestly influenced by their covenantal dimensions, although in fact they were looking for other things within them.

Not surprisingly, these municipal republics themselves often succumbed to the tendencies in Italian political culture to accept oligarchic rule on an organic basis, even while retaining a formally republican framework.[13] In a relatively short time, they accepted the "natural" elevation of certain principal families to what became hereditary positions of rulership. What can be said of these republics is that they preserved the Roman idea of the commonwealth as an association of people pursuing a shared concept of justice and a partnership in pursuit of common interests because these associations were contractual rather than covenantal, bound to each other out of common interest rather than linked as partners under heaven for some larger purpose.

What is extraordinary about the belt of cities that were municipal republics based on extensive networks of internal associations in the high Middle Ages is the degree to which the civic culture they fostered persisted despite all the vicissitudes through which the Italian territories and their inhabitants passed in the subsequent millennium, to remain today the centers of political and economic progress in Italy. Putnum shows that the single best predictor as to where to find the cutting edge of Italian political and economic progress is the spread of self-help societies in eleventh century Italy. He is attesting to the long-lasting character of culture and its power to shape society in general, and more specifically, to the power of this Italian civic associational culture to release for generations the energies of those who were and are its products, whenever conditions have been ripe to do so.[14]

Thus, Italian feudalism furnished important examples of the two major forms of feudal linkage: the vertical linkage in the south and the horizontal linkage in the north. Both were products of the feudal age; both had a degree of success, each within its own fundamental principles and terms of reference, and both have left legacies that have lasted a thousand years or more and are still having their consequences in very important ways. The first was hierarchical and the second contractual, and the differences speak for themselves.

France: The Ever-Hierarchical

France developed into an increasingly centralized state through the more or less uniform application of feudal principles throughout the territory which the Counts of Paris were able to conquer or otherwise acquire—not infrequently through personal covenants or compacts—in the name of the emergent French state. After an initial period of weakness, the kings of the new state were able to shift the balance of power and through a series of devices transform nominally hierarchical arrangements into real ones with the monarchy clearly at the top of the power pyramid and the nobility, subordinate to the king, increasingly concentrated in Paris and dependent on the royal court. This achievement made France the first nation-state in Europe, both chronologically and in terms of political and military power.[15]

The Franks transformed the feudal order into an embryonic state through two devices. One was the development of a system of feudal law, which took form in the Carolingian era and in the development of a strong and increasingly centralized administrative system. The feudal law of the Franks was both political and centralized; as such it was quite hierarchical. As Mitteis writes, "the king became the apex of the feudal pyramid so that his power as a monarch was reinforced by his position as a feudal overlord."[16] This feudal law also became an administrative code, which in turn assisted the development of systematic administration suited to Frankish character. Since in France Frankish law had no rivals, it shaped the state in the making from a relatively early period.

In order to hold the French state together, the French leadership fostered a myth about the French people that emphasized its organic character as a single nation, a myth whose fragility was visible in a variety of ways, impressed on France by a cultural imperialism imposed by Paris on the regions that maintained separate languages or dialects and separatist traditions well into the nineteenth century. At no time in this period did the French power elite seek to use contractual means to give expression to French nationalism. Even at the height of French feudalism, the contractual dimension played a secondary role, with naked power arrangements visibly determining the degree of fealty within French feudalism.

Frankish law had its influence beyond France proper, contributing to the development of more systematic administration in southern Italy and England as well. However, in both places its influence was limited by the existence of other approaches to law—Lombard law in Italy and Anglo-Saxon law in England. In Germany it never even really reached the stage of creating a common administrative structure. Such administrative machinery as did develop, developed in the individual Germanic states.

The Iberian Peninsula

In Spain, on the other hand, the antihierarchical dimension of covenantal politics was more pronounced even where feudal forms were preserved and contractualism was prevalent.[17] Even after hereditary succession became a fact in the twelfth century, in both Aragon and Castille it was still founded on the theory of compact. Thus, every new king of Aragon had first to take a coronation oath, administered to him by the judiciary at Saragossa, to maintain the laws and liberties of the realm before the title was his. The famous oath of fealty of the Aragonese to their king reflects this clearly: "We, who are as good as you, choose you who are no better than us, for our king and lord and pledge to you our loyalty and support provided you observe our laws and customs. If not, not."[18] This was particularly true in Christian Spain, although Muslim Spain was also feudal, albeit in a more simply hierarchical and contractual way.

The difference in the Spanish situation can be understood as a result of the moral and political aspects of the *reconquista,* the reconquest of Spain from the Muslims, and as a reflection of the pluralism in Spanish society at that time. The *reconquista* was a moral adventure conducted in the name of heaven. Hence, it bound those in the Christian population who participated in it to a common transcendent goal, thereby equalizing them through the pursuit of that goal. At the same time, the reconquest brought into the Christian kingdoms substantial populations of Jews and Muslims who retained rights of self-government in their respective communities.

Moreover, the *reconquista* required an allocation of the conquered territories. While feudal principles were used in the allocation, they were expressed through contracts between kings and those members of the nobility willing to go out and actually reconquer those territories, which gave the latter primordial rights as co-conquerors. They and their troops participated in the activity, "on shares" as it were, including a share in their own governance. What resulted was a network of *fueros,* or constitutionalized local liberties which, while fitting into feudalism, substantially transformed it in the direction of the contractual model. What emerged was a synthesis known in Spain as *foralismo* (from *fuero*)—the vesting of local liberties.

Robert Agranoff and others have referred to early medieval Spain as confederal Spain.[19] The regional entities of Spain were forged during the 700-year-long Christian reconquest of Spain from the Muslims, during which several Christian kingdoms emerged, including Asturias, which was never conquered by the Muslims; Castille-Leon; Aragon-Catalonia-Valencia; Portugal; Galicia; and Navarre. The Basque provinces maintained a separate identity because of their ethnic differences. In each of these, different languages were spoken, different customs and political systems were maintained. Their local rights were negotiated between kings and local citizens through *fueros,* charters of immunity, purely local, then provincial. In the Basque country and Navarre these *fueros* continued in modified form well into the nineteenth century and in some respects even to the present.

It was not until Ferdinand's conquest of southern Navarre in 1515 that Spain achieved even formal union within its present boundaries, and then the links between the kingdoms were dynastic and confederal in nature. In addition to having negotiated *fueros* to link the kingdoms within the crown of Aragon, the governmental system of Aragon was in many ways federal. The three subkingdoms within the kingdom—Aragon, Catalonia, and Valencia—had governments based on a theory of a constitutional compact whereby the Aragonese monarch was required to legislate only through the Cortes, which also voted all funding. After Navarre was conquered and annexed it not only had similar standing, but retained its own representative institutions, customs, and coinage.

At the other end of northern Spain, in the Basque country, another oath and pact society manifested itself through juntas formed in every parish and a *juntas generales* (general assembly) of Bizkaia, which met in Guernica (in the Basque language, *Gernika*) around the now-famed tree of Guernica. These juntas, developed locally, were then affirmed by the outside rulers of the Basque provinces as *fueros.* Accordingly, Basque provincial government was based on the idea stated in their tradition as "the king must obey our laws." These fueros and the juntas organized under them lasted until 1876, when they were abolished after the triumph of Madrid in the second Carlist War. Only the fueros of Navarre lasted longer.

It should be noted that with the introduction of the state of the autonomies in Spain in 1979 after Franco's death, the Basques established an autonomous community under the Spanish constitution of 1978 and the juntas were restored, albeit in modernized form. The tree of Guernica, itself just a protected stump, but with offshoots planted around the Bizkaia parliamentary buildings, has remained the symbol of Basque liberties. It was as such that Guernica suffered the first massive air bombardment in history, by the Fascists in the Spanish Civil War.

Thus, oath and pact societies flourished in a belt across the northern quarter of the Iberian Peninsula, each in its own way, in Catalonia, Aragon, Navarre, and the Basque country.

With the completion of the reconquest in 1492, the rulers of an increasingly united Spain began to subvert the medieval system, but it was so strong that it took them hundreds of years to effectively establish their absolute authority, and the peoples of Spain never gave up the principle of *foral* rights. Until the early eighteenth century even Hapsburg Spain basically followed this confederal system. In the eighteenth century a series of four Hapsburg-Bourbon wars and internal Spanish revolts led to the suppression of these constitutional arrangements, but local identity with the *patria chica* remained. It served as one of the bases for the numerous Carlist-sponsored efforts to revolt against the Spanish monarchy for the next hundred years or more. The issue resurfaced after the Napoleonic wars upset the established absolutism on the Iberian Peninsula. It was expressed through a variety of strange combinations in the nineteenth century. For example, the people of Navarre, who had been able to retain their *foral* rights throughout the period of absolutism, sided with the Carlist claimant to the Spanish throne in the Carlist wars of the nineteenth century and, when he lost, they lost most of those rights.[20] As the government of Spain modernized, more modern ideas of federalism became common coin and were even tried in the First Republic (1873–75). In short, even with the formation of the Spanish state, the nations of Spain continued to survive within it.

Today this foralistic approach has resurfaced in post-Franco Spain in both old and new ways, reinforced by certain aspects of Spanish culture, including Spanish political culture. It is present *de facto*, though deliberately not by name, in the new system of autonomous regions instituted under the 1978 Spanish constitution and is the key to the special Spanish approach to decentralization.[21]

Europe to the East

To the east of the Holy Roman Empire, settled polities only began to emerge out of tribal forms of government after centuries of tribal migrations westward. It seems that those polities were built out of a combination of organic and contractual arrangements, at least in the cases of Poland and Hungary, and as sheer despotisms based on conquest in its most naked form in the Slavic areas to their south and east. The Polish system, which was to become famous in later years as the worst possible form of government in Europe, rested on an assembly of nobles who chose the king and were involved in every important decision, operating on the basis of unanimity so that any one member could veto any action.[22]

Hungary was constituted by a compact among the southern Magyar tribes in 1001, under their founding King Stephen, who had also brought them to Christianity in the tenth century. In both cases, a nobility that had developed in more or less organic ways within each tribe or region compacted with one another in the name of their followers to organize a people or polity.[23] The Magyars, victorious after conquering the territory now known as the Hungarian plain, came together and made a pact to join together, accept Christianity, and proclaim Stephen their king. Subsequent generations of Hungarians have accepted this event as the starting point of their sacred history, the founding of their state and nation. In due course King Stephen became Saint Stephen, the patron saint of Hungary, thereby reaffirming the unity of the Hungarians' religious and national commitment.

What seems to be missing from this is carryover. The pact was a one-time act, not dissimilar from pacts among tribes in other times and climes. Stephen's crown was awarded him by the Pope and he built a state along German lines. The pact itself did not lead to the establishment or reinforcement of either a covenantal regime or political culture.

Notes

1. Paul Henri Mallet, *Northern Antiquities,* trans. Bishop Percy (New York: AMS Press 1968), "of the form of government which formerly prevailed in the north,"

chap. 7, 122-34; Heinrich Mitteis, *The State in the Middle Ages,* trans. H. F. Orton (Amsterdam and Oxford: North Holland Publishing Co., 1975), introduction, 3-23; Fritz Kern, *Kingship and Law in the Middle Ages,* trans. S. P. Chimes (Oxford: Basil Blackwell, 1956). On feudalism, see Rushton Coulborn, ed., *Feudalism in History* (Princeton: Princeton University Press, 1956); John S. Critchley, *Feudalism* (London: G. Allen & Unwin, 1978); and Fritz Kern, *Kingship and Law in the Middle Ages* (Oxford: Basil Blackwell, 1948).

2. Antony Black, "Society and the Individual from the Middle Ages to Rousseau: Philosophy, Jurisprudence and Constitutional Theory," *History of Political Thought* 1, no. 2 (Summer 1980): 145-66.

3. R. Eccleshall, *Order and Reason in Politics: Theories of Absolute and Limited Monarchy in Early Modern England* (Oxford: Oxford University Press, 1978), 10.

4. On the medieval Catholic church, see John A. F. Thompson, *Popes and Princes, 1417-1517: Politics and Polity in the Late Medieval Church* (London: G. Allen & Unwin, 1980).

5. Henry Maine, *Ancient Law* (London: Dent, 1965), 343ff; H. Silving, "The Oath," *Yale Law Journal* LXVIII (1959): 1329-90, 1527-77; Westermarck, *The Origin and Development of Moral Ideas* (London, 1912), I. 58-61 II, 118; A. E. Crowley, "Oath," *Encyclopedia of Religion and Ethics* IX, 206-09, 435; D. J. McCarthy, "Three Covenants in Genesis," *Catholic Biblical Quarterly* XXVI (1964), 181; A. Renoir, "The Heroic Oath in Beowolf, the Charism de Roland, and the Nibelungalied," in *Studies in Honor of A.G. Brodeur,* ed. S. B. Greenfield (Oregon, 1963), 266; Jan de Vries, *Heroic Song and Heroic Legend,* trans. B. J. Timmer (London, 1963), 181ff, 236ff.

6. Edward C. Banfield and Laura Fasano Banfield, *The Moral Basis of a Backward Society* (Glencoe, Ill.: The Free Press, 1958).

7. Filippo Sabetti, *Political Authority in a Sicilian Village* (New Brunswick, N.J.: Rutgers University Press, 1984).

8. Robert Putnam, Robert Leonardi, and Rafaella Y. Nanetti, *Making Democracy Work: Civic Traditions in Modern Italy* (Princeton, N.J.: Princeton University Press, 1993).

9. On Italian feudalism, see J. C. L. Sismondi, *Histoire des Republiques Italiennes du Moyen Age* (Brussels, 1809), 16 vols.

10. See chap. 5 of Putnam, Leonardi, and Nanetti, *Making Democracy Work,* for a detailed exposition of that documentation.

11. "Only a bold or a foolhardy subordinate, lacking ties of solidarity with peers, would seek to punish a superior" (215, in 18 April 1992 draft).

12. J. P. Canning, *History of Political Thought* 1, no. 1 (Spring 1980): 9-32.

13. On Italian city-states, see Edward Freeman, *History of Federal Government in Greece and Italy,* 2nd ed. (London: Macmillan, 1893), 562-63.

14. Putnam, *Making Democracy Work*; see especially chap. 5.

15. On French feudalism, see Charles Petit-Dutaillis, *The Feudal Monarchy in France and England* (New York: AMS Press, 1983).

16. Heinrich Mitteis, *State in the Middle Ages,* trans. H. F. Orton (Amsterdam and Oxford: North Holland Publishing Co., 1975).

17. On Spanish feudalism, see Roger J. A. Collins, *Early Medieval Spain: Unity in Diversity* (London: Macmillan, 1983).

18. As quoted in Henry Hallam, *History of Europe During the Middle Ages* II (New York: Colonial Press, 1900), 45.

19. Robert Agranoff, "Asymmetrical and Symmetrical Federalism in Spain: An Examination of Intergovernmental Policy" (unpublished paper for the joint conference of the International Association of Centers for Federal Studies and the Research Committee on Federalism and Federation, International Political Science Association; Kwa Maritan, South Africa, August 1993): 5-6. See also Henry G. Payne, *The Spanish Revolution* (New York: Norton, 1970); J. B. Trend, *The Civilization of Spain* (London: Oxford University Press, 1967); Ed Herr, *A Historical Essay on Modern Spain* (Berkeley: University of California Press, 1971); J. H. Pary, *The Spanish Seaborn Empire* (Berkeley: University of California Press, 1966).

20. On centralization and the dismantling of foral rights, see William C. Atkinson, *A History of Spain and Portugal* (London: Penguin, 1960) and J. Lee Schneidman, *The Rise of the Aragonese-Catalan Empire*, 2 vols. (New York: New York University Press, 1970).

21. See Daniel J. Elazar, *Exploring Federalism* (University: University of Alabama Press, 1987), 165-66; and Cesar Diaz y Lopez, "The State of the Autonomic Process in Spain," *Publius* 11, nos. 3-4 (1981): 193-216.

22. On the Polish regime, see J. K. Federowicz, *A Republic of Nobles: Studies in Polish History to 1864* (Cambridge: Cambridge University Press, 1982); Norman Davies, *A Short History of Poland* (Oxford: Clarendon Press, 1985); and Oskar Halecki, *A History of Poland,* 9th ed. (New York: D. McKay, 1976).

23. On the Hungarian pact, see Emil Lengyel, *1000 Years of Hungary* (New York: John Day, 1958); John Thayer Hitchcock, *The Magars of Banyan Hill* (New York: Holt, Rinehart, Winston, 1966); Carlile Aylmer Macartney, *The Magyars in the Ninth Century* (Cambridge: Cambridge University Press, 1930); Paul Teleki, *The Evolution of Hungary and Its Place in European History* (Gulf Breeze, Florida: Academic International Press, 1975).

4

The Holy Roman Empire

The Germans and the Holy Roman Empire

The Germanic tribes that invaded Europe in the latter days of the Roman Empire brought with them various proto-federal arrangements in the form of tribal confederations. Historians generally agree that their confederations were formed essentially to defend themselves against the Romans and were rarely more than defensive leagues. Since accounts of these arrangements were written by outsiders, mostly Romans, we know little or nothing about how they were structured or functioned, or about their political dynamics. As analysts, at least, we have to accept the fact that they were almost solely defensive leagues. By the beginning of the third century we begin to have a little more specific information that points to the defensive character of these leagues in specific territories. We have the most information about the Alemannic Confederation on the banks of the River Main. The confederated units were small groups based on ethnic and religious commonalities. Somewhat later the Frankish Confederation included Merovingians and Carolingians (in the sixth century), but again very little is known about it. Perhaps significantly, from the little information available to us, the fullest development of these proto-confederations was among the Alemannians, with the Franks not far behind. In both cases there were probably cultural influences that continued to affect what latter became Switzerland.

In Germany, on the other hand, the principle of hierarchy was accepted as the basis of the Holy Roman Empire, a peculiarly German institution, but the empire never succeeded in becoming more than a network of pacts between local hierarchs of varying degrees of power. Thus, within each feudal fiefdom hierarchical arrangements prevailed, while among the fiefdoms contractual arrangements were dominant. The linkage of these opposing approaches to political organization created a kind of schizophrenia in the German states that became characteristic of German society.[1]

The Holy Roman Empire's legal and constitutional structure passed through several stages. In the beginning, when the Germanic tribal tradition was still strong, the empire was conceived as a corporate community in which all of its associated members were jointly represented. Subsequently, after the empire adopted Roman law, it was understood to be a unitary political entity whose parts were dependent provinces. Finally, as the state system began to emerge, the empire came to be seen as no more than a roof organization encompassing various national units, equal in rank, with the emperor as *primus inter pares*.[2] At its height, the Holy Roman Empire consisted of over four hundred principalities, bishoprics, duchies, counties, seignorial estates, abbacies, and imperial cities with varying degrees of autonomy embracing the more or less autonomous manors of over 1,500 imperial knights.

The origins of the Holy Roman Empire lie in the Germanic tribes that streamed into Central Europe in the first centuries of the Common Era. These tribes were to a substantial extent oath societies, based on oath relationships between both equals and unequals. The importance of oaths to the Germanic tribes is seen in the fact that oath breaking was considered a crime like murder. Often it was common for Teutonic men to take oaths before engaging in battle or embarking on other common pursuits. Some of these oaths developed into long-term ties during the *volkwanderung* and from them emerged the later kingdoms of the Germans.

There is a dispute among historians with regard to the governance of the Germanic tribes. Nineteenth-century historians in particular looked with somewhat romantic eyes on the "primitive forest democracy" of the Germans. Subsequent historical studies have suggested that those tribes had very early acquired well-defined hierarchies of nobles and kings who were, however, bound to the entire community of warriors through oaths and pacts, leading to a number of continuing formal procedures that made it seem as if there was more equality than there was in reality. This combination was an ideal basis for what later emerged as feudalism and, indeed, for the tensions within the Germanic peoples to this day.

The theory of kingship implicit here was made explicit by Manegold of Lautenbach, an Alsatian priest:

> King is not a name of nature but a title of office: nor does the people exalt him so high above it in order to give him the free power of playing the tyrant in its midst, but to defend him from tyranny. So soon as he begins to act the tyrant, is it not plain that he falls from the dignity granted to him? Since it is evident that he has first broken that contract by virtue of which he was appointed. If one should engage a man for a fair wage to tend swine, and he find means not to tend but to steal them, would not one remove him from his charge?... Since no on can create himself emperor or king, the people elevates a certain one person over itself to this end, that he govern and rule it according to the principle of righteous government; but if in any wise he transgress the contract by virtue of which he is chosen, he absolves the people from the obligation of submission, because he has first broken faith with it.[3]

The German language had its own parallel term for *hesed, treue* (fealty), that describes the dynamics of this relationship. *Treue,* an allegiance based on oath taking, was the central concept in medieval Germany. As the product of a mutual pledge between kings, nobles, or chiefs on the one hand, and the knights and the people on the other, in which fealty to one another was based upon a common fealty to the law, it was distinctly different from obedience.

This concept was to survive within German political culture, to resurface in the post-World War II German Federal Republic as the constitutional principal of *bundestreue,* which establishes the dynamics of the relationship between the *bund* (federal government) and the *lander* (constituent states). It is a principle that the German constitutional court will invoke as necessary to assure the smooth operation of the federal system.

Nor was this the only covenantal concept within medieval Germany. Thus, Germans distinguished between an oath brotherhood or *gerschwurbruderheit,* which was considered the equal of blood brotherhood and required the expression of kinship loyalty or *frith* (a term that may actually be related to the Hebrew *brith*), and covenants among unequals (e.g., a chief and his thanes) known as *ger-gasinds* (fellow-travelers or comrades-in-arms); or in Latin, *comitatus.* These involved reciprocal obligations based on a service-and-reward system. The term *common speech* first came to mean kinship, but its original meaning had the sense of an inviolable bond, like the relationship of a kind of *brit shalom* (covenant of peace) rooted in *hesed,* or in German, *freode* (usually translated as friendship). Thus, it became the term used to describe relationships established among people by some covenantal act. Ultimately the German term for oath, *eid,* became the basis for its term for federal association, *eidgenossenschaft.*

The medieval polity as an association between persons (*personenverband*) reached its most complete form in Germany, where it existed both on the conventional feudal basis of lordship and vassalage and also as association between equals. The polity that these associations created was known in German as the *personenverbandsstaat* whose constitutional framework was a network of personal associations. This was also manifested in the way in which princes had companies of retainers known as *gefolgschaften.* Here too the polity was often described as a *konigsgefolgschaften,* in other words, a large company of retainers in the king's service.

It is important to note that historically, Germanic law was personal. That is to say, it adhered to members of the tribe or community wherever they happened to be, while Roman law was territorial. In other words, it was binding upon all who lived within a particular territorial jurisdiction. As it turned out, the combination of the two created feudalism and was mutually reinforcing.

The various Germanic tribes were linked through traditional tribal pacts during the centuries of their invasions of the West. While often presented as confederations, most of these were merely military leagues. Only in the case of the Belgae and the Alemanni is there a possibility that these leagues went beyond that. Unfortunately, lack of internal records and the necessity to rely upon external observers, principally Roman, prevent us from knowing enough about them to draw conclusions.

These Germanic tribes also had at least a quasi-covenantal concept of *kuith* as a social bond. Thus, one who committed a major offense against the public, especially against public safety, property, or religion, was declared an outlaw by being proclaimed "peaceless." This ban, equivalent to the biblical *herem,* severed connections of kinship as well.

The thin line between an oath society and a compactual one was frequently crossed by the Germans to the point where compilations of their laws were sometimes expressed in terms of a compact between prince and people. So, for example, they established the *pactus legis salicae alamannorum.* This early sixth-century enactment provides for the selection of a king by four electors after they had conducted lengthy discussions with the presidents of local assemblies.

The problem here for our investigation is how to distinguish between the various Germanic tribes. The example given above clearly refers to the Alemanni, whose political culture revolved around oaths and compacts. They were the ancestors of the Swiss Germans. It is not at all clear, however, that all German tribes were oriented in the same direction as the Alemanni. For example, the eastern Germanic tribes became monarchies early in their history and ultimately evolved into Prussians. Kingship among the eastern Germans was particularly strongly rooted in military command. Among other German tribes popular consent was a more powerful element. Tacitus's classic study, *Germania,* describes all of this in the early days of the Germanic migrations, but it must be remembered that his study is primarily focused on the southern German tribes who settled along the northern edge of Roman jurisdiction in territory now part of Switzerland.[4]

Tacitus's account also suggests that while kings were subject to popular control, the instruments of popular control such as the *witan,* which he refers to as the *concilium civitatis* or public assembly, were dominated by nobles whom he describes as priests as well. These primitive Germanic folk constitutions apparently were developed into the *curial* assemblies and diets of subsequent epochs, which were primarily aristocratic councils. Men of noble birth also served as justices, often on an itinerant basis, each within his *gau* (canton). While the judge's task was limited to formulating the question and proclaiming a judgement or refusing to do so if he considered it unjust, being first and last gave him tremendous power in shaping the outcome.

In the early and high Middle Ages, a clear right of resistance to "lawless" or incompetent kings was accepted as a by-product of the notion that fealty to the law worked both ways. This right of resistance did not take the form of formal action against such kings. Rather, the people simply abandoned them, absolved themselves from fealty, and chose a new ruler.[5] Thus, matters were usually settled by force of arms. In the fourth century the English barons formulated the principal involved in the exercise of this right by stating that their oath of fealty was due to the crown as "the unchangeable symbol of lawful magistry" rather than to its actual wearer and his individual caprices.[6] This idea was to come down through the ages to modern Great Britain to give content to the continued use of medieval forms in a republican age. Thus, today it is argued (especially by Scots) that it is the crown that bears sovereignty and unites the peoples and countries of that realm, while its bearer is merely an agent of the crown.

It has been argued that much of the apparent chaos in the Middle Ages had to do with the exercise of the right of resistance over real and pretended grievances. Since feudalism is based on military force, it never developed appropriate mechanisms for resolving disputes other than the sword. Since there was no way other than the judgement of battle to judge kings, the judgement of battle was frequently invoked. Hence, it is not surprising that the ultimate response to this was the development of the absolutist state whereby kings acquired monopolies over military force by hook or by crook—if only for self-protection—and proceeded to use those monopolies to establish their absolute rule.

The right of resistance was actually put into legal form on a contractual basis, thereby clarifying and strengthening what had earlier been an undefined right sanctioned by the law of the land. Under feudal law, if a lord denied his vassals justice, they could raise the feud against him. (The relationship of the term *feud* to *feudal* is unclear. On one hand, it can be used to describe a feudal relationship, yet in its other meaning it is derived from the Old English word for enmity). This led to a just war (*bellum iustum*), which was often concluded by a new contract whose terms reflected the results of the conflict. Thus, the right of resistance became a matter of public law enforced by military might.

All told, this was the way *pactum* tried to limit *imperium*. Since all pledges of fealty included mutual promises to respect hereditary laws and liberties, it was the nominal or actual breach of same that triggered the right of resistance.

While shifts in the locus of power ultimately run into the successful exercise of the right of resistance, that power had to receive theoretical justification. Once again the Church stepped in to provide it, arguing that under the original governmental contract provided in Roman law, once the people freely chose their king, the power they transferred to him was irrevocable. This shift from earlier Church doctrine that embodied the right of resistance to one that assisted the development of divine right came as a result of the investiture contest out of which the *lex regia* began to acquire adherents as the bulwark of absolutism.

As an argument for absolutism, the *lex regia* had a weak spot, and that was in positing popular sovereignty in a governmental contract to begin with. This view was developed in the eighth decade of the eleventh century at the height of the controversy over the *lex regia* by Manegold of Lautenbach, who went so far as to argue that the monarch was an employee of the community who could be dismissed for misfeasance or malfeasance.[7] The king's contractual right to dominion was real, but only so long as he did his duty. In a sense, sovereignty is lodged in the people, who make a compact with their ruler. Once they do, it is true that the sanctity of the compact binds both. If the king violates the covenant, the other authoritative officers can collectively interpose themselves between ruler and subjects. This is quite close to covenantalism since, of course, any compacts entered into between ruler and ruled were under God, who served at the very least as witness and guarantor. If the idea was too radical to have been widely accepted in the eleventh century, it was a precursor of the future. It would take two more historical epochs, approximately 600 years, before the idea would become dominant in European thought.

Here is where the weaknesses of medieval public law became most apparent. Medieval philosophers often argued the right of resistance, but like medieval society itself offered no remedy for the maintenance of that right other than the battlefield, which, as philosophers, they abjured. Having no other remedy, and tiring of the incessant warfare, the feudal polity gave way to the absolutist state, if only for the lack of an alternative.

Municipal Corporations

The exceptions in Germany were the municipal corporations that emerged from the mid-eleventh to the mid-fourteenth centuries, rising out of the framework of feudalism to transform the contractual elements of the feudal system into a basis for local liberties. These new municipal corporations were formed through contracts among those who settled them, and became unions of guilds. At the same time, they obtained charters from the feudal rulers in whose territories they were located or, if possible, from the Holy Roman Emperor himself so as to bypass and be freed of the local feudal hierarch.[8]

These charters, while nominally handed down by the superior in the feudal manner, were actually products of extensive negotiation, generally initiated by the city fathers. Hence, while in form they were unilateral acts of the monarch or ruler, in fact they were bilateral agreements with very explicit terms, not only defining the obligations of each to the other but limiting the power of the feudal superior to intervene in municipal affairs. These charters constitutionalized the relationship between the municipality and its feudal overlord in such a way that the municipality became substantially independent. Such charters were renewed on the accession of each new ruler, certainly through a formal ceremony, in some cases after actual renegotiation of their terms.

By the middle of the fourteenth century, central Europe from the Mediterranean to the Baltic was dotted with these medieval municipal corporations. They represented the cutting edge of the movement, which ultimately led to the transformation of feudalism and, after a period of absolutism, to the emergence of modern republicanism.[9]

Hamburg, for example, was founded in the tenth century but celebrates its existence as a city from 7 May 1189, when the Holy Roman Emperor Frederick I granted it the rights and privileges that were to make it the Free and Hanseatic City of Hamburg, its name to this day. The name itself suggests its federal connection. It is free and Hanseatic, part of the league of free cities of the Hansa. Today, as a city-state in the German Federal Republic, it is one of the anchors of the West German federalist tradition.

The medieval city was a civic association organized by its burghers to gain control of the political institutions that governed them from the former lords of the city. The burghers either acquired legitimacy for their civic association through a feudal grant on the part of the lords, often purchased, or through usurpation because they were economically powerful enough to do so. As the city evolved, the erstwhile lord would either decamp entirely or himself become a member of the civic association.[10] These civic associations were in turn brought into existence and strengthened as "sworn associations or oath-bound fraternities." Weber put it as follows, "The initial aim of the oath-bound fraternity was the union of locally resident landowners for offensive and defensive purposes, for the peaceful settlement of internal disputes, and for the safeguarding of the administration of justice corresponding to the interests of urban residents."

This system of oath-bound fraternities spread throughout continental Europe, where they became powerful enough, Weber says, that "whoever did not enter voluntarily was forced to join."[11] In Italy these bodies were known as *conjurationes* (*conjuratio* meaning oath of association), and north of the Alps as *guilds*.[12] By creating a new urban law and new forms of city administration they eliminated feudalism and conducted the affairs of each city with substantial independence. These *conjurationes* or guilds fulfilled the same functions as the clans and tribes around which the ancient city had been organized, but they were seen as artificial associations rather than organic kinship networks. The fraternity they created transformed the city into a public, something more than a municipal corporation, and made its residents into citizens. As Weber put it, "more than anything else, the fully developed ancient and medieval city was formed and interpreted as a fraternal association."[13] As polities, each of these cities shared a particular vision of public order and at its bottom it was either a survival of an older covenantal vision or the embryonic development of a new one.

In some cases, these municipal corporations had within them Jewish communities whose internal organization was covenantal, as described in chapter 2. Irving Agus argues persuasively that the medieval municipal corporation was strongly influenced by the patterns of Jewish community organization of the time and borrowed heavily from them in developing its own contractual framework.[14] In most cases, the relations between the Christian and Jewish communities within the city were like relations between separate municipalities occupying a common territory. Each had its own charter from their common feudal overlord, its own municipal organization based on an internal covenant or contract, and, of course, separate ways of life rooted in their different ethno-religious traditions.

Each of the various segments of Europe created its own combination of hierarchical, organic, and contractual dimensions of political organization. In each case, that combination ultimately led to the emergence of a state or nation whose political organization reflected that synthesis.

What is historically important about the experience of the Germanic peoples is that centuries later they were to embrace federalism as their solution to the problem of national integration. With the exception of the Swiss (treated separately in chapter 5), they did not do so easily, and not without trying other, more hierarchical forms of political integration. But, at the end of the modern or at the beginning of the post-modern epoch, after descending to the depths of hell, they turned to federalism as the only feasible way to democratization.

Two Reform Efforts: The Conciliar
Movement and the Imperial Diet of 1495

The one great challenge to this pervasive hierarchical system within
Christendom as a whole was the Conciliar movement of the fifteenth
century, a result of the "Babylonian exile" of the popes to Avignon in
1305 for nearly a century and the Great Schism of 1378 to 1417. Conflict between popes and emperors at the top of the medieval hierarchy
provided a modest opening for the conciliar approach to emerge. The
scandals accompanying these schisms encouraged a reform movement
that sought to reorganize the Church through conciliar mechanisms. Two
great councils were held, both in the Alemannic heartland of the surviving covenantal territory, the first at Constanz from 1414 to 1418, and
the second in Basle from 1439 to 1448. Both are cities of the German-
Swiss borderlands.

Both councils developed theories of conciliar government that attempted to republicanize the Church, according to new theories of republicanism as expressed in the works of Marcilius of Padua, Juan de
Segovia, Nicolas of Cusa, Jean Gerson, and Pierre d'Ailly.[15] One of the
best expressions of the central idea of the Conciliar movement was provided by Andres Diaz de Escobar, one of the leading theorists at the
Basle council: "The Church is a kind of mystical body, and a kind of
republic of the Christian people...that most holy republic is the universal church...and therefore it is a common affair of the Christian
people." Juan de Segovia referred to the ecclesiastical leadership as "the
presidency" and Conciliar leaders as "ministers of the republic." Jesus
Christ, as manifested through the Holy Spirit, was in Black's words,
"the true president of the council," with humans occupying positions
more republican in character. The mystical body of the Church was to
be reorganized along the lines of the university "colleges" with their
independent charters.

In the last analysis, Conciliar theory, while rejecting hierarchy, was
organic rather than covenantal. In their view, the Church was an organism, informed throughout by the Holy Spirit, governed by a mixed constitution in organic balance. Also, the Conciliar movement was entirely
ecclesiastical. Laity were excluded, in part to keep powerful princes
from manipulating the proceedings, and partly because even the radicals in the Church saw the right of free and open discussion so essential

to the Conciliar process as of necessity carefully restricted to those who could meet the highest standards of theological faith.

The Council of Constanz did result in a document that held that the pope was not absolute but dependent on a general council, but all it succeeded in doing was to depose three popes and choose a successor, Martin V, who secured his position by concluding separate agreements (concordats) with the five different "nations" (vernacular linguistic groupings—English, French, Italian, German, Spanish) represented at the Council. Once a new pope was elected and recognized, he resumed the papal powers, so the Conciliar movement failed. However, it did succeed in breaking down the medieval theory of hierarchy, opening the door to greater changes later.

The great failure of the Conciliar movement was connected in no small measure to its failure to develop a theory of Christian federalism to replace the theories of papal imperialism that it had shattered. The "national" delegations left the Council to pursue their own narrowly defined interests and ultimately to develop into separate nation-states. Perhaps a theory of federalism could have held them together; an organic theory that vested all power in ecclesiastical hands could not.[16] Intellectually more significant in the chain of covenantal tradition was late medieval nominalism. Heiko Oberman wrote of that movement that it involved

> an emerging new image of God.... God is a covenant God, His *pactum* or *foedus* is his self-commitment to become the contractual partner in creation and salvation.... In the nominalist view man has become the appointed representative and partner of God, responsible for his own life, society and world, on the basis of and within the limits of the treaty or *pactum* stipulated by God.[17]

From this and other sources it is clear that nominalism understood the covenant between God and humans as bilateral and conditional. Medieval nominalism seems to have originated as a revolt against the excesses of the Platonists in arguing for the preeminence of universals, emphasizing instead the particularities of words and things. Hence, covenantal thought was natural to them, with their emphasis on particulars and empiricism. Because Platonic and Aristotelian doctrines were part and parcel of orthodox Christian belief, there were those who suggested that nominalism was a heresy. At the same time, the thought of William Ockham was considered to have been connected with the nominalist school. Intellectually, Thomas Hobbes seems to have been influenced by nominalist thought in his understanding of words and concepts.

The problem with the effort to seek a nominalist link in the covenantal chain is that while nominalist ideas of covenant were present and in some ways even pervasive early in the sixteenth century, its basis in the Pelagian doctrine of justification would not at all have appealed to Bullinger. Moreover, Bullinger himself was educated in the *via antiqua,* while nominalism was considered the *via moderna.* Moreover, for our purposes, nominalist thought was philosophical-theological, rather far removed from the political.

The ideas of conciliarism and nominalism did come together in the thought of John Mair (sometimes known as John Major), the late fifteenth-early sixteenth century Scottish thinker whose political ideas are thought to have seriously influenced John Knox and George Buchanan.[18] While a monarchist, Mair saw political power as grounded in consent, either directly or indirectly. In trying to balance his monarchism with his theory of consent, Mair also returned to the Hebrew Scriptures to demonstrate that Adam, Noah, and their sons established government by consent. Mair sees them as in the same situation as settlers occupying a newly discovered island who come together to choose a ruler or rulers to govern them. They establish the relationship between rulers and ruled through an act of choice, that is, essentially a covenantal act, by "the people" or "a free people" or "the community," the three terms he uses to describe parties to the covenant. In this Mair posits a kind of communal democracy whereby the people or the community are collective bodies, not merely aggregations of individuals.

Mair, who lived half his life in France, was influenced by a French contemporary, Claude de Seyssell, the author of *Monarchie de France.* Seyssell, like Mair, was a monarchist but one who sought to anchor the monarchy in a constitution that provided for a separation of powers.[19]

Seyssell grounded his constitutional monarchy in a division of power into three spheres—*la religion, la justice, la police*—which could be read as a Christian equivalent of the *keter kehunah, keter torah,* and *keter malkhut,* the three domains of the biblical polity, even though Seyssell, unlike Mair, does not present his writings as theological and scriptural commentaries.

Seyssell's is a conservative position, opposing the growing absolutism of the French monarchy. So, too, is Mair's. It is a conservative position in the way that the Puritans were conservatives less than a century later. Both Seysell and Mair were too late in the sense that the Reformation was about to overtake them. Both, however, belong in the chain of transmission between at least quasi-covenantal medieval constitutionalism and the covenantal ideas of the Reformation.

A similar effort occurred toward the end of the fifteenth century in the realm of the Ceasars. After 1250, the office of Holy Roman Emperor became elective, with seven electors keeping the Emperor in check and preventing centralization of the empire's hundreds of feudal subdivisions. After long and fruitless struggle between the emperor and his princes, the empire's one and only substantial effort at constitutional reform was launched in 1495 by the princes to restrict the rapidly expanding powers of the new Hapsburgian dynasty. The reformers attempted to standardize imperial law, restructure the imperial territory, and introduce a strong imperial government jointly controlled by the Emperor and the princes. The first two met with partial success. The last failed entirely.

The imperial diet of 1495 that undertook the reform succeeded in replacing the medieval feud system with standardized court proceedings, including a supreme court (Reichskammergericht), which continued to operate with considerable success until the empire's dissolution in 1806, limited principally by its own bureaucracy and the territorial privileges of exemption. Six large imperial districts (reichskreise) were established—a number later expanded to ten—as the basis for territorial representation in the new imperial institutions. District diets (kreistage) were convened, district chanceries for the administration of the daily affairs of state were organized, and assemblies were held in the various estates. However, these districts remained more or less artificial administrative units, superimposed on the old structure, and failed to mediate between imperial and princely interests, thus sealing the fate of the overall reform effort.

The princes failed in their effort to make the Hapsburg Emperor submit to collective rule. Part of their failure was related to the princes' own reluctance to provide the revenues necessary for the maintenance of the new governmental institutions or to relinquish any of their own "sovereignty" in their respective territories. Efforts to install an imperial government (reichsregiment) were made in 1500 and 1521. Both failed within a few years.

Only the imperial diet, or reichstag, continued to exist. The 1495 reform movement had as its goal annual sessions of the diet with authority to determine foreign policy, imperial finances, and the maintenance of internal peace. But in fact the diet continued to meet irregularly and failed to set policy in all three fields. To no small degree this was due to the absence of even a reliable and binding register of reichstag members or a fixed constitution defining its functions. The emperor could convene the diet whenever it suited him.

The extent of the change was that from the beginning of the sixteenth century onward the emperor could no longer invite only those whom he pleased, but had to convene all those assumed to be members. But even that was a variable proposition because of constant changes in the nobility. While the imperial cities were to be invited to each diet as representative of the bourgeois estate, they had to fight again and again for the right to participate.

The diet was divided into three curia or colleges: the college of electors, the college of princes, and the college of the imperial cities. The first college, or *curia*, consisted of the seven electors. During the sixteenth century the noble curia (college of princes) numbered about eighty-five, including both secular and ecclesiastical figures, while the curia of the imperial cities had about fifty-five members. The princes each had one vote, while the counts and prelates sat on four curial benches, each of which had one curial vote. Even the imperial knights, not to speak of peasants and residents of the smaller cities and towns, were not represented at all. The three colleges assembled and voted separately, with the vote of the college of cities having consultative status only. The imperial chancellor had to harmonize the results of the votes of the two other curia, which result was then ratified by the general assembly.

Each of these curiae had their own bureaucracies. What made the system at all workable were the advisory committees in which the curial decisions were prepared prior to their formal presentation to the three colleges. In these committees the importance of the cities' economic power was recognized and they were granted full voting rights, which often made their votes decisive. Moreover, each member of the various colleges voted as an individual.

Between the emperor, the diet, and the supreme court, a certain separation of powers came to exist within the imperial structure. The emperor, assisted by his council of electors of which he was usually one, represented the executive power; the imperial diet served as a legislative body; and a supreme court oversaw the constitutional ties that bound the various territories of the empire together. Thus, the possibilities for a true imperial federal system existed by the sixteenth century, only to be destroyed by a series of conflicts within the imperial structure among the electors, the emperor and the princes, the princes themselves, and the old territorial elites and the emergent imperial cities. The Reformation and the wars of religion helped these controversies along, but the *coup de grace* was delivered by the Thirty Years' War (1618–48), which finally destroyed the old order and ushered in the modern epoch.

Each of these quarrelling groups sought to maximize individual autonomy or the autonomy of the political entity he or it controlled, preventing the development of an effective shared constitutional order. The Hapsburg emperors pulled the important territories of Austria, Bavaria, and Swabia out of the empire. The electors opposed the other estates in any attempt to increase the powers of the diet and its committees, which they saw as coming at their expense. All the nobility opposed the rising power of the bourgeoisie and fought any extension of powers to the cities. The cities, in turn, became the main source of imperial revenue to finance the election of new emperors; hence the emperors' support for maintaining their local constitutions.

The effort to reform the Holy Roman Empire failed for some of the same reasons that the Conciliar movement failed to reform the Roman Catholic Church. It basically attempted to lower the top of the pyramid, not to abandon the empire's hierarchical character. That not only went against the natural thrust of hierarchical polities, it failed to address the problems of political structure and culture that the hierarchical system inevitably perpetuated. In the end, the princes took their hierarchical status even more seriously and succumbed to the blandishments of the age of absolutism, devoting their efforts to becoming the absolute rulers of their respective territories. Those who were successful ultimately turned those territories into modern absolutist states, of which Prussia was to be the first and foremost within Germany.

Curiously enough, it was only after these events in the sixteenth century that the Holy Roman Empire reached its political peak under the Hapsburg Emperor Charles V. Charles united under his personal rule the traditional lands of the Hapsburgs plus the Spanish and Portuguese empires, which he personally inherited as a result of royal marriages. His was the first true world empire, including most of Central and Western Europe, the lion's share of the Western Hemisphere, and outposts in

Africa, South and East Asia, and the Pacific, all held together by the organic ties of personal inheritance, which brought Charles to his exalted position.

A careful, sober, and decent ruler, Charles generally respected the imperial constitutional traditions and especially the liberties of the imperial cities. Tragically, he was either unable or unwilling to take advantage of his opportunity to transform personal organic ties into institutionalized ones, which would have required some measure of consent. Moreover, he made a fatal mistake in that early in his reign he arranged for his brother Ferdinand to succeed to the imperial title while his son Philip was merely to inherit Spain and the Netherlands, thereby severing the organic tie between his domains. Although he tried to undo this arrangement before his abdication in 1555, his wishes were ignored by the German electors who did not want to be under the rule of a Spanish king. That plus the wars of the Reformation and the growing national rivalries within Europe made obsolete any possibility of uniting Europe through organic means.

Royal families, of course, continued to be interrelated and became even more so as the centuries passed, but with less and less consequence for political organization. The apotheosis of this came at the outbreak of World War I. Just about every major royal figure in Europe was a descendent of Britain's Queen Victoria, yet their countries all went to war with each other with enthusiasm. Thus, even in its secular dimensions the sixteenth century marked the end of the possibility of European unity on a hierarchical basis along feudal or monarchical lines. Charles exhausted himself in the effort, travelling constantly to different parts of his realm. As Hueglin put it:

> It was much more than just the self-righteous policy of a lonely emperor which failed: it was a political principle which proved wrong. The idea of a European "monarchia universal" failed, because it was simply impossible to govern any such vast conglomeration of different social, cultural, and political units as the Hapsburg empire in the highly centralized fashion of a unitary territorial state. Such a centralization either has to fall back upon the methods of despotism, as in the case of the Asian empires, or it must produce and depend on a predominant desire for overall homogeneity, as in the case of the United States of America. Europe, which had received its very strength and identity exactly from this existing socio-cultural variety, needed—and, for that matter, still needs—a different concept of integration.[20]

The imperial diet was convened for the last time in 1663. Subsequently, it was transformed into a permanent congress called the eternal diet, but it continued to be immobilized by the conflicts of interest among its members, between the imperial and princely interests, between the emperor and the various estates, and, from the eighteenth century onward, between Austria and Prussia. The Prussian kings successfully constructed a modern state in every sense of the word, one that ultimately embraced most of Germany through the so-called Second Reich, and which was nominally federal, but so much under Prussian domination as to almost neutralize federalism in practice.

The Hapsburg empire, on the other hand, survived until 1918 as a multinational political entity, the last on the European continent west of Russia, but it did not quite survive intact. It underwent constitutional reforms of a quasi-federal character. Unfortunately, the nationalism of its peoples, exacerbated by the mixture of ethnic groups within the territories of the empire, made simple territorial solutions impossible without massive population transfers.

Notes

1. On German feudalism and the Holy Roman Empire, see Heinz Kahler, *Rome and Her Empire* (London: Methuen, 1963); H. M. Gwatkin and J. P. Whitney, *The Cambridge Medieval History* I (Cambridge: Cambridge University Press, 1913–1943); Geoffrey Barraclough, *The Crucible of Europe* (London: Thames and Hudson, 1976); and James Westfall Thompson, *Fuedal Germany* (New York: F. Ungar, 1962).
2. Cf. Thomas Hueglin, "Johannes Althusius: Medieval Constitutionalist or Modern Federalist?," *Publius* 9, no. 4 and "Covenant and Federalism in the Politics of Althusius," paper presented to the Workshop on Covenant and Politics, 27–29 February 1980 (Philadelphia, Pa.).
3. Reinhold Laakmann, *Manegold of Lautenbach* (Hamburg: Hamburg University Press, 1969).
4. Cornelius Tacitus, *The Germania of Tacitus: A Critical Edition*, Rodney Potter Robinson, ed. (Middletown, Conn.: American Philological Association, 1935). Cf. also Cornelius Tacitus, *Tacitus on Britain and Germany*, a new translation of the "Agricola" and the "Germania" (Harmondsworth: Penguin, 1954).
5. Cf. Fritz Kern, *Kingship and Law in the Middle Ages* (Oxford: Basil Blackwell, 1956).
6. Ibid., 88.
7. Manegold based his argument on 1 Peter 2:13 and 2 Chronicles 22, 23 (the case of Jehoiada's intervention to save the constitution, see vol. 1); Manegold von Lautenbach, *Liber Contra Wolfelmum* (Weimar: H. Boehlaus, 1972).
8. On German municipal corporations and their charters, see Franz Baeuml, *Medieval Civilization in Germany, 800–1273* (Oxford: Praeger, 1969); Geoffrey E. D. Barraclough, *Medieval Germany, 911–1250* (Oxford: Blackwell, 1948); Horst Fuhrmann, *Germany in the High Middle Ages*, trans. Timothy Reuter (Cambridge: Cambridge University Press, 1986).

9. Cf. Hueglin, "Covenant and Federalism."
10. Cf. Max Weber, *The City,* trans. ed. Don Martindale and Gertrud Neuwirth (New York: The Free Press, 1958).
11. Ibid., 10.
12. See Lauro Martines, *Power and Imagination: City-States in Renaissance Italy* (New York: Knopf, 1979).
13. Weber, *The City,* 96.
14. Irving Agus, *Urban Civilization in Pre-Crusader Europe: A Study of Organized Town-Life in Northwestern Europe During the Tenth and Eleventh Centuries* (New York: Yeshiva University Press, 1965).
15. Anthony Black, *Council and Commune: The Conciliar Movement and the Fifteenth Century Heritage* (London: Burns and Oates, 1979); Antony Black, *Monarchy and Community: Political Ideas in the Later Conciliar Controversy 1430–1450* (Cambridge: Cambridge University Press, 1970); Paul E. Sigmund, *Nicholas of Cusa and Medieval Political Thought* (Cambridge, Mass: Harvard University Press, 1963).
16. Thomas O. Hueglin, "The Idea of Empire: Conditions for Integration and Disintegration in Europe," *Publius* 12, 3 (Summer 1982): 11–42.
17. "The Shape of Late Medieval Thought: The Birthpangs of the Modern Era," in *The Pursuit of Holiness in Late Medieval and Renaissance Religion,* ed. Charles E. Trinkaus, 3–25; Studies in Medieval and Reformation Thought 10 (Leiden: E. J. Brill, 1974), 15. On the *pactum* in nominalist thought, see Heiko A. Oberman, *The Harvest of Medieval Theology: Gabriel Biel and Late Medieval Nominalism* (Grand Rapids, Mich.: William B. Erdmans Publishing Co., 1967), 232–52.
18. Cf., e.g., Lord Acton, *Lectures on the French Revolution* (London, 1910) and Francis Oakley, "On the Road from Constance to 1688: The Political Thought of John Major and George Buchanan," *Journal of British Studies* 2 (1962): 1–131. Mair was concerned with both church and civil government. For a modification of this position, see J. H. Burns, "Politia Regalis et Optima: The Political Ideas of John Mair," *History of Political Thought* 2, no. 1 (Spring 1981): 31–61.
19. *Monarchie de France et deux autres Fragments Politiques,* ed. Jacques Poujol (Paris, 1961). His book was originally published in 1515.
20. Hueglin, "Covenant and Federalism."

5

Oaths and Covenants in the
Mountains and Lowlands

Feudalism had considerably less impact on four peripheral regions of Europe. Four, indeed, preserved or developed democratic-republicanism during the Middle Ages: the alpine lands of Switzerland, Frisia and the Lowlands, Scandinavia and the north, and parts of Scotland. All were covenantal societies. The heart of this territory runs right along the old line of division between the Roman empire and the Germanic tribes and encompasses that Romano-Germanic border region from Switzerland to Scotland. This at least suggests that some kind of creative synthesis took place during the 450 years from Julius Caesar's Gallic wars to the Roman evacuation of its northern frontier. It was in that region that four forces came together, each with its own contribution to make to the forging of a covenantal political culture—the Celts and the South Germans (Alemanni) with their orientations toward combining liberty and community through sociopolitical arrangements secured by oath, the Romans with their law of contracts and the sociopolitical order it represented, and the influence of the Hebrew Bible, which provided a framework of ideological legitimation for that political culture after the pagan tribes were Christianized.

Covenanters in the Mountains

On the European continent, the major exceptions to the feudal order were located in the heart of Europe, in the mountain valleys where liberty-loving people fled to escape the burdens of imperialism and feudalism and to carve free lives for themselves in their own communities. Like the glaciation of the ice ages that created the Alpine landscape, in the Middle Ages freedom in Europe was slowly forced back till it reached the heart of these Alpine regions. These communities became mountain republics in the Pyrenees, the Appenines, and the Alps. In the first, most were slowly absorbed by one or another of the voracious giants to their north and south, France and Spain. Only Andorra survived into modern times, through either a deliberately or accidentally brilliant use of federal principles. The Andorrans came under the joint sovereignty of the Spanish bishop of Urgel and the king of France. By playing off those two external forces against one another, the Andorrans were able to maintain their own republic of equals, the assembly of all citizens, which elected a council of twenty-four and two syndics to conduct its affairs. They still do.[1]

The same model was maintained in the mountain republics of the Appenines. The Appenines survivor, San Marino, differs from Andorra only in that it sits on the top of a mountain instead of in a valley. It is governed in similar fashion, electing a great council of sixty members and two appointed regents.[2]

Coniuratio Helvetica

It was in Switzerland, however, that mountain republicanism took root and survived as more than an isolated phenomenon.[3] Nominally under Burgundian or Hapsburg rule, by the thirteenth century the Swiss valley communities were in revolt against any attempt to translate that nominal rule into reality. In order to further their cause, the three mountain republics of what is today central Switzerland, Uri, Schwyz, and Unterwalden, came together in 1291 to establish a confederacy, originally known by the medieval Latin term *coniuratio* (those bound by a shared oath) and the German term *bundesbrief*.

The act of confederation, a covenant and oath, signed and sworn on the field of Rutli in the canton of Uri, on the banks of the Vierwaldstattensee (Lake Uri—an extension of Lake Luzern) became the foundation of the Helvetic Confederation which, over the centuries, expanded into the twenty-seven cantons and half-cantons of contemporary Switzerland. It was the people of these three mountain cantons who, in resisting the Austrian efforts to subordinate them to imperial control (as distinct from nominal suzerainty), brought about the 526 year war that led to the establishment of the territorial integrity and independence of modern Switzerland.

After 1291, freedom began to spread outward through federalism, slowly reconquering the European continent over the next seven centuries, a reverse ice age indeed, even if its movement at times seemed glacial. For many years the Swiss confederation was the only substantial free territory on the continent. In 1332, forty-one years after the original pact at Rutli, the city-state of Luzern at the northern end of the lake joined the original three confederates; Zurich joined in 1351, Glarus and Zug in 1352, and Berg in 1353, so that two generations after the founding of the confederation it had grown to eight cantons covering the country's alpine heartland. It was these cantons that waged the battle for liberty for the next four generations, until five more cantons to the northwest and north of the eight joined between 1481 and 1513 what became regarded as the old confederacy. The cantons to the south, southwest, and east did not come into the confederation until the time of the Napoleonic wars, between 1803 and 1815.

David Lasserre, in his book *Die Schicksalsstunden des Foederalismus,* argues that the main importance of the covenant of 1291 was not so much a military but a legal one. To be sure the military aspect cannot be neglected, but modern scholarship has quite convincingly established that the military part of the conjuratio goes back to another compact, the physical evidence of which has been lost. Thus, the innovative parts of the covenant of 1291 are the clauses dealing with the claim of the Swiss of having judges elected from among the people inhabiting their area and the ones that codify the criminal law of the time. Codification of this sort could be found throughout Europe at that time and reflected the desire of the people to put down on paper, in a time of turmoil and widespread insecurity, the principles of law hitherto handed down orally.[4]

This decision of the covenanters to resort to law rather than violence in the resolution of conflicts among them has its parallel in the arbitration clause. That clause provided that if there should be litigation between two or more parties, those not involved should offer their services as arbiters. In case one of the parties did not implement the arbiters' ruling, all the other contracting partners were to support the harmed party. Clauses of this sort were included in all the subsequent covenants and, as Lasserre points out, frequently were put to use. As notable examples he cites the conflict between the city of Zug and its rural hinterland, the latter of which was supported by Schwyz. Another example is the war between the city of Zurich and Schwyz, during which there were numerous attempts at arbitration. Besides these most notable examples, there is evidence of more than 100 cases where the arbitration clauses were put to use.

Arbitration was not used only by the Swiss. What made their way of using it exceptional was that the arbiters were other partners in the covenant. By avoiding the then common custom of calling on a well-known aristocrat to resolve the dispute, the Swiss could secure a strong internal stability and keep outside influences at a minimum. Additionally, the very important notion of arriving at a compromise, or a majority solution for that matter, and the acceptance of the compromise or the solution by those whose position did not prevail, became a part of Swiss political life from its very beginnings. It was to become rooted in Swiss political culture and to be of invaluable importance for the survival, despite occasional grave differences among the federal partners, of the Confederation and of the present Swiss federal system.[5]

The Covenantal Basis of Swiss Federalism

The Swiss invented or reinvented federalism in Europe and, indeed, represented the greatest expression of federalism in the world between the time of the Israelite tribal federation and the establishment of the United States of America. Until the Napoleonic wars, the constitutional design of Swiss federalism involved a series of overlapping bilateral and multilateral covenants that knit together the various territories comprising the confederation. Those covenants were renewed annually on the appropriate days so as to continue to rest on the consent of the governed. These multilateral and bilateral pacts were true covenants in the sense that they were more than international treaties since the people who made them saw themselves at least in some way bound as parts of a common proto-national whole. Indeed, their maintenance relied far more heavily on moral commitment than on formal or informal uses of power.

The covenanting Helvetic states were themselves federations or confederations of independent communes, some of which remained separate republics for all but the most limited purposes until the Napoleonic wars. For example, Gersau, a village of a few hundred families on the Vierwaldstattensee, remained an independent republic until 1817. This constitutional scheme of covenantal networks was appropriate to the medieval constitutional outlook, which did not seek single overarching frameworks, but rather webs of allegiances.

The development of Swiss federalism is a classic case study in the use of covenants as devices to promote federal political integration. The importance of these documents lies in their role in the Swiss nation-building process. As in ancient Israel, 2,500 years earlier, and the United States, 500 years later, nation building in Switzerland preceded state building. The Swiss experience was more like that of ancient Israel since 700 years of nation building passed before a full-fledged state emerged.

The heyday of covenanting was the period from the founding covenant of the three *Waldstaten* in 1291 until the beginning of the sixteenth century, when the Reformation disrupted many of the formal relationships among the Swiss republics. During this period the early confederation of thirteen was consolidated through three kinds of pacts: (1) those that dealt with the addition of other rural republics and cities to the original pact of 1291; (2) covenants that regularized or expanded intercantonal relations within the confederation; and (3) the *combourgeoisie* treaties that constituted the first step toward the expansion of the confederation by establishing what today we would call associated state arrangements with polities immediately adjacent to it. These covenants were used to adapt the terms of membership to the characteristics of each potential candidate, including its geopolitical position, its past and present diplomatic relations with the confederation, and its socioeconomic composition.[6]

The usual process for the expansion of the confederation was for the confederates to first develop mutual *combourgeoisie* agreements with their neighbors and then to transform those agreements into confederal ones after a period of testing through the implementation of the original, more limited, ties. Following biblical terminology, first the peripheral entities were made *baalei brit*—league partners—and then after that worked, there was a recovenanting to make them *bnai brit*—confederates. As a result, each accession was tailored to the particular situation. Zurich was leagued with the three original cantons by the agreement of 1315, and was not turned into a confederate until 1351. Lucerne was added in 1332 and Glarus in 1352, followed by Zug. Berne joined the confederation in 1353 by signing three different pacts with the members of the existing confederation in order to accommodate the terms of Berne's earlier treaty with Austria.

This confederation of eight continued until 1481, at which time other polities applied for membership but were obliged to wait. In 1481, two long-time allies of the confederation, the cities of Solothurn and Fribourg, were admitted as confederates over the opposition of the five rural members, who were afraid of adding two more cities to give the three existing confederated cities parity in the confederal Diet. Since the cities had larger populations and were wealthier, a parity of numbers would mean city dominance. Again, a compromise was found in special covenants with each new member that kept both from full membership for a period while at the same time limiting their ability to undertake foreign policy initiatives that might adversely affect the rest of the confederation.

Zurich was the first free city of the empire to enter the confederation in 1351 and did so primarily because it did not like the terms offered it by Austria. It was very much an agreement of mutual interest, one that worked out well despite the civil wars of the Reformation era. Even the religious schism was relatively manageable in that it divided both the country and city confederates rather than creating a city-country polarization, but the Reformation was vitally important to Zurich, developing the "Zurchergeist," the special Zurich mentality of spirit that truly developed after Zurich's defeat at Kappel in the civil war. Zurichers turned from politics to economics and adopted sobriety as their dominant mode. In the first phase it became a great religious center, which may have come in the place of its previous efforts at political expansion. Then bourgeois economics took over. As people became more oriented toward economic profits and the industry that it took to bring them, many of those Zurichers with a more cultural bent even found it desirable to move elsewhere in Switzerland. At the same time part of the new Zurchergeist was a commitment to the Swiss Confederation as a whole, which certainly helped to sustain the latter through the stormy period of transition that followed the Reformation. All of this was deeply embedded in a covenantal sense of things, which meant that as Zurich became dominant in Switzerland, it did not become greedy for power and certainly not political power, thereby further protecting the small country and its covenantal character both.

Only when Basel was admitted to full membership at the beginning of the sixteenth century were Solothurn and Fribourg given that status as well. With Basel, the confederation had no choice. It was the biggest city in Switzerland, attractive both for its wealth and for its geographic location. It, too, was accepted through a special covenant. Schaffhausen and Appenzell were added in the early sixteenth century as well to make Switzerland a confederation of thirteen when the Reformation came.

All told, there were four principal covenants that formed the basis for the Helvetic Confederation between 1291 and 1647: the Priests' Charter, the Covenant of Sempach, the Covenant of Stans, and the Treaties of Defensional. The Priests' Charter, signed in 1370, was the first covenant to try to reshape the internal arrangements of the confederation by harmonizing the laws of all the cantonal units. It was the first document to use the term *unzer eydgnossenschaft* (our confederation) and brought that term into common use. It also provided for a common internal federal function, the protection of traffic along the major roads passing through the confederation.

Twenty-three years later, in 1393, the Covenant of Sempach became the federation's first multilateral treaty, establishing a common code of conduct during war. Among other things, it was an attempt to standardize military instruction, regulate the distribution of pillage and war profits, and forbid private warfare initiatives. It was only partially successful.

The *Staner Verkommnis* (Covenant of Stans) was not signed until nearly a century later in 1481. It, too, was directed toward the safeguarding of internal order. Reconfirming the two former covenants, it included arrangements for governing occupied territories, the division of military gains, and increased coherence in the common foreign policy. Partners to the Covenant swore not to attack each other or to assist in the subversion of each other's internal regimes. This *Staner Verkommnis* became the basic constitution of the confederation. As such it included a provision for reaffirmation by public oath on the part of the members every fifty years, perhaps an echo of the biblical Jubilee.

These three great covenants were supplemented by the network of *combourgeoisies,* treaties that were somewhere between confederal pacts and international agreements. These were mutual defense pacts of indefinite duration, principally between cities, hence their name. They included provisions for mediation in case of potential conflict, and economic arrangements. This was the first step toward the admission of new members to the confederation, providing for a trial period of mutual relations before the full marriage.

William E. Rappard, in his book *Du Renouvellement des Pactes Confederaux,* examines the habits of periodically renewing and repledging the old covenants.[7] Introduced for the first time in 1351, the reasons and the procedure for this institution are outlined in the charter:

> Afin que ce pacte soit toujours mieux connu de tous ceux, jeunes et vieux, qu'il concerne, il est aussi decide que tous les dix ans, vers le debut de mai, a la demande d'une des Villes ou d'un des Pays, il faudra, en vertu de nos serments, lire publiquement et renouveler ces engagements et l'alliance, avec les formules, les textes, les serments et tout ce qui s'y rapporte. Tout homme ou garcon age a ce moment d'au moins seize ans devra alors jurer d'observer eternellement ce pacte, avec toutes les clauses qui sont designees dans cette charte; sans aucune reserve.

This institution was not invented in 1351. Rappard lists, as one among many, the covenant between the cities of Bern and Fribourg (1243), which contained a like clause. But by 1351 it was used for the first time in one of the covenants that were slowly building up Switzerland. Additionally, it came to be an indispensable clause for the subsequent covenants. Later, one particular weekend was designated during which all the members of the alliance would have renewal ceremonies in their respective seats of government and send envoys to all the other members in order to "receive the pledge." It seems that these ceremonies were held fairly regularly without adhering, however, to rigid intervals. There were some controversies as to where some of the smaller communes had to send delegates in order to fulfill their duties (this relates to the custom that the rural communes sent delegates to the cities as their representatives to participate in the ceremony) and as to the status of some members of the alliance, namely Fribourg, Solothurn, and Schaffhausen which, for a time, felt that they were treated as minor members.

The Reformation put an end to this institution. 1520 was the last time that all the members exchanged pledges. Five years later the Catholic cantons refused to receive the delegates of, or send their own to, the cities of Basel and Zurich which, in the interim, had adopted the new Reformed faith. With the further spread of Reformed Protestantism, the wars that ensued between the members of the two religious camps further disrupted established procedures.

In Basel, for the sake of unity, a superficial acceptance of the new reality, particularly on the Catholic side, led to numerous attempts to reestablish the old custom. Elaborate compromises were offered by those cantons that were divided in their religious composition or put political considerations above religious differences. In the latter camp were the cantons that, because of their geographical location, were most vulnerable to external intervention and, therefore, most concerned about maintaining an undivided Switzerland.

All the attempts failed, however, because the Catholics insisted that the covenants had to be renewed according to the old formula in which "God and the saints" were mentioned. The Reformers, on the other hand, were not about to invoke the saints. Thus, the covenants remained unrenewed from 1520 until the eve of the French invasion of Switzerland in 1798. Then, significantly, they were ceremoniously renewed in a revival of the old way in an attempt to show unity in the Swiss effort to resist a potential invader. As it turned out, this attempt came too late.

In the interim, after four generations of religious wars and tension, two general covenants cut in the mid-seventeenth century reconstituted the confederation and gave it the formal framework that lasted until the Napoleonic conquest in 1798. The latter set in motion the processes that culminated in 1848 in the transformation of Switzerland into a federation.

Upon conquering Switzerland in 1798, Napoleon tried to impose a unitary government on the Swiss, which he named the Helvetic Republic, transforming the existing confederated republics into cantons, a term designed to show their subordination to the new national government. Because most of the cantons had fallen into the hands of patrician oligarchies in the late seventeenth and eighteenth centuries, eliminating the older medieval democracy in all but name, Napoleon's revolutionary effort was not entirely rejected by the Swiss, but they did reject his efforts to establish a unitary government. After five years he was forced to partially restore the old confederation through the Act of Mediation (1803).

In 1815, with Napoleon's fall, the old confederation was substantially restored, but on an enlarged basis. Graubunden, previously an independent confederation of communes loosely allied with the Helvetic Confederation, was incorporated into Switzerland as a single canton and eight other cantons were added as well, including Vaud, Aargau, and Ticino, which had been ruled as subject territories, and Valais and Geneva, which had been allied under the combourgoisie system. The Treaty of Paris guaranteed Switzerland's perpetual neutrality.

The 1815 restoration also restored much of the prerevolutionary patrician rule. It was not until the 1830s that the Radical parties (in the European sense of bourgeoisie liberalism) in most of the cantons were able to establish democratic governments. Since the Radical party was also secularist in its orientation, it aroused Catholic opposition, which led to the Sonderbund War in 1847, the result of which was the transformation of Switzerland from a confederation into a federation through the constitution of 1848. That constitution combined American influences with Swiss traditions such as the plural executive. With it Switzerland fully entered into the modern epoch.

What Made the Swiss Special

What made the Swiss special remains an unanswered question. We know several things. The original Helvetians were a Celtic people. Once again, we are in the presence of the Celtic cultural tradition, which seems to have had a predisposition to covenantal forms.

Fifty years after the Roman withdrawal in 401 from what is now Switzerland, much of the country was overrun by Burgundians, an East Germanic people who had earlier settled in Savoy. Like other East Germanic peoples they tended to favor pyramidal political and social structures. But their period of dominance in the area of Switzerland was foreshortened by the arrival of the Alemanni after the year 500, who continued to advance for the next 200 years until they became the region's dominant group. As the Alemanni arrived, the Franks conquered the Burgundians, so that the Frankish rulers confronted an Alemannian population. The Franks brought Christianity; the Alemanni, liberty. It has already been noted how the basis of Frankish government was feudal in its most hierarchical sense, but under the Merovingians and Carolingians, still rather benevolently so. In the end the Alemannian element proved the stronger, reinforcing older Celtic residues (which may even have been reinforced by the fact that Irish monks had a significant share in bringing Christianity to the Alemanni). Celtic covenantal foundations were strengthened with the elements of Alemannian oath politics.

We also know that on the eve of the modern epoch, Switzerland gave birth to the Protestant Reformation in its most covenantal form, drawing heavily on the Bible for political inspiration. Although it is dangerous to draw facile judgments about that since the original republics of the Swiss confederation remained Catholic and Reformed Protestantism was essentially an urban phenomenon, it may be that the Reformation strengthened covenantalism in the cities, where it was most in danger of turning into something else. Third, there is the tradition of commitment to freedom and independence on the part of mountain people, which

seems to be well-nigh worldwide. For example, the closest thing to republicanism one finds in south Asia before the twelfth century were the
mountain polities in the foothills of the Himalayas, settled by people
who fled oppressive rulers in India proper. In any case, the Swiss experience in the Middle Ages demonstrated the difference between real
covenantal polities and the feudal synthesis of hierarchy and contract.

Swiss covenantalism is based on the twin pillars of a federal political
culture and a strong religious tradition. In a sense they represent what
Alexis de Tocqueville was later to say about the United States, that felicitous combination of "the spirit of liberty and the spirit of religion"
marching hand in hand. This is evident in every sphere, from the cantonal anthems such as the "Ode to God" of Appenzell that attributes that
republic's liberties to its people's covenant with God, to wines such as
the Vin de la Republique, developed in honor of the reestablishment of
the republic of Valais in 1798, to the Swiss constitution. This combination was forged in the Middle Ages and reforged during the Reformation and again in the seventeenth and nineteenth centuries at each
reconstitution of the Swiss federal polity.

In 1991 Switzerland celebrated 700 years of Swiss confederation.
The commemoration started at the beginning of the year in Ticino and
ended in September in Basel. The actual anniversary day, 1 August,
was marked on the field at Rutli where the confederation was initiated
by a covenant between the three organized mountain republics. In
Ticino and Basel, the focal point of the commemoration was a tent of
meeting (called exactly that, including the biblical name) designed by
Switzerland's leading contemporary architect around thirteen arches
representing the thirteen republics of the original confederation. It was
designed to be portable, as a tent of meeting would be. In the Rutli
area itself, the Swiss constructed a cantonal path covering 35 kilome-
ters, with each canton allocated a section in proportion to its population (so many millimeters per individual inhabitant), which it will be
responsible for building and maintaining.

Much emphasis was placed on *heimmat*, which means original home.
Every citizen has a *heimmat*, an original home in one of Switzerland's
3,072 communes, and the right to return to it. Even if a person was not
born there, the *heimmat* must accept him. *Heimmat* is a living principle
maintained in contemporary Switzerland as in the past—shades of the
biblical idea of permanent family and tribal allotments.

Today the Swiss are probably the most federal people in the world in terms of their political culture. Somehow they have internalized the proper combination of individual autonomy and commitment to group effort that is essential for successful federal arrangements and is quite covenantal in its orientation. One can assume that the Swiss of today are perpetuating cultural patterns established centuries ago, since there was little in the modern world to encourage them to develop those patterns.

The Low Countries

The Netherlands or Low Countries were another peripheral area in medieval Europe. Just as some liberty-loving people fled to the mountains, others fled to the marsh and swamplands along the coast of the North Sea, where they developed an urban civilization based upon commerce, manufacturing, shipping, and fishing, and the most advanced agriculture in medieval Europe. They organized themselves into communities around the necessity to fight against flooding to keep the North Sea back and, indeed, to claim land from it so as to extend their own settlements.

These communities united on a regional basis into provinces, tied together by reclamation districts that were to be known as *poulders,* the earliest form of government beyond the commune. In due course these regional reclamation associations became provinces. These original associations were based on pacts, pure and simple. By the definitions used here they can be defined as compacts involving practical arrangements supported by mutual pledges in which the role of a transcendent power is not particularly manifest.

Unlike Egypt and China, where control over scarce water resources led to despotism, the necessity to organize control over an abundance of water led in the Netherlands to republicanism, which was to emerge on the threshold of the modern epoch in the form of a confederation, the United Provinces of the Netherlands. In the history of political development, the United Provinces was to be a transitional form between medieval and modern federal arrangements.[8]

The most covenantal of the Netherlandish peoples were the Frisians, who apparently were the very first settlers in the region and may themselves be an admixture of Celtic and Germanic influences. Like the Alemanni, the Frisians were a Germanic people who flourished in Roman and medieval times and who became submerged within a larger grouping during the Middle Ages but not entirely. They settled an area in the very northern part of the Netherlands where they were most isolated from interfering neighbors. Frisland itself was originally an island archipelago off the coast of Europe, part of which was connected with the mainland through diking, which claimed land from the sea. The Frisians engaged in cattle raising and dairying. Frisland extends along the coast of the North Sea from the westernmost of the West Frisian Islands in what became the Netherlands, north and slightly to the west of Amsterdam, to the northernmost of the North Frisian Islands in Denmark. The Frisians ultimately were submerged within a kindred people, the Dutch, just as so many of the Alemanni were transformed into Swiss. The consciousness of Frisian, like Alemannian, origins has remained within those larger peoples and it seems to have some prominent connection with their covenantal political cultures.

Frisians are known to have been located in those territories as early as 200 B.C.E., when they already were herders and fishermen. They were conquered by the Romans, who made them *foederatii*. Their most important moment in history came between the fifth and ninth centuries C.E. when Frisia became a leading maritime power, dominating trade and commerce from southern France to Finland, so much so that the North Sea was known as the Frisian Sea. While they continued to be active in commerce throughout the Middle Ages, after the ninth century the North Frisians came under the influence of the Danes, the East Frisians the Germans, and the West Frisians the Dutch. The latter became a Netherlands province by joining the United Provinces in 1579. While later absorbed into the Dutch polity, the Frisians maintained their own ethnic subculture and language well into modern times. There are still scattered pockets of Frisian speakers.

The Frisians were not converted to Christianity until the late eighth century. They were the first to resist outside authority after 1493 against the Burgundians and then the Hapsburgs. Only in 1523 did Charles V subdue them. They quickly adopted Reformed Protestantism in the sixteenth century. In the Netherlands they are linked with the Dutch or Independent Reformed Churches. It was during that resistance that Frisland split into three, West Frisland ultimately became a Netherlands province, East Frisland became part of Germany after 1454, and North Frisland a part of Denmark.

In the early centuries the Frisian language had an influence on English. This influence is especially visible in the development of English covenantal language.[9]

In the early years of the settlement of the Low Countries, these communities were under the nominal or at times more than nominal rule of the House of Burgundy, which merged with the Hapsburgs in the fifteenth century. However, it was not until the sixteenth century that these rulers tried to transform the network of authoritative links, which bound the communities of the Low Countries to them, into a state. Whereas the Burgundians were content with the looser connections wherever they ruled (western Switzerland was also under nominal Burgundian suzerainty in the same period), the Germanic desire for order led to the effort to impose central institutions—political, financial, and judicial—over the preexisting local and provincial polities. For about a century they succeeded, only to provoke revolution.[10]

As usual, the Hapsburgs laid the foundations for their own destruction, in this case when Charles V, who was the Holy Roman Emperor in 1519, at the very beginning of the sixteenth century, extended Hapsburg dominion to the five outermost provinces of the Netherlands, which had hitherto been outside of Burgundian-Hapsburg rule. They, along with Holland and Zeeland, were to become the core of the anti-Hapsburg revolt and the initiators of the United Provinces of the Netherlands and to become independent before the century was out. Charles's misguided effort was modified only by his general care to preserve the forms of urban autonomy, which were very strong in the Lowlands. The story of that revolt and its consequences will be told in chapter 11.

Notes

1. On Andorra, see Peyret J. Corts, *Geography and History of Andorra* (Spanish) (Barcelona, 1945).
2. On San Marino, see G. Rossi, *San Marino* (San Marino, 1954).
3. For the history of Switzerland, see J. F. Aubert, *Petite Histoire Constitutionelle de la Suisse* (Bern: Francke Editions, 1974); Andre Siegfried, *Switzerland,* trans. Edward Fitzgerald (New York: Duell, Sloan and Pearce, n.d.). Cf. also Benjamin Barber, *The Death of Communal Liberty: A History of Freedom in a Swiss Mountain Canton* (Princeton: Princeton University Press, 1974).
4. David Lasserre, *Die Schiksalsstunden des Foederalismus: Alliances Confederales, 1291–1815* (Zurich: Erlenbach-Zurich Editions, 1941).
5. On Swiss culture and political culture, see Denis de Rougemont, *La Suisse: Ou L'Histoire D'un Peuple Heureux* (Paris: Hachette, 1965) and Daniel J. Elazar,

Federal Systems of the World (London: Longman, 1991). Edgar Bonjour, *A Short History of Switzerland* (Oxford: Clarendon, 1952).

6. On the camourgeoise treaties and the Swiss method of federal expansion see Aubert, *Petite Histoire*; Klaus Schumann, *Das Regicrungassystem der Schweic* (Koln: C. Heymann, 1971); Ernst Gagliardi, *Geschichte des Schweizerischen eidgenossensehaft* (Leipzig: R. Voigtlaender, 1912).

7. William E. Rappard, *Du Renouvillement des Pactes Confederaux, 1351–1798* (Zurich: Gebr. Leeman, 1944).

8. Paul Henri Mallet, *Northern Antiquities,* trans. Bishop Percy (New York: AMS Press 1968), chap. 7, "of the form of government which formerly prevailed in the north," 122–34.

9. The best concise source about the Frisians in English is the article "Frisians," in *Harvard Encyclopedia of American Ethnic Groups,* ed. Stephan Thernstrom (Cambridge, Mass. and London, England: The Belknap Press of Harvard University Press, 1980), 401–03.

10. Heinrich Mitteis, *State in the Middle Ages,* trans. H. F. Orton (Amsterdam and Oxford: North Holland Publishing Company 1975), introduction, 3–23; Cornelius Tacitus, *The Germania of Tacitus: A Critical Edition,* Rodney Potter Robinson, ed. (Middletown, Conn.: American Philological Association, 1935); Fritz Kern, *Kingship and Law in the Middle Ages,* trans. S. P. Chimes (Oxford: Basil Blackwell 1956).

6

Oath Societies in Greater Scandinavia

The Scandinavian Polity

On Europe's northern rim, the Nordic peoples developed military, political, and religious organizations based upon oaths of mutuality that were only partially feudal. These were classic oath societies that reached their apotheosis in the new territories settled by the Norsemen. The most articulated of these, Iceland, strikingly resembled the early Israelite polity without the moral dimensions of monotheism.[1]

For three hundred years, from the middle of the eighth to the middle of the eleventh centuries, a full epoch in human history, the Norsemen represented a great power in Europe, moving outward from their Scandinavian base in every possible direction. To the east they opened up Russia for trade, penetrating from the Swedish Baltic ports across the Russian steppes to the Black Sea and into the Mediterranean. Their influence was so great that the very name of the Russian people is derived from the word *Russ,* which is Norse for trader. To the west, the Norse moved down the North Sea and through the English Channel, conquering and settling territories on both sides, then continuing down the Atlantic coast of France and Spain into the Mediterranean as far as Sicily.[2]

While the origins of the Norsemen or Vikings are lost in the mists of prehistory, archeological evidence suggests a strong influence of Iranian culture, which, in turn, was influenced by the earlier Assyrian culture. Iranian peoples such as those in Iran and the Scythians to the north of it seem to have contributed much to the artifactual and ritual culture of early Scandinavia until the Vikings themselves picked up Celtic influences as a result of their expansion into the Celtic world. Were the Scandinavian tribes that became the Vikings themselves originally from an Iranian people, perhaps a branch of the Scythians? We do not know,

but there is reason to speculate in that direction. One hopes that continued studies of prehistorical archeology and anthropology will throw
additional light on the matter. If that were the case, it would do much to
explain Viking oath-culture and the society it produced.[3]

The Scandinavian countries themselves began as congeries of independent polities. As Mary Wilhelmine Williams put it, "Each river valley, coastal plain, peninsula, and island had a distinct governmental
system." Over the centuries these local polities were gradually combined, "sometimes through mutual agreement, but more frequently as a
result of the successful military campaigns of ambitious chieftains or
aggressive kings."[4] By the close of the ninth century Denmark, Norway,
and Sweden had more or less achieved sufficient territorial delineation
under a common government.

It was as a result of the completion of the political consolidation of
Norway under King Harold Fairhair that the Icelandic republic was
founded. From 874 onward, those who were unwilling to submit to
Harold, including many of the country's best people, fled to Iceland to
reestablish a classic Norse commonwealth. There they reintroduced the
system of local republics until in 930 they combined in what may best
be called the republican union of Iceland with a common *althing* (general assembly), while the local political units remained the centers of
day-to-day governance.[5]

In Scandinavia proper, a thousand years of localism could not be
eliminated overnight. Most of the formerly independent republics were
reconfirmed as local governments, known as *lands* (as Haalogaland) or
rikes (as in *raumarike,* meaning dominion). Kings only emerged as chief
executive officers after the ninth century. Even at that they remained in
many ways no more than first among equals until the thirteenth century
or later, long after the Viking age had passed. Along with the process of
election or acceptance of kings went a real right of resistance, documented in the Nordic sagas.[6]

While Norwegian kings obtained office through inheritance, in Denmark and Sweden they were usually elected. In Denmark kings were
elected by the towns, led by Viborg, Ringsted, and Lund, the three leading towns of the time. In Sweden they were elected by a popular assembly called the *morathing*. After election the new king of Sweden had to
travel to each province and submit himself to approval of the local assemblies whose task it was to satisfy themselves of the legality of the

candidate's claim. The king, in turn, was required to swear "to strengthen the laws and to preserve peace," after which the presiding officer of the local *thing* proclaimed him to be the rightful ruler and the local population then swore allegiance to him. This procedure reaffirmed the system of popular assemblies, which continued to exist.

Things were always assembled in the open, in a valley or a plain known as the *thingvol,* or field of assembly. This procedure survives on the Isle of Man (which was under a prolonged period of Norwegian rule), where the Manx parliament still meets in a valley out in the open and proclaims new laws from Tynwald hill. The lawspeaker who presided over the *thing* stood on a low hill or knoll in the middle of the assembly area.

Meetings of these political assemblies usually took place during the summer and were the focal point of popular gatherings of two weeks or more. They involved not only political decision making but religious festivals and commercial activities. In essence the equivalent of fairs, much private business was done as well. These encampments were called *thingsteds*. At the site of the *thingsted* each family had the shell of a booth that they would recover during their weeks of residence.

Attendance at the local *thing* was compulsory, with some exemptions, such as sole farm workers, for example, who could not leave their farms. Even they were required to be present at special assemblies convened to deal with murder cases, tax equalization, or the militia. Each local assembly had to send a specific number of men to the regional assemblies, and so on.

While the Scandinavian countries had social aristocracies, it seems that aristocratic privilege did not carry over into their political institutions. Other than some exemption from taxation and military service granted to certain noble families, no feudal system of manors, tenants, or serfdom was developed. The major landowners were more like English landowners before the Norman conquest. Customary law controlled king, aristocrats, and commoners. In most cases these were local customs. Indeed, it was not until Magnes the Sixth, known as the Lawmender (1263–80), that the king was able to begin to standardize the different provincial customs, 400 years after the unification of Norway.

Sweden was even slower to consolidate; law enforcement and the maintenance of peace (along the same notion as the Germanic peoples) was a provincial responsibility. The first national code of law was not issued until 1347 by Magnes Eriksson. In Denmark the process took even longer. Even in Norway the kingly inheritance did not necessarily pass to the eldest son. Rather, a consortium of sons would rule until one was selected.

The biggest factor in increasing centralization and the consolidation of the monarchy was the Church. Whether because of their worries that local customs encouraged the people to revert to paganism or because they had become ideologically committed to hierarchical government, the clergy threw all their influence behind strengthening the centralized institutions of the monarchy. In the end their intervention was decisive and power was centralized in the throne, destroying the Scandinavians' customary local liberties.

The real change came in the fourteenth century. The king's office-holders, by then an aristocracy, acquired the status of a hereditary nobility. Kings were strengthened and centralization of law and administration increased. Military power passed from the popular militias (*ledung*) to feudal armies in Sweden and Denmark. As the military system became feudalized, there was a partial feudalization of government. Still, feudalism remained at best rudimentary. As was characteristic of the feudal age, the distribution of military power shaped the distribution of civil authority.

The key to the diffusion of power in the Scandinavian countries lay in the broad distribution of military power among local levys. The Vikings were unique in that theirs was a militia fleet. Each locality (*herred*) was responsible for providing from one to four ships whose crews were headed by a *styraesman* (helmsman or ship's captain, reminiscent of the Greek cabarnit, from whence the Latin word *gubernare* and the linguistic association between governing and steering a ship). Members of the local levy paid dues to build and maintain the ship, but the *styraesman* had to have greater private means to provide a larger share needed to maintain his office.

The power of these *lethanges* or levys remained great during the 300 years of Danish Viking ascendancy, although for the last several generations of that period kings gained in strength. On at least two occasions, in 1074 and 1104, the Danish *styraesmen* were responsible for electing the kings of Denmark. It was only after the Danes lost England and gave up large-scale forays across the sea for more than a century that the *lethanges* began to lose their power.

When Denmark resumed its military activity, the king had formed a new military nucleus out of his immediate retinue, the *hird*. In the latter part of the twelfth century, private forces began to develop. Under the Jutland law, the position of *styraesman* was hereditary, passing to sons or brothers, thus recognizing the existence of notable families. The *lethanges* had been like marines—oarsmen and infantry. New conditions of land campaigning required cavalry whose cost was beyond what ordinary yeomen could bear. These cavalry were furnished by the new nobility and became the basis of their power. Within the next century and a half, the bulk of the yeomanry lost their liberty and were confined to farming, burdened with heavy taxes, and increasingly lost their freeholds and became tenant farmers. The new nobility appropriated the old name *fri-hals* (freeneck—a term applied throughout Scandinavia to those not in servitude as a sign of the special liberties and tax immunities they acquired).

The Norse word for king, *konungr,* like the general Germanic term, carried the basic meaning "man of noted origin." The early kings were essentially umpires in legal matters, applying customary law, and only much later acquired a role as sources of law. Indeed, they had a very limited role in law enforcement. The exception was Sweden, where the law defined a number of offenses as *epsorisbrot* or sworn oath offenses—crimes which, if unpunished, were interpreted to mean that the king had failed to keep the oath he swore on his accession to the throne to maintain peace. Later these laws were to provide the opening for greater royal power. For our purposes, what is significant is that the only national law had to do with oaths and their violation.[7]

The system of Swedish kings ascending to the throne only after mutual oath taking was continued even after hereditary kingship was introduced, down to the end of the seventeenth century, if not later. As part of the king's accession to the throne he had to grant charters, hierarchical versions of constitutions, and bind himself by those charters. The great Gustavus Adolphus, for example, only gained the crown in 1611 by binding himself by a charter, which even began to resemble a modern constitution.[8]

Upon the death of Gustavus Adolphus in 1632, Sweden took another step toward replacing medieval charters with modern constitutionalism. As in the past, the charter he granted ceased to be operative when he died. Two years later the king, in consultation with the Swedish *riksdag* (assembly), promulgated the first *regeringsform* (form of government) as a basic law designed to continue to be in force without regard to who occupied the throne. In a sense, this was the beginning of modern constitutionalism in Sweden. The term *regeringsform* is still used to describe the principal Swedish constitutional law. The *regeringsform* emphasized the organization of the government and said relatively little about the prerogatives of the legislative body or the rights of the people.

Between 1680 and 1718 the Swedish kings reigned as nearly absolute monarchs, but in 1719 a new *regeringsform* was promulgated as part of a new charter. Since then, Sweden has been under some constitutional instrument. Royal charters given at the king's accession to the throne continued until 1772. *Regeringsformer* were issued in 1720, 1772, and 1809, with the last still being in force, having been subsequently supplemented by *grundlager* (constitutional laws) dealing with the organization of the legislature (*riksdag-sordning*), succession to the throne (*successionordning*), and liberty of the press (*tryckfrihetsforordning*).

The very language of the *regeringsformer* reflects the continuity of Swedish constitutionalism. From the eighteenth century onward, the emphasis has been on the organization of the executive powers and the relationship of those two branches of government according to the idea that the separation of powers is the best protection of individual rights. Although the right to do so is not clearly specified, the Swedish courts have claimed and at least modestly exercised the right to declare statutes unconstitutional, completing the balance of powers in the system.

Each century has contributed to the underlying theoretical presuppositions of the Swedish polity. In the seventeenth century, the idea of fundamental law became normative. In the eighteenth, fundamental laws were viewed as codifications of the social contract. The nineteenth century introduced the idea of a flexible constitution. The twentieth century added a strong social dimension to constitutional interpretation. Swedish constitutionalism today, then, is a continuation of its medieval legacy.

Cultural Continuities

Marcus Hanson, in his classic work on immigration to the New World, *The Atlantic Migration*, emphasizes the cultural differences between the coastal peoples along the west coast of Europe, what he calls the "Celtic borderlands," and the interior peoples, suggesting that even in countries like Norway, not to speak of those further south, this represented a cultural divide. He uses the distinction for his purposes, but it is an important tracer for ours as well, for there seems to be a serious cultural factor involved here.[9] The regions Hanson points to are those that were the heart of Viking oath culture. It was from those lands that the Danish and Norse Vikings set sail for Britain, conquering great parts of the English north country, the west coast of England, and the Scottish seacoast, particularly to the west, beginning in the eighth century, settling long enough to establish a culture that would later be conducive to new forms of covenantalism.

The Norse settlements in Scotland blended in with the local Scottish culture to strengthen the latter's covenantal impulses. Danish settlements in East Anglia, which became part of the Danish world for several generations, undoubtedly influenced that region's general and political cultures and contributed to it becoming the center of Puritanism hundreds of years later, of which more is discussed in chapter 7.[10]

Compare the maps of Viking penetration and Puritan congregationalism 600 years later and the convergence is too unmistakable to be accidental. It was then that the influence of the pre-biblical oath society of the Northmen found its most elevated expression in the biblically based religious ideology of Puritanism. The Northmen conquerors may themselves have been an oath culture but their behavior and habits were those of barbarians, striking fear into the hearts of the peaceful folk who lived in the areas of their conquest. It remained for a new synthesis to tame their barbarism while retaining the commitment to freedom, independence, and equality embodied in their oath societies. The coming of the Reformation, with its Puritan expression in England and its Presbyterian expression in Scotland wedded a biblical morality, outlook, and expectations to a culture waiting for such a mode of expression, just as was the case with the original Israelites in the oath cultures of the Fertile Crescent.

The Norse conquests in France led to the creation of a mixed people, the Normans, who combined feudal and contractual elements in their political culture and polity and then took those elements down into the Mediterranean world, conquering Sicily and reshaping it.[11] As late as the early nineteenth century, the local liberties of Sicilian villages rested upon the original compact between the Norman conquerors of the country and on the rights of their ancestor founders as *commilitones* (comrades-in-arms) or co-conquerors in the tenth century. Only the imposition of the new-style modern absolutist system developed by Napoleon for France, by the Kingdom of Naples at the end of the Napoleonic wars, ended that system of local liberties. It was driven underground to re-emerge as the compact of Sicilian families known as the Mafia, which was initially organized through what had become traditional Sicilian instruments of oath and compact to resist foreign usurpation of estab-lished Sicilian rights and only later was transformed into the criminal vehicle we know today.[12]

Iceland: An Oath-Bound Republic

The crowning achievement of Norse society was Iceland. As we all know now, Norsemen sailing to the west in the tenth and eleventh cen-turies discovered the new worlds of the Faroes, Iceland, Greenland, and Vineland (North America), and attempted to establish settlements in all four. They succeeded in the Faroes, but their greatest success was in Iceland, the closest of the large new territories to the European main-land and the one most capable of supporting a settled population that could still remain in communication with the motherland.[13]

In those lands, the Norsemen had an open frontier in which their basic institutions could develop without having to compromise with an existing population, as was true in the other areas into which the Norse advanced. Moreover, the influence of the frontier in Iceland and Greenland, two of the territories that were actually settled, was the same as it later was in North America. That is to say, it encouraged the sense of equality among its settlers, who came together as equals to form civil societies and who had neither the time for the organic development of governing institutions nor the inclination to establish hierarchical frame-works that would deny or interfere with that fundamental equality. Tenth-century Iceland was already a full-blown democracy based upon a shared compact and embodied in a shared law. This polity was reaffirmed an-nually by an assembly of all Icelanders to reaffirm their mutual oath to one another and to listen to the law speaker recite to them their funda-mental law.

Serious settlement of Iceland began in 874 as many of the finest people from Norway left rather than submit to consolidated monarchical rule. Until 930 they and those who joined them lived in small groups scat-tered around the island. Each settlement became an independent republic, a miniature democracy, protected then as subsequently by the fact that as a distant island Iceland had no problems of military security, so it did not have to maintain a standing army. With no military organization necessary, no hereditary commanders emerged, as was true in the mother country at that time, so no basis for hereditary civil rule developed.

Nevertheless, by 930 intergroup disputes and the need to undertake certain tasks in common led to the establishment of the Republic of Iceland through the formation of the Althing, a general assembly for the island as a whole, that supplemented the local democratic republics but did not replace them. The original communal settlements known as *bygd* became *godords,* in effect townships with political and religious functions. When the Icelandic republic was founded, the number of *godords* was reduced to thirty-nine. They were grouped into four quarters, three with nine *godords* each and the north quarter with twelve. Groupings of three *godords,* which functioned for certain administrative purposes, were known as *thridings,* from whence came the later *riding* for electoral district.

At the head of each *godord* was a *godi,* a combination of civil chieftain and priest. Each built a temple on his own land, which became the nucleus around which the community grew. He officiated at the temple's religious functions and out of that priesthood acquired responsibility for a full range of civil duties from poor relief to legislation. He was the customs and immigration officer. It was he who protected foreigners and arranged for their accommodation. He also managed the foreign relations of his district, served as supreme magistrate, and presided over the local assembly.

Godi (plural *godar*) means a man in some special relationship with the gods or a priest. It is almost exclusively an Icelandic term. The first *godar* were drawn from the notable families of the first period of settlement. In some cases members of those families retained the office during the whole period, until the end of the twelfth century, and the relationship between them and the other free farmers was a central element in the law code to which all agreed in the 920s. *Godar* had few special rights but did have special duties which, if neglected, could lead to prosecution, fining, and deposition.

In return for his protection of the men of his *godord,* the *godi* could require them to accompany him on his journeys through the *godord* or to accommodate him when he visited them. He could also require at least one-ninth of the men of the *godord* to accompany him to the Althing. The *godi* was supported principally by the temple dues, supplemented by fines and fees.

The closest this came to feudalism was that the *godi* could in fact force weaker members of the community to bequeath their property to him in return for his support and protection. On the other hand he was limited by the fact that his jurisdiction was personal and voluntary and extended only over those who chose to place themselves under his protection as *thingmen* or temple men. Men could shift from one temple to a neighboring one if it suited them, by mutual agreement.

The fundamental political relationships in Iceland were based on all free men being in thing with a *godi*, a relationship that was established by mutual consent and guaranteed mutual support. Until 965 a free man could covenant with any *godi* he liked on the island, but one of the reforms of that year was to limit the freedom to choose for both *godar* and *thingmen* to the *godords* in one's own quarter.

At the Althing, each man was required to state to which *godord* he belonged and to be recognized by that *godi*. After the formation of the Icelandic republic, the *godis'* civil functions began to diminish, while their religious functions apparently became of comparatively greater importance.

Perhaps as early as the eleventh century and most certainly in the twelfth, the *godart* passed into the hands of a few families, thus establishing oligarchical rule within the republican framework. This acquisition was apparently as much by purchase of rights as anything else. This gave those few families the right to nominate most of the *godar*, who acted at the various assemblies. In great part it was this move to oligarchical rule that made Icelanders willing to submit to the Norwegian crown in the thirteenth century. The corruption of the *godar* system subsequently enabled the Norwegian king to replace them with *syslumenn*, or royal officers, by the end of the thirteenth century.

The only official serving the entire Icelandic commonwealth was the lawspeaker, elected by the Althing for a term of three years. As in the case of other Scandinavian countries, the lawspeaker was the special guardian and repository of law who also served as the chairman of the Althing, both a legislative body and a court. His election required the unanimous vote of the entire Althing. If that was impossible then one of the quarters was chosen by lot to make the choice, which had to be unanimous within that quarter. The lawspeaker received an annual salary of 200 ells of wadmal and half of the fines imposed by the courts.

The lawspeaker had to have a thorough knowledge of the law, since he had to recite aloud the body of Icelandic law in the presence of the majority of those present at the Althing over the course of his three-year term with certain sections, such as those having to do with the rules of the Althing itself, to be recited at every meeting, and others to be recited over a three-year cycle. By and large Icelandic law was not preserved in writing, so it had to be transmitted orally in this manner. Hence some of the laws were rhymed for mnemonic purposes.

As the living voice of the law, the lawspeaker was able to issue special regulations binding only during his period in office. If a particular lawspeaker was reelected repeatedly, something that occurred twice in the history of old Iceland, his edicts became as binding as regularly enacted laws and were recorded in the law books when legislation began to be written down. Thus, the lawspeaker was the guardian of the republic. Similar offices existed in other parts of Scandinavia in earlier times, but they lost power as the kings gained strength. In Iceland, the lawspeaker retained his critical role until the island came under Norwegian control.

The Althing assembled annually in a valley called Thingvellir. Under the Icelandic code its sessions had to open not later than when the sun could first be seen from the hill of laws where the lawspeaker stood shining on a cleft in the western hills, at which point the members of the Althing marched to the site with the lawspeaker in the lead, followed by the *godar* and other officials and then by the members. The *godi* of the district in which the Althing was held served as convener of the assembly. The task of consecrating the national assembly belonged by inheritance to the *godar* from the family of Ingolf, Iceland's first permanent settler, who bore the ancient title of *allsherjargodi* (priest of all the host).

Upon convening the Althing, the lawspeaker would consecrate the gathering and proclaim the boundaries of the thingsted. Those boundaries established the peace of the thingsted, and within them even outlaws were safe. Every man laid down his weapons, which could not be picked up until the moment of the assembly's dissolution. Once in session, thingmen were required to be in constant attendance and it was against the law to be outside of the boundaries of the thingsted for even one night. Each assumption of responsibility was accompanied by an appropriate oath.

The role of the Althing was to adopt general legislation and to deal with the major judicial issues confronting the commonwealth, including interjurisdictional quarrels between individuals from different *godords*. It also served as a court of appeals from the local courts. The order of business for the Althing as a whole was determined by casting lots. Most of the work, however, was done through committees and separate courts.

Legislative affairs were handled by the *logretta*, the principal legislative committee, which assembled on the hill of laws. Its nucleus consisted of the thirty-nine *godar* plus nine others, also *godar*, nominated by them to form an inner committee of forty-eight. The functions of the latter were limited to the Althing. They sat on the middle bench of a group of three, arranged concentrically on the top of the hill. Forty-eight men sat on each of the other benches as well. They served as counsellors for the *logretta*, with each of the inner forty-eight consulting the two men in front of and behind him.

This assembly of 144 constituted the Icelandic legislature, which dealt with matters of general concern and legislation. In order to act at least forty-eight men had to be present. When there were absentees from the inner committee, the lawspeaker who presided over the *logretta* could coopt men from either of the other benches to fill the vacancies so as to enable the body to continue to act. In order to be approved, a measure had to have a majority of the middle bench, after which the whole *logretta* would assent to it and then the new law would be promulgated by being proclaimed to the entire gathering of thingmen by the lawspeaker from the hill of laws.

As a judicial body, the Althing functioned through a number of courts, at first four, one for each quarter, organized in 965. The *logretta* nominated the judges for the four courts. Decisions in each court had to be unanimous.

A fifth court was instituted after 1000 as a court of equity, after the other four courts became so bound by legal form and influenced by technicalities that the spirit of justice was often lost. In this respect, Icelanders succumbed to the tendencies of contractually oriented societies to emphasize technical form. The new court was comprised of men from each quarter and, hence, acquired a national character. It was given special jurisdiction over cases that could not be settled elsewhere. Its members were bound by a more stringent oath and decision making was by a majority. However, by the time it was instituted, the government of Iceland had fallen into the hands of a powerful oligarchy, so its influence was less than its founder, Njal, a famed Icelandic statesman, had anticipated.

The Althing sat until all cases had been tried, necessary legislation enacted, and the required parts of the old law recited by the lawspeaker. It was then adjourned until the following year. Its closing was marked by the *vapnatak,* namely, the resumption by the thingmen of the weapons that they had laid aside at the opening of the assembly, which they proceeded to shake, thereby proclaiming the end of the session.

Law enforcement then passed into local hands, dependent to a great extent upon public opinion to enforce subsequent court decisions and the fact that someone who resisted a court decision would become an outlaw for the entire community. A key element in the Icelandic system was trial by one's peers in case of serious criminal offenses, whereby the aggrieved parties would appear before their friends and neighbors for a trial to determine guilt or innocence, presided over by a third-party arbitrator.

In local assemblies, three *godar* would act together, one of whom would consecrate the assembly at its beginning and function as its priest. The three *godar* nominated local judges, apparently each nominating twelve. So too did the *logretta* nominate the national judges for the four courts organized as part of the reforms of 965, and later the fifth court introduced after 1000. There is some evidence that the Norse settlers of Iceland were joined by Irish of Celtic stock who reinforced all the predispositions of the northlanders, but also added a dimension of high culture and literacy to what was then still a rather raw population. If this were the case, it would be easier to explain Iceland's special character.

The Icelanders maintained their independence for a full epoch, for three hundred years from the mid-tenth to the mid-thirteenth centuries. They then were forced to accept Norwegian suzerainty, which gave way to Danish rule as a result of mergers back in Scandinavia proper. It was not until 1944, in the middle of World War II, when Denmark was occupied by Germany, that Iceland became fully independent once again under the protection of the United States and Great Britain and then as part of NATO. Throughout that whole period, however, the Icelanders maintained home rule and through it their own particular brand of democratic institutions.

Why Did the Scandinavian Countries Become Lutheran?

With their long and deep history of oath-based societies, why did the Scandinavian countries become Lutheran rather than Reformed during the Reformation? That the Northmen opted for the Reformation is not surprising. G. R. Elton said it clearly: "It would seem that the Viking Northmen never became fully assimilated to Mediterranean Christianity."[14] The answer lies in the political struggles that took place in Scandinavia in the sixteenth century that ended in the princes using Lutheranism to consolidate their power over the aristocracy and forcing the new faith on their subjects.

In 1397, the Union of Kalmar united all of Scandinavia under the Danish crown. Danish authority extended from Finland to Iceland but local sentiments for independence, coupled with the problems of governing territories of such size and inaccessibility, meant that the monarchy was quite limited. In fact, Denmark, Norway, and Sweden (which included Finland), are better described as aristocratic republics and Iceland a democratic republic, all of whom shared a common king as their nominal ruler. As such they were more like a confederacy than a kingdom, but without more than nominal common institutions.

The Union was further rent by the negative influences of a neighboring confederacy, the Hanseatic League, whose interest in controlling the Baltic Sea led them to intrigue to keep the rival Scandinavian kingdom-confederacy from consolidating. Ironically, as the Hanseatic League prospered, its need for unity diminished. That, combined with the growth of territorial states in northern Germany and the Netherlands, led to its effective demise in the sixteenth century.

Christian II (reigned 1513–23) of Denmark tried to step in to fill the regional power vacuum and strengthen his territorial state as well, but he overreached himself. In 1521, Sweden revolted and within two years won its independence, appointing Gustavus Vasa, the leader of the revolt, as its new king. Christian was driven out of Denmark, only to launch repeated attempts to return over the next decade. In the years of upheaval that followed, Protestantism spread in Denmark, with Lutheranism coming in from Schleswig and Lubeck to compete with an indigenous Bible-oriented Danish Reformed Church.

In 1536 Christian's son, Christian III, finally succeeded to the throne and found that he could solve his financial problems best by confiscating the properties of the old church, which he did by establishing a state church. Since he wanted to be a strong prince and Lutheranism was clearly the religion of princes, he brought in Lutheran doctrines that fostered political hierarchy and civil obedience, forcing the teachings of the original Danish church into the realm of folk religion. Since Denmark continued to control Norway and Iceland, Christian foisted the same system on those two countries in the face of what Elton calls "a mixture of violent opposition and surprised non-comprehension."[15]

Thus, Lutheranism was a tool for consolidating the Danish monarchy by breaking the church and the nobility both. But the state religion was only a surface phenomenon in the three countries, a fact that was only to become clear in the nineteenth century when secularization and emigration altered the balance of power, the former at home and the latter in the New World where Norwegians, Danes, and Icelanders remained nominally Lutheran but restructured their congregations and religious ideas on covenantal lines.

Sweden underwent a similar process with Vasa, the new king, who also found the royal treasury bankrupt. Since the people supported his revolt against Denmark for their own reasons but were not interested in a new overlord who would tax them, he, too, sought relief by confiscating the Church properties. Intending to establish dynastic succession, which he did, a religion that supported princes was very much to his liking. Thus, Lutheranism was the best vehicle for him for the same reasons as it was for Christian III. The Reformation was accomplished between 1527 and 1544 against a certain amount of populist resistance among those who opposed the strengthened monarchy far more than they supported the old Church. There was a subsequent effort to promote Calvinism in Sweden, but the king ended that effort. Thus, more than in any other place in Europe, the Reformation in Scandinavia was imposed by the princes from above and took on the characteristics of same. The not-entirely Christian populations were left to their own devices within the new state churches.

The state churches stood for the next four centuries. In the nineteenth century the necessity to maintain such orthodox attachments contributed to the great emigration from Scandinavia to the New World. There the emigrants either broke away from or restructured the hierarchical churches. Some went so far as to secede and form what they refer to in the United States as covenant churches where, in the Reformed tradition, congregations were created by individuals and families covenanting with one another. But even where Lutheranism was maintained, the churches were reorganized on a congregational model. This was most true in connection with the Norwegian Lutheran Church, almost as much with the Danish and, perhaps least but still significant, with the Swedish. The distinctions remained visible as long as the churches remained separate.

Conclusion

The Swiss, the Dutch, and the Scandinavians preserved covenantal ideas and practices on the European continent in the Middle Ages, each population in its own way. In all three cases necessity played its role and in all three it can be said that covenantalism suited the external conditions in which they found themselves, but in none was it foreordained. Indeed, among the Scandinavians it ultimately lost out to stronger pressures, external and indigenous, toward centralization and hierarchy. It was perhaps most principled among the Swiss, whose covenantal system was rooted in Latin law, biblical teachings, and Alemannic culture, as well as their own psycho-cultural dispositions toward liberty and equality. Having all the requisite dimensions, Swiss covenantalism has lasted longest and has become an integral part of the Swiss political culture and its institutional and behavioral manifestations. Dutch covenantalism grew out of the same or very similar tribal traditions and individual psycho-cultural predispositions, but its expression was more influenced by technical necessity than political aspiration. When a different political technology came along that seemed to meet their needs, they adopted it with relative ease.

Scandinavians brought with them a traditional oath culture. Indeed, because they maintained it so late into the historical era, we have a more complete picture of their oath culture than of any other, although we can imagine that theirs was little different from other pre-literate oath cultures in other places and at other times. As long as the environment supported that culture it survived and, in any case, because it did represent a culture and not just a system of organization, it became part of the deep structure of the Scandinavian peoples to a greater or lesser degree; but, because it did not develop any legal, ideological, or institutional base, when the Scandinavian peoples entered history it was overwhelmed by imported ideologies, institutions, and laws to survive as a residue only. Studying it we can see both primitive patterns of culture and learn that such patterns are not enough.

Notes

1. On medieval Scandinavian politics and society, see Johannes Brondsted, *The Vikings* (Baltimore: Penguin, 1965); C. A. Vansittart Conzbeare, *The Place of Iceland in the History of European Institutions* (Oxford: James Parker, 1877); Eric G. Oxenstierna, *The World of the Norsemen,* trans. Janet Sondheimer (London: Weidenfeld and Nicholson, 1957); Rudolf Poertner, *The Vikings: Rise and Fall of the Norse Sea Kings,* trans. Sophie Wilkins (New York: St. Martin's Press, 1975); Alan Small, ed., *The Fourth Viking Congress* (Aberdeen: University of Aberdeen, 1961); Gabriel Tur Ville-Petre, *The Heroic Age of Scandinavia* (London: Hutchinson's University, 1951).
2. The Norse epoch is described in Peter G. Foote and David M. Wilson, *The Viking Achievement* (New York: Praeger, 1970); P. H. Sawyer, *The Age of the Vikings* (London: Edward Arnold, 1971).
3. Exhibit of Viking artifacts, Paris, 1992.
4. Mary Wilhelmine Williams, *Social Scandinavia in the Viking Age* (New York: MacMillan, 1920; New York: Kraus Reprint Co., 1971); Paul Henri Mallet, *Northern Antiquities,* trans. Bishop Percy (New York: AMS Press, 1968).
5. Edward Henriksen, *Scandinavia Past and Present* (Denmark, 1959).
6. Fritz Kern, *Kingship and Law in the Middle Ages,* trans. S. B. Chimes (Oxford: Basil Blackwell, 1956).
7. Ibid., 84.
8. Nils Herlitz, *Sweden: A Modern Democracy on Ancient Foundations* (Minneapolis: University of Minnesota Press, 1939), 4.
9. Zacharias P. Thundyil, *Covenant in Anglo-Saxon Thought: The Influence of the Bible, Church Fathers, and Germanic Tradition on Anglo-Saxon Laws, History,* and the poems *The Battle of Maldon* and *Guthlac* (Madras: The MacMillan Co. of India Ltd., 1972).
10. Marcus Hanson, *The Atlantic Migration, 1607–1860, A History of the Continuing Settlement of the United States,* ed. with a foreword by Arthur M. Schlesinger (New York: Harper, 1961).
11. On the Normans, see *The Norman Conquest: Its Setting and Impact* (New York: C. Scribner Sons, 1966); John Herbert Le Patourel, *The Norman Empire* (Oxford: Clarendon Press, 1976).
12. Fillipo Sabetti, "Covenant Language in Canada: Continuity and Change." Paper presented to the Covenant Workshop on Language of Covenant, Center for the Study of Federalism (Philadelphia, Pa.: Temple University, December 17–18, 1980).
13. On Iceland, see Conzbeare, *The Place of Iceland.* Njal's saga of Iceland deals with the relationship between oath, covenant, and law [trans. Carl A. Bayerschaff and L. M. Hollander (New York, 1955), 219–20].
14. G. R. Elton, *Reformation Europe 1517–1559* (Huntington, N.Y.: Fontana Library, 1963), 125.
15. Ibid., 129.

7

The British Isles: Frontier, West, and Borderlands

On the western peripheries of feudal Europe, a somewhat different combination of organic and compactual arrangement emerged. In the British Isles, England and Wales went from an early compactual phase to an emphasis on organic development, while Scotland preserved a strong compactual basis throughout the medieval period. As elsewhere, Celtic peoples seemed to be more oriented toward covenantal arrangements than other Europeans.

England: Pacts and Feuds

As migrating groups from the Asian heartland and the Mediterranean continued moving westward, some of them crossed the Channel or the North Sea or came up the Atlantic to the west coast of Britain and to Ireland until they reached a point where they could go no further without crossing the ocean. Thus, what may have been the most adventurous of the Asian westerers, among those most likely to have preserved and fostered covenantal forms, reached Britain within relatively recent historical time. There they mixed with other groups who had migrated with them or before them to create a situation that combined frontier and borderlands to provide the requisite environment for fostering covenantal or oath relationships.[1]

The covenant tradition has played a significant role in the political history of England since earliest times, albeit not consistently throughout the country or in all periods. Historically, the strongest manifestations of that tradition were to be found in East Anglia and in the northwest. An exploration of its sources helps explain why. Covenantal or oath political cultures came to England in three separate waves: apparently with the Celtic ancient Britons, among whom there is also a tradition of Mediterranean origins; with the Germanic tribes that became the Angles and the Saxons; and with the Northmen in England, most particularly the Danes.

The Celtic influence is hard to pin down beyond the facts of later history where those western borderlands that retained a Celtic presence were predisposed to covenantal ideologies, institutions, and forms of behavior. With them we are left with the same mystery that we are with the Celts in Helvetia or on the borderlands of continental Europe.

Matters are more easily identifiable when it comes to the Angles and Saxons. They brought with them their Germanic heritage with an oath political culture. In this there are signs of particularly strong Frisian influences, an influence that played a similar if not greater role in the Netherlands. The most oath oriented of these tribes seem to have arrived in the fifth and sixth centuries. With them the first linguistic evidence suggesting a covenantal language appears, apparently influenced by the spread of Christianity. That, however, is not a sufficient explanation since the mainstream of Christianity in those centuries was hardly covenantal; indeed, it was far from it. The fact that the Anglo-Saxons may have translated their own cultural heritage into biblical language and concepts still marks them off. At the same time it is reasonably clear that their oath culture would not have taken on a covenantal dimension without their encounter with biblical sources, much as in Germany proper.

Perhaps the best evidence for all of this is to be found in the evolution of Old English and in the earliest writings that we have from the period. Not only do we find Old English adaptations of the familiar German and Latin terms, but the very word "free," which becomes so important in the history of England, may well have had origins in the covenantal *freo*, with its implications of being at one and the same time unbound (in the sense of shackled) and at liberty to bind one's self through oath.[2]

A good and usually unnoticed example of the pervasiveness of covenantal thought and terminology in a covenantal system is the trial jury. A jury is a body of sworn people. To be a juror is to be someone who has taken an oath (as witness the idea of non-jurors, those English and Scottish clergymen who refused to take an oath to William III after James II was deposed in 1688).

As we learn in studying the history of the jury system, juries are the popular branch of the judiciary, just as elected magistrates are of the executive and elected legislatures or at least lower houses of legislatures are in the legislative branch. They were introduced precisely to democratize, at least to some degree, the three branches of government. Juries are still chosen in the old way, at random, from among the eligible citizens, and then they are sworn in as members of the court, becoming part of the judicial branch for a limited period by virtue of their oaths. Thus, it is no accident that the jury system, while not by any means universal among covenantal peoples, exists only in those polities that grow out of the covenantal tradition in one form or another.

In England, after the Roman withdrawal, political power flowed to a number of regional kings whose petty kingdoms were slowly consolidated through marriage, treaty, and conquest into what is today England. While the first kings gained power through conquest, they were only able to pass it on through compact. For whatever reasons, out of the process grew a network of local magnates rooted in the countryside throughout the emerging England, who acquired effective exercise of most of the political power in the country. Consequently, the compacts were essentially marriage contracts uniting or linking families, which gave the entire system an organic cast. It was only after the Norman conquest in 1066 that a sharply defined feudal framework was introduced with all the appropriate hierarchical elements, which had to be reintegrated into the organic-contractual framework over the next century and a half.[3] Magna Carta, wrung from King John by the barons in 1215, can be understood as a compact or covenant that marked the turning point in that development, permitting organic frameworks to reassert themselves against hierarchical ones. Ideologically it had clear covenantal origins.[4]

English feudalism was modified by Anglo-Saxon traditions of the oath society. This is reflected in the venerable Bede's *Historia Ecclesiastica and Anglo-Saxon Chronicle*—works that describe both suzerainty and vassal treaties; in connection with *Beowulf,* parity treaties and oaths of personal allegiance. Bede uses the standard Latin terms *comitas* (fidelity oaths) and *comitautatus* (a group of retainers) to describe the feudal networks based upon such fidelity oaths. Anglo-Latin also includes the terms *foedus, pactum,* and *testamentum* to describe covenantal relationships, while Old English has its own terms, *frio* and *waer.* The pervasiveness of the oath society is seen in such Old English terms as wedlock to describe marriage, a compound of the term *wed,* a pledge, and *lac,* a gift. In old England, fidelity oaths superseded kinship to establish new ties.[5] The Anglo-Saxon term for promissory oath, *ao',* appears more than one hundred times in Anglo-Saxon law.[6] The conversion of the Anglo-Saxon peoples to Christianity may well have been seen by them as a covenanting act, with baptism as its seal, establishing a vassal treaty between God and the Anglo-Saxons.[7] There is considerable evidence that the Anglo-Saxons understood their relationship to God as being covenantal.[8] St. Martin of Braga referred to conversion as a *pactum* with God in his work, *De Correctione,* written around the year 572.[9] So too, Alcuin describes the conversion of Edwin as a covenant between God and the king in *Dei Pontificibus et Sanctis Ecclesiae Eboracensis.*[10]

The venerable Bede is, of course, the primary exemplar of this old Anglo-Saxon literature and *Beowulf* its classic expression. That Bede belonged to the covenantal school of Christianity is more than reasonably clear. The very fact that he was a monastic put him among those who sought *comunitas* through *koinonia* rather than hierarchy (see below). Moreover, he has left us his discussions of the Noahide covenant and its importance for determining the human fate and destiny, or in other terms, morality and behavior. A thorough study of the ideas that form his writings is likely to reveal a commitment to the covenantal foundations of the world no less comprehensive than that of the Puritans of nearly a millennium later, if not as systematic and profound. The saga of *Beowulf,* as well as such similar period works as *Guthlac* and *The Battle of Moran,* reflect the more primitive dimensions of Germanic pagan oath societies, although with *Guthlac* Thundial claims that a Christian covenantal dimension is already apparent.[11]

Bede was particularly conscious of this covenantal dimension and wrote extensively about it in his biblical writings, referring to the Hebrew term *brit.*[12] He understood the biblical narrative of creation and the fall of man as a covenantal document, followed by the Noahide covenant, which he saw as cosmic in character and a prefiguration of the new covenant with Jesus. Bede claimed that he followed the church fathers who accept the old covenant and new covenant as inseparable from one another, and suggested it is heresy to reject either. He emphasizes that the Gentiles have the Noahide blessing through Japhet. In this respect as in others, he serves as the nexus between the church fathers and medieval theologians.[13]

Beowulf refers to the *ealderiht,* which is the Old Testament or natural covenant of Noah (*Beowulf,* I, 2328). Guthlac emphasized *coinonia,* the Greek word for fellowship, which he understood as a two-sided relationship or a covenant state. He himself equated it with the Hebrew term *hever,* seeing *coinon,* a fellow, as a *haver.* He advocated living a life of *coinonia* with men and with nature and saw monasticism as one expression of *coinonia.*

These older Anglo-Saxon influences might have been stamped out by the feudalism imported from the European continent were it not for the invasions of the Northmen, particularly the Danes who for three centuries ruled and settled in East Anglia and other eastern and western peripheries of Britain. These Northmen brought with them the forms and culture of their oath society.

Theirs, the third great wave, was the dominant force on the English scene between the mid-eighth and the mid-eleventh centuries. During those three centuries, when the Norsemen were at the height of their powers, they repeatedly raided, invaded, and settled different parts of the British Isles, leaving their mark on every aspect of the lives of the peoples they encountered. In England the Danes actually established a settled polity of their own in what is today East Anglia, where they were able to leave their imprint with a special consistency. That imprint was later to reappear through Puritanism, whose center was in the same region of England.

If the east coast of Britain was open to the Danes, in the same measure the west coast was open to the Norwegians to almost the same degree, although Norwegian penetration did not have the same impact as that of the Danes in England. As a forthrightly oath society with a deeply entrenched oath culture, the Norse had a great impact on those parts of England that fell under their influence. Thus, by the time of the Norman invasion in 1066 and the beginning of the last major demographic and cultural synthesis in the making of England, significant sections of the country already had a strong latent covenantal culture.

The Scandinavian influence extended beyond the 300 years of Norse dynamism. In the British Isles it joined with other older covenantal influences to leave its mark. So, for example, the Icelandic *thriding,* referring to a district with political representation, became the English *riding,* or constituency. The tradition of Scandinavian lawsayers who presided over the popular assemblies evolved into the idea of the speakers of the legislative bodies of the English-speaking world. There is a dispute with regard to the source of trial by jury, whether it came directly from the Danes or from the Normans. In either case a Norse influence is involved. Certainly the Danelaw became a fundamental influence.[14]

In political organization, perhaps the most significant development under the Scandinavians was the Confederation of the Five Boroughs. Centered in East Anglia, each borough had its own council based upon the *wapentake,* or the local militia, and the five borough councils sent representatives to the general council of the Confederation. The pattern should sound familiar since it is almost exactly the same as that found in the biblical tribal federation and in many of the Germanic and Scandinavian confederations described above, only without the strong hierarchical dimension of the Germanic experience. The federation continued under English kings after Danish rule ended, and centuries later the areas embraced by the five boroughs became the heartland of English Puritanism.

Systemic feudalism came to England after the Norman conquest of 1066. Despite their Norse origins, the Normans had imbibed French culture to the point where their political and social order was entirely feudal, albeit with a stronger contractual basis than in Frankish France. Conquering England as they did at the end of the epoch of Norse domination, it was relatively easy for them to impose this system on the unwilling English, who after all had not been entirely immune from feudal influences even prior to the coming of William the Conquerer.

The struggle between Norman feudalism and Saxon liberties became the substance of legend in the England of a latter day, faced with a similar conflict between entrenched interests and a new spirit of modern liberty. While the Normans won, those contractual elements of the feudal way of life that were most conducive to maintaining liberty in some form were part of their heritage and within a century and a half came to the fore in the form of Magna Carta (1215), where the barons raised the idea of the right of resistance against King John to extract that foundation of English liberties from him.

Magna Carta may itself be at least partially a product of the doctrine of covenantal interposition. England's leading archbishop during the latter part of the reign of King John, Stephen Langton, held to the doctrine of interposition, building on the same biblical precedents as

Manegold, especially II Chronicles 22–23. Using that doctrine he encouraged the lords, ecclesiastical and temporal, to take the steps they took to make King John accountable in light of his scriptural obligations.

The vast majority from both groups, both the nobles from the various parts of the country and the clergy, came together following the pattern proposed by Langton, covenanted among themselves, and appointed Robert Fitz Walter to function as their Jehoiada. Under Fitz Walter's leadership and initiative, John was forced to make the famous concession at Runnymede, which they understood to be a covenant between king and lords for any specified protections he owed the Church, the nobles, and the people.[15]

Wales: Pacts and Tribes

Wales during this period was essentially Celtic tribal territory, the degree of whose unity remains in dispute among historians. At most, the country was a network of tribal confederations of a more or less traditional character. It was only after the conquest and absorption of Wales by England and the destruction of those tribal confederations that the Welsh turned to an organic expression of their nationhood, essentially through their common language and culture.[16]

There were two, perhaps three, sources of covenantal influences in Wales. One was the Celtic background of the Welsh. The second probable one was the invasion of the Mediterranean people that came up the west coast of Britain and certainly influenced the early settlement of Wales. The third came with the Norsemen, whose invasions penetrated at least as far as northern Wales, though their influence was less than that of the Danes in England.

The Welsh ethnocultural synthesis is based on the intermingling of an early migration from the Iberian Peninsula, perhaps 3,000 years ago, referred to in Welsh as "the little black-haired people" (pobl fachddu) and the tall, ruddy Celts who invaded the area about 500 B.C.E. and became known as Britons. "Welsh" means "foreigners" in Old Anglo-Saxon, and these Britons who had been Romanized were given that name by the Anglo-Saxon invaders sometime between the fifth and seventh centuries C.E.

Most of the Britons were absorbed into the general population in England and southeastern Scotland but those who retreated to mountainous areas of what is today Wales and continued to speak their own Celtic language, Cymraeg, became known as Cymry, or fellow countrymen. Wales or Cymru united politically with England in 1536. The Welsh remain, however, part of that Celtic belt that includes the Cornish, the Manx (from the Isle of Man), the highland Scots, and the Irish.

In the process of becoming Welsh, the people developed a tribal society apparently based on oaths and covenants that, in turn, generated an appropriate political culture. The Reformation would link that covenantal political culture with a covenantal religion, especially after the evangelical revival in 1735 when most Welsh joined covenantal churches—Baptist,. Calvinistic Methodist, or Independent (Congregational).[17]

Scotland: Pacts to Covenants

If England was partly influenced by covenantal ideas, Scotland was informed by them from one end to the other.[18] The Scots as we know them today are an amalgam of at least four peoples: the Picts, the Scots, the Britons, and the Angles. Scotland as a whole was the last frontier of the British Isles. Even Ireland was settled earlier, and settlers from Northern Ireland provided one of the forming groups for the Scottish. Christianity came to Scotland from Ireland and, hence, was monastic rather than hierarchical, a matter of considerable importance in determining the character and influence of Christianity in Scotland.

At the same time the vital part of Scotland, the part that was crucial in determining Scottish history and culture, was the lowlands area, itself a borderlands, first between the Romans and the Britons and then between England and Scotland on one side and the lowland Scottish and highland Scottish on the other. Hence, there was an especially strong combination of factors encouraging the covenantal tradition.

Each of the four peoples that went into the Scottish amalgam had its own contribution to make to that tradition. The first, the Britons, were Celts with all that implied. The Picts and the Scots preserved a tradition that they were Scythians from central Asia who came to Scotland via the Mediterranean after a sojourn in Spain. There is evidence of a Mediterranean race having come up the west coast of Scotland and settled there, perhaps the same Mediterraneans who settled the west coast of England and Wales. The Angles brought with them their Germanic tribal tradition in its Frisian version. All this was reinforced by the Norse invaders, particularly in the north and west and most particularly in the offshore islands, although they were less influential on the Scottish mainland than the Danes were in England because they were less interested in colonization and the encounter with them was therefore less intense and enduring.

As in England, the original foundations of the covenantal tradition came out of pagan oath societies and cultures, but it was reinforced by the brand of monastic Christianity that captured the country. In the first epoch of Christendom, between the fifth and eighth centuries, there was a struggle within the Catholic Church between the hierarchical demands emanating from Rome and the monastic emphasis on multiple centers, each seeking *koinonia* as represented by the monasteries. In many respects, Ireland was the fountainhead of monastic Christianity, with the impact of proselytizing Irish monks felt at least as far as Switzerland and very heavily in Scotland.

For our purposes, the differences between the two forms of Christianity were extremely important. Monasticism not only involved a noncentralized Christianity with independent monasteries dominating and setting the tone for Christian life in different localities, but membership in the monasteries was voluntary. For them the highest principle of the Church was the voluntary acceptance of a bond. Here, too, we find that monastic Christianity found the fertile soil upon which to grow in those countries and regions that were cultural and linguistic means to express overtly covenantal ideas, Scotland very much among them.

As bearers of the Christian message, these monasteries became powerful forces in the Christianizing of Germanic, Celtic, and Norse Europe. In the Mediterranean world, on the other hand, with a few exceptions, they played a secondary role to a hierarchical church established within the framework of the old Roman Empire as well as upon its ruins. Inevitably there was a struggle between the bishops, headed by the Bishop of Rome, and the monks, a struggle that the bishops ultimately won, imposing their hierarchical structure at the same time that the secular powers imposed feudalism on peoples less than willing to accept that double yoke.

It is important to note that these monasteries were not unisex bastions of celibacy in the period under discussion. Rather, it was accepted practice for married men to play a leading role in the monastic movement, since its aim was not isolation and self-denial per se, but *koinonia* or *communitas*. The strict rules of celibacy were imposed later by the hierarchical church in a successful effort to subordinate the monasteries and transform them into subsidiaries of the Roman Catholic edifice. In this way a movement that could not be eliminated was coopted with substantial changes. The monks were shunted to the side and isolated from the world, both socially and physically, as the monasteries were transformed from worldly instruments of the church triumphant, to other-worldly hermitages.[19]

Meanwhile, the peoples of Scotland through war and marriage were forging themselves into a new nation, one bound by a network of oaths and pacts, from military leagues to a kingdom. Kings appeared relatively early in this process, but while the principle of a royal family was accepted, succession to the throne was determined by the notables, who chose the new king from among all the descendants of the predecessors of the previous king through the fourth generation (great grandchildren). Normally this offered a range of choices that could provide a competent occupant for the throne.

The principal responsibilities of the king were to lead his people in battle. Most governing, such as it was, was carried on through traditional forms under local auspices. Only in the next epoch were kings able to begin to establish something akin to the king's justice administered by the king's emissaries, the sheriffs. It was in that epoch that kingship was transformed into a more conventional-style monarchy with strict lines of descent and without the notables having their say except in cases of disputes, where conspiracy and war were the devices used to reach a decision.

The medieval theory of popular sovereignty under God was more real in Scotland, where kings themselves were much weaker, than on the continent. The Scots were able to transform their early traditional network of tribal confederations into a kingdom with an elected king. Kingly authority and powers rested on the nobility or heads of the Scottish clans, who themselves were usually in a state of turbulence. Together, this prevented the introduction of absolutism, although at great cost to the stability and independence of the country. Thus, while the style of the times dictated what from the outside seemed to be hierarchical organization, in fact the Scottish polity remained essentially contractual in character, with its contractual arrangements having a tribal or clan base in its peripheral regions.[20]

Centuries later, in the Protestant Reformation, Scotland was to emerge as one of the major bases of the covenantal expressions of that Reformation. The Scottish example was widely admired in Puritan England. John Milton describes it in his famous *Tenure of Rings and Magistrates:*

> The Scots, in justification of their deposing Queen Mary, sent ambassadors to Queen Elizabeth and in a written declaration alleged, that they had used towards her more lenity than she deserved; that their ancestors had heretofore punished their kings by death or banishment; they the Scots were a free nation, made king whom they freely chose, and with the same freedom unkinged him if they saw cause, by right of ancient laws and ceremonies yet remaining, and old customs yet among the Highlanders in choosing the head of their clans or families; all which, with many other arguments, bore witness that regal power was nothing else but a mutual covenant or stipulation between king and people.[21]

Scottish society retained many of its tribal characteristics even after it had developed more articulated political institutions. The Scottish clans remained significant political-military forces until the end of the first generation of the eighteenth century, when they brought disaster upon themselves in the last of the Jacobite wars. But even in the lowlands, tribal republicanism remained a force until the consolidation of the monarchy in the last generation of the eleventh century or perhaps even later. The Scottish military forces were local militias, heirs of earlier tribal ties, and power was shared among local chiefs whose relationship with their followers was one of voluntary bond. While these bonds were to some extent a mixture of kinship and consent, they were affirmed and reaffirmed through strong leaders, usually in the military sense, who could attract the support of bands of followers.

On the other hand, as towns began to develop they acquired corporate rights and, in time, subcorporations or guilds developed within them so that each town was a federation or union of guilds as on the continent. Even after a stronger dynastic monarchy developed, Scotland remained a country of many power centers. It was the rare king who could consolidate power for his reign, and it was almost never possible to pass on his successes to his successors.

To the extent that feudalism influenced Scotland, it was primarily in the lowlands, brought in by Anglo-Normans as part of the English effort to extend its dominion over its northern neighbor. Virtually all of Scotland had been left outside of Roman England. Indeed, the northernmost line of Roman fortifications was virtually identical with the later English-Scottish border. While the Romans occasionally penetrated northward beyond those defenses and border wars continued after the Romans evacuated Britain, systematic efforts on the part of the English to conquer Scotland really began after the Norman conquest.

The thirteenth century was an especially difficult time for Scotland, but by the early years of the fourteenth, the Scots had liberated themselves from the English, in the process forging their national legend based on the exploits of Wallace and Bruce, and had adopted their first national covenant, the Declaration of Arbaroth. That document, addressed to the pope by the assembled leadership of Scotland in an effort to obtain papal recognition of Scottish independence, still a formal necessity even on the fringes of medieval Christendom, and of actual worth as well in establishing the legitimacy of the Scottish king, makes the essential points that were to accompany Scottish national life from then on.

[A]mongst other peoples of renown our Scottish nation has been distinguished by many tributes to their fame. We passed over from Greater Scythia across the Tyrrhenian Sea and beyond the Pillars of Hercules, and sojourned for many a year amid the most savage races of Spain; but nowhere could any people, however barbarous, reduce us to subjection. From there, twelve hundred years after the Departure of the Children of Israel, we came to our abode in the West where we now dwell. The Britons were driven out: the Picts were utterly destroyed; we were assailed again and again by Norse, Angle and Dane: but by many a victory and with endless toil we established ourselves here, and, as the historians of old bear witness, we have ever held our land free from servitude of every kind. Within this our realm there have reigned one hundred and thirteen Kings of our native royal dynasty, and not one of alien birth.

[O]ur nation lived in freedom and in peace, until that august prince, Edward, King of England, the father of the present King, finding our realm without a king, and our people innocent of evil intent and still unused to the assaults of war, came to us in the guise of a friend and ally and then made a hostile attack upon us. As for the wrongs he inflicted upon us—the slaughter, violence, pillage, conflagration, prelates imprisoned, monasteries burned down and their inmates robbed and slain, and all the other outrages which he perpetrated on our people, sparing neither age nor sex nor religious order—none could describe nor even conceive these things unless he had actually experienced them.

From these innumerable evils, with the aid of Him Who woundeth and His hands make whole, we have been delivered by our most valiant Prince and King, Robert; who, that he might free his people and heritage from the hands of the enemy, rose like another Joshua or Maccabeus, and cheerfully endured toil and weariness, hunger and peril. He it is that by the providence of God we have made our Prince and King, not only by right of succession according to our laws and customs, which we are resolved to maintain unto the death, but also with the due consent and assent of us all. Unto him, by whom salvation has been wrought unto our people, we are bound for the preservation of our liberties, both by force of law and out of gratitude for all he has done; and unto him we are determined in all things to adhere. But were he to abandon the task to which he has set his hand or to show any disposition to subject us or our realm to the King of England or the English, we would instantly strive to expel him as our enemy and the betrayer of his own rights and ours, and we would choose another King to rule over us who would be equal to the task of our defence.

For so long as one hundred men remain alive, we shall never under any conditions submit to the domination of the English. It is not for glory or riches or honours that we fight, but only for liberty, which no good man will consent to lose but with his life.

Possible Sources of Covenantal Culture

The case of the British Isles helps us clarify the origins of the cultural predisposition toward covenant. All three elements that seem to be influential are present: migration to a new frontier, borderlands of cultural contact and interaction, and ethnic groups with an oath and pact anthropology. The need for at least two of the three, if not all three factors, is demonstrated by the difference between the situation in Ireland and in Scotland.

Both the Irish and Scots are of Celtic stock, with the predisposition to covenantalism that seems to be a part of the Celtic heritage. Yet, while the Irish contributed to the formation of a covenantal social order in places as varied as Scotland and Switzerland through Irish monks propagating their particular monastic and non- if not antihierarchical brand of Christianity, Ireland itself never became a covenantal society. At most it retained a latent predisposition to be converted to the covenantal way that was to manifest itself a millennium later in the integration of Irish emigrants to the United States.

In the Middle Ages, however, the Celts in Ireland had neither an intensive frontier experience, nor did they confront a borderlands situation. There may have been an initial frontier dimension to Irish history when the island was first settled by a combination of Celts and unknown people from the Mediterranean (assuming that they were not one and the same), but it ended quickly and the population of Ireland stabilized, having settled the whole island. Even though Ireland was not politically united, Irish society and culture were quite homogeneous. Until the Northmen inaugurated temporary settlements along the Irish coast in the ninth century, there was no possibility for a borderlands situation to develop. While the Danes had some influence, they were in Ireland for too short a period to make a lasting impact under the circumstances.

Contrast the situation in Scotland. The dominant group in Scotland actually developed out of a migration from Northern Ireland to the Scottish west coast. The Celts, however, encountered other peoples, similar in many respects but still a generally heterogeneous environment. Moreover, these peoples were almost all placed in a borderlands situation, first with regard to the Romans and Anglo-Romans and then with regard to the other peoples of medieval England. Under such circumstances, the latent Celtic cultural predispositions toward covenanting easily came to the fore, reinforced by concrete situations in which pacts and oaths were useful and even necessary devices for survival.

The Survival of Covenant

The thirteenth century was a decisive one in the history of covenant and liberty in Europe.[22] One of its founding events was the English Magna Carta, the first major and successful effort on the part of the barons to constitutionally curb a king (as distinct from the ebb and flow of actual power within kingdoms and empires). During the course of the century, an increasing number of cities emerged as corporations with local liberties, with constitutionalized contracts between their burghers and the ruling monarchs to establish their rights. Among European Jewry this was a century in which the principles of local communal autonomy were given *halakhic* form and established as the constitutional basis for dealing with the new condition of scatteration and fragmentation by then characteristic of European Jewry. The last generation of the century began with the establishment of the *coniuratio* of the three Swiss mountain republics and concluded with the Declaration of Arbaroth and the establishment of the independence of the united Scotland. In every one of these cases, principles of oath, pact, and covenant were present and vitally important.

The medieval free cities, the only pinpoints of liberty on the European continent other than the mountain republics until the foundation of the United Netherlands in 1569, gained their liberties through covenants and alliances with authoritarian rulers whose suzerainty over them was thereby limited. Important as they were, they did not constitute substantial free territories on the map of Europe and were limited in the exercise of their freedom, very much unlike the Swiss who, by being willing to fight to remain free, were able to do so and to exercise free control over an increasingly larger territory within the heart of Europe through their network of covenants. The next such free territory, the United Provinces of the Netherlands, emerged in much the same way in the latter third of the sixteenth century. Interlocking parts in a common covenant forged a confederation out of these lowland provinces that successfully revolted against Spain.

All told, medieval Europe was a network of polities organized by charter, oath, or covenant. In its heartlands it was feudal, with its feudalism tamed by capitulations (*capitulo* meaning chapter), the Latin term for those charters; in its Norse peripheries by oaths; and in its mountain fastnesses by occasional covenants. These were *de jure* ways of recognizing and constitutionalizing *de facto* realities.

A principal characteristic of feudalism and, indeed, the ancillary political arrangements in the Middle Ages, was that political ties were personal rather than territorial. That is to say, persons were bound to governing institutions through contracts or oaths binding them to other persons, either of their own making or which they inherited. Citizenship or, more accurately, fealty or subjecthood did not go with the territory. That is why there could be a wide variety of political arrangements for different people occupying the same territory, what became known as the estates and guilds of medieval times. This system lends itself to contractual arrangements.

The double key to the hierarchical character of the system was, first of all, its emphasis on fealty whereby lower ranks were bound to support higher ones. In a warrior society, feuding and fighting were necessary preoccupations that both tested and rewarded fealty. They provided a basic status for all those able to carry arms, giving them a right to contract, as it were.

It was the convergence of the three major elements that were synthesized to develop medieval European civilization—the Roman, the Germanic, and the Christian—that reinforced this hierarchical approach. Rome, which had begun as a republic of equals, had long since become the quintessential imperial hierarchy while preserving the notion that the emperor was somehow bound by agreement to the citizenry. Western Catholic Christianity had adopted this Roman system by degrees, moving from a community of bonded equals to a network of communities dominated by bishops, who became an aristocracy of equals within the Church (the College of Cardinals of today is an extension of that system), to a hierarchy in which the Bishop of Rome was first acknowledged as *primus inter pares* and then later as Pope or father at the top of the hierarchy. By the time Christianity was solidly established as the state religion of Rome, the old Christian community of equals had long since disappeared; and by the time that feudalism was in full sway, the hierarchical principle had been well established in the church. All together then, these three streams tended to reinforce that particular combination of hierarchy and contract that came to be known as feudalism.

It is not surprising that as times became more settled this system evolved into a bureaucratic as distinct from a military structure. Still, the contradiction inherent in that synthesis tended to mean that the structures formed through it were almost invariably out of balance. Either the hierarchical element dominated, in which case the contractual element was well-nigh meaningless, or the hierarchical element was so weak as to be meaningless in the face of the contractual, in which case the principles of the system were violated.

Nevertheless, in at least some parts of Europe, the synthesis helped preserve a spirit of covenanting, particularly where the political culture was so oriented that it was able to surface again in the sixteenth century, and in the process transform Christendom, if not Christianity. That transformation was not to be based upon Roman roots, any more than Greek. It was to involve a return to Scripture, particularly the Hebrew scriptures.

The medieval period offers us opportunities to test three dimensions of the covenant tradition: (1) the covenant as an operative concept in any political order, even one apparently far removed from covenantal principles; (2) oath societies as parallels to covenant societies, and the intersection of the two forms; and (3) how the covenantal tradition may survive in a hostile environment. Precisely because the medieval period was in its fundamentals so uncovenantal, it offers a hard case test with regard to covenant as an operative concept. The period from the fall of Rome to the Reformation was a period of confrontation between the concepts of *imperium* and *pactum,* with imperium having the upper hand, albeit modified by *pactum* in a confrontation between Roman and Germanic law and tradition.

In this struggle, the Church stood behind, with, and in the vanguard of *imperium,* pressing for hierarchical arrangements from the Sahara to the Arctic. Indeed, the history of the period can be seen as a history of the Church leading the vanguard in efforts to impose hierarchy on previously nonhierarchical tribes and peoples, beginning with the Berber peoples of North Africa and the Germanic peoples of Central Europe and extending as far as the Scandinavian peoples of the far north. The Church, in this respect, was in conflict with primordial oath societies.

Perhaps because those primordial societies were pagan and the Church had to Christianize them, it wished to establish hierarchical arrangements to enable its leadership to exercise the control necessary to achieve that religious transformation. Or it may be that the Church chose to extend its own sphere of influence by aligning itself with a few principal secular power holders, strengthening them by making their authority a matter of religious obligation and thereby gaining benefits from them in return. In some cases it may simply have been that by the time these confrontations took place, the Church itself had become so hierarchical that its leaders knew of no other way to organize society. In any case, the struggle between hierarchy, imperial or sacral, and equity, primordial or covenantal, was a principal feature of the Middle Ages.

Imperial hierarchy was most substantially modified where the imperium confronted primordial oath societies. These latter played a role parallel to that played elsewhere by covenantal societies. Feudalism itself represented a series of agreements based more on oath than on compact. The concept of fealty was developed to provide for oath-established relations within a hierarchical structure. Fealty, as distinct from obedience, is a conditional pledge in which the party higher on the hierarchy as well as the lower party establish mutual obligations based upon overall fealty to the law. Indeed, it is the conditional character of fealty that makes it into a modification of hierarchy rather than simply its reinforcement. Thus, oath societies were more compatible with feudalism and became prominent in this period as a substitute. Norse society, in particular, was an oath society, but one based more on equity than hierarchy. Hence, Norse domination of the medieval world from the mid-eighth to the mid-eleventh centuries strengthened covenantal tendencies within it. Indeed, it was only subsequently, beginning a century and a half later, that the Church was able to impose its hierarchical structures on the northlands themselves.

The other notable thing about this period is that despite the powerful pressures toward hierarchy, covenantalism survived, at least at the peripheries of European society. The history of that survival reflects the degree to which covenantalism is organic to some peoples—it is their "way" and they will hold on to their covenantal tradition at virtually all costs—while at the same time it is so much a part of the human experience as to be at least partly unavoidable even in hostile situations. This played itself out on two levels. The first principle was at its strongest among the peoples of Helvetia, the Netherlands, the Scots, and the Jews. It was given something of a boost by the Norsemen.

There was also the latent federalism of the Holy Roman Empire. Although its beginnings were initiated by the Church in an effort to reestablish Roman-style hierarchy, in fact because the Holy Roman Empire's core was in the lands of the Germans, it leaned toward federalism. In its first stage it was really a corporate community in which the imperium presided over many local and regional corporations tied together by pacts. Only after its first 300 years was the Church able to transform the Empire into a unitary political entity in theory, if not always in practice. That gave way after 300 years to an empire transformed into a roof organization for national units, a framework it continued to maintain until its virtual demise in the Thirty Years' War and actual demise in 1806.

This last stage already brings us into the age of modern state building and the struggle between etatism and federalism. At various points in its history, the Holy Roman Empire could have been transformed into a European federation of sorts based upon its medieval foundations. Perhaps the greatest of those opportunities came at the end of the fourteenth and beginning of the fifteenth centuries with the Conciliar movement and the Council of Constanz (1414-18), which attempted to lay down the basis for what we would today call a federal empire. The failure of the Conciliar movement and the subsequent seventeenth-century failures to revive the idea of imperial federalism on a more secular basis, opened the door to modern European statism, a modern manifestation of imperium, and temporarily reduced the role of pactum to a low never reached under feudalism.

It remained for the revolutionary movements of modernity to revive the covenantal tradition and to give them a new secularized expression associated with modern democracy, even if they were unable to shake the impact of modern statism. In the meantime, in those peripheral regions of the Empire where covenantalism had survived as the central operative principle, the Reformation bridged the medieval and modern worlds, giving covenant new meaning and covenantalism new form to establish a covenant connection between the two worlds that continued through the transformations of the modern epoch.

Notes

1. On the settlement of England in ancient times, see Nicholas Howe, *Migration and Mythmaking in Anglo Saxon England* (New Haven, Conn.: Yale University Press, 1989) and Albert L F. Rivet, *Town and Country in Roman Britain* (London: Hutchinson, 1978).
2. Felix Lieberman, *Die Gesetzeder Angelsachsen,* 3 vols. (Berlin: University of Berlin Press, 1960).
3. On England in the Middle Ages, see Frank Barlow, *The Feudal Kingdom of England, 1042–1216,* 4th ed. (London: Longman, 1988); Henry Buckle, *History of Civilization in England* I (London: Longmans, Green, 1908); and Henry Mayr-Hartung, *The Coming of Christianity to Anglo Saxon England* (London: B. T. Batsford, 1977).
4. In his paper *Multipolarity and Covenant: Toward a Biblical Framework for Constitutional Safeguards* (Cambridge, England: Jubilee House, 1989), B. G. B. Logsdon argues that the "Magna Carta, itself the immediate forebear of modern constitutionalism, thus has a biblical heritage more significant than is widely known."
5. See *Beowulf* 2, 2614-56; H. M. Chadwick, *The Heroic Age* and Socrates Sizomen, *Ecclesiastical History,* trans. and ed. Wace and Sholt (New York, 1891), IX, IV, 421.
6. Cf. Liebermann, *Die Gesetzeder Angelsachsen* II, 374-75.
7. Zacharias P. Thundyil, *Covenant in Anglo-Saxon Thought* (Madras: Macmillan Company of India, Ltd. 1972).
8. Cf. Liebermann, *Die Gesetzeder Angelsachsen* I, 278, 300; Bede, *Historia Ecclesiastica* III, XXIV, 180 on the Mercians; also 177-78 and IV, XVI, 236-37 on Caedwalla.
9. St. Martin of Braga, *De Correctione* 15, 2-3.
10. Thundyil, *Covenant in Anglo-Saxon Thought.*
11. Thundial, ibid., chap. 5.
12. Bede, *Inbibrum Gen,* cap. xviii (ed. Giles, VII. 187), "Notandum antem quod ubieumgue in Graeco legimus testamentum, ibi in Hebraeo sermone sit foedus, sive pactum, idest berith."
13. See Bede, *Hexaemeron* IV, *PL,* 91, 163 for his view of narrative of creation and fall of man as a covenant document; Bede, *In Pent.,* VIII, *PL,* 91, 225 for his view of Noahide covenant as cosmic covenant and prefiguration of the covenant with Jesus.
14. On Danish influence in English, see John H. S. Birch, *Denmark in History* (London: J. Murray, 1938), and *Danish Medieval History,* ed. Niels Skyum-Nielsen and Niels Lund (Copenhagen: Tusculanum Press, 1982). Cf. also Shakespeare's *Hamlet.*
15. Logsdon, *Multipolarity and Covenant.*

16. On Wales, see James Frederick Rees, *Tudor Policy in Wales* (London: G. Bell, 1935); William Rees, *South Wales and the March, 1284–1415* (Bath: C. Chivers, 1974); and Gwyn A. Williams, *The Welsh in Their History* (London: Croom Helm, 1982).
17. *Harvard Encyclopedia of American Groups,* Welsh, 1011.
18. On the history of Scotland, see J. D. Mackie, *History of Scotland* (Hammondsworth, Middlesex: Penguin, 1969).
19. W. R. Jones, "Medieval State-Building and the Churches of the Celtic Fringe," *Journal of Church and State* (Autumn 1974): 407–19.
20. On medieval Scotland, see Geoffrey W. S. Barrow, *The Anglo Norman Era in Scottish History* (Oxford: Clarendon Press,1980) and Edward L. G. Stones, *Anglo Scottish Relations, 1174–1328* (London: Oxford University Press, 1970).
21. John Milton, "The Tenure of Kings and Magistrates," in *Political Writings* (Cambridge: Cambridge University Press, 1991).
22. In this section I draw upon the categories developed by Aaron Wildavsky in his book, *The Nursing Father: Moses as Political Leader* (University, Ala.: University of Alabama Press, 1984).

Part III

Reformation Federalism

8

Federal Theology and Politics in the Reformation

*"Catholicism is a religion of priests, Lutheranism
of theologians, Calvinism of the believing
congregation."*

—Charles Beard
The Reformation of the Sixteenth Century

The opening of the sixteenth century ushered in the second great age of covenantal politics. If there is a single moment when that century can be said to have begun, it was in 1517 when Martin Luther nailed his *Theses* to the church door. Luther's act precipitated the revolution within the Catholic Church that had been in the making for at least a generation. While he was far from being a covenantalist, there were other Reformers who were, principally in the republics of Switzerland and the Netherlands. Great Britain, France, and Germany also were centers of the covenantal revival in both its theological and political expressions until the exponents of covenantalism were overwhelmed by militarily stronger forces.

Within Protestantism, covenant emerged as the central concept of a school of Reformed (as opposed to Lutheran and Anglican) theology that became known as *Foderaltheologie,* or Federalism. This federal or covenant theology movement derived its name from the Latin word *foedus,* meaning covenant, from which comes the English word *federalism.*

Given the intense belief of Protestant Reformers of all stripes in the depravity of man and the inability of humans to achieve salvation on their own through reason or works or some combination of the two and

147

their total dependence upon God's grace and their faith in that grace, it seems rather amazing to find covenant at the center of the Protestant Reformation as a whole and Reformed Protestantism in particular. For many—Lutherans for example, or many of the free churches, and ultimately even one wing of Reformed Protestantism—the covenant was entirely a covenant of grace, in some respects a contradiction in terms or even an oxymoron. For the mainstream of Reformed Protestantism, however, covenant was covenant in the true sense whereby humans had to accept it and enter into a commitment to undertake God's tasks and will as His partners. The ability to do so in a system that emphasized human depravity and predestination was a major issue in Reformed theology until well into the nineteenth century. Even today when Protestantism is committed to a more "optimistic" view of the world, playing down views of original sin and human depravity, Protestant theologians must still wrestle with this issue, albeit it is one that occupies a very diminished place in their thought.

Their problem was much less intense in Reformation political theology, and certainly in its political science. With even its theology covenantal, there was much more room for humans to behave freely as partners in its politics, albeit within theologically imposed limits, but those limits became wider as time went on. Again, this was especially true of Reformed Protestantism, here including even those Reformed Protestants who relied most heavily on theological covenants of grace. So while the covenantal ideas growing out of Lutheranism either diminished substantially in the political realm and in the theological realm stayed more strictly theological, emphasizing theological covenants and ignoring political ones, Reformed Protestants combined both theology and politics into a strong covenantal tradition.

Part of this was possible because of the translation of the medieval Catholic doctrine of the two swords into a Protestant doctrine of the two kingdoms, earthly and temporal on the one hand, and heavenly and eternal on the other. At least for Reformed Protestants, both had to be governed ultimately by God, so both had to be covenantal. In a sense the two kingdoms were the theological equivalent of a dual monarchy. They saw the purpose of the kingdom of heaven as to lead humans to love God, while the purpose of the earthly kingdom was to lead humans to love and serve their neighbors. Clearly the two are connected. Through covenant they form a kind of federal union. Thus, where Lutheranism stopped with the dual monarchy, Reformed Protestantism transformed it into a federal union.

This geopolitical doctrine became the godfather of later ideas of civil society. Among the Protestant Reformers it was held that if all people had faith, all people could be empowered. This opened the door to later theories that if all people have the same nature and needs, all must be equally empowered.

Students of political philosophy have clearly demonstrated that the Protestant Reformers' attitudes toward government agreed with those of the medieval antipapalist theorists, particularly Wyclif, Marsilius, and Ockhmam.[1]

Huldreich (Ulrich) Zwingli (1484–1531) was the founder of Reformed Protestantism. A Swiss contemporary of Luther, Zurich was his stage. While a priest and a humanist, he was drawn back to the Bible, particularly the "Old Testament," and became convinced that Christianity had drifted from biblical religion and had to be purified through the restoration of the biblical way.

Reforming Zurich at the same time as Luther and his Reformation, he published his ideas in *Architeles* in 1522 and *Sixty-Seven Theses* in 1523. In them he rejected the extensive ritual and use of images of the Catholic Church, celibacy in the priesthood, and the governance structure of the Church including the papacy and monasticism. He emphasized individual responsibility and the construction of the holy commonwealth.

Winning over the civil authorities of Zurich, which gave him a power base, he redesigned the constitution and regime of that city in conformity with his ideas. He broke with Luther over doctrinal matters (Zwingli held that the Lord's Supper was merely a commemorative feast, not a transubstantiation). Busy with civic and political affairs, Zwingli did not develop a full-blown theology before he was killed at the battle of Kappel. His teachings were absorbed by John Calvin, who based Calvinism in part upon Zwinglian doctrine.

Johann Heinrich Bullinger, Zwingli's successor as chief pastor of Zurich, was one of the first, if not the first to develop this line of thought. Bullinger's work, *De testamento sue foedere Dei unico et aeterno*, appeared in 1534, three years after Zwingli's death. McCoy and Baker describe it as "the first treatise to be focused thematically on the covenant and contain political and theological views that are explicitly federal."[2] The movement later reached its most thorough articulations in the works of Johannes Cocceius, *Summa doctrinae de foedere et testamento Dei* (1648) and Hermannus Witsius, *De oeconomia foederum Dei cum hominibus* (1677) on the Continent and in the works of a number of the Puritans in England and New England as well as Presbyterians in Scotland.

The federal theology movement, which revived the idea of covenant in the sixteenth century, emerged in the Rhineland area of German Switzerland, mainly the areas dominated by the cities of Zurich, Basel, Bern, and Schaffhausen, and in French-speaking Geneva, later the center of Calvinism, immediately upon the heels of the Lutheran Reformation.[3] Its simultaneous emergence in five Swiss cities was hardly accidental. Ideas of a covenantal-federal nature have deep roots in Switzerland, beginning at least with the pact of 1291 that set the Swiss on the road to civil liberty and their modern federal union. The great Swiss Reformers, Huldreich Zwingli, Heinrich Bullinger, and John Calvin, drew upon the Swiss experience as well as the biblical idea of covenant to describe and define the relationship between God and man and accordingly prescribe the proper religion and politics for humanity.

The heart of the new covenantal politics was to be found in the city republics of Zurich and Geneva, where religious reformation and political transformation went hand in hand. They developed the most sophisticated systematic theories of covenant, theological and political, in the history of the idea. Parallel to them was an extensive application of those theories to the organization of public life.[4]

From Switzerland, this new covenantalism spread up the Rhine valley to Strassburg, westward into France and northward into the Low Countries. From there it jumped across the North Sea to Scotland and England where it took root in East Anglia and those parts of the British Isles that had been colonized by Norsemen—Danes and Norwegians—600–900 years earlier. From Britain it would jump across the Atlantic to North America a century later. By the end of the sixteenth century there was a "covenant belt" in Europe, a strategically located strip bisecting the European heartland.

Perhaps the greatest achievement of the new covenantalism was to restore the alliance between religion and liberty that had been sundered when Christianity became the established church of the Roman Empire 1200 years earlier. Precisely because it was so daring in giving man a role to play as God's partner, however junior, covenant theology emphasized human liberty in matters of faith which, once established, would be extended to other spheres, including the political sphere. There is a paradoxical element here. Covenant theology as it spread throughout the world in its Calvinist form emphasized predestination, that is to say, God's a priori decision as to who was saved and who was not, based upon His granting of His grace to certain humans—the greatest possible contradiction to the idea of liberty. Later covenant theologians who appreciated the relationship between religion and liberty as much as the doctrine of predestination would grapple with this paradox and attempt to reconcile the contradiction inherent in it. Regardless of how well they succeeded intellectually, it is a historical fact that those groups that accepted the covenant theology and made it the cornerstone of their faith were also the groups that became committed earliest to human liberty and contributed most to its advancement.

Political Developments and the Reemergence of Covenantal Ideas

The sixteenth-century revival of covenant occurred under circumstances in many ways similar to those surrounding the emergence of covenant in ancient Israel. Indeed, the reformers, both religious and secular, portrayed it as even more similar than it may have been. Like the Israelites, the reformers rebelled against a pyramidally structured social order, in this case, dominated by a hierarchical church that claimed a position of dominance in an organic society by divine and natural law. If civil and ecclesiastical leaders did not claim to be gods like the pharaohs, they did claim certain divine rights and special proximity to God. Likewise, the majority of people were serfs, servants, and peasants embedded in the rhythms of nature and circles of kinship. All were considered subjects of those selected to *rule* by birth, ordination, or coronation rather than elected to *govern* by popular consent.

To reformers, this system produced more evil and corruption than ancient Egypt. The Egyptian elites had ruled in the name of false gods; but the Christian elites had the temerity to rule in the name of the true God. If this characterization of the late Middle Ages is more overdrawn than the historical record may support, the point is that the reformers saw it that way and drew the analogy.[5] The analogy was strengthened by the fact that biblical theology also linked religion and liberty as a result of the prominent role that the Exodus played in the foundation of both. Thus, the Reformers most influenced by the Hebrew Bible were those who drew upon that ancient synthesis against the conservatism of the existing religious establishment.

One of the major conceptual channels that the Reformed theologians used to connect the Reformation with the Hebrew Scriptures was the *ius regnum*, the Latin translation of *mishpat hamelekh*, which for them as for ancient Israelites provided Divine guidance with regard to civil powers. Just about every Reformed political theologian noted the *ius regnum* and used it as an argument for the limitation of royal powers or even as justification for tyrannicide.[6]

The reformers continued that analogy in developing their response to these perceived evils. In revolting against the established ecclesiastical polity, reformers faced the necessity to refound their politics as did the Israelites in the Sinai desert. To do so, they had to develop a new ideological foundation for church and polity and then reconstitute both.

By undermining hierarchic authority, the Reformation splintered much of civil society and encouraged the formation of multiple religious groupings, often despite the intentions of the original reformers, who retained much of the monistic outlook of the old Church. The accompanying individualization and pluralization of society, along with frequent outbreaks of bitter civil strife, frightened many reformers as well as the supporters of the *ancien regime*. Such conditions required reassertions of civil and religious authority. They also encouraged some leaders of the Reformation to adopt autocratic measures in order to hold on to their flocks against the centrifugal forces of emerging denominationalism and republicanization. As a result, many early Reformation leaders did little more than convert existing rulers to Protestantism or replace old elites with new Protestant ones. With a few exceptions, this was not the case with those who established the Reformed tradition. Autocratic as some of them were, they sought even to establish republics. They took the first steps in both theology and political science toward dispensing with princes altogether.

The latter required a fundamental reconceptualization of civil society along covenantal lines, a development stimulated by at least three factors. First, certain of the reformers discovered in the course of their work that not only was the church corrupt and filled with simony and sinecures, so was civil society. At the same time, their efforts to rethink the religious polity also encouraged drives to reconceptualize the civil polity in line with Protestant teachings. Consequently, the establishment of Protestantism became as much a political as a religious matter.

By the early sixteenth century in most polities, politics was clientelistic, law was regularly subordinated to personal influence, and authority was autocratic and arbitrary. The constitutional aspects of feudalism, whatever the reality at the height of the Middle Ages, had virtually disappeared. The growth of new centralized organs of state governance, the prevalence of interstate warfare, and the concomitant rise of military expenditures encouraged authoritarian measures. As a result, nearly all of the larger governments were also in debt; but because their creditors were usually the lesser nobles and merchants, these debts were often left unpaid. In trying to stay solvent, therefore, the lesser nobles simply squeezed those below them. The *taille* on peasants, for example, increased substantially in many areas of early sixteenth-century Europe.[7] In the pecking order of things, each lower social class was regularly compelled to lay out gifts, favors, fees, gratuities, and loans to those above for services that were not always forthcoming. Debts contracted and agreements negotiated between social unequals were frequently broken by the superior parties, leaving the inferior parties with virtually no effective appeal to courts of law or higher authorities, except by giving still more gifts to curry favor in a circular system.

As a result, the lesser nobility began to slip into debt and some lost their estates. Merchants experienced similar problems. Smaller businessmen, moreover, had to compete with monopoly enterprises chartered by crown heads of state. At the same time, the Reformation touched off a scramble for church lands, while taxes and changing land-use patterns began to push more people into towns and cities.

These developments placed considerable pressure on local and provincial governments, which were in some disarray in any event. Medieval republicanism had given way to the privatization of the polity. Absentee rule was a major problem in both the church and civil government; public policies were arbitrary or nonexistent; and struggles between Catholic and Protestant authorities, religious and secular authorities, local and imperial authorities, town and country authorities, and merchants and nobles only exacerbated the plight of those subject to these authorities.

In this chaotic milieu, the revived idea of covenant became a way of rationalizing and ordering civil society along lines of more consistent lawfulness, popular sovereignty, and constitutional choice. Covenant provided reformers with a way of reconceptualizing civil society as being founded upon a voluntary compact rather than conquest, divine bequest, or organic evolution. Instead of regarding civil society as a private thing, a system of personalistic favoritism and clientelism, the new covenantalism construed civil society as a republic in the original sense of the Latin term *res publica,* meaning a public thing.

Perhaps the greatest contribution of Reformed federalist thought to the development of democratic republicanism was the federalists' insistence that sovereignty rests with the people and not with the ruler. Writing at the same time as Jean Bodin, the great theorist of centralized indivisible sovereignty, the federalists offered a clear alternative that became the coin of the realm of the great Reformed republics of Switzerland, the Netherlands, and the United States, and strongly influenced other polities where the Reformed Protestant tradition was strong.

At the same time, just as Reformed political thought denied the a priori authority of rulers, it also did not foster the principle of the self-evident rights of individuals. The people, for the federalists, was a body politic, usually an association of associations. Their starting point was the question: What is the vocation of any particular association and how can the association be organized so as to fulfill its vocation? Frederick Carney puts it: "Authority (or rule) becomes a function of vocation; and great care must be taken to provide constitutional structures, both ideological and institutional, that authority not become unduly weak or corrupt.... Calvinist associational thought involves at its very roots both the acknowledgement of a high calling and the recognition of ever-present finitude and sin."[8]

The linkage of popular sovereignty and political organization through the polity of associations dedicated to fulfilling high vocation, organized and framed through a proper constitutional law, resting upon covenant, in which the appropriate covenants were those in service of the right vocation, still remains the basis of a proper political morality for democratic republics to no little extent. The voluntary dimension here is of the utmost importance. Johannes Althusius was to develop the theory of the polity as an association of associations more systematically, but the roots and basis of Althusian theory are in the Federalist view of theology and politics.

Even more basically, covenant was a way of requiring and obligating men to live up to their promises, not only to God, but also to each other in the manner of God's covenants with humanity. As God is consistently faithful and forgiving even in the face of human infidelity, so too must individuals be faithful to their covenants with each other. So essential was this feature of covenant that when Thomas Hobbes initiated the process of secularization of the covenant idea, he made out the third law of nature and the fountain of justice to be *"that men perform their covenants made*; without which covenants are in vain and but empty words."[9] This, according to the "new political science," is not simply the proper foundation of civil society, but the only foundation, any other arrangement being a state of war.

The covenant idea had potential appeal to all, perhaps, but the court and the nobility that constituted the upper classes had the most to lose under a system that would empower their erstwhile inferiors. The emerging middle classes had strong interests in covenantal arrangements that satisfied their new self-perception as citizens in the polity and would provide them political representation, resource to impartial courts, and freedom to trade. In an increasingly capitalistic economy, commercial interests especially needed systems of government that would honor and enforce business contracts.

The lower classes also had interests in developing covenantal political arrangements, which they expressed through religious and political protest movements. Most of the Reformed churches became more open to "saints" of all classes; and a number of those associated with federal theology emphasized the obligation to minister to all. As Martin Bucer wrote in *Everyone should live not for himself but for others, and how men may fulfil this* (1523):

> One must make no difference between men but have the same love and desire to procure for each all the good to which he is responsive. From this it follows that the best, the most perfect and blessed condition on earth is that in which a man can most usefully and profitably serve his neighbor.... To conclude...according to the order and commandment of the Creator, no one should live for himself but each man should out of love for God live for his neighbor and by all means be of service to him in matters pertaining to both the spirit and the body; that this obligation rests above all on those who were called and established to promote public usefulness, both spiritual and secular.[10]

It is not unfair to say that the federal republicanism that emerged from the Reformation covenantalists came at just the right time, when medieval constitutionalism had given way to an absolutism that was no less a dictatorship for being legitimized through monarchy. Reformation federalism in that sense was the cure for an advancing disease—a cure that would ultimately triumph over a mutated form of the disease. The federalist politics of the Reformation was an answer to two older theories of Christianity and the political world. One, dominant among Roman Catholics and to a great extent among Lutherans as well, held that princes possessed absolute and unlimited civil power; and the other, the pietistic theory of the first Christians revived by the Anabaptists, that denied that civil government filled any significant role for Christians. The federalists sought the Christian commonwealth, recognizing the importance of civil government for maintaining the fabric of human society against human vices, especially greed, overweaning ambition, and lawlessness.

In the last analysis, Reformed Protestantism was overwhelmingly middle class in its orientation. Its understanding of government was in keeping with that orientation. It is no accident that Reformed Protestantism was strongest among the French bourgeoisie, among the Swiss commercial and artisan classes, among the burghers along the Rhine in the Netherlands, and among the rising middle classes in England. Later it served as one of the principal foundations of the United States as a great commercial republic.

The Reformation Community

One of the most pronounced characteristics of the polity of the Reformation covenanted community was the link between the religious congregation, the civil government, and the university, with the universities in Reformed Protestant polities serving as centers for theological and doctrinal development. Never before in history had universities played such a prominent role in a major social movement. The founders of Reformed Protestantism were, to a man, university educated and much influenced by their various teachers along the lines of religious reform, as well as well trained in the classics and often in Hebrew studies as well. For them the university was a natural intellectual home. Hence, it is not surprising that they should have sought either to capture existing universities or to build universities of their own as the seats of the new learning. Theirs was an intellectual movement from the first and so it remained. Thus, Calvin included doctors along with preachers, elders, and deacons as the principal officers of the proper Christian commonwealth. Pious as they were, they were far removed from pietism. Concerned as they were with matters of the spirit, they were as far removed from the spiritualistic approach to religion as they were from such an approach in politics. Thus, the university was both an intellectual anchor and an intellectual bastion.

A second great dimension of Reformed Protestantism was the great effort to enforce what was understood to be God's law in every aspect of life, in matters of personal behavior and sumptuary laws as well as in the realms of clearly public policy. This was part of the same theory of federalism that seeks the integration of every part of the commonwealth with every other that tends to be a feature of covenanted societies, especially in their most actively religious phases. In an age when church and state intervention in the private lives of individuals was the norm, when crimes were vigorously prosecuted, and torture and barbaric execution were ordinary aspects of public policy, the fact that the Reformed commonwealths used these methods was unexceptionable, even though they justified them on a different basis.

To accomplish these goals the Church was transformed into the congregation (or congregations), the assembled or gathered faithful. Rather than a reified organic body that was presumed to exist independently of its members, who had to conform to rituals and doctrines determined by a self-selected and self-perpetuating bureaucracy, the new religion called for communities of the faithful who believed themselves to be called to pursue Divinely ordained vocations and who could accordingly assemble together (congregate) to form associations of believers obligated to themselves and to God. This new model congregation was in the tradition of the biblical *edah* (assembly) and postbiblical *beit knesset* (synagogue), the general and local manifestations of the antihierarchical thrust of covenantal organization.

One of the major sources of schism within Reformed Protestantism had to do with the nature of the congregational polity. Presbyterians favored the *edah* model, whereby local congregations are "gathered" into regional and national bodies on a federal representative basis (what contemporary political science, reflecting its hierarchical biases, refers to as "from the bottom up"). Congregationalists believed that the religious community should be composed of independent local congregations "gathered" on a face-to-face basis and essentially standing alone, perhaps at the most with some kind of associational or confederal links between them. These questions of church polity were properly of the utmost importance in Reformed Protestantism.

Still, in the first phase of the covenantal revival, the theologians too often overemphasized the spirit. This led to the second phase, in the seventeenth century, when secular philosophers turned to focus on the body—sometimes to the exclusion of the spirit—to emphasize the quality of all "bodies" in nature and the desire of all bodies for, as Hobbes put it, commodious well-being. Locke, for example, specifically designed his system with the intent of raising the income levels of all citizens.

Zwingli versus Luther

When Martin Luther (1483–1546) opened the Reformation, however, the idea of covenant was still submerged within the *Corpus Christianum*. At best, there were medieval notions of contracts of government between the people as an organic body and their rulers, which some early federal theologians developed more explicitly, but these were narrow in scope, limited in application, and of little policy relevance. Although Luther discussed biblical covenants, they assumed no important role in his theology. Likewise, although he advocated greater lay participation in the church, in civil affairs he left most matters to the German princes and directed his appeals for religious reform to them. As a result, perhaps, he rejected social change as a legitimate dimension of the Reformation and supported the political status quo. Indeed, his role in the suppression of the peasants' revolt by the Protestant princes from 1525 to 1526 decreased his base of popular support. In 1548, however, two years after Luther's death, the Admonition issued by the Lutheran town of Magdeburg argued that a king may become illegitimate by violating and persecuting the true religion. Under such conditions he may be resisted by lesser magistrates who have a measure of independent power because they too are instituted to do God's will.[11]

Ideas of covenant began to surface almost simultaneously with Luther's groundbreaking actions, in the sermons and writings of John Oecolampadius (1482–1531) in Basel; Huldreich Zwingli (1484–1531),

Johann Heinrich Bullinger (1504–75), Konrad Pellikan (1478–1556), and Leo Jud (1482–1542) in Zurich; and Martin Bucer (1491–1551) and Kaspar Hedio (1494–1552) in Strassburg. On the more Lutheran side of things, Philipp Melanchthon (1497–1560) advanced the idea of a state contract as early as 1523.

Historians of the Reformation have paid particular attention to the contrast between the Swiss and the Saxon Reformations, the first being that of Zwingli and Calvin, and the second that of Luther.[12] Lutheranism emerged out of Saxony in North Germany while Zwinglism was a product of the Alemannian Germans. This accepted ethnic distinction suggests a cultural distinction of particular importance in our discussion.

Charles Beard, the noted student of the Reformation, gives pride of place to Luther in the overall history of the Reformation, but he acknowledges that it was the Swiss Reformation in its Calvinist form that actually conquered Europe for Protestantism, with Lutheranism confined to North Germany and the Scandinavian countries. Already in 1888 Beard suggested that the ethnic backgrounds of the two groups of reformers played a significant role in the different forms the Reformation took among each. This was clearly reflected in the political processes associated with each. In the last analysis Lutheranism succeeded because of Luther's alliance with the North German princes and Scandinavian kings, who imposed it on their subjects.

Matters were very different in the already republican Swiss cities. As Beard describes it: "Each step in the process of the revolt against Catholicism, or the adoption of Protestantism, was marked by a public debate, and a solemn decision arrived at by the authorities of the city. The change in religion, with all it involved, was the will of the people, and therefore held to be binding upon the people, in the same way as any regularly enacted law, and legally concluded alliance."[13]

While Calvin has become the Reformed analog to Luther in Protestant history, in fact the founder of Reformed Protestantism was Huldreich Zwingli. As G. R. Elton points, out, the Zwinglians combined Puritanism and intellectual elegance.[14] Zwingli's premature death in battle in 1531 removed him from the scene in his prime. Hence, he was never able to fill out his more humanistic system of the Reformed Christian commonwealth. We will never know what the impact of Zwingli's death really was. In place of Zwinglism came Calvinism. While Calvin, like Zwingli, shared an affection for the classics along with theology, he had a darker view of human nature, reflected in his more severe teachings, which became even more severe in the hands of his successors.

Because the Reformation in Switzerland combined political and religious goals, Zwingli had an important political program to achieve. In the fifteenth century the Swiss, whom Beard describes as brave but poor, had become Europe's mercenaries, providing armies for pay for foreign rulers. Having proved their mettle against the Hapsburgs, selling their swords for the Italian wars was a natural next step to earn the keep of the Swiss confederates. This was both demoralizing and bleeding the Swiss, and Zwingli took the lead in opposing that system. Hence, Zwingli's political program was to end Swiss economic dependence on providing mercenary armies and "concentrating the life of the confederacy within its own frontiers."[15] He was able to break Zurich of the habit before he died.

With all Zwingli's efforts to end Swiss military adventures abroad, he drew heavily on his own military experience in the construction of his new religious doctrines. Thus, his doctrine of sacraments is based on his understanding of the word *sacramentum*, the military oath of fidelity whereby each sacrament is a form of renewal of the oath of covenant, what Beard refers to as "visible marks of Christian allegiance." Zwingli's understanding of the sacraments was a key factor in his break with Luther, who held to a more mystic view that Zwingli simply could not accept as consistent with his puritan understanding of Christianity.

Switzerland: The Concrete Expression of Covenantal Theo-Politics

The Swiss Reformation was the revolutionary movement that addressed the problems that had accumulated in the Swiss republics throughout the fifteenth century, particularly their economic weakness. There was no common government, only a council of confederates. The locus of government remained fully with the individual republics, rural and urban. Through this republicanism the civil authorities first consented to and subsequently kept control of the Reformation in their cities.

It is hardly surprising that Switzerland became the motherland of the federal theology. All of Swiss political tradition and culture had emphasized contractual arrangements from its earliest origins, perhaps even as far back as the Celtic-Helvetic lake peoples who created the first civilization in what is today Switzerland, and certainly from the time of the emergence of the medieval mountain and valley republics. Covenanting was second nature to the Swiss, the basis of their political organization in every arena.

While the outside world sees the Swiss as very much of one piece, the Swiss themselves understand the Swiss confederation as a *coincidentia oppositorum,* "a community embracing all the individualities and self-interests of the various cantons."[16] As Peter Stadler points out: "Each canton has assumed this Swiss identity in its own identity. Historically considered, Switzerland is a kind of mutual insurance society that has developed over the centuries, and for very real ends: the individual joined it because in the event of adversities he is covered by a system of indemnification that exceeds his own unaided capacity. This sober reasoning lies at the heart of every confederation."[17]

It would be easy to conclude that Reformed Protestantism was simply a natural next step for the Swiss. Unfortunately, matters are never so simple. When the Reformation came, federal theology and its politics were most attractive to the cities of Switzerland and the lowland villages surrounding them and not attractive at all to the rural communities in the mountain cantons where the Swiss confederation had been born in the thirteenth century. The latter, indeed, held fast to both their direct democracy and confederal politics and to Catholicism, and fought successfully, particularly against Zurich, to retain both. It may be that their rural character produced a religious conservatism that was further reinforced by the fact that organized Catholicism in the mountains was so peripheral to the Church and its hierarchy that it never became an oppressive instrument in the eyes of the locals, or it may be that the mountain republics were simply interested in resisting the domination of Zurich; and, since Zurich had become Protestant, they resolved to stay Catholic.

The new religious division cut across the other division into German-speaking and French-speaking republics and communities. There were Protestants and Catholics in both camps. The federal theology developed in the German-speaking states of the Swiss confederation but took form as Calvinism in French-speaking, fully independent Geneva, which remained outside the Confederation until the end of the eighteenth century. When the dust settled at the end of the sixteenth century, the country was divided, with about 60 percent Protestant and about 40 percent Catholic. Nevertheless, the Confederation held together, in great part because of the prior commitments of all segments of the Swiss people to federal arrangements, which enabled compromises that allowed each republic to preserve its own religion and language while remaining united with its sisters. In the interim, the Swiss did give birth to both a federal theology and federal political theory.

Zwingli, the father of Reformed Protestantism, initiated a theological break with Luther over the Eucharist, which led to the separate development of Reformed Protestantism with its own theology. He also developed a body of followers, some of whom founded the federal theology movement. Zwingli saw God as the giver of the covenant, who promises thereby to be our God. In turn, he regarded baptism as the *signum foederis* or *pacti*. Zwingli placed great emphasis on the Bible rather than the church as the source of authority, and also on the responsibility of individuals before God. His main contribution was to turn to the Hebrew Scriptures—for him, the Old Testament—for models upon which to base the reformed polity of Zurich. Drawing upon these models, he sought to build a replica of the biblical commonwealth. He regarded the Elect as being the chosen people, who have a responsibility to follow the example of Christ and disseminate the faith.[18]

Zurich: Zwingli's Covenantal Community

Politically, Zwingli organized the Reformation in Zurich between 1519 and 1531 and also fostered it in Bern in 1528 with the assistance of Oecolampadius. Zurich, already an aristocratic republic, retained its republican character in its effort to become a holy commonwealth. In a tight marriage of church and state, those who professed belief in Zwingli's version of the faith were permitted to participate in Zurich's government while Catholics were excluded and Anabaptists were persecuted, with some being executed. Authority and power were vested in the hands of God-fearing magistrates on the biblical model as interpreted by Zwingli and his followers.[19] While not a democrat, as a Swiss Zwingli was a republican. He displayed far greater sympathy toward peasants than Luther.

Reformed Protestantism gained additional strength as a result of the dispute between the Zwinglians and the Lutherans over how best to cope with Charles V and the Holy Roman Empire. Luther and his supporters, representing the heartland of the Holy Roman Empire, opposed going to war with its emperor while Zwingli and his supporters, representing the Swiss, who had been at war with the empire for centuries, had no such qualms. Strassburg and the south German reformers followed Zwingli. They were reinforced by Hesse, whose Prince Phillip tended to be impetuous in such matters. Phillip did make one more attempt to bring the two together in October, 1529, but there the serious differences of opinion that had developed over the meaning of the sacraments led the meeting to break up in anger.

Zwingli then turned to consolidating Switzerland behind him by trying to force the rural cantons to abandon Catholicism and join the Protestant city republics. He sought to establish a league of all Protestants, called the Christian Burgher Rights, against the House of Hapsburg and the Pope. Although the scheme failed, a smaller Schmalkald League was formed in 1530. At the same time, Zwingli tried to introduce his teachings into the forest republics of Uri, Schwyz, Unterwalden, Luzern, and Zug, which had formed the core of the original Swiss confederation and remained Catholic. This led to war. Two years later Zwingli was dead at Kappel where the soldiers of the forest republics destroyed the army of Zurich. Zurich's policy reverted to one of coexistence with the Catholic cantons, which had been the preference of its civil magistrates all along, and the peace of Kappel was signed in 1531 to that end. The peace treaty essentially permitted each republic to retain the religion of its choice, but required that Catholics be tolerated in Protestant cantons, while Protestants could be excluded from Catholic cantons.

In 1536 Swiss Protestants united around Zwinglian doctrine in the First Helvetic Confession (written by his successor, Bullinger), which lasted until Calvin became the dominant figure in the Swiss Reformation. He negotiated the agreement of Zurich (1549) to supersede the Confession. The two views of the Reformed Church were somewhat reconciled in the Second Helvetic Confession initiated by Bullinger in 1566, which established the Swiss Reformed Church. Zwinglianism was forced to retreat from much of south Germany and gave way as a separate doctrine to Calvinism. Outside of Switzerland the more somber Calvinist doctrine was to go from strength to strength. Within Switzerland, however, much of Zwinglian humanism remained to modify Reformed religion.

Theological reformation and political activity went hand in hand. Zurich was the first free city in Europe to accept the Reformation and to make it the basis for its political community. Hence, one of the problems it faced was to avoid isolation as a Protestant island in a Roman Catholic sea. The spontaneous emergence of similar movements in Basel, Schaffhausen, and St. Gallen prevented this from happening.

It was the Reformation that led to the development of what is known in Switzerland as the *zurchergeist*, the spirit of Zurich, which in essence has meant disenchantment with expansionist politics and sobriety in all things. Zurich's efforts to expand the influence of its brand of Reformed Protestantism came to an end at the catastrophic Battle of Kappel. Its cantonal territory became fixed and had to be consolidated in both the governmental and religious spheres with the latter taking first place because it set the tone for the body politic. Internal politics became primary, especially for the next two centuries. In true covenantal spirit the people of Zurich, once they had their covenant, turned inward.

Bullinger himself recognized the connections between the Swiss Confederation and the new federal theology. As early as 1528, in his *Admonition*, he discussed the need for a reformation of the entire confederation along the lines of biblical covenantalism. That connection was to become central to the Swiss experience, with Zurich as its major source.[20]

With its territorial expansion ended, Zurich became an international center of Protestantism in the years of Bullinger's rule. In keeping with Reformed Protestantism, sumptuary laws and a new religious attitude ended showy apparel, most of the festivities that had been part of the Catholic age, bombastic architecture, and theater, which was considered particularly demoralizing. Zurich was a city but, by today's standards, a small town. Even in the eighteenth century it had only 10,000 inhabitants. Within the context of reformation, the city's old guild constitution was formally preserved but the guilds were undermined, to be controlled first by religious oligarchy and then, in the eighteenth century, by a mercantile one that grew rich on banking, trade, and industry.

Basel had joined the Swiss confederation in 1501 when its citizens had implemented reforms of a democratic character that abolished the civil powers of the local bishop and reduced those of the nobility. In 1517, the Reformation was introduced by Wolfgang Capito (1478–1541), a precursor of the federal theology movement. Capito, however, left Basel in 1519 and moved to Strassburg where, by 1523, he became a leader of the Strassburg Reformation with Martin Bucer and Burgermeister Jacob Sturm. The Reformation was brought to fruition in Basel by John Oecolampadius, who arrived in 1522.

Although not generally regarded as a great theologian, Oecolampadius was apparently well regarded as a spiritual and political leader. In writing on Isaiah in 1525, Oecolampadius held that God's eternal covenant with man entails the law of love being written on the hearts of men at creation. This law is then applied and elaborated through the written law of the Scriptures. In order to keep this covenant, humans are obligated to obey this law. For Oecolampadius, the covenant was a kind of natural law very similar to Hobbes's first law of nature, *"that every man ought to endeavor peace, as far as he has hope of obtaining it,"* and Locke's law of nature, that "no one ought to harm another in his Life, Health, Liberty, or Possessions." He understood this natural law as the basis for a contractual relationship between the people and their rulers, who then establish a system of civil law to apply the general law of the covenant to particular cases.

It remained for Zwingli's disciple and successor, Heinrich Bullinger, to articulate a theology of covenant and, with it, a political theory of the covenantal commonwealth, becoming the first of the Reformers to do so. Bullinger's work not only preceded that of Calvin, but went farther toward the enunciation of a theo-political federal doctrine. Bullinger gave Protestant covenantalism its first major theological expression. As Zwingli's successor in Zurich, Bullinger was an influential figure whose ideas were known to theologians and philosophers throughout Western Europe.

Bullinger developed the idea of covenant as a bilateral agreement first made between God and Adam and Eve after the Fall, specified for Israel in the covenant between God and Abraham, and fulfilled by Jesus Christ, who opened the covenant to non-Jews. The covenant is also conditional upon man's faith and love of both God and man as further elaborated in the Sinai covenant, or Ten Commandments. This law of love is the eternal moral law, tantamount to the natural law ideas of the philosophers. In turn, it is the basis of civil society and civil law.

Bullinger believed that God preferred "a republic, a democracy," though other forms of government, including monarchy, were acceptable so long as they adhered to God's covenant scheme and constitutional stipulations in the Ten Commandments. Bullinger's model of civil society in Zurich was that of a close community of the faithful governed by town magistrates possessing sovereign authority over religious and civil matters so as to enforce the obligations of the covenant, which is the higher law constitution for both public and private behavior.[21]

Although today the theocratic overtones of the model of the polity developed by the Swiss are often viewed as "undemocratic," even "authoritarian," in fact, by placing the force of religion behind republican government, it represented a major step forward toward democratic republicanism. Reformed teachings were adopted by the citizens and their representatives from the various towns and cantons as a matter of constitutional choice, just as the people of the forest cantons chose to retain their Catholicism. Here there developed another parallel with biblical Israel.

In many cases, local majorities, caught up in religious fervor and believing that reformation meant renewal of their covenant with God, eagerly embraced, as a kind of expression of their general will, the most comprehensive regulations for what they regarded as the common good. The age of possessive individualism, after all, was yet to come, and people still sought communal redemption through community. Moreover, those receptive to covenantal teachings were culturally more oriented to communitarian approaches to life.

This mode of regulated public life, while much more secularized now, can still be found in many Swiss communities; yet Switzerland is generally regarded as a free society. The covenantal ideas revived by the theologians also corresponded with the movement toward federal democracy already underway among the Swiss. In sum, Switzerland became one of the first European nations to institutionalize the concept of a free society resting upon a strong system of local participatory democracy and united along federal lines.[22]

The Reformation initially brought disruption and civil war to the Helvetic Confederation as its members chose between Protestantism and Catholicism. The Confederation had thirteen members at the time of the Reformation. A majority were Catholic, but the population and wealth of the Protestant ones were greater. For a while it looked as if the conflict generated by the Reformation would break up the Confederation. The treaties binding the members were renewed for the last time in 1526, nine years after the Reformation had begun. Periodic subsequent efforts to formally renew them failed, although they continued to be generally observed because a sense of solidarity had already developed among the Swiss as Swiss. Thus, while there was some conflict, serious civil wars were avoided. All members remained fearful of external enemies, particularly France, and shared a common economy. Hence, at the end of the Thirty Years' War the Swiss, too, were ready to take the next step in their federal development.

In 1647 the thirteen cantons signed a pact that ended the process of separate intercantonal agreements. This *vil defensional* for the first time established a common federal instrumentality with emergency authority and a council of war (*kriegsrat*) to coordinate the armies of the members. A federal army of up to 12,000 men was established to guard the common frontier. In 1668 this pact was recast, but except for the army of border guards, the other provisions of the two pacts proved to be unenforceable because of internal religious conflict.

The Reformation energized Switzerland and, after the religious wars ended in 1648, brought prosperity to at least the urban areas of the country, which flowered in the eighteenth century. The intensity of the Reformation was burned out after the mid-seventeenth century; covenant ideas remained but sank into the background. The eighteenth-century Enlightenment, in Switzerland as elsewhere, led to a secularized form of covenantalism embodied in associations to stimulate "progress" such as the Helvetic Society.

The confederal tradition was modernized through such devices as Lavater's "Schweizerlieder," patriotic lyrics that were influential at least for a century or more. The famous painting "The Oath of the Rutli" by Pusselly was from that period; although, significantly, Pusselly painted it after emigrating to England where he was influenced by their covenantal tradition. Pestalozzi captured the spirit of the Enlightment in his political, geographic, and educational writing in which the idea of the autonomous individual, child as well as adult, who was yet part of a community, was featured.

The eighteenth century in that sense created the sense of "Swissness" that was to lead to the adoption of a federal constitution to replace the confederation in 1848. That constitution was the culmination of the secular or compactual phase of Swiss covenantalism. Still, it was the movement from a republic of guilds and congregations to an oligarchy of merchants, industrialists, and bankers that contributed most heavily to the breakdown of the old order.

The confederation was successfully insistent on complete neutrality during the Thirty Years' War, a policy that it has maintained to this day, and which its neighbors have come to respect. The only subsequent violation of that neutrality was in 1798, when Napoleon led the French armies into Switzerland, conquering the country. While it is unlikely that the confederation forces could have stood up against Napoleon even if they had been united, the fact is that the weakness of their common institutions, the individual jealousies of the members, and their zealous defense of their own sovereignty made Napoleon's task an easy one. Thus ended the historic Swiss confederation. When the Swiss regained their independence a few years later, they decided to rebuild their institutions on a new, more modern, basis.

The new federal Switzerland internalized covenantal politics and even imprinted them on its remade landscape. Like all good federations, Switzerland does not have a capital, only a seat of government, and, characteristically, it is the fourth city of the country. Part of the "federal understanding" (a Swiss term) of the reconstituted Switzerland of the nineteenth century was that each of the major cities of Switzerland would have its own role. Zurich became the great commercial metropolis; Basel, the trade fair center; Geneva, the host of international organizations; Berne, the seat of the federal government.

Notes

1. Leo Strauss and Joseph Cropsey, eds., *History of Political Philosophy* (Chicago: Rand McNally, 1963), particularly Duncan B. Forrester, "Martin Luther and John Calvin," 277–313.
2. Charles S. McCoy and J. Wayne Baker, *Fountainhead of Federalism: Heinrich Bullinger and the Covenantal Tradition* (Louisville, Ky.: Westminster/John Knox Press, 1991), 11.
3. See Kyle C. Sessions, ed., *Reformation and Authority: The Meaning of the Peasants' Revolt* (Lexington: D.C. Heath, 1968); Rupert Eric Davies, *The Problem of Authority in the Continental Reformers: A Study in Luther, Zwingli and Calvin* (London: Epworth Press, 1946); Robert Herndon Fife, *The Revolt of Martin Luther* (New York: Columbia University Press, 1957); Luther Hess Waring, *The Political Theories of Martin Luther* (Port Washington, N.Y.: Kennikat Press, 1910); Ernst Walter Zeeden, *The Legacy of Luther* (London: Hollis and Carter, 1954); Walter Zimmerman, *Die Reformation als Rechtlich-Politisches Problem in Den Jahren 1524–1530* (Goeppingen: Kuemmerle Verlag, 1978); Emile G. Leonard, *A History of Protestantism*, ed. H. H. Rowley (London: Nelson, 1965); Paul Tillich, *The Protestant Era*, trans. James Luther Adams (Chicago: University of Chicago Press, 1957); Thomas Sanders, *Protestant Concepts of Church and State* (New York: Holt, Rinehart and Winston, 1964); John Dillenberger and Claude Welch, *Protestant Christianity, Interpreted Through Its Development* (New York: C. Scribner's Sons, 1964); Lewis William Spitz, *The Protestant Reformation,*

1517–1559 (New York: Harper and Row, 1985); Hans Joachim Hillerbrand, ed., *The Protestant Reformation* (New York: Harper and Row, 1968); Henry Daniel-Rops, *The Protestant Reformation* (London: J. M. Dent, 1961); D. J. Callahan, H. A. Oberman, and D. J. O'Hanlon, eds., *Christianity Divided: Protestant and Roman Catholic Theological Issues* (London: Sheed and Ward, 1962); Henri Hauser, *La Naissance du Protestantisme*, 2nd ed. (Paris: Presses Universitaires de France, 1962).

4. Steven E. Ozment, *The Reformation in the Cities: The Appeal of Protestantism to Sixteenth-Century Germany and Switzerland* (New Haven, Conn.: Yale University Press, 1975); Jacques V. Pollet, *Huldrych Zwingli et la Reforme en Suisse* (Paris: Presses Universitaires de France, 1963); Merrick Whitcomb, ed., *The Period of the Later Reformation*, rev. ed. (Philadelphia: University of Pennsylvania Press, 1902); Henri Naef, *Les Origines de la Reforme a Geneve* (Geneve: A. Jullien, 1936); Jill Raitt, ed., *Shapers of Religious Traditions in Germany, Switzerland and Poland, 1560–1600* (New Haven, Conn.: Yale University Press, 1981).

5. Cf. Michael Walzer, *Exodus and Revolution*, and Michael Walzer, *The Revolution of the Saints: A Study in the Origins of Radical Politics* (London: Weidenfeld and Nicolson, 1966); Dilbert Hillers, *Covenant: The History of the Biblical Idea* (Baltimore, Md.: Johns Hopkins University Press, 1985).

6. In 1647, Wilhelm Schickard of Tubingen wrote *Mishpat Hamelekh Ius Regium* to present an exhaustive list and discussion of rabbinic sources dealing with the concept. His work stands as only one visible measure of its importance.

7. See Perez Zagorn, *Rebels and Rulers, 1500–1660* (Cambridge: Cambridge University Press, 1982); H. G. Koenigsberger and George L. Mosse, *Europe in the Sixteenth Century* (London: Longmans, 1990).

8. Frederick S. Carney, "Associational Thought in Early Calvinism," in D. B. Robertson, ed., *Voluntary Associations: A Study of Groups in Free Societies* (Richmond, Va.: John Knox Press, 1966).

9. Thomas Hobbes, *Leviathan* (Oxford: Blackwell, 1946), 93.

10. Martin Bucer, *Everyone should live not for himself, but for others, and how men fulfill this*, 1523.

11. L. H. Waring, *The Political Theories of Martin Luther* (Port Washington, N.Y.: Kennikat Press, 1910); Cynthia Grant Shoenberger, "Luther on Resistance to Authority," *Journal of the History of Ideas* 40 (January-March, 1979): 3–20; Davies, *The Problem of Authority.*

12. Charles Beard, *The Reformation of the Sixteenth Century in its Relation to Modern Thought and Knowledge* (Ann Arbor: University of Michigan Press, 1962), especially chap. 7, "The Reformation and Switzerland."

13. Ibid., 237–38.

14. G. R. Elton, *Reformation Europe 1517–1559* (London: Fontana Library, 1963), 73.

15. Ibid, 32.

16. Peter Stadler, "The Zurich Mentality and Swiss Identity: Convergences and Divergences," *Swissair Gazette* 7 (1986), 13.

17. Ibid.

18. Ulrich Zwingli, *Zwingli and Bullinger,* selected translations with introductions and notes by G. W. Bromiley (Philadelphia: Westminster Press, 1953); Davies, *The Problem of Authority.*

19. Ibid.

20. Heinrich Bullinger, *Anklag und einstliches ermanen Gottes Allmaechtigen/zuo eyner gemeynenn Eydgnoschafft/dys sy sich vonn jren sunden zuo ymm keere* (Zurich, 1528).

21. J. W. Baker, *Heinrich Bullinger and the Covenant: The Other Reformed Tradition* (Athens, Ohio: Ohio University Press, 1980).

22. Ibid., and cf. Benjamin Barber, *Death of Communal Liberty: History of a Swiss Mountain Canton* (Princeton: Princeton University Press, 1974). The Swiss remain fundamentally covenantal to this day in a way that is noticeable even to very contemporary and even somewhat casual commentators on the Swiss scene. For example, in 1986 Swissair, in its monthly *Swissair Gazette* for July of that year, devoted the issue to the city of Zurich, then celebrating its bimillennium. In it the authors emphasize the Puritan character of Reformation Zurich and its continued influence on the contemporary city.

9

The Political Theology of Federalism

The Tenets of Federal Theology

The tenets of federal theology are difficult to summarize generally and succinctly because not everyone who used the concept of covenant was a federal theologian per se. The movement was also diverse. No single person emerged as the preeminent Federalist to establish an orthodox school and line of disciples; instead, each theologian developed his own system within the general language of covenant discourse. In an era of the "priesthood of the laity," when nearly everyone was encouraged to read the Bible, additional diversity was introduced by the fact that not every Federalist was a "theologian"; a number were preachers, propagandists, political activists, would-be philosophers, jurists, or some combination of these. Key figures in the movement, from Calvin to Althusius and beyond, were political scientists as well as political leaders. Furthermore, the movement developed both independently and conjointly in different countries and spanned a period of nearly three centuries of extraordinary intellectual ferment. In effect, such circumstances produced a truly "federal" theology.[1]

Albeit, beneath the diversity and sometimes extraordinarily elaborate arguments of the federal theology movement lies the central concept of covenant. In this system as opposed to other theological systems, covenant is the organizing principle. Humanity's relationships with God, from Adam to the present, are seen as having always been covenantal. Covenants are the means by which God establishes authoritative relations with humanity, reveals His law, and manifests His extraordinarily gracious benevolence in light of man's sinfulness. According to Bullinger: "God, in making leagues, as he doth in all things, applieth himself to our capacities.... And therefore, when God's mind was to declare the favour and good-will that he bare to mankind...it pleased him to make a league or covenant with mankind."[2]

This emphasis on covenant derived in part from the extraordinary importance that Reformed Protestants attributed to Scripture as the source of authority over against the church and tradition. In turning directly to the Bible for new guidance, reformers were bound to rediscover covenant. This appears to have been brought home to them by at least four routes.

First, many Reformed theologians gave unprecedented attention to the Old Testament, where the covenant theme is so explicit and prominent. Here was the history of God's relations with man before the visible advent of Jesus Christ in human affairs. Indeed, given the persecutions of the period and the perception of a new covenant through Christ, some Protestant groups, especially the Puritans and Scottish Covenanters, regarded themselves as new Israelites. As a result, federal theology contributed greatly to the development of modern biblical studies.[3]

One of the most important elements in all this was the Christian Hebraist movement, which preceded the Reformation by a generation and continued for nearly a generation after the Reformation began, until it was persecuted and virtually stamped out as a Judaizing heresy. In the late fifteenth century, Christian theologians discovered what they called the Old Testament in its original Hebrew language. In distrusting the Vulgate and Septuagint Bibles, Reformed Protestants also sought ever more pristine translations that would be as close to the original texts as possible. To do so, many theologians and scholars learned Hebrew and other ancient languages.

This whole enterprise was given great impetus by the invention and spread of printing. In 1524 and 1525, only seven years after the beginning of the Reformation, Daniel Bomberg, a Christian printer in Venice who specialized in publishing Judaica, published the work of Jacob ben Haim ibn Adoniya of Tunis, one of his proofreaders, which consisted of the Hebrew Scriptures, its most famous Aramaic translation, and the classic medieval Jewish biblical commentaries, under the title *Mikraot Gedolot*. *Mikraot Gedolot* made the Masoretic text and Jewish biblical commentary widely available to Christian Hebraists and became a cornerstone of their studies. It emphasized textual accuracy in every respect, which fit into the mystical ideas prevalent at the time regarding the necessity to reach God through an utterly uncorrupted biblical text.

Josephus's and Philo's analyses of the biblical polity also were widely available and read.

Hebraic studies became particularly popular with those Christian theologians who joined the Reformation, particularly those who embraced covenant theology. Reformers sought to defend the purity of the Hebrew texts against the Vulgate and Septuagint and to use new translations to defend particular points of view. More than that, they discovered the later rabbinic literature of the Jews, particularly the Talmud, the Midrash, and the Kabbalah (Jewish mystical literature). One such scholar was Johann Buxtorf in Basel, whose son and then grandson followed in his footsteps. Basel became a center of Hebrew studies for covenant theologians and, indeed, there was a conflict between the University of Basel and the University of Wittenberg, whose theological faculty had embraced Lutheranism, over this very issue, in the 1540s.[4]

The Federalists in particular paid attention to matters Hebraic, contributing thereby to a renaissance of Christian Hebraic studies in the sixteenth century, especially in Switzerland and England.[5] This included not only the study of Hebrew, which many believed was the actual language of God, but also the study of the history and cultures of the Old Testament period.

A number of very influential figures began to study the languages and the texts themselves with Jewish scholars, who were in some demand at the time as various theologians sought them out as teachers. Finally, a few Jews converted to Reformed Protestantism and brought their knowledge of Jewish sources with them. For example, John Immanuel Tremellius (1510–80) became a Calvinistic Protestant in 1541 at the urging of Peter Martyr. Subsequently, Tremellius went to England at the invitation of Archbishop Thomas Cranmer and succeeded Paul Fagius as the King's Reader of Hebrew at Cambridge University in 1549. After the death of Edward VI in 1553, he became a professor of Old Testament studies at Heidelberg. When Louis VI expelled him, the Duc de Bouillon appointed him professor of Hebrew at his new college in Sedan. There, between 1569 and 1579, Tremellius produced a Latin translation of the Bible from Hebrew and Syriac that long served as a Latin standard for Protestants.

For the Federalists, covenant performed the important function of bridging the Old and New Testaments. Without abandoning the distinction between the two, the covenant theme common to both showed them not only the history of God's salvation plan, but also the process and continuity of that salvation from Adam onwards. This provided a certain sureness and certainty about the steadfastness of God's promise of eternal life for man as well as man's dependence on God for salvation. In so doing, Federalists read Christ back into the Old Testament, and covenant into the New Testament, much more strongly than other theologians.

Federal theologians did this, in part, by focusing on the two covenants that became prominent in Reformed theology: the Covenant of Works and the Covenant of Grace. While no two Federalists seemed to agree precisely on the nature, meanings, and differences between these two covenants, they were important; and thoroughgoing federal theologians derived their entire systems from them. Generally, the Covenant of Works was regarded as a covenant between God and man, specifically Adam, the representative man, before the Fall. Although the Old Testament does not speak of such a covenant, the idea appears to have been derived from Hosea 6:7 rendered as: "But like Adam they have transgressed the covenant." Paul also spoke of a law of works and a law of faith, or two covenants (Galatians 4:24).

The first covenant involved God's promise of eternal life being given to man on the condition that mankind observe the law, the first being the prohibition against eating the fruit of the tree of the knowledge of good and evil. This, for the Federalists, was tantamount to a covenant insofar as it entailed some mutuality between God and man in which man received the enormous benefit of eternal life. While this was the blessing for obedience, the arrangement also included curses for failure.

Adam, of course, violated the law and broke the covenant of his own free will, thereby bringing about the terrible Fall that has made all humans liable to sin and misery. Since then, men and women can be saved and given eternal life only by an unconditional grant of love through Christ. The Covenant of Works, namely, obedience to the law, is no longer a sufficient route to salvation. Although humans are still obligated to obey the law, they must suffer the penalties of Adam's disobedience unless redeemed by Christ, namely, the Covenant of Grace (*foedus gratuitum*).

In the eyes of the Federalists, this covenant already existed in the Old Testament as promise. For some Federalists, it had existed for eternity as a covenant of redemption between Father, Son, and Holy Spirit. Because humans are fallen beings who can no longer act on their own behalf by obeying the law to achieve salvation, God consented, according to His promise, to offer his Son to act on their behalf by suffering all the penalties of man's disobedience unto death and by fulfilling the law. To accomplish this, God entered history by uniting divinity and humanity in the person of Jesus Christ who thereby became the *representative federal* head of His spiritual community in a manner similar to Adam's role as humankind's *natural* head. This, for the Federalists, is God's outstandingly gracious covenantal act. On God's side of the covenant, there is grace and mercy, which gives people, according to Bullinger, a "holy and wonderful liberty." The ultimate blessing is eternal life. On man's side, there is merely faith, repentance, and an obligation to walk in the ways of the Lord.

Generally, those redeemed are termed the Elect—the chosen ones or new Israelites—though their certain identities are known only to God. For many theologians, the *foedus gratuitum* pertained to a fixed portion of humanity who are saved by predetermination by God, almost regardless of visible faith and works. For others, the covenant is made available to all for a period of time, but with only some individuals then securing salvation. As a result, there were also differences of opinion as to the parties to the covenant. Cocceius, for instance, regarded the parties as being God and Christ, with Christ being man's representative. Witsius saw God and the elect as being the parties, though through a double covenant between God and Christ, the Mediator, and then between God and the elect. The more Arminian Federalists regarded God and all men as the parties.

There were also differences about the basic nature of the covenant. Many Federalists treated it as a mutual agreement, a contract, a bargain with respect to something. Others, including many early Scottish and Puritan Federalists, saw the covenant more as a promise, a very sure and stable promise.[6]

Regardless of the fine points of debate, there were certain important areas of agreement. God's relationship with humanity has always been covenantal, thereby suggesting a similar design for human relations. Since covenant entails direct relations between God and individuals—God's choosing the Elect and their responsive faith—the power of the church and importance of tradition are reduced considerably. Covenant, moreover, is not a decree; it is an agreement and/or promise involving responses by both parties. Likewise, covenant, not command, is the basis of law. The Puritans especially linked law and covenant and saw covenant as reasserting the moral obligations and responsibilities of individuals. Thus, in these respects, the covenant idea served to undermine the models of *Corpus Christianum* and *Sacrum Imperium*.

Federal theologians wedded their covenantal thinking with a new methodology known as Ramist logic. This method was developed by the French logician Peter Ramus at the time of the Reformation. Carney describes the Ramist system as follows:

> [He] made use of the two traditional topics of logic: invention and disposition (or judgment). What was largely new with Ramus, however, was the manner in which he employed these two topics. Where invention had previously been understood as the processes for combining predicates with subjects in debatable propositions, under the influence of Ramism it also came to denote the processes for determining what material belongs to subjects as scholarly disciplines. And where disposition had previously referred to methods of arranging propositions into syllogisms or inductions, and these into discourses, with Ramism it also came to refer to the methods of organizing material appropriate to any given discipline. The change that has occurred is one in which logic is used to clarify not only what may be said for or against propositions and combinations of propositions, but also how a field of study may be "logically" organized. An assumption inherent in Ramism is that proper organization of materials is valuable not only for teaching and learning purposes, but also for the discovery and clarification of knowledge.[7]

Following Aristotle (*Posterior Analytics*), Ramus claims that the law of justice indicates that each art or science has its own purpose that determines what is proper to it and allows us to exclude all that is improper, and that the law of truth indicates that every art or science consists only of universal and necessary propositions or precepts, requiring that those that are true only in certain times and places should be eliminated. This Ramist emphasis on method gives works influenced by it an architectonic quality so that wise and methodic works "descend from the most general idea to the various divisions thereof, and thence to the particular cases it comprehends."[8]

Covenant also introduced a strong historical dimension to Christian thinking, which was another of the Federalists' lasting contributions to modern theology. As opposed to the often timeless, metaphysical quality of predestination in mainstream Calvinism, covenant linked the idea to God's historical dealings with humanity. When one method failed at the outset of history, God tried another, more extraordinary way to reach man. This attitude continued the experimentalist approach evident in the Hebrew Scriptures. Cocceius especially emphasized the history of redemption and its present reality. It is by means of covenant that the Kingdom of God is actualized in history. Indeed, given the intense religious fervor at various points during the Reformation, some believed that "reform" meant an earthly establishment of the Kingdom of God.

The Calvinist Deviation

In Geneva, the Reformation developed somewhat independently under John Calvin (1509–64), whose teachings came to dominate the tradition of Reformed theology worldwide. Calvin, indeed, was the great figure of the Protestant international, shaping both the theology and church government of the French Huguenots, the Scottish Presbyterians, and the English Puritans, as well as Geneva and the Swiss. Calvin's Geneva became "a fortified post of the Reform, to be held against all comers, and within whose walls, always open to attack, the sternest discipline was necessary."[9]

The story of Calvin's Geneva is well-known—almost too well-known in the sense that Calvinism has come to be used synonymously with Reformed Protestant theology as if Calvin were the sole originator of that worldview.[10] By reaching an agreement with Bullinger at Zurich in 1549, the *Consensus Tigurinus,* Calvinism became the accepted theological system of Protestant Switzerland. As a result, federal theology has tended to be submerged within this stream, and scholars have usually regarded the Puritans, for example, as dour Calvinists when they were really more federalist in the Bullinger pattern. The principal influences on the formation of the Puritans' covenant theology came not from Geneva, but from Zurich, Basel, and Strassburg. While Calvin was regarded by most as the leader of the Reformed tradition, his teachings were not always followed exactly, enabling the several schools of federal theology to develop within this general tradition.

Since the sixteenth century there has been a controversy among covenant theologians as to the degree to which Zwingli, Bullinger, and the Zurich school—which came to include the English Puritans—and Calvin and the Geneva school represent different understandings of the biblical covenant, with the former emphasizing its mutuality, its call for a greater human responsibility, and its downplaying of rigorous predestination, while the latter emphasize God's unilateral promise and a rigorous division between the elect and the reprobate. In the twentieth century, this question has become the focus of scholarly dispute ever since Perry Miller wrote his essay "The Marrow of Puritan Divinity" in 1935, and the first volume of his classic work *The New England Mind,* published in 1939, reviving the emphasis on covenant in Reformed and Puritan political thought.[11]

A scholarly debate was initiated by Leonard J. Trinterud in a 1951 article, "The Origins of Puritanism."[12] Trinterud stated the two different theory thesis and suggested how it applied to English Puritanism, especially through the influence of Tyndale and Frith, assisted by Hooper and many of the Marian exiles who fled to the Rhineland in the 1550s (see chapter 12). Trinterud summarized the two views of covenant as follows:

Zwingli/Bullinger:
1. The covenant is bilateral involving God's conditional promise and the response of the human partner.
2. The burden of fulfilling the covenant rests on the human partner.
3. The covenant was fulfilled in the obedience of the human partner and God's reciprocal reward.

Calvin:
1. The covenant is unilateral: God's unconditional promise.
2. The burden of fulfilling the covenant rests on God.
3. The covenant is fulfilled with the incarnation, death, and resurrection of Jesus Christ.

Those supporting the Trinterud thesis, which became the dominant one in the years following its original publication, included Jens Moller.[13] He, too, stresses the difference between Zurich and Geneva, as does William Clebsch, who takes issue with Trinterud over holding that it may have been an independent development. The Zwingliites had a concept of covenant that placed "the believer and God in a contractual relationship that obligated God to bestow rewards for the performance of the Divine law."[14]

Richard Greaves accepted the general view in his article, "The Origins and Early Development of English Covenant Thought,"[15] arguing that in English Puritanism the separatists leaned more toward Calvin and the nonseparatists more toward Zwingli. Others supporting the two-visions view included Kenneth Hagen, in "From Testament to Covenant in the Early Sixteenth Century,"[16] and J. Wayne Baker. Baker argues that while the germ of the Zurich idea was to be found in Zwingli, it was actually Heinrich Bullinger who gave it full development.[17] Baker also argues that the difference between the two is that in the Zwingli-Bullinger school the covenant was a mutual pact while for Calvin it was a unilateral testament linked to absolute double predestination, while the ritual pact was linked to election only. Furthermore, these differences were minimized to maintain unity among the Reformed churches in Switzerland later in the century. Even the opponents of this view recognized that it has a clear basis. Their argument is that in the last analysis, both schools also partake of the views of the other one.[18]

We need not try to determine the fine points of theology here. It is sufficient to know that there is another covenant tradition, derived from Zurich and the Rhineland, that influenced Reformed thought, particularly political thought, and that had its own direct impact on the formation of English Puritanism and Puritan political thought.[19]

The differences manifested between Zwingli and Bullinger, on one hand, and Calvin on the other, may be even more clear cut in the federal thought of Melanchthon in his years at Wittenburg. Melanchthonian theology opposed the strict Calvinistic doctrine of predestination and its theological federalism grew out of that opposition.[20] This position was argued by Heinrich Heppe in his *Dogmatik des Deutschen Protestantismus im 16ten jahrhundert (Goethe)* (1857).[21]

Although there is some evidence that this was a particularly German Reformed view and was not spread among any of the important Swiss theologians, in fact, its consequence was to oppose predestination and covenant theology, something that all the Swiss emphatically avoided only by clever argument. Even in that case, however, the idea of covenant functioned to modify the idea of predestination.[22]

It has been argued that Zacharias Ursinus provided a German Reformed bridge between the two positions. Ursinus, a very close student and even disciple of Melanchthon, developed the idea of the covenant of creation to bridge between Melanchthon's reliance on natural law and Calvin's emphasis on the covenant of law (*foedus legale*).[23] To pursue this any further would lead us into the more arcane aspects of Protestant theology and not significantly advance our understanding of the political idea of covenant and its uses, even in the Reformation. Ursinus's covenant of creation essentially emphasized the belief that what others called natural law was built into creation and made part of God's covenant with Adam.

A larger question is whether Calvin's teachings include a covenant of works or only a covenant of grace, the latter which suits the conventional understanding that Calvin emphasized the unilateral character of God's promise rather than mutuality of the pact between God and man.[24] Calvin's victory, as is usually the case in such matters, came more as a result of his political and organizing abilities than of the validity or elegance of his theological views. Both the Reformation and the covenant idea had been well launched by the time Calvin published his *Christianae Religionis Institutio* in Basel in 1536 and arrived in the independent republic of Geneva that same year. The Reformation was introduced into French-speaking Geneva by French preachers under protection from Bern. Calvin also was French. Geneva, which did not become a full member of the Swiss confederation until 1815, had negotiated a pact of co-citizenship with Bern and Fribourg in 1526. The patriotic party, known as the Eiguenots (from *Eidgenossen,* meaning confederates,) had sought such an alliance in order to promote reform in Geneva and protect the city against the Duke of Savoy.

Calvin himself was trained at the Faculty of Arts in Paris and the Faculties of Law at Orleans and Bourges in what today would be called political science, rather than in theology. His first published work was a commentary on Seneca's *De Clementia*. It was unquestionably a work of Renaissance political science. Thus, his concern with the political order and problems of government preceded his theological concerns. Hence, it is not surprising that his influence on the theory and practice of government has been so great. It is not unfair to say that the man who succeeded in institutionalizing the federalism of Reformed Protestantism was as much a political scientist as was his counterpart, James Madison, who succeeded in institutionalizing the federalism of the American founding. Calvin's legacy includes a great deal of political exposition in his biblical commentaries, sermons, pamphlets, and, most of all, the *Institutes of the Christian Religion,* his magnum opus.

After agreeing, reluctantly, to remain in Geneva at the invitation of local reform leaders, Calvin vigorously applied himself to a strict organization of the Reformation. However, resistance from the citizens and a controversy with Bern led to his banishment in 1538. Calvin then moved to Strassburg for several years, where he became friendly with Martin Bucer, whose views influenced his new edition of the *Institutes* in 1539. After his partisans gained power in 1541, Calvin returned to Geneva and ruled it for the next twenty-three years. Calvin organized a theocratic regime well known for its severity and made infamous by its executions of, among others, Jacques Gruet in 1547, Raoul Monnet in 1549, and Michael Servetus in 1553.

Covenant in Calvin's theological system is more a matter of unilateral action than of mutual agreement as in Bullinger's. It has been described as *testamentum* rather than *foedus*. As such, attention is focused more on the omnipotent sovereignty of God, the sinfulness of humanity, the certitude of salvation for the elect, absolute predestination, and justification by faith without works. By so emphasizing the glory and power of God, Calvin eliminated the role of humans as effective covenant partners with God and interpreted covenant as God's way of stipulating obedience from His servants. Likewise, in stressing the continuity of covenants between the Old and New Testaments, Calvin gave clear priority to the Covenant of Grace over that of Law in the Old Testament.

Nevertheless, Calvin's attitude toward and use of the Old Testament closed a circle, since he emphasized the unity of the Hebrew and Christian Scriptures through a dual act—Christianization of the Old Testament on one hand and Judaization of the New on the other. In this he relied heavily on the Epistle to the Hebrews and the tradition it represented, which had been rejected in the ideological struggles of the early Church. The influence of his model was to be widespread, especially among the English-speaking peoples, where the Hebrew Scriptures came to command an eminence granted no other source.[25]

Politically, Calvin was a brilliant and effective leader whose influence extended far beyond Geneva, which Sully called "the holy city of Jerusalem." By organizing the Academy of Geneva with assistance from his friend Theodore Beza, Calvin was also able to train missionaries in his system. Calvin's model of civil society was that of a highly unified, well-regulated, and busy Holy Commonwealth established, if necessary, by a spiritual prince, such as Calvin, and ruled by ministers and magistrates devoted to the service of the sovereign Lord. Whereas in Germany Lutheran churches became national churches subject to secular political authority, though in tension with it, in Geneva the church became dominant.

There was, however, a covenantal element of constitutional choice here, insofar as those willing to profess the faith and abide by the laws could become members of the commonwealth. Indeed, during Calvin's reign, some 6,000 Protestant refugees fled into Geneva from many areas of Europe. At first, the magistrates treated them as outsiders and temporary guests among the city's regular 13,000 citizens; but Calvin pressured the town council into granting most of them citizenship. At the same time, under the circumstances, many citizens were more or less compelled to profess the faith and obey the law lest they be banished or executed, though most were given opportunities to leave first.

Calvin sought strong but constitutional government and he was prepared to learn about the organization and conduct of civil government from the classic world and the classic writings on the subject. In his commentary on Genesis 4:20 (Ada bore Jabal; he was the father of such as dwell in tents and have cattle), he justified doing so on natural law grounds as long as the knowledge gained was within the framework of Scripture. As in Jewish and classic medieval Christian thought, reason became the handmaiden of God's word. Thus, God reveals himself through nature and history as well as through His direct word. Natural law is that which God has engraved on man's conscience (*Institutes* IV, XX:14 commenting on I Timothy 2–3.) The decalogue embodies and summarizes the convergence of these expressions of God's law (*Institutes* IV, XX:16). A political constitution or basic law is the adaptation of God's law to the physical and psychological needs of each particular people and polity. It both empowers and binds magistrates, who are responsible for the maintenance and execution of justice and the prevention of collective sin.

Whatever the quality of Calvin's covenantalism in his theology, his commitment to covenant was manifest in his politics as reflected in his 1551 sermon on I Samuel. He insisted that the citizens of Geneva should join together in a political covenant to affirm the city's political and ecclesiastical ordinances. A polity's constitution flows from its three-way covenant between the people and the magistrates in the sight of God. So committed was Calvin to the covenantal foundations of the polity that he sought ways to explain even absolute monarchies as having some kind of implicit covenant at their base, albeit one that had gone wrong. In this respect he did not separate polities on the basis of the three models of their origins. Rather, he combined all three, at times speaking in platonic terms of the body politic as an organism and at times emphasizing the necessity for hierarchy within it, even as he derived its very existence from covenant.

Within that framework he had a scale of better and worse regimes, with tyranny the worst and the Christian commonwealth the best. Examples of that commonwealth, while drawing on Scriptural blueprints, need not and should not be mere copies of the polity of biblical Israel since each must be designed to suit local conditions. In this, magistrates need to hearken to the minister interpreters of Scripture in the way the kings of ancient Israel were required to hearken to the prophets.[26]

Geneva Becomes Calvin's Republic

To understand the political impact of the Reformation in Switzerland it is important to note that from the end of the fifteenth century the city governments in Switzerland and south Germany assumed greater responsibilities in the religious domain. In Geneva, the city council began regular interventions into the management of a school founded by Francois de Versonay, particularly in the selection of its faculty. It was in this school that the Reformation first penetrated into Geneva, beginning in 1523 when the priests were ousted from its directorate by the council, which also began to exercise stricter controls over the monasteries of the mendicant monks.

In 1526 Geneva entered into a treaty of friendship and alliance with Berne and Fribourg in the face of the opposition of the local bishop and the Duke of Savoy, the city's nominal overlord. This treaty initiated the political revolution that was to culminate in Calvin's republic. Through the treaty Geneva assumed political sovereignty, establishing a Council of 200 as its basic governing body, taking over the civil courts and giving them and a newly established governor's tribunal exclusive jurisdiction within the city. The newly independent city republic began to mint its own coins.

At this time propagation of the new ideas of the Reformation was confined to rather narrow circles of German merchants who traded in the city. Only in the early 1530s, when Guillaume Farel, Antoine Froment, and Pierre Viret began to openly preach in the city, did Geneva move toward acceptance of the Reformation. Its partner Berne's acceptance of the new religious doctrine in 1528 was influential as well. In June, 1535 there was a formal theological debate between the reformers and the established

Church and, as a result, on 10 August of that year the Council of 200 provisionally suspended celebration of the mass. The Roman Catholic bishop had already left the city several years earlier. Finally, on 21 May 1536 the citizens were asked to vote in a public referendum to confirm the abrogation of mass, which they did. Roman Catholics were expelled from the city and none were allowed to live in Geneva until 1803. It was Farel who recruited Calvin in July, 1536 to the service of the city, shortly after the latter had published his magnum opus, *The Institutes of the Christian Religion,* while living in Geneva to escape persecution in France.

Calvin and Farel began to formulate a confession of faith for all citizens to sign, based on Calvin's plan for organization of the new church. The civil magistrates opposed their efforts to impose an ecclesiastical order on the city and actually exiled the two reformers in 1538. Calvin was allowed to return only three and a half years later, after agreeing to a compromise in the organization of the Protestant republic.

In the framework of that compromise, he became the spiritual father of the three basic laws that formed the constitution of Protestant Geneva: the ecclesiastical ordinances, approved on 20 November 1541, a constitution for the internal organization of the Genevan Church that also defined its relations with the civil authority; the political edicts, approved on 28 January 1543 and revised in 1568, the frame of government that established the structure and offices of the civil government and their electoral procedures; and the civil edicts first adopted in 1542, completed in 1546, and then reformulated in 1568 to govern the social life of the city. These three texts served as the constitution of Geneva until 1791, when under Napoleonic rule the Code Genevois was adopted to replace them. They were supplemented by the sumptuary ordinances adopted in 1558, which forbade luxurious dress or food. After 1646 they were enforced by a Chambre de la Reformacion.

The Ordonnances Ecclesiastiques included provisions for assisting the poor and caring for the sick. It governed the city's principal charitable institution, the Hospitale Generale, founded in 1535, to unite all the welfare and charitable institutions and programs in the city, to improve and extend their services. It survives today under the name Hospice Generale and specializes in assistance to refugees.

The other great institution to emerge as part of the Reformation polity was the Academy of Geneva. From the first, the Reformed tradition emphasized literacy so that all could learn Scripture. On the same day that the citizens of Geneva resolved to accept the Reformation, they also resolved to appoint and pay a schoolteacher so that even the poorest Genevans could learn to read and write. He was "to instruct children to live in accordance with God and His word." In 1559 the Academy of Geneva was founded after the leading professors of the Academy of Lausanne, including Theodore de Beza, had to flee from the wrath of the Bernese government. With them Calvin established a complete educational system, with the college providing elementary education and the Academy higher education. Its curriculum was built around biblical languages, theology, law, and belles lettres. Today it survives as the University of Geneva.[27]

The Triumph of Calvinism

Although many of these features of Calvin's regime are often regarded as narrow mindedly authoritarian, they are essentially the same as Locke's liberal theories of consent, the social compact, and the right of emigration. According to Locke, anyone except atheists, who, lacking fear of God, could not be relied upon to keep the moral commitment that formed the basis of the civil compact, may live in a compactual society as long as they abide by the laws, that is, the terms of the compact as determined by the majority of resident citizens. Whereas Calvin required explicit consent in the form of a profession of faith, Locke required only "tacit consent" by choice of residence. Likewise, according to Calvin and Locke, anyone unhappy with the majoritarian compactual arrangement can simply emigrate to another civil society, or establish a new one on a wild frontier.

The difference is that, unlike Calvin and Hobbes, Locke separated church and state, limited government sharply, and sanctioned a right of revolution as a last resort. Calvin sanctioned only passive resistance to tyrants, primarily on the part of lower magistrates sincerely convinced of a constitutional mandate to resist an unjust and, especially, unholy ruler. Albeit a century later, many English Calvinists of Locke's day were vigorous proponents of revolution. Indeed, Locke's caution about revolution was probably derived, in part, from the reckless boldness of some of his Calvinistic contemporaries.

In the end it was John Calvin who put his stamp on Reformed Protestantism, which took his name as its appellation, often using it even when they did not more than partially accept his doctrines. Under the banner of Calvinism, the Reformed churches conquered much and became the major force in Protestantism after 1546 (the year of Luther's death). Calvinism became a revolutionary ideology even while Calvin was alive. We have seen how his movement became the first "revolutionary International," as per his intentions. Geneva was his "city-upon-a-hill"; his experiment there was not to be conducted in isolation but was to be a model for the reformation of the world.

Why did Calvinism succeed? The answer to that question tells us much about the role of covenant in Western civilization. In aligning itself with the princes, Lutheranism opted for what was rapidly becoming the past, while Calvinism allied itself with the forces that were rapidly becoming the future. Luther and his followers tried to fit into the late medieval political-social system at a time when, unbeknownst to them, that system had reached the end of its road and was within a century of being replaced by modernity. Whatever Calvin and his followers' intentions, their adoption of a covenantal worldview with its emphasis on the congregational republic meant that they were not only in tune with what was about to occur but became a major factor in making it happen. It is corny to say that they were on the side of history, but there is truth in the fact that both their ideas and their polity were in tune with the trends of the times.

Moreover, they had a far more flexible set of political tools and technologies for organizing wherever adherents of the Reformed faith could be found. Covenants and congregations are superb vehicles for advancing a new idea and movement in concrete ways. They are eminently portable and highly participatory. They offer the moral challenge necessary for people to change their behavior and to willingly, even gratefully accept new burdens and challenges. They are flexible and they can be linked with one another in a network of "cells" that can undertake concerted action on the one hand, yet remain self-sufficient on the other. In other words, setbacks to some would hardly affect the others in their ability to survive and spread once again.

All this adds up to the combination of a revolutionary idea with the "delivery system" required to transform it into a movement. In the history of Western civilization, almost every time there has been a revolutionary situation whose thrust was in the direction of what we today refer to in general terms as democracy, the revolutionists have turned to covenantal ideas and vehicles as the best means of expressing their aspirations and have been willing to make the greatest sacrifices in the name of those ideas to achieve those aims.

Another advantage of Reformed Protestantism was that it offered a doctrine attractive to people who today would be known as academics and intellectuals, a doctrine that came to serve as the basis of an intellectual "camp" whose members could carry its ideas far and wide and who in interacting with each other reinforced and deepened, as well as spread, those ideas. Moreover, Calvin used the academy as a major vehicle for spreading his ideas. Among the major functions Geneva served in the spread of Calvinism was that it not only was a place of refuge for persecuted Protestants but it was a place where they came to learn the new doctrines of Calvinism. When they returned to their respective homes, they carried those doctrines with them, even if they modified them in the process.

Particularly in the decade from Charles V's victory over the Schmalkaldic League in 1547, which led to the forced imposition of rigorous Lutheranism on Strassburg the next year, through the persecutions in France (1547–59), England (1553–58), and Scotland (1546–58), at least 5,000 refugees, most of whom were politically or intellectually influential, flocked to Geneva. Naturally they were all ardent Protestants, prepared to learn at the feet of the master. The Lutheranization of Strassburg had the additional effect of putting an end to that city's role as the intellectual center of Protestantism, a role that Geneva picked up.

In the last analysis, the influence of the new religious ideology, although great, was tempered by those older cultural strands. Much of the difference between Zurich and Geneva can be accounted for by the different cultures of German-speaking and French-speaking Switzerland. The Germans had a tradition of local self-government and federalism while the French already had a strong tradition of centralization and holism, or monism. Each of those traditions found religious expression in its culture area.

Covenant and the Radical Wing of the Reformation

The third grouping in the Reformation was its radical wing. There, too, a sharp distinction developed between the Germans and the Swiss. The German radicals were more extremely militant than the Swiss. The latter, on the other hand, developed their adaptation of covenant principles in the idea of what the English sectarians were later to call the "gathered church," that is to say, a voluntary, self-selected community of believers who accepted the lordship of Christ as adults through baptism and, as such, became free of responsibility toward the civil order, being required by their beliefs to obey only God.

In general, this wing of the Reformation was known as the Anabaptist movement, referring to their opposition to infant baptism. Anabaptists appeared in Zurich at the very beginning of the Reformation, but within a decade had been driven out of the city by Zwingli's persecution, which began in 1526. The Zurich exiles provided leadership for much of the Anabaptist movement in the German-speaking world. Most met their deaths through executions for heresy and civil disobedience.

Because of their radical individualism, these Anabaptist groups tended to reject all authority, in the most radical form even the authority of Scripture, relying only on God's inner light shining in each individual. Hence, they were considered enemies to civil society. Whatever their congregational organization owed to covenantal ideas, at a certain point they went beyond the original idea of covenant to religious anarchy.

On the other hand, some of them developed a level of communal collectivism that has preserved them to this day, especially in the New World whence they migrated in the seventeenth and eighteenth centuries. As G. R. Elton put it: "It is not, therefore, surprising that in the long run the proper place for these sectarian ideas came to be the empty continent of North America—rendered empty if found occupied—but not only the English Puritans but later also Moravian, Dutch and Swiss brethren found not so much a refuge as a Canaan."[28] There, protected by a more comprehensive, almost covenanted society, they could live out their own limited communitarian covenants.

One of the byproducts of the Reformation was to divide the German-speaking peoples into those who over the next centuries increasingly pursued more hierarchical approaches to governance and political organization and those who pursued more federalistic approaches, the former culminating in the second and third German Reichs and the latter in the Swiss confederation. On the other hand, Swiss confederal ideas also modified French centralism, in the sense that Calvin wanted to be the dictator of a city but believed in the small republican ideal that Geneva represented.

The Wider Impact of the Reformed Idea

One of the most important contributions of Reformation thinking to the secular world was the refinement of the concept of "calling" or "vocation" as the religious legitimation of all worthy human endeavor. Medieval Catholicism had emphasized the separation between priests and laymen, while the Reformation, especially Reformed Protestantism, moved back toward the original Jewish concept of the holiness or chosenness of all believers. Under the latter circumstance, those who accepted God's rule, "the yoke of Heaven," were called by Him to pursue their vocations, whether nominally religious or nominally secular. They were responsible to Him for doing their very best, whatever occupation they pursued, thereby hearkening to God's will and gaining signs of His favor.

Vocation is a covenantal concept par excellence, but one that can be extended into the political, economic, and social realms, as well as the religious, where it introduced the application of covenantal principles far beyond the confines of any church. The concept of calling worked in two directions. It emphasized that humans need not leave or abandon this world in order to serve God, while at the same time it required them to remold their secular pursuits along the lines of God's law and will.

The idea of vocation was not the vulgar notion later attributed to it by some, that money making by capitalists was a sign of God's favor, but the idea that economic enterprise as a calling could be pursued as long as it was done in the spirit of God's commandments. Neither Max Weber nor R. H. Tawney properly understood this in their classic works. *The Protestant Ethic and the Spirit of Capitalism* (1904; English translation 1930) makes Protestantism the engine for unrestricted capitalist expansion, while *Religion and the Rise of Capitalism* (1926) sees Protestantism as coming to an already incipient capitalism and perverting itself through the endorsement of the freebooting spirit of profit making. In fact, Protestant covenantalism came close to the classic Jewish covenantal position on such matters. Enterprise and profit making are useful and thereby good, provided that they do not become ends in themselves, only the means to pursue the tasks for which God covenanted with humanity.

This begs the question as to the closer identification of Reformed Protestantism with the new states in Europe where commerce and industry were most fully developed. Here the same question can be asked as must be asked with regard to issues of political liberty: Which came first, the chicken or the egg? Contemporary social science has backed away from this kind of question of causation, suggesting that relationships are much more reciprocal than matters of cause and effect. As they interact, they mutually reinforce one another. Thus, political liberty, religious covenantalism, and the spirit of enterprise combined as mutually reinforcing principles strengthening one another and responsible for one another. Reformed Protestantism strongly defended frugality, diligence, careful living, and doing one's duty, but condemned luxury as well as idleness, exploitation of economic advantage as much as sloth.

The development of the covenant as a device for the organization of religious congregations and communities was paralleled by the development of the idea of contracts among equals in the economic and commercial realms. In the medieval world, pacts were made within the hierarchical system, and continued to emphasize the relationship between superior and subordinate, even if, through subsidiarity, the pacts actually served to modify prior hierarchical ties. In the sixteenth and seventeenth centuries, medieval notions were replaced by the principle that equals enter into contracts with one another or, put differently, that to be able to enter into a contract one had to at least be equal with the other contractors for the purposes of the agreement. This idea led to the spread of voluntary associations, corporations, and partnerships in European towns and the countryside.

Notes

1. On the federal theology, see Frederick Carney, "Introduction to Johannes Althusius," *The Politics of Johannes Althusius*, trans. Frederick Carney (London: Eyre & Spottiswoode, 1965); William Johnson Everett, *God's Federal Republic* (New York/Mahwah: Paulist Press, 1988); and Perry Miller, *The New England Mind: From Colony to Province* (Cambridge, Mass.: Harvard University Press, 1953).
2. As quoted in Everett H. Emerson, "Calvin and Covenant Theology," *Church History* 25 (1956): 137.
3. On the Protestant notion of covenant and its connection with the Hebraic concept, see: Champlin Burrage, *The Church Covenant Idea: Its Origins and Development* (Philadelphia, 1904); Peter Ymen DeJong, *The Covenant Idea in New England Theology, 1620–1847* (Grand Rapids, Mich.: W. B. Erdmans, 1964); Delbert R. Hillers, *Covenant: The History of a Biblical Idea* (Baltimore, Md.: Johns Hopkins

University Press, 1969); E. Brooks Holifield, *The Covenant Sealed: The Development of Puritan Sacramental Theology in Old and New England* (New Haven: Yale University Press, 1974).

4. See Dagobert D. Runes, ed., *The Hebrew Impact on Western Civilization* (New York: Citadel Press, 1965), especially Abraham I. Katsch's article "Hebraic Foundations of American Democracy," 1061.

5. Leon Roth, "Hebraists and non-Hebraists of the Seventeenth Century," *Journal of Semitic Studies* 6 (Autumn 1961).

6. Jean Calvin, *Calvin: Commentaries,* trans. and ed. Joseph Haroutunian, with Louise Pettibone Smith (Philadelphia: Westminster Press, 1958); Henri Clavier, *Etudes sur le Calvinisme: La Parole de Dieu et l'Unite de l'Eglise d'Apres Calvin* (Paris: Librairie Fischbacher, 1936); Rupert Eric Davies, *The Problem of Authority in the Continental Reformers: A Study in Luther, Zwingli and Calvin* (London: Epworth Press, 1946); Basil Hall, *John Calvin: Humanist and Theologian* (London: George Philip, for the Historical Association, 1956); Robert McCune Kingdon, ed., *Calvin and Calvinism—Sources of Democracy?* (Lexington, Mass.: Heath, 1970); George Lachmann Mosse, *Calvinism: Authoritarian or Democratic?* (New York: H. Fertig, 1971); Thomas Henry Louis Parker, *John Calvin: A Biography* (Philadelphia: Westminster Press, 1975); George Richard Potter, *John Calvin* (New York: St. Martin's Press, 1983); Albert Marie Schmidt, *Jean Calvin et la Tradition Calvinienne* (Paris: Editions du Sueil, 1957); John Thomas McNeill, *The History and Character of Calvinism* (New York: Oxford University Press, 1954); Everett H. Emerson, "Calvin and Covenant Theology," *Church History* 25 (June 1956): 137.

7. Frederick Carney, *The Politics of Althusius,* translator's introduction, xvii.

8. Peter Ramus, *Dialectique* (1555), 4.

9. Charles Beard, *The Reformation of the Sixteenth Century in its Relation to Modern Thought and Knowledge* (Ann Arbor: University of Michigan Press, 1962), 245.

10. Fred W. Graham, *The Constructive Revolutionary: John Calvin and his Socio-Economic Impact* (Atlanta: J. Knox Press, 1971); Stefan Zweig, *The Right to Heresy: Castellio Against Calvin* (New York: Viking, 1936); Harro M. Hoepfl, *The Christian Polity of John Calvin* (Cambridge: Cambridge University Press, 1982).

11. Perry Miller, "The Marrow of Puritan Divinity," republished in *Errand into the Wilderness* (New York: Harper Torchbooks, 1964), and *The New England Mind* (Cambridge: Harvard University Press, 1953).

12. Leonard J. Trinterud, "The Origins of Puritanism," *Church History* 20 (March 1951): 37-57.

13. See particularly his article, "The Beginnings of Puritan Covenant Theology," *JEH* 14 (1963): 46-67.

14. William Clebsch, *England's Earliest Protestants, 1520–1535,* Publications in Religion, 11 (New Haven: Yale University Press, 1964).

15. Richard L. Greaves, "The Origins and Early Development of English Covenant Thought," *Historian,* 31 (1968): 21-35.

16. Kenneth Hagen, *Sixteenth Century Journal* 3 (1972): 1-24.

17. J. Wayne Baker, *Heinrich Bullinger and the Covenant: The Other Reformed Tradition* (Athens: University of Ohio Press, 1980).

18. Lyle D. Bierma, "Federal Theology in the Sixteenth Century: Two Traditions?" *Westminister Theological Journal* 45 (1983): 304-21.

19. R. L. Greaves, *Society and Religion in Elizabethan England* (Minneapolis: University of Minnesota Press, 1981).

20. Peter Alan Lillback, "Ursinus' Development of the Covenant of Creation: A Debt to Melanchthon or Calvin?," *Westminister Theological Journal* 43 (1981): 247–88.

21. Vol. 1, 139ff, 188ff.

22. See Heinrich Heppe, *Reformed Dogmatics* (Grand Rapids, Mich.: Baker, 1978). Heppe advances ideas to argue, quite falsely, that the covenant idea originated among German Reformed Protestants rather than among the Swiss.

23. Zacharias Ursinus, *Institutes* 2, 11, 4; Commentary on Jeremiah, 32:40.

24. Ford Lewis Battle's Concordance to Calvin's Corpus Reformatorum Edition of the *Institutes* indicates that the term *foedus* appears 155 times, *pactum* twenty-nine, *compactum* four times, and *contractum* three times—a sufficient frequency to allow those who argue for Calvin's strong reliance on covenant to make their case, especially since their opponents often claim that Calvin never even used the term. [Note the English articles listed in p. 271, footnote 80, of the Ursinus article.]

25. Emil G. Kraeling, *The Old Testament Since the Reformation* (New York: Schocken Books, 1969, chap. 2, 21–32). It should not be entirely surprising to find that Calvin's covenantalism showed a great reliance on the Epistle to the Hebrews in the New Testament. After all, the Epistle was written, like the other missionary literature of the New Testament and subsequently, to reach the people to whom it was addressed, and in the case of the Epistle to the Hebrews it was addressed to Jews. In a curious way it is testimony to the fact that the Jews continued to be so heavily embedded in the covenant tradition that those who sought to separate them from their Judaism had to appeal to that tradition and its ideas to make their case.

26. Stanford Reid, "Calvin and the Political Order," chap. 14 of *John Calvin: A Contemporary Prophet, A Symposium*, ed. J. T. Hoogstra (Grand Rapids, Mich.: Baker Book House, 1959), 243–57. This is a flawed article in that it identifies all of Reformed thought with Calvin and attributes to Calvin affects that belonged to the entire Swiss Reformation.

27. Catherine Santschi, "Geneva, City of the Reformation," *Swissair Gazette* 5 (1987), 25–27.

28. G. R. Elton, *Reformation Europe 1517–1559* (Huntington, N.Y.: Fontana Library, 1963), 89.

10

The Aborted Spread of Reformed Federalism in Germany and France

From Switzerland, federal theological and political ideas and practices spread along the Rhine River Valley through western Germany, eastern France, Belgium, and the Netherlands, wherever Reformed Calvinist and Protestant Free churches established themselves. It spread slightly northward into the North Sea areas of Scandinavia, eastward among Protestant groups into Bohemia and Transylvania, and strongly westward into Scotland, England, and Ireland. From many of these countries, federal theology ideas were then carried to the New World—what is now the United States and Canada—to Australia and New Zealand, and to South Africa by the Dutch. For others, powerful opposing forces, for the most part hierarchical, aborted the Reformed revolution and in its place began to move down the road toward modern absolutism and, in some cases, totalitarianism.

Germany: The Struggle Between Covenantal and Hierarchical World Views

In Germany, the heart of the Holy Roman Empire, covenant ideas originated in Strassburg, less than a hundred miles downriver (north) from Basel. The early theologians who revived these ideas included Martin Bucer (1491-1551), Kaspar Hedio, Wolfgang Capito (1478-1541), and Peter Martyr Vermilii (1500-62). Strassburg became the center of the Reformation in southwestern Germany and the bridge between the Swiss and German non-Lutheran reformers. Bucer and Capito, the leaders of the Reformation in Strassburg, were influenced by the Reformation in Basel, further up the Rhine, and especially by Johann Oecolampadius (1482-1531), its leader.

The Basel and Strassburg reformers were more peace oriented than Zwingli or Calvin. Their cities were more vulnerable to attack than Zurich or Geneva. Strassburg especially sat astride one of the major imperial highways. It began to receive refugee evangelical preachers in 1523 and in 1524 reformed its local institutions, but it was not until 1538 that its religious institutions were completely reformed and it joined the larger Reformed movement. Through Basel, Strassburg was linked with the Zurich reformers, and by the late 1520s it was clear that they would not join with Luther. The major differences between them and the Lutherans were expressed in covenantal terms and reflected the foundations of covenantal polities: stronger civil government and a greater role for the civil magistrates, more republican rather than princely polities, as well as the doctrinal differences. Zwinglian reformers built up strength among the guilds then reaching the height of their powers in the Swiss and south German cities.[1] From Strassburg, the idea of federal theology was taken up by theologians in Augsburg, Herborn, Muhlhausen, and Emden.

The most influential figure appears to have been Martin Bucer, who emphasized covenant as the law of love.[2] In fact, Bucer devoted himself to various efforts to effect unions, reconciliations, and accommodations among rival religious and regional forces. One of his achievements was the Wittenberg Concord of 1536 between Luther and the Protestants in south Germany who were being influenced by Swiss ideas. In the process, however, Bucer displayed a certain pragmatic flexibility about religious principles that made him suspect as a systematic theologian. Generally, Bucer viewed the church as a congregational society of the faithful whose members covenant together to become as "one body" with each member fulfilling appropriate roles in support of that body. In effect, these congregations are visible manifestations of the invisible church of the Elect through which Christ advances His Kingdom. In turn, the church in a Christian republic has the responsibility, with lay participation, of establishing ordinances of discipline to guide the faithful.

In 1530, Bucer became president of a newly created church council that was the highest ministerial authority in Strassburg. Four years later, he introduced the lay presbytery, and then confirmation, in 1539. He also founded a gymnasium in 1538 and a seminary in 1544. However, when Protestant-Catholic conflicts made things politically uncomfortable for him in 1549, Bucer moved to England with his friend Paul Fagius at the invitation of Archbishop Thomas Cranmer.

In England, Bucer came to exert considerable influence on both Anglicans and the emergent Puritans as well as the Edwardian commonwealthmen. His influence can also be found in Milton, who employed Bucer's ideas in his treatises on divorce. King Edward VI asked Bucer to retranslate the Bible into Latin and appointed him Regius Professor of Divinity at Cambridge (with Fagius being appointed to the chair in Hebrew). In 1550, Bucer was asked to review the Book of Common Prayer. Against opposition from bishops who still leaned toward Rome, many of his suggestions were adopted, thereby giving the Book some Reformed nuances and casting the Eucharist in a more congregational mode than the mass, which term was dropped at this point. That same year, Bucer also wrote his last major work, *De regno Christi,* which expressed his idea of God's Kingdom and how it might be realized in England. Buried with great honor at Cambridge in 1551, his body was exhumed and burnt in 1556; then, in 1560, his life was memorialized by Queen Elizabeth.

German covenantalism made at least one major contribution to the developing federal theology in developing an emphasis on the prelapserian covenant of works alongside the postlapserian covenant of grace. According to this thesis, God covenanted with Adam before his fall (i.e., prelapserian). Salvation by nature was through a covenant of good works. After Adam's fall humanity could only be redeemed by God's grace, a redemption brought about by the coming of Jesus Christ, the second Adam, with whom God made the postlapserian covenant of grace, which involves the redemption of the elect only.

This motif originated between 1560 and 1590 in the Palatinate, then the other intellectual center of covenantal thought. It was first proposed in 1562 by Zacharias Ursinus, to resolve a decade of controversy over the nature of God's sovereignty and Adam's fall. Between 1584 and 1590 it became commonplace in the theology of Ursinus and was developed by four theologians: Caspar Olevianus, Thomas Cartwright, Dudley Fenner, and Franciscus Junius, all of whom were connected with Ursinus and the Reformed Church of the Palatinate. After 1590 federal theology spread throughout Europe and the idea of the two covenants spread with it. Over eighty years after Calvin's death, the Westminster Confession of Faith adopted the two covenants' federal theological system and proclaimed it part of Reformed orthodoxy.

The special character of the Alemannians among the Germans was perhaps a contributing factor in the decisive political event of early Lutheranism, the so-called Peasant Wars. Taking advantage of the revolutionary ideas in the air, the yeomanry and smaller craftsmen in the towns of the Black Forest who were of Alemannian background but located in Germany rather than Switzerland, rose up in June 1524, starting a rebellion that spread rapidly through southern Germany. This uprising is misnamed. In fact both leaders and followers were principally from the propertied lower orders. It was triggered by a combination of new economic pressures and new efforts by regional rulers to interfere with customary local self-rule. The rebels' program was presented in the twelve Articles of Memmingen, which combined demands for local economic relief with the demand that congregations be allowed to elect their own pastors and that the body politic be founded in Scripture and God's law.

By May of 1525 the princes' military response brought the rebels to heel supported by Luther, who sided with the power elite, thereby setting the course for Lutheranism. Luther's stand opened the door to the rapid conversion of many of the rulers of northern and central Germany to Lutheranism, assuring its separate development from Reformed Protestantism along distinctly hierarchical and pietistic, rather than covenantal, lines. The Rhineland cities, on the other hand, moved into the Reformed camp.

After about 1550, the federal theology movement lost steam as a significant force in Germany, except for pockets of expression, mainly in Strassburg, Herborn, and Emden, concentrated in their universities. Covenant ideas did survive in Germany for another century in the realm of political theory, beginning with Johannes Althusius, the great synthesizer of covenant theology and the federalist political worldview, and continuing through the seventeenth-century theorists who sought to revive the Holy Roman Empire on a federal basis, such as Ludolph Hugo and Leibniz. All three came from the covenant belt in western Germany and studied in either the Netherlands, Switzerland, or both. All were essentially ignored by their countrymen, at least insofar as they emphasized covenantalism and federalism.[3]

Enter Romantic Nationalism

In the middle of the eighteenth century, a new current captured the minds of liberal Germans, fostered by the Enlightment, and by the end of the century it developed into a synthesis of Jacobinism and German romanticism to advocate a more democratic, organic state and society, in many respects the antithesis of the covenanted community sought in earlier generations. Although it embraced German cultural figures such as Beethoven, Goethe, and Schiller, perhaps its most important spokesman was the German philosopher Johann Gottfried von Herder (1744–1803), who actually built his organic philosophy of nationhood out of a transformation of covenantal materials. For example, he emphasized ancient Israel and the Jewish people as the model of organic nationhood by shifting biblical covenantal ideas in the direction of organic expression.[4]

There was one attempt in the nineteenth century, principally by Otto Gierke, to revive the covenantal political ideas of sixteenth- and seventeenth-century Germany through reissuing the works of Althusius and through Gierke's own histories of medieval and late medieval German political thought. It either had no influence or was twisted to emphasize the Romantic theories of organic German nationhood that were part of the German political tradition and, thereby, fed the trends that led to the emergence of Nazism.[5]

In the last analysis, covenant ideas could not be readily employed in the practical religious and secular politics of Germany because of the importance of Lutheran and Catholic ideas which, despite the doctrinal conflicts between the two churches, were politically and socially much the same. Both emphasized society as organic in origin and hierarchical in form, leaving little or no room for theories of liberty and equality. Both churches allied themselves with the princes, thereby retaining or restoring the old tie between organic religion and reactionary politics.

Eventually, what came out of Germany as an internationally influential political idea in the nineteenth century was not a theory of covenanted polity, but the theory of the bureaucratic state made academically respectable through Max Weber and others. Essentially, Lutheranism had replaced ecclesiastical law with civil law administered by the servants of princes. If a layman was his own priest on Sunday, he was a faithful servant of the state during the rest of the week.

Nevertheless, German unification came about through federal arrangements, however reluctantly, because there was no other choice given the entrenched character of the German states, a holdover from medieval times. However, this unification could only be achieved once one German state, in this case Prussia, had emerged as dominant and could impose its will—by force if necessary—on the others, so that federal principles were applied only through authoritarian means. Prussia itself was described by Voltaire as an army in the guise of a state and was opposed to federalism temperamentally and in every other way.

Covenant ideas remained a minor theme in struggles between liberal and illiberal forces in which authoritarian conceptions of "the state" came to the fore and finally culminated in Nazism. A strong case can be made that the Nazis drew upon certain aspects of both Catholicism and Lutheranism to strengthen their own political theology. Moreover, the transformation of Nazism into a messianic political faith, anti-Christian and therefore satanically anti-Jewish, was a logical outcome of the mainstream German experience, Lutheran and Catholic, from the Reformation onward.[6]

After World War II, the Rhineland regions that represented the heartland of covenantal ideas and Reformed religion in sixteenth-century Germany and had become peripheral to the Prussian-centered unified German Reich of the modern epoch became the nucleus for the German Federal Republic constituted in 1949 under the pressure of the American, British, and French occupying powers. This was done by first reconstituting the three Allied zones of occupation into eleven *lander*, or federal states, which then came together to draw up a federal constitution and form the federal republic.

While covenant ideas or orientations may or may not have played a direct role in the founding of the federal republic, they were revived indirectly through the federal and constitutional foundations of that polity. Over the next forty years, federalism once again became very much a part of the West German landscape, so much so that when, in 1990, the opportunity came for the Federal Republic to embrace East Germany (until then the German Democratic Republic, a highly centralized communist state that carried on the habits of Prussianism with what was ostensibly a new vision), the Federal Republic did so by first reviving the five *lander* in the east that had been reduced to mere administrative districts by the GDR and then arranging for the five to petition to join the other eleven *lander* in a unified German state.

Today, covenant ideas find expression not only in German federalism but in various constitutional devices. For example, in efforts to adjudicate intergovernmental disputes, the supreme constitutional court of the GFR has introduced the concept of *bundestreue,* which is a modern civil equivalent of the biblical idea of *hesed* in covenant. The concept calls for a certain federal friendship and loyalty among the constituent states (*lander*) and between them and the federal government, which requires the various partners to go beyond the letter of the law in certain disputes so as to promote more effective intergovernmental cooperation.[7]

Immediately after reunification, it became apparent that there were real cultural differences between eastern and western Germany, with the east Germans bringing the same hierarchical, even authoritarian, outlook for which they had been traditionally noted. The West Germans had their work cut out for them. It must be said that the issue is still in doubt.

France: Huguenots and Resistance to Tyrants

France, the first home of statist absolutism in Europe and later the home of the Jacobin antithesis to federal ideas, became the battleground between those espousing covenantal ideas and those vehemently opposed to them at the time of the Reformation. This battle took its primary form in the struggle between Catholics and Protestants, although at first matters were not so simple as that division would suggest.

Between 1559 and 1629, covenant ideas were advanced by the Huguenots in their struggles for religious freedom. Although certain tenets of the Reformed tradition in France can be traced to Jacobus Faber whose *Sancti Pauli Epistolae xiv...cum commentariis* of 1512 expressed the idea of justification by faith, the Huguenots emerged from the exile congregation that had been established by French Protestants in Strassburg under Calvin's leadership in 1538. Calvin, who had fled France in 1534, still seemed to have in mind a reformation of France when he addressed the first edition of his *Institutes* to his persecutor, Francis I. In 1546 the first Protestant congregation was organized at Meaux along the lines of the Strassburg community. In 1556 a church was finally established in Paris. Early growth led the emboldened Protestants to convene a synod at Paris in 1559, where they framed a doctrinal and governmental constitution for themselves. Fashioned after Calvin's Geneva constitution, it became an influential model for Presbyterian governance.

The Huguenots established a confederal democratic system. Final ecclesiastical authority was held to belong to the people, who then selected elders to administer church affairs and call pastors. In this respect, each local congregation was an independent polity. To attend to matters of common concern, mutual assistance, and defense, nearby local churches formed a local council, or *colloque*. On a still wider plane, local congregations were organized into regional associations, each governed by a provincial synod having equal numbers of lay and pastoral delegates from each church. In turn, the provincial synods elected lay and pastoral representatives to the national synod.

Fifteen churches were represented at the synod of 1559. By 1561, it is estimated that the body had grown to 2,150 congregations. The next year, however, a wave of persecution began with the killing of a number of Huguenots at worship in Vassy. Huguenot leaders quickly assembled at Orleans to issue a call to arms. While declaring loyalty to the Crown, the Huguenots held that they had a right to worship freely and were bound by conscience to defend that right. Years of civil war followed.

After the civil war was concluded in 1570, peace and toleration seemed at hand. However, on the night of 24 August 1572, many Huguenot leaders were assassinated in what became known as the St. Bartholomew's Eve massacre. Thousands of Protestants were slain throughout France and war broke out anew. The Huguenots organized a political party as well as their own underground republic.

In 1598 Henry IV, who had been a Huguenot but accepted Catholicism as the price of inheriting the throne ("Paris is worth a mass"), issued the Edict of Nantes, which brought an end to hostilities. The Edict of Nantes granted liberty of conscience and the right of private worship to all, liberty of public worship wherever it had been previously granted, royal subsidies to Huguenot schools, and the right of Huguenots to fortify and garrison approximately 200 cities. The underground republic of the Huguenots was thereby legitimized, in order to serve as a guarantee of their other rights. A state within a state was created, which flew in the face of the dominant political culture in France. War broke out again in 1624 and continued until the Huguenots were defeated in 1628. The peace of Alais ended the French religious wars in 1629. The Huguenots lost their political privileges and their republic within the state, but were able to preserve the freedom of worship granted in the Edict of Nantes.[8]

One of the reasons the Huguenots were able to hold their own in France for as long as they did was that the administration of the French government in the sixteenth century was highly decentralized.[9] The fifteenth and sixteenth centuries were exceptional in French history in that the provincial parliaments were the true loci of domestic governmental power, sometimes sharing it with the governors appointed by the king and sometimes not. It was possible through control of the organs of provincial government to become essentially autonomous for domestic purposes. During the civil wars, Huguenots controlled the provincial parliaments in the areas where they formed the majority. Hence, they had a separate governmental base as well as political power vis-à-vis the king and the Catholic loyalists. In the seventeenth century, this situation would give way to the centralization of the kingdom through the intendent system introduced by Louis XIV at approximately the same time that he revoked the Edict of Nantes and destroyed the Huguenot presence in France.

The fullest expressions of this decentralization were to be found in the codifications of French customary law of the fifteenth and sixteenth centuries, which carefully codified local customs and usages bailiwick by bailiwick or, in cases such as Brittany and Normandy, province by province, in deference to the strength of provincial autonomy. The combination of powerful provincial parliaments with the new codifications of customary law established through the public consent of each community for a moment gave France a constitutional basis more or less appropriate for the covenantal religion that was sweeping its more advanced sectors, but in the end this could not be maintained in the face of the absolutist and centralist tendencies of the French crown. Still, at the end of the ancien regime there remained sixty-five general customary laws and approximately 300 local ones, this after what Filhol calls "a severe pruning of local customs had taken place."[10] These codifications remained in effect until the introduction of the Napoleonic Civil Code in 1804.[11]

There is an aesthetic dimension here that needs further exploration, especially in the case of France where aesthetics plays such an important role in directing philosophy. J. Huizinga has suggested that what characterized artistic works of the fifteenth century was a love of detail and an acceptance of infinite variations at the cost of the unity of the whole.[12] On the other hand, the new commitment to science and rationalism that characterized the seventeenth century may well have influenced the desire for uniformity and "rational" order that characterized the absolute monarchs of that period.[13]

While the rank and file of French Protestants were drawn from the ordinary people, the movement was given special strength and impetus through its strength among the aristocracy and particularly those associated with the noble leadership of Navarre. In the first half of the sixteenth century, much of the territory of southwestern France consisted of lands under the rule of the Navarre nobility. Spanish Navarre was the last independent kingdom on the Iberian Peninsula, one which was to jealously guard its *fueros,* the feudal political compacts that guaranteed its independent standing then and subsequently. Was there a connection between this Navarrese dimension, so deeply entrenched in the medieval analog of a pact and oath society and the covenantal predisposition of those who were to become the Huguenots?

During these bloody conflicts, Huguenots invoked covenant as a revolutionary principle justifying resistance to tyranny. Three works in particular were influential in presenting this view: Francois Hotman's *Franco-Gallia* (1573), Theodore de Beza's *Du droit des magistrats* (1574), and the *Vindiciae contra tyrannos* (1579), written under the name Stephanus Junius Brutus, supposedly a Celt, but frequently attributed to Philippe Du Plessis Mornay ("the Huguenot Pope") and/or Hubert Languet.

Hotman (1524–90) was a jurist who converted to Reformed Protestantism in 1547 and became an acquaintance of Calvin. His *Franco-Gallia* is essentially an attempt to reconceptualize the French polity as a covenanted commonwealth. To do so, Hotman argues that France had been such a commonwealth before the present era of corruption and royal usurpation. The Francogallic commonwealth had been founded not by conquest, but by the free, voluntary consent of "our forefathers" who then elected a magistrate for life. Thus, the monarchy was originally an elective public office. The later tradition of succession by male descent, which Hotman does not reject in principle, occurred by custom or tacit consent, not by rights of heredity or of the realm being the personal property of the royal family. The polity, therefore, is properly a republican commonwealth and there is a compactual tie between the people and their monarch involving a relationship of *mutua obligato.* When the king violates the terms of that relationship, the people have a sovereign right to remove him.

Even more to the point, the monarch did not rule alone in antiquity. He was, in effect, a strong chief executive who shared power with a public council consisting of three Estates: the kind, the high nobility and public officials, and the people as represented by deputies from the commonwealth's provinces and towns. Thus, the ancient polity was a mixed commonwealth combining Aristotelian principles of the mixed regime, that is rule by the one, the few, and the many, as well as the federal principle of territorial democracy. This council, according to Hotman, possessed all the sovereign authority customarily associated with government and modern parliaments. While no longer effective in fact, the council still existed by right, not only because of its constitutional basis in the compact of antiquity, but also because such concilar arrangements belong to the common law of all peoples.[14]

Although Hotman's historical account is dramatically inaccurate in many respects, his book created quite a stir when it appeared in 1572 and it is an excellent example of the historical concerns of covenant thinkers during this period. In trying to transform church and society, they tended to read covenant back into history, even inappropriately, so as to place the very origins of the polity on a covenantal foundation and thereby establish a tradition where none, perhaps, had existed before, and to show that present arrangements were not natural or divinely ordained, but rather contrived corruptions. This honorable tradition of the forefathers could then be invoked to help legitimate revolutionary covenantal activity in the present.

While Reformed theologians tended to draw these ideas from the Old Testament, more secular thinkers like Hotman drew from both the Bible and the ancient Greek and Roman republican periods. As a jurist, for example, Hotman had been trained in the classics and was a professor of Roman law. As a Huguenot and associate of Calvin, Hotman was also educated in the Reformed tradition's focus on the Old Testament's covenant tradition.

This is further evident in the work of Theodore de Beza (1519–1605), a jurist, theologian, and spiritual leader of French Protestants after Calvin's death. Beza was associated with Calvin and Hotman in Geneva, which he visited on several occasions and where he taught in 1558. In his first political work, *De Haereticis a civili magistratu puniendis* (1554), Beza defended the burning of Michael Servetus in Geneva while, at the same time, upholding the principle of resistance that had been expressed in the Magdeburg Admonition of 1548.

In his *Right of Magistrates,* published two years after the massacre of St. Bartholomew's Eve, Beza articulated a more general theory of constitutional resistance, again like Hotman, on the basis that there is a compact of mutual obligation between the people and their monarch. In supporting his view that the king is created by the people, Beza argued that the ancient Israelites elected their kings and that this practice was common among ancient peoples, including the French. Beza also held that "the people" exist as a community prior to the monarchy. Although they create a monarchy for the common good, it is a risky enterprise subject to corruption, as pointed out by Samuel and the prophets in the Old Testament. Therefore, it is unreasonable to expect the people to delegate rights and powers to a monarch unconditionally. Instead, they impose conditions that serve as the constitutional basis of resistance.

Beza distinguishes two kinds of resistance. Against a usurper, the right of resistance belongs to every citizen as an obligation. Against a monarch who abuses power, the right of resistance belongs to the Estates and lesser magistrates who represent the people in their communal capacity. Because the monarch is created by the community of the people, not by individuals, he must be deposed by public communal processes, not by private citizens acting on their own initiative. The final right of deposition, according to Beza, belongs to the Estates.[15]

The Vindiciae contra tyrannos, which seems to be based on many ideas of Beza and John Knox, presents a more impassioned argument and adds two new elements to the Huguenot theory of resistance.[16] First, the Vindiciae speaks of two covenants. One is between the people, the king, and God for the purpose of advancing and defending the true religion. The second is between the people and their chosen monarch for the purpose of promoting the common good. In the first covenant, the king and people promise to be God's servants; in the second, the king promises to serve the people. Therefore, the people have the right to resist a monarch who violates the first covenant by persecuting the true religion, or violates the second covenant by abusing his authority. Like Beza, the Vindiciae holds that a monarch must be deposed by public procedures rather than private initiative, though the process may be initiated by individual magistrates. Unlike Beza, however, the Vindiciae gives the lesser magistrates, rather than the Estates, the decisive role in deposing a monarch by agreement among themselves.

In sum, by 1579, Huguenot theorist-practitioners had advanced a sophisticated compactual theory of civil society seventy-two years before Hobbes's Leviathan and ninety years before Locke's Two Treatises. Huguenot ideas were widely disseminated throughout Western civilization through frequent contacts and communication with Protestants elsewhere on the Continent, the British Isles, in North America, and southern Africa.

In tracing the history of the rise of the radical movement or position among the Huguenots in the second half of the sixteenth century, W. Standford Reed argues that John Knox, the founder and great leader of Scottish Presbyterianism, was the first of the monarchomachs, those who fomented resistance against the French monarchy and as such had a major direct influence on the Huguenots. Indeed, Reed argues that by taking this step Knox broke with Calvin's ideas of submission to constituted civil authority to propound the idea of the legitimacy of religiously motivated resistance. Knox based his break on his understanding of covenant theory which, to him, justified the common people taking up arms against a tyrannical and idolatrous ruler. Whatever his impact on the Huguenots, which seems to have been very real, Knox had even greater impact on his own people the Scots, who began their century-long path toward seeking covenantally based political solutions to their religio-political problems. Developed first for the Huguenots in the 1550s, Knox's views became dominant among the Huguenots after the St. Bartholemew's Massacre in 1572 and in Scotland in the late 1560s and early 1570s.

It must be recalled that in those days there were close ties between Scotland and France, and French troops even occupied certain points in Scotland; Knox himself had his first serious exposure to the French when he was imprisoned on board the French galley Notre Dame in 1547. Certainly his views in opposition to monarchic tyranny were reinforced by his opposition to Mary Queen of Scots.

Unfortunately, the French establishment did not take to those ideas, drawing its intellectual justification instead from the works of Jean Bodin, who was writing at the same time to present his quite contrary view of undivided sovereignty vested in a single authority who governed a reified state, thereby providing full justification for the kind of absolutist monarchy by Divine right which became the hallmark of early modern France. Later, in the eighteenth, nineteenth, and twentieth centuries, there were French political philosophers who excelled at developing sophisticated theories of liberty, fraternity, republicanism, and federalism—Montesquieu, Alexis de Tocqueville, P. J. Proudhon, and Alexander Marc, for example—but they were utterly incapable of putting them into practice. At best, French federalist thought has served to influence and even inspire citizens of other, more fortunate, lands pursuing those same goals. In France itself, continual conflict and a new round of persecution under Louis XIV, who revoked the Edict of Nantes in 1685, led some 400,000 Huguenots to flee France during the seventeenth century and settle in England, Holland, Prussia, Switzerland, British North America, and southern Africa.

The last gasp of Huguenot resistance in France itself came, ironically, from Protestant peasants, the Camisards, who conducted a rebellion against religious persecution between 1702 and 1710. Less fastidious than their noble counterparts, they fought a successful guerilla war in the Cevennes of France until they were forced into submission by overwhelming royal power.

Only after 1815 did French Protestants experience a final cessation of persecutions. Perhaps because of the absence of an external threat, the Huguenot Church split in 1872. In 1907 a National Union of Reformed Churches was established; and it, in turn, affiliated with the Protestant Federation of France.

The Huguenot Diaspora

Wherever they settled, the Huguenots made a significant contribution to the flowering of federal liberty and covenantal ideas. In the Dutch colony at the Cape of Good Hope they became the intellectual, religious, and political leaders, and to this day the vast majority of the Afrikaner establishment bear Huguenot names. In British North America, they either assimilated into the upper echelons of the existing Puritan society in New England or established themselves and their ideas in the southern colonies, reinforcing Reformed Protestantism in the South.

As it turned out, in both southern Africa and southern North America, the Huguenot emigres were able to combine their commitment to federal liberty for themselves with the enslavement of black Africans, which gave them the unenviable position of fathering or building exclusivist covenanted communities that reflected one of the dark sides of Western civilization. In both South Africa and South Carolina, they erected elaborate intellectual edifices to justify their acts—an abuse of the spirit of covenant.

Elsewhere in Europe the Huguenots also assimilated into the local Reformed establishments, usually also at the higher levels because most of the emigres were principally from the French upper classes. Their traces can be found wherever Reformed Protestantism was present.

Notes

1. B. Moeller, *Reichstadt und Reformation* (Schriften des Vereins Fur Reformationsgeschichte, 1962).
2. Heinrich Bornkmann, *Martin Bucers Bedeutung fur Die Europaische Reformationsgeschichte* (Gutersloh: C. Bertelsmann, 1952); Basil Hall, "Diakonia in Martin Butzer," *Service in Christ: Essays.*
3. Patrick Riley, "Three Seventeenth-Century German Theorists of Federalism: Althusius, Hugo, Leibniz," *Publius* 6, no. 3; Thomas Hueglin, "Johannes Althusius: Medieval Constitutionalist or Modern Federalist?," *Publius* 9, no. 4; Thomas Hueglin, "Covenant and Federalism in the Politics of Althusius." Paper presented to the Workshop on Covenant and Politics, 27–29 February 1980 (Philadelphia, Pa.).
4. Johann Gottfried von Herder, *Sprachphilosophische Schriften* (Hamburg: F. Meiner, 1975); see also Frederick Mechner Barnard, *J. G. Herder on Social and Political Culture* (Cambridge: Cambridge University Press, 1969).
5. Otto von Gierke, *Natural Law and the Theory of Society*, trans. Ernest Barker (Cambridge: Cambridge University Press, 1950); *Political Theories of the Middle Age*, trans. with an introduction by Frederic William Maitland (Cambridge: Cambridge University Press, 1927); and *The Development of Political Theory* (New York: Norton, 1939). See also Sobei Mogi, *Otto von Gierke: His Political Teaching and Jurisprudence* (London: P. S. King, 1932).
6. Cf. Hayim Greenberg, *The Inner Eye: Selected Essays* (New York: Jewish Frontier Association, 1953). See Uriel Tal, "Political Faith of Nazism Prior to the Holocaust," and "Structures of German Political Theology in the Nazi Era," the first and second annual lectures of the Jacob M. and Shoshana Schreiber Chair of Contemporary Jewish History, Tel Aviv University, 1978–79.
7. P. H. Merki, "Executive-Legislative Federalism in West Germany." In *The Origin of the West German Republic* (New York: Oxford University Press, 1963); Christa Altenstetter, "Intergovernmental Profiles in the Federal Systems of Austria and Germany," *Publius* 5, no. 2; G. Braunthal, "Federalism in Germany: The Broadcasting Controversy," *Journal of Politics* 24 (August 1962): 545–61; S. Drummong, "Lander and German Federal Politics," *Political Studies* 16 (February 1968): 89–94; A. J. Heidenheimer, "Federalism and the Party System: The Case of West Germany," *American Political Science Review* 52 (September 1958): 809–28.
8. On the Hugeunots, see Guy Howard Dodge, *The Political Theory of the Huguenots of the Dispersion* (New York: Columbia University Press, 1947); Hillel Schwartz, *The French Prophets* (Berkeley: University of California Press, 1980); Nicola Mary Sutherland, *The Huguenot Struggle for Recognition* (New Haven: Yale University Press, 1980).
9. D. C. Gaston Zeller, "Royal Administration Before the Intendents: Parliaments and Governors." In Henry J. Cohen, ed., *Government and Reformation in Europe, 1520–1560* (New York: Harper and Row, 1971).
10. Rene' Filhol, "The Codification of Customary Law in France in the Fifteenth and Sixteenth Centuries." In Cohen, *Government and Reformation in Europe*, 282.

11. Ibid., 265.
12. J. Huizinga, *The Waning of the Middle Ages* (Harmondsworth, Middlesex: Penguin Books, 1968).
13. See J. E. King, *Science and Rationalism in the Government of Louis XIV, 1661–1683* (New York: Octagon Books, 1972).
14. On Francogallia, see *Constitutionalism and Resistance in the Sixteenth Century: Three Treatises by Hotman, Beza and Mornay*, trans. and ed. Julian H. Franklin (New York: Pegasus, 1969). For the Latin text, see Francois Hotman, *Francogallia*, ed. Ralph E. Giesey (London: Cambridge University Press, 1972).
15. On *Du droit des magistrats*, see Julian H. Franklin, trans. and ed., *Constitutionalism and Resistance in the Sixteenth Century: Three Treatises by Hotman, Beza and Mornay.*
16. On the *Vindiciae contra tyrannos* see Harold J. Laski, ed., *A Defense of Liberty Against Tyrants: A Translation the Vindiciae Contra Tyrannos by Junius Brutus* (New York: Burt Franklin, 1972).

11

The Netherlands: The Covenant
and the United Provinces

The Covenantal Roots of the Revolt Against Spain

By the middle of the sixteenth century, Calvinism had become the predominant religious force in the Low Countries, and by the early seventeenth century, federal theology became the dominant source of ideas in the newly independent United Netherlands.[1] Federal theology was given its most thoroughly systematic formulations by such theologians as Johann Kloppenburg (1592-1652) at the University of Franeker; his student, Johannes Cocceius (1603-69) at Bremen and Franeker; Franciscus Burmannus (1628-79) at Utrecht and a student of Cocceius; Hermannus Witsius (1636-1708) also at Utrecht and a student of Burmannus; Melchior Leydecker (1642-1721) at Utrecht; Solomon van Til (1643-1713) at Dort and Leyden; and Friedrich Adolph von Lampe (1683-1722) at Utrecht. As university theologians rather than public leaders like many of their predecessors, these Dutch thinkers were concerned primarily with theology rather than politics. However, they emerged within a thoroughly Calvinistic, federal political climate and their work had a wide and varied influence.

Within the realm of theology, Cocceius, Burmannus, and Witsius are generally regarded as the most exemplary, systematic representatives of the school of federal theology. In them, the movement reached its intellectual high point. Indeed, this school established itself so firmly as a variation on mainstream Dutch Calvinism that it became customary for the next three centuries to appoint one Federalist to each university in Holland.

These covenant ideas played a significant role in the establishment of the United Provinces in 1579. The Dutch revolt can be seen as Europe's third great covenantal war of independence, after that of the Swiss in the thirteenth century and the Scots in the fourteenth. It was federalist through and through in both theology and politics.

The rise of the Dutch republic is intimately linked to the failure of Charles V to transform the Holy Roman Empire into a functioning federal system. Not surprisingly, the consequences of his failure were first felt in the Lowlands, whose inhabitants already had a federal political culture. In the Netherlands, the strength of the *stadholders* (provincial governors) had developed into a form of late feudal independence that ultimately gave the rebels an important governmental and administrative base from which to launch their revolt. Moreover, each province had its own estates (legislature) with the power to give or withhold consent to imperial taxes locally.[2]

Local power grew during the reign of Charles V and his immediate successor, not by royal design but because of the realities of the political situation. While Charles was respectful of local liberties to a point, in 1531 he introduced central administration into the Lowlands under a governor-general with three collateral councils and provincial *stadholders*. This effort, which he saw as merely a matter of increasing the efficiency of his government, struck at the libertarian sentiments of the locals and led to twelve years of resistance which, from time to time, included the taking up of arms.

The greatest of these risings was that in Ghent in 1539–40, which the Empire crushed. In 1539 Ghent rebelled against Charles's effort to impose a tax to which it had not consented, nearly bringing all of Flanders to arms. The rebels executed some loyal burghers and expelled others, armed the local population and organized them into a civic guard, and tore up the *chalfvel* (or *kalfvel*, as the 1515 declaration of Charles V was called because it was written on calf skin to preserve it as a covenant between the emperor and the city). When negotiations failed, the emperor himself returned to the Low Countries to deal with the matter. On 14 February 1540, he and his army reentered the city without resistance. In a development foreshadowing the French Revolution, the revolutionaries had allied themselves with the poor and the mob to take over the city, thereby alienating the burghers of property, who were still strong enough to welcome the king. He, in turn, meted out punishment to the rebels and on 29 April abolished the city's traditional privileges and self-government. The city was disarmed and garrisoned by imperial troops so that no resistance was possible. By 1543 provincial resistance to the new regime came to an end.[3]

Recognizing that crushing the resistance was not enough, in 1548 Charles granted the Netherlands special status in the Holy Roman Empire as the Burgundian Circle. This might have held the line for the Empire had Charles not abdicated seven years later. In the subsequent division of the Empire, the Lowlands remained Spanish possessions and came under the rule of Philip II. Almost immediately there followed a war with France. When it was concluded in 1559 and Philip returned to Spain, the Spanish governors of the Low Countries began a new round of civil and religious repression, exacerbated by the spread of the Reformation. In 1561 Cardinal Granvelle, the real power in the Lowlands Spanish government, introduced changes in the church structure, but they were not enough. In 1565 King Philip bluntly rejected the demands of the Netherlands' nobles for preservation of local rights and an end to religious persecution.

At first the resistance was essentially conducted by the great nobles led by William of Nassau, the Prince of Orange. They dominated the local Council of State and opposed the Consulta headed by Cardinal Granvelle, which had become the real government of the country. This in turn triggered the lesser nobility and the common people, who were suffering from the economic crisis that plagued the Lowlands and further fueled their dissatisfaction, to take steps toward revolt.

Early in December, 1565 a group of the younger noblemen, mostly of lesser ranks, came together in Brussels to hold Reformed religious services. At their meeting they established a league of resistance known in the language of the time as a *compromise* (that is, bound by a common oath), to which noblemen from every part of the Low Countries became signatories, including some Catholics and some of the higher-ranked nobility. All signatories swore an oath which, inter alia, contained the following:

> We have decided to form a holy and lawful confederation and alliance by which we promise to bind ourselves mutually by solemn oath to use all our efforts to prevent the reception or introduction of this Inquisition in any way.... We have promised and sworn and do now promise and swear to uphold this confederation and alliance as sacred and inviolable for all time without any break as long as we live. We take God the sovereign Lord as witness of our consciences that neither in deed nor in word, neither directly nor indirectly, will we knowingly and willingly contravene this confederation in any fashion whatever. And in order to ratify this alliance and

confederation and to make it stable and firm for all time, we have promised and do promise each other full assistance with our bodies and our goods as brothers and faithful companions, joining hands so that none among us and our confederates may be investigated, harassed, molested, or persecuted in any way, either in our lives or in our property...because of this present confederation.... We agree and mutually promise that...each of us will follow the common opinion of all his brothers and allies or of those who will be given such duties in order that this sacred union may be maintained among us, that what will be done will be more certain and stable because it is done with common agreement, in witness whereof in assurance of this confederation and alliance we have invoked and do invoke the most sacred name of God, the sovereign Lord, who created the sky and the earth, as our judge who sees into our consciences and thoughts and knows that this is our decision and resolution. We most humbly pray from His power from on high he will keep us firm and steady and give us such prudence and discretion of spirit that, always possessing good and mature council, we may achieve our purpose with a good and happy success, bring glory to His name, to the service of his majesty the king, and to the welfare and safety of the public. Amen.[4]

The catalyst for this *compromise* was the resistance to religious persecution and the introduction of the Inquisition into the Low Countries, which the signatories saw as an assault both on their religious practices and on "all public law and order and all equity...the ancient laws, customs and ordinances which have been preserved from time immemorial.

Independence and Federalism

In 1566 the economic situation worsened, bringing actual famine. Calvinists, in an effort to gain heavenly favor, began prayer meetings in the fields (*hage preken* or head sermons). Believing that the authorities were preparing to stop those services, on August 10 in Steenvoorde, a small town in western Flanders, a mob of Calvinists destroyed the town church. Their act stimulated others which spread throughout the provinces, reaching Groningen in the extreme north a month later. The efforts are known in Dutch history as the *beeldenstorm* or image-breaking. The Catholic religious art of the churches was destroyed because it was viewed as idolatry, in opposition to the plain worship required by the more puritan Reformed tradition, but the riots also involved the awakening of the impoverished common people, thereby alienating at least a part of the nobility.

King Philip, for his part, decided to crush the resistance in the Low Countries once and for all. To that end in 1567 he sent the Duke of Alva with a strong force of Spanish regular soldiers. Alva's behavior completed the alienation of the nobility, which had begun to have second thoughts after watching the mob during the *beeldenstorm*.

Alva threatened all self-government in the Netherlands. Consequently William of Nassau himself reluctantly became leader of the resistance, which was to transform him and his life. In his commission to his brother, Count Louis of Nassau, issued on 6 April 1568, to resist the Spaniards by force of arms, he emphasizes the Spaniards' daily violations of "the contracts, leagues and privileges...upon which the prosperity of this country is wholly dependent and which his majesty has affirmed, confirmed, and sworn by solemn oath" and ties that with "the Spaniards' further endeavor...to extirpate the pure word of God." Part of William's justification for taking up arms was the attack on the religious liberty of the Huguenots in France.[5]

Alva countered by bringing in German mercenary armies and in the four years following 1568 seemed to triumph everywhere. But on 1 April 1572 the tide turned when a band of seaborne guerillas, the *gueuxdemer* or water beggars (the term *gueux* or beggars, which had originally applied to the rebels in contempt, was adopted by them as a proud designation), a militant Reformed Protestant group, captured the Dutch port of Denbriel on one of the mouths of the Rhine. Aligning themselves with fierce Calvinists on the land, they moved inland to capture one town after another in Holland and Zeeland, where Alva had left only a small garrison. Two weeks later, on 14 April, William of Orange, who had taken refuge in his castle at Dilenberg in Germany, issued a call to rebellion.

In mid-July a revolutionary assembly met in Dordrecht and took the name "The States of Holland." That body had never before assembled at its own initiative. In true covenantal fashion they sought to establish resistance to Spanish rule on a legal basis. Hence, the assembly proclaimed itself "The Lawful States of Holland" on the grounds that they represented the will of the people as expressed through the existing local and provincial authorities. Their claim to legitimacy was that the king could not govern without popular consent and certainly not against the popular will.

The chief instigator of these meetings was Philip of Marnix, advisor to Prince William. Through him the prince set the tasks for the new assembly in instructions read to it on 19 July. The assembly recognized William as *stadholder* in Holland against the king's designee. In addition to calling upon the states to recognize his authority, William also asked them to provide for raising and maintaining military and naval forces for the resistance, to develop a system of communication to "maintain good agreement and correspondence with one another," to draw up a policy for the resistance while reaffirming their loyalty to the king himself, to "bind themselves and promise the others never to enter into any accord, agreement or compact, be it with the king himself or anyone bearing the orders or commission of his majesty, nor to do or decide anything else concerning the generality" without securing his advice, consent, and agreement. He, in turn, agreed to the same. These provisions were to be established by a mutual oath. The assembly thereby recognized William as the *stadholder*.[6]

Alva launched a counteroffensive, which had limited success, but as long as the rebels continued to control the waterways there was no way to subdue them. When the emperor intervened in an effort to persuade both sides to make peace, he, too, failed since by then the rebels, including William, had developed an even stronger commitment to Reformed religion and even greater hatred of the Spaniards and distrust of Philip, plus William's more mundane needs of having to pay off mercenaries and reluctance to depend upon outside intervention. The decisive connection between the Reformed religion as the true word of God and the privileges and liberty of the lowlanders became the cornerstone of the revolt, anticipating Alexis de Tocqueville's description of the felicitous situation in the United States where the spirit of religion and the spirit of liberty walked hand in hand. In its own way the same was true of the Netherlands during the revolution. This combination meant that the bearers of a covenantal political culture had found a powerful covenantal political ideology to reinforce their political orientations. Herbert Rowen describes the results:

> We may see this by looking first at the special role of the Calvinists in the revolt—so special, indeed, that modern Dutch Calvinists still look upon the rebellion, and the Dutch state and nation which emerged from it, as deeply and truly their own and no one else's. The Calvinists were part of an international movement of religious transformation and reinvigoration which, despite the initial distaste of Calvin himself for political violence, became a powerful revolutionary force transcending the boundaries of single states. Moved by a fervent conviction that they and they alone possessed the truth of God's word (a conviction shared, to be true, with most other religious groups of that time), they sought to gain freedom of religion at the cost of tremendous exertions and a readiness for sacrifice. But it was freedom for themselves, as, in their own eyes, the only true church; it was not freedom for those

who held false doctrines.... The most essential task of the state, in their eyes, was to serve God's church against its enemies; and the meaning of the revolution to which they devoted their goods and their lives was to put 'pious men'—that is, good Calvinists—in the seats of power.[7]

The Calvinists were powerful but they were not the only people involved in the revolt. Indeed, William sought to bring together Reformed and Catholic residents of the Low Countries in an independent united Netherlands, but they and their Reformed Protestant religion became the driving force in the revolt, principally because their covenantal ideology was so suited to the struggle for liberty and the political culture of the Netherlanders.

A temporary respite in the war came in 1576 when, on 8 November the parties agreed to the Pacification of Ghent. The rebels' demands were recognized: the Spanish soldiers were to leave, the country was to have self-government, there was to be religious peace on the basis of toleration with Calvinism to be the established religion in Holland and Zeeland, and limited Spanish sovereignty would be acknowledged. A new governor-general, Don Juan of Austria, was required to swear to uphold the Pacification before he was accepted. The pact was known as the *traite* and *confederation.*

Don Juan almost immediately violated the Pacification of Ghent to the point where the moderate Catholics in the southern provinces appealed over his head to Mathias of Hapsburg, the young archduke and heir to the throne of the Holy Roman Empire, to come to the Netherlands to replace him because Mathias was known for his moderation in religious matters. William and his followers accepted the new governor-general and the Prince of Nassau even became his lieutenant general.

Mathias negotiated a second pact, the Peace of Religion, signed in Antwerp on 22 July 1578 by the parties involved, which reaffirmed the terms of the Pacification of Ghent and in a long series of clauses detailed specific actions that were required or forbidden with regard to religious liberty and tolerance, designed to keep the peace. Mathias then returned to Austria and turned over his powers to the Duke of Parma, Alexander Farnese, who arrived on 15 October 1578 to begin the methodical reconquest of the Low Countries. Parma combined a policy of moderation with a firm assertion of Spanish control. Over the course of the next seven years he drove William and his supporters out of the southern Netherlands, but could not dislodge them from Holland and

Zeeland. The result was the beginning of a separation of the Netherlands into the two states of today, Catholic Belgium to the south and the overwhelmingly Protestant northern Netherlands to the north.

In 1579 two covenants established the division—the Union of Arras, in which the Walloon provinces pledged their support to Parma, and the Union of Utrecht, through which the northern provinces reaffirmed their adherence to Reformed Protestantism and declared their commitment to maintaining their liberties.

Assembling at Utrecht, the representatives of the seven northern provinces adopted the Union of Utrecht, a covenantal political constitution, and established the United Netherlands in the north. In response, the southern Netherlands provinces adopted their covenant, the Union of Arras, separating them from their northern brethren. If the declaration of Dordrecht was the United Provinces' founding covenant, the Union of Utrecht was the constitution of the new confederation, one which remained in force until the fall of the Dutch republic in 1795. It was not yet a modern constitution. Hence, it was more like a treaty among the provinces and had the curious ambiguity of confederal constitutions, pointing at one and the same time toward a league of provinces and, on the other hand, toward some form of perpetual union. The articles of union provided that

> the aforesaid provinces will form an alliance, confederation, and union among themselves...in order to remain joined together for all time, in every form and manner, as if they constituted only a single province, and they may not hereafter divide or permit their division or separation by testament, codicils, donations, cessions, exchanges, sales, treaties of peace or marriage, or for any other reason whatsoever. Nevertheless each province and the individual cities, members, and inhabitants thereof shall retain undiminished its special and particular privileges, franchises, exemptions, rights, statutes, laudable and long-practiced customs, usages and all its rights.[8]

The partners of this union were *bondgenoten,* literally parties bound by covenant. Officeholders of the confederacy were bound by a common oath "to follow and maintain this union and confederation and each article therein."[9]

The problems of the confederation were what could have been expected in a highly noncentralized system. The states-general could not provide the policy direction, funds, or manpower for pursuing the war of independence, and each province and city tended to go its own way. In the meantime, the provinces in revolt became a haven for other persecuted members of the Reformed church. Huguenots in particular came north to participate in the conflict.

A year later Philip II declared William an outlaw. This led the States to renounce the sovereignty of Phillip in 1581 and elect the Prince of Orange as the head of their government. The basis for renouncing King Philip's sovereignty was that he had broken his covenants with his provinces and therefore had lost any legitimate right to rule them. This was spelled out in the Act of Abjuration. Implicit in it was the principle that ultimate sovereignty resided in the host state assemblies of the individual provinces. While not exactly a declaration of independence, it involved a transfer of sovereignty to a new "shepherd." The recitation of grievances against King Philip in justification of the abjuration can only be understood in the context of a covenantal politics. The Act closes with a statement of the terms of the new "contract and agreement" with the Duke of Anjou to replace the old agreement with King Philip, which contract reaffirms the power of the states-general and the provincial councils.[10]

Clearly, the idea of national independence was still too bold even for the rebels, and over the next decade they experimented with entrusting nominal sovereignty first to the French Duke of Anjou and then to the English Queen Elizabeth through the Earl of Leicester. Both turned out to be no better than the Spanish. Finally, in 1588 the Dutch provinces threw off all pretense to allegiance to any outside authority and became independent.

The war continued throughout the 1580s, but by 1588 the Dutch republic was clearly independent and on its way to becoming a major European power. Between 1588 and 1598 all the northern provinces were liberated from the Spanish and an advance southward began. Parma died in 1592, John von Oldenbarnevelt took over the political leadership of the United Provinces, and the military leadership passed to William's second son, Maurice of Nassau. (William had been assassinated at Spanish initiative in 1584.) France and England recognized the independence of the United Provinces and a truce with Spain, which involved de facto acknowledgement of the separation of the United Provinces, was reached in 1609 to effectively end over a generation of warfare in Dutch victory.

Unfortunately, the coming of peace in 1609 only exacerbated the religious conflict between the different wings of the Reformed church, even leading to the execution of John von Oldenbarnevelt on the grounds that he espoused doctrines that were not faithful to the Reformed faith. That act shocked the Dutch back to a more even keel in religious matters.

The final peace came through a treaty concluded at Munster on 30 January 1648 after two years of negotiation. The princes of Orange, Frederick Henry and his son and successor William II, opposed it because it confined them to the northern provinces when they still hoped to reclaim all of the Netherlands. The leadership of the extreme wing of the Reformed Church also opposed it because it was a pact with the Spanish papists. Even the province of Zeeland opposed it because through their West India Company they were profiting from a tax on Spanish and Portuguese territory in Latin America that would lose its legitimacy once there was peace. Nevertheless, the peace party led by the province of Holland prevailed.

The Heyday and Decline of the United Provinces

No sooner had peace been established when William II sought to expand his power through a new war. Opposed by Holland, which demanded a reduction in the size of the Dutch army, William tried to engineer a coup d'etat against the provincial government, including an assault on Amsterdam. His plans failed almost by accident, but the ability of the local and provincial citizens to defend themselves through their citizen militias prevented him from trying again. His sudden death from smallpox opened the way for Holland's vindication, to the point of preventing William's infant son from being named to his father's offices. Strengthened by a disastrous war against England that was concluded by terms of peace in which Oliver Cromwell demanded that the Dutch put an end to hereditary succession, the treaty lasted for seven years until the English restoration of Charles II and almost succeeded in fully republicanizing the United Provinces.

The argument against dynastic succession was essentially a "states' rights" argument based on the original and continuing right of the provinces to select their own *stadholders* from among the generality of the population. "Therefore all healthy republics...have always taken into consideration the nobility of houses and illustrious families, but have never given it as much weight as the nobility of the persons themselves who are to be called to the leadership of the republic."[11]

The restoration of the House of Orange was argued by the Lord States of Zeeland who declared "that the repose and peace of the low countries in general and individually can never be maintained without employing heads and lords of eminence in the leadership of the common cause." They argued "that these lands, considered in general and as part of the German nation from ancient times, not just during the past 800 years but for centuries before, have not had any other form of government than one which gave these heads power and authority which was sometimes greater and more absolute and sometimes lesser and more limited." What followed was not only a series of fateful political decisions, but a philosophical debate over republicanism of no little significance that emphasized the degree to which the Dutch as merchants should be committed to republicanism rather than monarchy, which emphasizes the military virtues.[12] Parts of that debate was translated into English and French and had some influence on eighteenth-century republicanism.

Perhaps the best description of the fully federal character of the United Provinces of the Netherlands in the seventeenth century was provided by Sir William Temple, the British Ambassador to The Hague, in his *Observations upon the United Provinces of the Netherlands* (1672):

> It is *evident* by what has been discoursed in the former chapter concerning the rise of this State, (which is to be dated from the Union of Utrecht) that it cannot properly be styled a commonwealth, but is rather a confederacy of Seven Sovereign Provinces, united together for their common and mutual defence, without any dependence one upon the other. But, to discover the nature of their government from the first springs and motions, it must be taken yet into smaller pieces, by which it will appear, that each of these Provinces is likewise composed of many little states or cities, which have several marks of sovereign power within themselves, and are not subject to the sovereignty of their Province; not being concluded in many things by the majority, but only by the universal concurrence of voices in the Provincial States. For as the States-General cannot make war or peace, or any new alliance, or levies of money, without the consent of every Province; so cannot the States-Provincial conclude any of those points, without the consent of each of the cities that by their constitution has a voice in that assembly. And though in many civil causes there lies an appeal from the common judicature of the cities to the provincial courts of justice; yet, in criminal, there lies none at all; nor can the sovereignty of a Province exercise any judicature, seize upon any offender, or pardon any offence within the jurisdiction of a city, or execute any common resolution or law, but by the justice and officers of the city itself. By this a certain sovereignty in each city is discerned, the chief marks whereof are, the power of exercising judicature, levying of money, and making war and peace; for the other, of coining money, is neither in particular cities or Provinces, but in the generality of the Union, by common agreement.[13]

The Dutch remained without a *stadholder* from 1650 to 1672 and then again after William III died without an heir in 1702 until 1747, when the Dutch debacle in the War of the Austrian Succession led to the restoration of the House of Orange under Prince William IV. As *stadholders* they played a limited role, but in the intervening years the several thousands of regents who governed in the town and provincial assemblies had become a self-perpetuating oligarchy, holding the power of the polity and controlling virtually all political power.

The seventeenth century was the heyday of the United Netherlands. During that century, it was the best example in the world of a functioning federal system. It became a great world power in which Reformed religion and political liberty went hand in hand within the limits of the time. The Dutch built a world empire but in the process overreached themselves, and after the Treaty of Utrecht of 1714 never recovered their power. In the eighteenth century not only did they recede on the world scene but their republic was slowly transformed into an oligarchy, with a hereditary *stadholder* after 1747. By the time the French invasion overthrew the old regime in 1795, few tears were shed for the old system.

By the time of the American Revolution, a democratic movement had developed and, although it lost to the conservatives in 1787, eight years later it came to power with the assistance of the French, but only at the expense of the abolition of the 200-year-old confederal regime. The Patriots, as the democratic party had come to be called, were much influenced by the American as well as the French Revolution. Some had even assisted the fledgling United States of America in its effort to borrow money in the Netherlands. Thus, the mantle of federal republicanism was almost literally passed from the Dutch to the Americans. Unfortunately the Dutch themselves, under the influence of French ideas and a reaction against the provincial oligarchies, rejected federal democracy on behalf of a Jacobin program, which was put into effect in 1795. Even after the fall of Napoleon, the restoration in the Netherlands left the Jacobin victory at least partially intact in the sense that the unitary state remained, albeit with constitutional provisions for decentralization.

Dutch independence brought with it the organization of the great trading companies that were to expand Dutch influence around the world and were to be among the pioneer institutions of modern capitalism. The first of these, the General Dutch-Chartered East India Company, better known as the United East India Company (VOC or Verendigde Oost-Indische Compagnie), was chartered by the states-general in 1602. The new company was a product of the necessity for the Dutch to find new ways to gain access to the new worlds once they ceased to have access as Spanish subjects. It was followed by the West Indies Company.

The terms under which the companies were organized and ships sent out were entirely contractual as constitutionalized by the original charter. The right to invest in the company was open to all the inhabitants of the country, who were to share proportionally in the profits as were the captain, officers, and crews of the ships that the company sent forth. To enable them to pursue their trading efforts the Dutch had to defend the principle of freedom of the seas, a task undertaken by Hugo Grotius, a man who had been strongly involved in the Reformed tradition to the extent of having been imprisoned during the Arminian controversy.

Grotius's argument was based upon the law of God and the law of nations, emphasizing that international trade was "this most praiseworthy bond of human fellowship" that provided "opportunities for doing mutual service." He argued that "surely no one nation may justly oppose in any way two nations that desire to enter into a contract with each other." While Grotius brings biblical examples and emphasizes that freedom of the seas is God's will, most of his examples are drawn from classical Greek and Roman literature, philosophy, and experience which strengthen the principles of the law of nations. As such he already is a transitional figure in a transitional time, already moving toward the secularization of covenant as compact and contract.[14]

The United Netherlands soon became a leader in world trade, and Dutch traders, in the manner of other covenantal peoples throughout history—the Jews and the Swiss in the past and New England Yankees in the future—got the reputation of being very shrewd and sharp, at the very least driving a hard bargain if not taking advantage through some kind of casuistic interpretation of the meaning of a negotiation.

In the last analysis, the Dutch were the first to break the tradition of exploiting the new worlds through state or imperial monopolies by introducing private initiative and enterprise. In this respect, there may have been a connection between covenantal religious beliefs and the rise of capitalism as suggested by Werner Sombart, R. H. Tawney, and Max Weber.[15] While the problems of the "religion and the rise of capitalism" theory have been explored in considerable depth to demonstrate that it rests at least in part on specious assumptions, it would be foolish not to recognize that it also contains elements of truth. There is little doubt that the notion that humans have a role to play as partners of God in developing the world's resources and that they should do so through pacts among equals had its carryover into the economic realm, at the very least to counteract the notion that all resources belong to monarchs by divine right and that the organization of their use should be accordingly hierarchical.

Beyond that, the moral ideology that God rewards the elect, a particular feature of Calvinism, no doubt had its influence as well in justifying the pursuit of economic success. It is, however, a mistake to overestimate the importance of economic success to those who shaped Reformed Protestantism who, when all was said and done, emphasized moral and theological goals first and foremost and political goals secondarily as necessary to the achievement of the true religion on this world. In that respect economic goals were present but were certainly in no more than third place.

The covenantal basis of Low-Country politics in both its prerevolutionary and revolutionary phases was widely reflected in the common political vocabulary of the times. Even under the Empire, the ceremony (dating back to the middle of the fourteenth century) whereby each new emperor swore the traditional oath to uphold local liberties, was referred to as *blijdeinkonnst* or joyous entry. The 1566 covenant among the nobles that initiated serious resistance to Philip II was known as a *compromise* or common oath. The phrases used in connection with prerevolutionary agreements with the imperial sovereign included "contract, league, and privilege" between the sovereign and subjects, and "the liberty and privileges of the country." After the revolution began, the terms shifted to confederation and alliance, confederates, or simply confederation to show that these were relations among equals. All of these were introduced by oath. The aim of these oaths were to establish communities and commonwealths. Many emphasized the Dutch equivalent of *hesed* to characterize relationships in the Netherlands.

The Dutch also distinguished between *bnai brit* and *baalei brit*. The Dutch term for the former, *bondgenoten*, is used in the Union of Utrecht and during the entire subsequent history of the Dutch republic to designate member provinces. Allies, on the other hand, are designated *geallieerden*. In international matters the phrase used was *traite y con-*

federation, treaty and confederation. In short, an appropriate language of covenant developed along with the application of covenantal principles in Dutch nation building.

Religion and Politics in the Netherlands

The republic of the United Provinces practiced, for its day, a relatively wide religious tolerance, which included admission of Jewish refugees fleeing persecution in Spain, Portugal, and elsewhere. The Pilgrim Fathers were given refuge in Leyden between 1609 and 1620. There were also close contacts between the English Puritans and the Dutch Calvinists and Federalists. William Ames had come to Holland in 1610 and served as a professor of theology at the University of Franeker from 1622 until his death in 1633. When necessary, English and Scottish Calvinists found refuge in the Dutch republics.

In contrast with its tolerant attitude toward non-Christians, the Dutch Calvinists maintained a restrictive policy or worse toward non-Calvinists. Catholics ("papists" in Reformed terminology) were considered a potential fifth column during the Dutch struggle for independence against Catholic Spain, not without reason. Socinians, who denied the doctrine of the trinity, and Lutherans were also opposed. Papism and Socinianism were to be repressed while the rights of worship of the Anabaptists were at the very least to be restricted. It was only the intervention of the Prince of Orange that kept the Calvinists on something of a leash.

Far worse in Calvinist eyes were such "heresies" as Arminianism, a more optimistic interpretation of Protestant Christianity that also had its roots in the Reformed tradition, but which rejected Calvinist orthodoxies. Arminianism, which rejected Calvinist predestination, was closer to Zwinglian doctrines. The Calvinists persecuted, expelled, and occasionally even executed Arminians in displays of religious zeal under state sponsorship. These persecutions were less a reflection of covenantal exclusivism than the general human penchant of ideologues who believe that they have the whole truth to persecute those whom they believe to be undermining that truth when they have the power to do so.

The intimate connection between federal theology and federal republicanism in the Netherlands was to have considerable influence on the emergence of federal political thought. Althusius was directly influenced by the Dutch experience with republican government. The Dutch

jurist and political philosopher Hugo Grotius drew upon federal republican principles for his work, while Baruch Spinoza, one of the Jews
living under the tolerant Dutch regime, linked ancient Jewish federal
republicanism with that of the contemporary Netherlands to become
one of the founders of modern political thought.[16] All three were intimately associated with the Dutch Calvinist and Federalist scholars.

Grotius, indeed, built his theory on the linkage of natural law and
covenant:

> Since it is conformable to natural law to observe contracts [stare pactis]...civil
> rights were derived from this source, mutual compact.

> For those who had joined any community or put themselves in subjection to any
> man or men, those either expressly promised or from the nature of the case must
> have been understood to promise tacitly, that they would conform to that which
> either the majority of the community or those to whom the power was assigned
> should determine.[17]

John Locke lived in exile in Holland between 1683 and 1689 and published his most important political work, *Two Treatises of Government,*
upon his return to England in 1689.

The Dutch Republic lasted until its defeat by the French in 1795. The
French made it a client state and reorganized its government, first along
the centralized lines of the French Revolutionary regimes, and then as a
centralized monarchy under Joseph Bonaparte in 1805. After the fall of
Napolean, the Netherlands became a decentralized unitary monarchy.
Later in the nineteenth century, there was a revival of covenant as an
explicit political force, primarily through Abraham Kuyper (1837–1920),
a Calvinist theologian turned statesman, who reorganized the Dutch
polity as a liberal parliamentary democracy structured along consociational lines.[18]

The Subsequent History of Dutch Covenantalism

The post-Napoleonic reorganization of the Netherlands and its church
included the concentration of ecclesiastical authority in the new central
government in a manner coincident with the centralistic trends of modern statism and very much in conflict with covenantal federalism and
power sharing. From 1815 onward there were struggles within the Church
until 1834, when those who rejected this new centralization seceded. As
a result of the struggle that followed, a substantial number of the seces-

sionists emigrated to the United States, principally between 1846 and 1850, settling in southwestern Michigan, Chicago, and central Iowa, then at the edge of the American agricultural frontier, where they laid the foundations for Reformed communities of the kind so characteristic of Reformed Protestantism elsewhere.[19]

The migration itself was clearly in the spirit of Abraham and the English separatists, Pilgrims and Puritans. In other words, it was a covenantal migration undertaken to live up to the terms of God's covenant and manifested in new communal congregational covenants in the New World. Grand Rapids, Michigan became the capital of Dutch American Calvinism, which remains centered around Lake Michigan. In time, Dutch Reformed communities spread westward to southwestern Minnesota, southeastern South Dakota, the Gallatin Valley in south central Montana, southern and central California, and Washington.

They developed a particularly Dutch combination of pietism and Reformed orthodoxy. Thus, they were and remained fundamentalist in their teachings, yet intellectual in their orientation, seeking an educated ministry and laity and concentrating their efforts on their separate school system from kindergarten through college. In the main politically conservative and ethnically separatist, for them their covenant is both a bond uniting the members of their community and a boundary separating their community from other Christian communities. In this they stand in sharp contrast with the outreach-oriented Christian denominations in the United States such as Methodism. At the same time their pietism has led their theologians and church historians to distance themselves from Puritanism, which to their mind has placed too much emphasis on human covenants with one another.

From the Hebrew prophets these Dutch Calvinists have taken the idea of the righteous remnant and have emphasized it to explain their survival in America theologically. In this search for survival they have emphasized the role of the family, both from a covenantal perspective and because it is reflective of an ethnic minority condition. In another dimension of their covenantalism, rather than emphasizing baptism, they have emphasized the Lord's Supper as a sealing covenant from the nuclear family to the larger "household of faith," going back to the tradition of the covenantal meal as a critical element in covenanting and covenant renewal.

Meanwhile, back in the Netherlands, many of these same themes were played out among those faithful Calvinists who stayed home. After mid-century they found a leader in Abraham Kuyper, who became the foremost religious and political figure in the nineteenth-century Netherlands. Kuyper recognized the changed situation of his country and the necessity to come to grips with modern post-revolutionary pluralism. At the same time he sought ways to preserve the Reformed community within this new order.

In a brilliant political invention, Kuyper introduced what Arend Lijphart later labelled consociational government into the Dutch polity.[20] Dutch civil society was recognized as being organized around three pillars; in his time Reformed, Catholic, and Liberal (later Socialist), each of which maintained a complete range of social and communal as well as religious institutions. The institutions of government were to be shared among all three by democratically determining their respective shares of political strength in the country as a whole and on that basis their leaders would negotiate a fair share of governmental power. Under this arrangement the state supported the basic institutions for each pillar. In the twentieth century, this included support for separate radio and television networks.

Every Dutch citizen had to find his or her place in one of the pillars in order to participate in social and political life and to gain the full benefits of citizenship. The result was an important extension of covenantalism in the form of a nonterritorial federation whose sole territorial manifestations were in those local and occasionally provincial arenas where there was sufficient homogeneity so that one pillar dominated the territorial institutions of the polity.

Kuyper became prime minister of the Netherlands and held office for a generation. Within the Reformed pillar, he emphasized the role of the family and indeed made the principle of household suffrage basic to the country as a whole. In his theology he emphasized that Christians were bound by the Noahide covenant, reviving its principles as important elements in Calvinism.

The consociational system that Kuyper devised remained the form of the Dutch regime for two generations, from the 1880s to the 1960s, that is to say, from the middle of the last generation of the nineteenth century to the middle of the second generation of the twentieth. It only became unraveled as a result of the events of the 1960s, which broke down the social order that tied people to their respective socioreligious or socioideological communities.

The history of the United Netherlands strengthens the thesis presented earlier in this volume. The lowlanders were a borderlands people going back to time immemorial, with Frisians, Zeelanders, and Hollanders especially being products of ethnic, cultural, and geophysical borderlands as fragments of earlier ethnic groups that had fled their conquerors until they reached the edges of Europe, where they were in constant conflict with the sea. That conflict also made them frontiersmen of a sort, having to reclaim land from the sea in order to survive. The region was a political borderlands in Roman times and, with the coming of the Reformation, a religious borderlands dividing Protestants and Catholics. At the right historical moment these factors came together to produce a felicitous synthesis of covenantal ideas, culture, and behavior that has left its enduring mark on Western civilization.

Notes

1. James Skillen, "From Covenant of Grace to Tolerant Public Pluralism: The Dutch Calvinist Contribution," and James W. Skillen and Stanley W. Carlson-Thies, "Religion and Political Development in Nineteenth-Century Holland," *Publius* 12, no. 3 (Summer 1982).
2. See Paul Rosenfeld, "The Provincial Governors of the Netherlands and the Minority of Charles V to the Revolt." In Henry J. Cohen, ed., *Government in Reformation Europe, 1520–1560* (New York: Harper and Row, 1971), 257-64.
3. Herbert H. Rowen, ed., *The Low Countries in Early Modern Times: A Documentary History* (New York: Harper and Row, 1972), 21-25.
4. Ibid., 31-33.
5. Ibid., 38.
6. Ibid., 44.
7. Ibid., 48.
8. Ibid., 70.
9. Ibid., 74.
10. See Act of Abjuration, Rowen, ed., *The Low Countries in Early Modern Times,* 92-105.
11. Ibid., 196.
12. Cf. Pieter de la Court, *The True Interests and Political Memoirs of the Republic of Holland and West Friesland* (London: n.p., 1702).
13. Rowen, ed., *The Low Countries in Early Modern Times,* 214-15.
14. Hugo Grotius, *De Jure Belli et Pacis,* 1625, trans. Louise R. Loomis, *The Law of War and Peace* (New York: W. J. Black, 1949.)
15. See Werner Sombart, *The Jews and Modern Capitalism* (Glencoe: The Free Press, 1951), and *Der Moderne Kapitalismus* (Muenchen: Duncker and Humblot, 1928); R. H. Tawney, *Religion and the Rise of Capitalism* (Harmondsworth: Penguin, 1966); Max Weber, *The Protestant Ethic and the Spirit of Capitalism,* trans. Talcott Parsons with a foreword by R. H. Tawney (New York: Charles Scribner's Sons, 1958).

16. Benedict Spinoza, *Political-Theological Tractate* in *Writings on Political Philosophy*, trans. R. H. Elwes (New York: Appleton-Century-Crofts, 1937).
17. Grotius, *De Jure Belli et Pacis, Proleg.*, para. 15.
18. On Kuyper, see Skillen, "From Covenant of Grace to Tolerant Public Pluralism," and Skillen and Carlson-Thies, "Religion and Political Development in Nineteenth-Century Holland." Cf. also "Abraham Kuyper and the Rise of Neo-Calvinism in the Netherlands." In *American Society of Church History* XVII (1948).
19. Robert P. Swerenga, s.v. "Dutch." In *Harvard Encyclopedia of American Ethnic Groups*, 284–95.
20. Arend Lijphart, "Consociational Democracy," *World Politics* 21 (1968–69): 205–25.

Part IV

Puritans and Covenanters

12

English Puritanism

The third great intellectual-social movement of the Reformation federalists, after Zwingli and Bullinger in Zurich and Calvin in Geneva, was English Puritanism. In certain respects, it was the greatest of the three, particularly in its political thought and the political ideas and movements to which it gave birth, of which covenant was a central teaching. Reaching its apotheosis four generations after the beginning of the Reformation, English Puritanism had an opportunity to bring together all of the threads of thought and action of the previous century at the edge of the modern epoch. It was, on one hand, the last great sociopolitical movement of its own late medieval epoch and also the cornerstone of much of modern political thought, developing at the crossroads of premodern aristocratic republicanism and modern federal democracy. It began toward the middle of the sixteenth century, reached its peak in the middle of the seventeenth century, and receded after the Glorious Revolution.

Covenant in the English political tradition is derived from two sources. The first, which was explored in chapter 7, derives from the medieval and premedieval English experience that combined Celtic and Briton origins with selected Christian influences, as synthesized in such early expressions of English culture as *Beowulf* and the works of Bede.

Perhaps the greatest impetus to the spread of the covenant idea among the Puritans was the translation of the Bible into English. In every translation, beginning with Tindale's first translation in 1532, the Hebrew term *brit* and the Greek term *diatheke,* with all the numerous variations of each, were translated as "covenant." Moreover, particularly in the Tindale and Geneva Bibles (1560), where the word "covenant" was not used directly, terms with clear and unambiguous covenantal implications were used in the translation that was most appropriate and in the spirit of the Hebrew original. Thus, the idea of covenant was given original standing as the word of God. Perhaps the major change introduced by the Reformed Protestants, especially the Puritans, was to move the primary covenant of concern back from Abraham to Adam, thereby universalizing it with Adam as the "federal head of the human race," a favorite phrase of the times.[1] William Ames referred to this covenant with Adam, which was considered a covenant of works, as "God's special constitution for...mankind...His providential plan for creation."[2]

In the end, however, the Puritans relied more heavily on the covenant of grace, the New Testament addition to Christian covenant theology. After Adam's fall, according to their view, it required faith in Christ for humans to be redeemed. They even projected the covenant of grace back into what they referred to as the Old Testament, which focused on the elect nation of Israel rather than the elect members of the church. As the Westminister Confession of 1647 put it: "There are not two covenants of grace differing in substance but one and the same other various dispensations." Of course, the reliance on the graciousness of Jesus has the potentiality of eliminating much of the mutuality of covenant, which is the truly covenantal dimension. Several Puritan writers saw the covenant of grace as also achieved through bargaining between God and his elect. As one Puritan preacher stated in 1641, "the word covenant in our English tongue signifies a mutual promise, bargain, and obligation between two parties."[3]

The same Puritan divine used, to justify this, a statement that this bargaining nature was true of all covenants both divine and strictly human. While almost all agreed that God, not man, initiated the covenant of grace, the process of its adoption was the result of a bargain between God and man in which human will played a significant role. This was the view of such English Puritans as William Perkins, William Ames, Richard Sibbes, John Norton, John Preston, and Thomas Gataker, and their New England counterparts, Increase and Cotton Mather and Thomas Sheppard, among others.[4]

These were further peppered by medieval Jewish contributions to emerging English commercial law. It is from these sources that such terms as "writ of covenant" entered English law and legal practice[5] and the concept of "star" from the Hebrew *shtar* entered English contract law. Much of this dimension is hidden in the mists of time. More of it can be recovered than we have thus far if the effort is made.

The Essence of Puritan Covenantalism

The essence of Puritan covenantalism was individual moral reformation more than institutional restructuring, with the latter necessary in their eyes only insofar as it was the key to the former. As Collinson said, "For most church Puritans, the Presbyterian polity, or any other scheme for the extensive reparation of the church's structure, institutions and ministry, became a remote and irrelevant idea. By 'reformation' they tended to mean the pursuit of a piety or a moral order with a Puritan type, not the establishment of the external forms and symbols of a reformed church."[6]

This ultimately led the Puritans in two directions: (1) to reconstitution of local congregations from an episcopal to a congregational polity; and (2) to become a national movement for political revolution in the name of Reformation against the English monarchy for lack of an alternative. After great initial success, however, they were unable to solve the problems of self-government under a nonmonarchic regime and, hence, Puritanism collapsed entirely, leaving a legacy of the spirit but not a Puritan polity.

When push comes to shove, the English, like other peoples, do not want to be reformed in a Puritan or other manner that requires them to abstain from their normal pleasures or even the mild perversion of those pleasures. Thus, theo-political covenants in the end either make their mark by encouraging certain "habits of the heart," including certain approaches and attitudes toward political organization and political life, or they fail.

For historians and for our inquiry, the history of the transformation of Puritanism (between the late sixteenth and the mid-seventeenth century) from a movement of strictly moral reformation to one with political goals is at the heart of the story of English Puritanism. While that transformation took a somewhat different, in certain ways even reverse, course from the Israelite experience, there are real resemblances that can teach us about the problem of covenantal politics. In ancient Israel, the original moral reform movement established by Moses was established in a republican polity. As the Israelites also asserted their demands for common pleasures and misbehavior, a second reform movement gave its support to the establishment of kingship, perceived to be needed for external security purposes in any case. Thus, the Davidic monarchy received the support of the prophets as well as statesmen while republicanism was relegated to the ash heap as morally inferior, a regime in which "every man did what was right in his eyes."

In the end kingship did no better because kings and their families are as prone to normal human failings as ordinary people. Six hundred years later what became the system of normative or rabbinic Judaism, designed to give the desired habits of the heart the force of God's commandments, began to emerge in all its detail and did indeed have somewhat greater success, in part because of the circumstances of the destruction of the Jewish state with its Temple and the resultant exile, at least among those people who remained the avant garde of the Jewish people, not that there was not much reassertion of the drive for ordinary pleasures and misdemeanors throughout the ages.

In England it was just the reverse. Since the Puritan reform movement developed in an already existing monarchy, Puritan covenantalism sought political remedies in republicanism on the grounds widely shared by Reformed Christians throughout the Reformation period that it was monarchy that reinforced misbehavior. But in the end they had no better luck than the Israelites, except that the popular pursuit of ordinary pleasures reasserted itself sooner under a weak republican regime and led to the restoration of the status quo ante except insofar as leading forces in the regime (or, at least, major contending ones) had internalized Puritan habits of the heart, including covenantalism and republicanism.

In order to do this the Puritans had to invest themselves massively in political action. Their effort to detach their Reformation from politics without its being accompanied by a system of religious law such as that developed in time by the Jews simply did not succeed beyond a very narrow circle. Before the Civil War, they did try to influence the Elizabethan monarchy by many references to the old Israelite kings, especially those that attempted to introduce reform through covenants.[7]

What followed in the seventeenth century was the use of covenants to achieve moral reform on an extensive basis, for a limited number of people only, distinguishing between the "Ishmaelites" or unreformable people and the "genuine children of Abraham."[8] This, in turn, led to the reemergence of a political Puritanism and covenantalism that led to the English civil war.

As William Perkins put it, "God's couenant [sic] is his contract with man, concerning the obtaining of life eternall, upon certen condition.

This couenant consists of two parts: God's promise to man, man's promise to God."[9]

Shakespeare fully embraces the Puritan idea of covenant for Puritans combining the ideas of covenant and commission, as did John Winthrop later in giving an ideological and constitutional direction to the Puritans emigrating to New England. The biblical prophets also used marriage as a model for covenantal relationships (Hosea and Malachi particularly), but Shakespeare continues to contrast the covenantal bonds of marriage with the new contractual bonds that are emerging in economic relationships. A number of commentators including Fisch have pointed out this theme in Shakespeare. Together, Shakespeare seems to be saying, we have a covenant of grace that can protect us from the problematics of the new covenant of works. Shakespeare was not a Puritan, but he was not unsympathetic to Puritanism even as he was repelled by the hypocrisies of individual Puritans. As usual, he gets to the heart of the matter and offers us a larger understanding of Puritan covenantalism and its social and political implications, which not only is worth bearing in mind, but is worth exploring for an understanding of how covenantalism became part of the modern project and, as Shakespeare suggests, not only in England.

Puritanism moved from an almost purely theological and church-oriented doctrine to a theo-political one partly as a result of Puritan experiences in sixteenth-century England and partly as a natural consequence of its covenantal basis. Three political positions emerged, each with its doctrine of church government and the relationship between church and state: independency, Presbyterianism, and Erastianism. Advocates of independency sought to reform the Church of England congregation by congregation and to retain church governance on a congregational basis within the framework of (hopefully) an increasingly light-handed established national church. Advocates of Presbyterianism sought to establish structured Presbyterian church government throughout England parallel to the state and with enough state-granted independence to handle church matters through the presbyteries and synods as well as the congregations that would be so established. The Erastians saw the proper political order as one that involved a union of church and state, whereby church governance would be vested in the institutions of the state, which would thereby have to be transferred to Puritan hands. In addition there was a more radical wing of separatists who sought to separate church and state and give each congregation a completely separate standing.

With the exception of the radical separatists, what distinguished the three main camps on matters of relationships between church and state was whether the state was simply harnessed to support one or another form of church governance or actually took on itself the structuring and maintenance of churches. In any case, the state was to prevent or repress heresy and protect true religion by virtue of its physical and political powers. In many respects the struggle came down to the degree of independence and political power of the Puritan ministers. This has not been uncommon in human history when a new group seeking power has built a case on the disenfranchisement of the people they represent or speak for rather than making their claims directly. Nor is it unusual for clergy to take that position at different times and in different places.

A cynic can easily describe all the great religious reformations as efforts on the part of leading individuals to use religious belief and its claims to advance their own power positions. While it would be a mistake to view human behavior, even of this kind, as motivated by other than a mixture of principles, interests, and sensibilities, in all the myriad studies that have been done of the Protestant Reformation in its various forms, we have found no justification for any such cynical claim, even if we understand the difference between manifest and latent consequences or even more mixed motives. The leaders of the Reformation were sincere believers, highly motivated by their beliefs.

At the same time there was an irony in what flowed from this whole complex. As an increasing number of ministers presented ever greater variations of Puritan belief, a natural development in a free church in which doctrinal matters were so important, the church leadership developed more confidence in the magistrates to retain some kind of discipline and perhaps orthodoxy than in the ministry. While the ministers, whatever their ideas, had a greater stake in doctrinal correctness than in order, the magistrates were of a reverse mind. Order was for them the most essential, and to maintain it, compromises could be made on everything else. Too much emphasis on order at the expense of doctrine could alienate the Puritan ministers, but up to that point the magistrates could be relied upon to keep society going and in line.

Perhaps in recognition of Puritan doctrine's grant of very extensive powers to ministers, many Puritan divines also developed the theory that ministers were to "administer righteousness" and not interfere with civil power. Their explanation of this was that the ministers of the Reformed church should not be like the pope, who interfered regularly under the principles of church and state alike, even though some Puritans accepted a version of the "two swords" doctrine (although most looked to the experience of ancient Israel for their political doctrines, which involved much closer connections among the religious and civil authorities but subordinated the civil authorities to God more fully). They did so by calling for a much sharper separation between the two.

In the end, the independents supported the authority of the magistrates over the churches and sufficient magisterial power to make that authority meaningful. They had no other way to insure sufficient uniformity in the polity. In this, the difference between them and the Erastians came down more to one of degree and justification than substance. Only the Presbyterians tried to suggest a different path, one which not only would remove authority from the magistrates and give it to the covenanted national church but would provide the latter with the power necessary to make that authority work.

The fact is that after the middle of the seventeenth century, when the steam ran out of both English Puritanism and Scottish Presbyterianism in their pure Reformed formulation, none of the three approaches really preserved the idea of a kingdom of the saints. The problem was not so much with the kingdom as it was with the saints. Too much sainthood was expected for the ordinary people to accept and they preferred the old kingdom whose human corruptions surpassed its lip service to piety as more productive of both order and ordinary liberty. The triumph of the saints in both Scotland and England was brief, but the standards that they set continued long after the polities and political arrangements for which they strived had disappeared. Ultimately, those standards brought down kings as well as saints.

The Marrow of Puritan Divinity

The Puritans' efforts to purify the English Church led in a Reformed direction, with a strong federalist rather than Calvinist orientation. Like the Huguenots and Covenanters, the Puritans quickly applied the idea of covenant to politics as well as theology and developed republican conceptions of the polity in their battles against Anglican episcopacy and royal absolutism.[10] Their success came a century (or three generations) after their emergence as a movement and, while temporary from the perspective of government power, it changed the face of the Western world.

Unlike the Scottish covenanters, whose political culture was already attuned to pact-based political organization and behavior, the Puritans had to struggle within and against a society that prided itself in its organic evolution as a polity and whose current rulers sought to impose a hierarchic structure on that organic polity as the next stage in its development. Even in their triumph, the Puritans remained a minority in England, able to gain allies because of the rash efforts of the Stuart kings to impose their power pyramid on England's organic civil society, but never able to win over a majority of Englishmen to the covenantal approach, which involved more formal acts of constitution, more equality, and more leveling than the English sociopolitical order could absorb. Indeed, some of the Puritans realized this even before the Civil War and drew the appropriate conclusion that only in an entirely new world could they build their "city upon a hill" based on their federal theology and politics. They emigrated to North America to do so.

The matter was further complicated by the peculiar character of England's Reformation, instituted as it was by King Henry VIII for personal reasons. King Henry capitalized on a general climate to achieve a personal goal. Hence, the Church he erected, while anti-Roman Catholic, was not Protestant either, and so it remains to this day. The task of the Puritans then was to purify an already nominally reformed Church as a minority from within. Their work was to be spiritual, but they soon discovered that to be spiritual they had to be political. They had to actually seize control of the commonwealth—through its designated leaders if possible, against them, if necessary.

Because of their inability to appeal to deeply held indigenous traditions, the Puritan leaders had to develop a substantial body of thought through which they would try to persuade their compatriots. That body of thought was of the highest intellectual quality. Not only does it stand as a monument to English Puritanism, but it was seminal in its impact on the modern epoch through its ideas.

Despite their ultimate failure as a movement, the Puritans had a profound and lasting impact on the constitutional tradition in England, on the "new political science" of the political compact, and on the constitutional development of the United States. Eventually, through migrations and the influence of the British Empire, elements of the covenantal-federal tradition were also institutionalized in varying ways in Canada, Australia, New Zealand, India, Nigeria, and South Africa as well as the British Commonwealth system as a whole, which involved, among other things, a gradual covenantalization of what began as conquest relationships.

William Haller puts it well:

> The result was not reformation but the emergence of an articulate vernacular public, free from many of the inhibitions and impediments of customary attitudes and sanctions. This insurgency, giving unforeseen application and force to the doctrine of calling and covenant, made possible the seizure of initiative in the state first by parliament and then by the army. The theory of the social contract might be of dubious validity as law or history, but its acceptance by the public which came forward in the Puritan Revolution pointed to the inescapable condition of all government in the age to come. Kings and magistrates would henceforth in fact be compelled to exercise their authority under the constant impact of complaint and criticism by all who could command the means to evoke and direct the opinions and passions of men for their own purposes, means which could only with difficulty be denied to anybody.[11]

If government with the consent of the governed within a constitutional system is a primary feature and achievement of the modern epoch, the English Puritans and their covenantal/federal ideas were a major force introducing those principles into the modern world.

John Witte, Jr. describes the Puritan achievement as "the transformation of the idea of covenant from a subsidiary biblical theme to an organizing principle."[12] While Witte's suggestion that this subsidiary biblical theme relates to the New Testament rather than the Old is faulty, his general point has merit. The Puritan transformation of the universe into a network of covenants was a powerful explanatory motivating idea. It is one of those moments of truth in human history that transform human affairs. Covenant was what Perry Miller referred to as "the marrow of Puritan divinity," *marrow* being a seventeenth-century term meaning core or essence, combining the meanings of core, essence, summary, and distillation.[13]

The Puritan premise was stated by William Perkins in a 1624 sermon: "We are by nature covenant creatures, bound together by covenants innumerable and together bound by covenant to our God. Such is our human condition. Such is this earthly life. Such is God's good creation. Blessed be the ties that bind us."[14]

Back to the Bible

Puritan covenantalism was a "back to the Bible" movement in the best sense, fostered by the publication of great English translations of the Bible. Beginning in the sixteenth century, the early English translations of Tyndale (1532), Coverdale (1535), Matthew (1537), the Great Bible (1539), and the Geneva Bible (1560) translated *brit* and *diatheke*, the Hebrew and Greek terms respectively, and their numerous derivations and variations, as covenant. Beyond that, the translations were annotated to increase comprehension, particularly in the case of the Tyndale and Geneva Bibles. Many of those annotations interpret those Scriptural passages in covenantal terms, even where the word itself does not appear.[15] Thus Scripture, particularly the Old Testament, set out an accurate path for those who became Puritans, indeed for all English readers of the Bible.

The earliest origins of Puritan federalism can be found in the works of such reformers as William Tyndale (1494–1536), John Bale (1495–1563), John Hooper (1497?–1555), John Frith (1503–33), and John Bradford (1510?–55).[16] The work of Tyndale is especially important. Tyndale's influence was first felt through his novel translation of the New Testament (1525), which seemed to undermine the authority and position of the church by, for example, translating *ekklesia* as "congregation" rather than church and *presbyteros* as "senior" and, later, "elder." Tyndale's early theology was informed by a strong Lutheran perspective with its emphasis on the Gospel; but by the 1530s, his work increasingly focused on the Reformed ideas of law and covenant.

Tyndale came to regard all of God's promises as being conditional and, thereby, began to employ covenant as a means for stressing the moral obligations of humans to obey God's ordinances. "The general covenant," wrote Tyndale, "wherein all others are comprehended and included is this: If we meek ourselves to God, to keep all his laws, after the example of Christ, then God hath bound himself unto us, to keep and make good all the mercies promised in Christ throughout all the scripture."[17] Since men and women must know God's law in order to obey it, they must have free access to the Bible, translated into their own tongues, and the Word of God must be preached throughout the realm. Tyndale championed the idea of the priesthood of all believers and held the faithful to be a community of "brethren" in Christ. To this end, Tyndale's translation of the New

Testament was very influential, and thousands of copies were smuggled into England from Holland and Germany.

Politically, however, Tyndale remained more traditional. In his *Obedience of a Christian Man* (1528), he wrote: "He that judgeth the King, judgeth God and damneth God's law and ordinance." In this world, he continued in a manner later echoed by Hobbes, the King is "without law; and may at his lust do right or wrong, and shall give accounts to God alone." On the other hand, he did not hesitate to criticize and admonish the king for not pressing matters of reformation much farther in England. Although Tyndale's political ideas were not as radical as his religious ideas, later Puritans radicalized both as they turned away from royal absolutism.

Tyndale did, however, help to set in motion a number of currents that became important in later Puritan political conceptions. The idea of congregationalism eventually had a leveling effect on hierarchic conceptions of civil society. Tyndale also developed close ties with certain merchant groups interested in civil as well as religious reformation, some of whom helped to import and distribute books written by English and other Protestants on the Continent. Many merchants, small businessmen, and new, middle-class elements became linked with the Puritan movement and played central roles in democratizing English civil society.

Tyndale's emphasis on scriptural rather than ecclesiastical law and on popular rather than priestly interpretation became a basis for construing the Bible as a kind of higher law constitution and, in turn, for the idea of human constitutionalism. While Protestants are frequently criticized for seeming to buttress their religious and political positions through hairsplitting interpretations of Scripture, this enterprise is essentially no different from that of secular constitutional interpretation. If Protestant interpretations can be circumlocutious, they are often matched by those of the judges and justices who interpret the modern civil constitutions.

The Public Edifice of Reformation

On the political front, matters also shifted in the direction of covenantalism. As it turned out, the concept of covenant provided the basis for a relatively smooth doctrinal transition from feudalism to modern theories of political compact within England, leading to the foundation in the sixteenth and seventeenth centuries of English republican-ism within a context that continued the form of the realm's traditional institutions, but transformed their content.

Since the proximate cause of the English Reformation was to be found in King Henry's personal difficulties, it fell to his chief minister, Tho-mas Cromwell, to undertake the task of constructing the public edifice of Reformation, and it was Parliament that was called upon to enact the appropriate legislation, which it did through a chain of acts. One of the major statutes in this chain, the Act in Restraint of Appeals (24 Henry VIII Cap. 12) enacted in 1532 to define the relationship between church and state, presented a secular definition of the English polity that linked the feudal elements of medieval England with what was to come under the Puritans. It stated that "the realm is a body politick compact of all sorts of degrees of people divided in terms and by names of Spirituality and Temporality." In short, England under Henry VIII saw itself as a compound polity. While still more feudal than covenantal in origins, the connection was there.[18]

The brief restoration of Catholicism under Queen Mary, Henry's suc-cessor, which led to the exile of England's leading Protestant theolo-gians, ended up strengthening the most active anti-Catholic elements in English Protestantism. Fleeing from Mary, most found refuge in Swit-zerland and the Rhineland cities that had come under the Swiss Re-formed tradition. During their five years of exile they absorbed the new doctrines at their source and came back committed to Calvinistic theol-ogy and Presbyterian church organization.

With the return of the Marian exiles in 1559 and publication of the Geneva or "Breeches" Bible in 1560, covenant became firmly and dis-tinctively embedded in English Puritanism (which term came into use at about that time). The Geneva Bible, which proved to be popular and influential, used the word *covenant* more often than earlier English Bibles and included a Calvinistic covenant commentary written by its transla-tors, who included William Whittingham and Anthony Gilby. This emerg-ing covenant orientation of non-Anglican Protestants was reinforced during the reign of Edward VI when a number of continental theolo-gians came to England and disseminated the covenant ideas associated with Reformed Protestantism.

During the reign of Elizabeth (1559–1603), the Puritans intensified their reform efforts against Anglican uniformity. Their struggle was at least in part against the Elizabethan settlement, which retained papist ceremonies and episcopal rule, both Catholic dimensions of the Anglican Church. While nearly all remained loyal to both the crown and the idea of religious uniformity and sought to work their reforms through Parliament, a number urged separation and began to organize independent congregations and governing bodies. A more formalized system of federal theology began to be constructed around the covenant idea by such theologians as Dudley Fenner (1558-87) and William Perkins (1558-1602), Lecturer at Great St. Andrews. Theologian Richard Hooker (1554?-1600) has remained the most famous of those Elizabethan divines who introduced covenantal ideas into the political realm. In his "Of the Law of the Ecclesiastical Polity," he summarizes his position:

> Two foundations there are which bear up public societies: the one, a natural inclination whereby all men desire sociable life and fellowship; the other, an order expressly or secretly agreed upon touching the manner of their union in living together.... To take away all such mutual grievances, injuries and wrongs [sc. as prevailed when there were no civil societies], there was no way but only by growing into composition and agreement amongst themselves, by ordaining some kind of government public, and by yielding themselves subject thereunto; that unto whom they granted authority to rule and govern, by them the peace, tranquility and happy estate of the rest might be procured.[19]

Hooker remained committed to the established church, hence he remained acceptable to Anglican Tories throughout the period of the Puritan revolution. Hence, John Locke, a century later, found it advantageous to formally base his political thinking upon Hooker's work to gain authority for those ideas.

Puritan ideas of covenant and contract also began to appear in English literature, including the works of Shakespeare [(1564-1616); see, in particular, *Measure for Measure*] and later, of course, John Milton (1608-74).[20] Shakespeare's treatment of Puritans and Puritanism was critical, to say the least, in the sense that he understood where their doctrinal dogmatism took them. In essence, he accused them of not being willing to come to grips with the realities of human nature. Nevertheless, he absorbed much of the political essence of their covenantalism, even if he rejected its harsher religious elements. Milton, on the other hand, was himself moved by the Puritan vision. He sought to build a religiously grounded theory of political liberty on covenantal ideas drawn from Puritan thought.

Milton put it in this manner:

No man who knows aught can be so stupid to deny that all men naturally were born free, being the image and resemblance of God himself, and were, by privilege about all creatures, born to command and not to obey; and that they lived so, till from the root of Adam's transgression falling among themselves to do wrong and violence, and foreseeing that such courses must needs tend to the destruction of them all, they agreed by common league to bind each other from mutual injury and jointly to defend themselves against any that gave disturbance or opposition to such agreement.... The power of kings and magistrates is only derivative, transferred and committed to them in trust from the people to the common good of them all, to whom the power yet remains fundamentally, and cannot be taken from them without a violation of their natural birthright.[21]

Puritanism spread among the people as well as among the intellectuals. Puritans gathered strength in every diocese and once Archbishop Grindel refused to suppress their prophesyings, as they termed their religious conferences that had become the chief means for disseminating Puritan ideas, they achieved a kind of recognition. While Grindel's successor, Whitgift, did try to suppress these gatherings, he also devised the nine Lambeth Articles (1595), which emphasized the five points of Calvinist doctrine.

Despite tensions through much of the sixteenth century, it seemed as if Puritan ideas of religious reform could be absorbed by the political establishment in that both sides would find common ground. Indeed, the biggest barrier to doing so was to be found among elements of the Anglican hierarchy, but they were subject to royal manipulation. With the beginning of the seventeenth century, however, the situation changed radically, leading to a sharp confrontation between the Puritans and the Stuart kings.

Throughout the sixteenth century it was the continental Reformed theorists who elaborated on a political theory of covenant, with some overlap into Scotland. Only one English Puritan of note, Dudley Fenner, made an attempt to develop a systematic covenantal political theory. He wrote his tract on the continent in Latin, and it was never translated into English or even printed in England. Only in the seventeenth century did leadership in covenantal political theory pass to the English Puritans. Once again this illustrates the extent to which covenantal political theory, like all other, is a response to political necessity, which did not arise in England until the efforts of James I and Charles I to impose absolutism on the kingdom.[22]

It was only after the English Puritan divines developed the idea of a covenant of works, which they identified with the Ten Commandments, that they could distinguish the chosen from the merely called (as Michael McGiffert put it), and formed the former into "a covenanted constituency and rallied them into a party, especially graced and obligated" to unblock the process of reform that had been blocked at the top by the end of the sixteenth century.

The book that launched the process was written by a pastor in Suffolk, Nicholas Bownde, who called for the strict observance of the Sabbath under the terms of the Fourth Commandment. Thus, it was sabbaterianism that launched political covenantalism in England.[23]

James I (1603–25) coldly rejected the Puritans' Millenary Petition of 1603. As king of Scotland, James had learned Presbyterianism from the inside, enough to understand that it threatened his absolute rule as king. Nevertheless, Calvinism was so strong within the Anglican Church that he himself had to send representatives to the Synod of Dort. Still, separatist sentiment became more widespread.

During this period, the basic ideas of congregationalism and political compact came to the fore hand in hand as Puritans turned away from the crown and toward Parliament as an instrument of reform. William Ames (1576–1633) encouraged the formation of independent local churches within the established Church of England; others urged complete separation. Ames wrote that a church is formed by believers "joining together by covenant" and that "the same believing men may join themselves in covenant to make a city or some civil society when their immediate concern is for the common civil good." In 1613, Henry Jacob described the church as "a Spiritual Body Politike" and held that the people have the "power of free consent in their ordinary government" as well. In *A Confession and Protestation of Faith* (1616), Jacob argued that a church is created "by a free mutuall consent of Believers joyning and covenanting to live as members of a holy Society together in all religious and vertuous duties as Christ and his Apostles did institute and practise in the Gospell. By such free mutuall consent also all Civill perfect Corporations did first beginne."[24]

Thus, like the Huguenots, the Puritans began to read covenant back into history, sometimes as an historical reality, and sometimes as a theoretical construct for explaining the proper origins of civil society much like Hobbes, Locke, and Rousseau were to do. Some of the most radical

Separatists placed virtually every aspect of life on a covenantal basis. All congregations and civil systems had to be founded upon mutual agreement and all doctrinal teachings, forms of worship, and civil laws had to be instituted by the consent of the majority, which was free to change its mind at any time. The agreements of one generation could not bind another generation, and continual revolutions could be introduced into church and society.[25]

The Four Covenants

The English Puritans, like the other great Reformation-generated covenanted communities, followed the example of ancient Israel in seeking to anchor their polity in a national covenant. For them, a complete covenantal framework involved building a covenanted community resting on four basic covenants—national, political, ecclesiastical, and marital. The first was the most comprehensive, the one that established the people in question as a nation in partnership with God. Institutionally, the national covenant was to be made operative through government, church, and family. National covenants were covenants of the people before God, with God as witness and guarantor.

The political covenant was an agreement between governors and governed before God to establish a civil authority to represent God's majesty in this world and to apply God's will and law. The task of the governors was to lead the people by example in the fulfillment of their tasks under the terms of the national covenant. Responsible for implementing God's justice, the civil ruler was also to exercise mercy as appropriate. Reflecting God's discipline, he also was to reflect God's benevolence. The civil governors were responsible for promoting virtue and preventing vice. In their role as protectors of Christian norms, they were to fight against both immorality and heresy.

Increasingly, the people were deemed responsible for choosing their rulers. Indeed, in covenantal systems the ultimate sovereignty of God and the proximate sovereignty of the people seemed to go hand in hand. Whatever the extensive powers of civil rulers to lead the people along the right paths, the people had similar powers vis-à-vis the civil rulers. In England, Parliament was formally elected, albeit through a system of virtual representation and extremely limited suffrage, but Reformed Protestants as a group believed that civil rulers even could be deposed by the people by force of arms if necessary, a view that the English Puritans, above all, accepted and ultimately put into practice. As Witte put it,

> such an understanding of the political covenant helps to explain the Puritan's passion and concern for law and politics in the seventeenth century period. The political covenant ultimately made them responsible for the law and politics of the realm. They were to ensure that the civil ruler was a godly ruler and that the civil law reflected divine law and instituted godly order, discipline, and reform.[26]

Not all Puritan groups required ecclesiastical or church covenants a priori. The congregationalists and the independents required every gathered group that sought to become a congregation to do so through a congregational covenant; the Presbyterians sought one great ecclesiastical covenant to establish the church polity parallel to the civil polity. For the English Puritans these covenants were ways to rebuild the national church from within, although in fact the system of church covenants did not reach its fullest development in England, but among the English Puritans who crossed the ocean to the New World.

For the Puritans, the marriage covenant was the more intimate counterpart of the national covenant. As Witte puts it,

> this covenant, though formed by the mutual consent of a man and a woman, was also ultimately founded in the creation and the commandments of God. For God had created man and woman as social beings, naturally inclined to one another. Yet required them to help, nurture, love, and serve each other as 'friends,' 'partners,' and 'companions.' He had commanded them 'to be fruitful and multiply' and endowed them with the physical capacity to join together and beget children. By declaring their marital vows, the Puritans taught, the couple affirmed and accepted these obligations.[27]

Thus was created the covenanted family, the building block of the covenanted people through church and civil society.

Perhaps paradoxically, the Puritan covenantal understanding transformed the predestination of Reformed Protestantism into a condition where freedom of choice actually superseded it. Individuals were, for all intents and purposes, free to choose whether to accept the covenant and its obligations. Only free people could be covenantal partners with God. Of course, once the choice was made, they were obliged to live according to its terms. Indeed, once made, they were obliged to live up to it to the fullest degree because the order of the universe depended on fulfilling covenants and contracts. Moreover, since every covenant, no

matter how small, was part of the great covenantal chain that went back
to God and creation, any breach of covenant threatened the world with
chaos. Hence the peace and order of the world depended upon the fulfillment of covenant obligations. More than other forms of Reformed
Protestantism, English Puritanism emphasized man as a free moral agent,
able to choose and responsible for the consequences of his choice, free
to make the bargain. For the Puritans, as for all biblically oriented peoples,
human rights flowed from covenantal obligations. Unlike the philosophy of feudal theorists, those obligations were not hierarchical to other
humans but transcendent to God. Hence they were potentially equal for
all humans. This opened the door to the notion of equal human rights,
which in time were made prior to and then independent of all obligations, a very different situation than that required by the Puritans.

In sum, English Puritanism became a powerful, comprehensive
worldview, encompassing both civil and religious life involving the individual, the family, and the community. Its roots were in Calvinism,
but, de facto, it transformed Calvinist doctrine from one of rigid predestination to one that emphasized freedom of human will and choice and
the human acceptance of obligation and the responsibilities that flow
from being obligated. As Haller points out, covenant was an idea "which
had often been advanced in the pulpit in mitigation of the stark determinism of the pure doctrine of predestination."[28] In other words, the
elect could strive to improve the world, and if they succeeded it was a
sign that they indeed were among the elect. The covenant with the Lord
enabled them to keep "their part of the bargain, if they expected Him to
keep His, as He surely would do if they never failed Him even in the
greatest trials."[29]

In the biblical manner, Puritan doctrine was national and civil as much
as it was ecclesiastical. The separation between the two spheres was
much reduced in Puritan thought. The four primary covenantal associations—people, polity, church, and family—were closely intertwined.
The Old Testament was as important as the New, since both law and
gospel were essential instruments of grace.

Covenant was also a vehicle through which to temper God's absolute
sovereignty. Because of the covenant, God adds a "mercifull qualifica-
tion" (from Edmond Calamy in his sermon, "England's Looking Glasse,"
22 December 1641) in the exercise of His will because He "indents and
covenants" with every people, providing that if they repent, so will He.

On that same day, Stephen Marshall, in another sermon, "Reformation and Desolation," based on II Kings 23:26, outlined a meaning of calling and covenant as applied to the leaders of a people. "The Lord hath tied Himselfe in his covenant to reward every man according to his owne worke, and not according to the worke of another," a clear diminution of Calvinist predestination in the name of Puritan covenantalism. The last in this set of sermons on 4 January 1642, by Simion Ashe, "A Support for the Sinking Heart in Times of Distresse," took as his proof text the story of the sacrifice of Isaac to state that "whatsoever Promise is registered in the book of God...Jehovah will set all his attributes on work, for the full and seasonable accomplishment thereof unto His own people by special covenant."[30]

God remained incomprehensible and omnipotent, yet He was willing to enter into partnership with potentially depraved humans in such a way that those humans who accepted that partnership were, willy-nilly, redeemed. It could be that the acceptance of the covenant was not a redemptive act for Puritans so much as a sign that those who accepted partnership with God had been predestined for redemption, but that was more in the order of a quibble to get around the problem of predestination in a system that could not but emphasize freedom. Under this doctrine, human rights flowed from covenantal obligations as equal rights, kept within moral boundaries by the primary sense of obligation to God.

Notes

1. Why they went to Adam and not Noah for this universalization is another question since the Bible states that God entered into a covenant with Noah and the matter has to be inferred in connection with Adam.
2. William Aimes, *Medulla Theologica* 1:10 (1623), translated as *The Marrow of Sacred Divinity* (1642), from whence Perry Miller's felicitous description of the biblical idea of covenant as "the marrow of Puritan divinity." Perry Miller, "The Marrow of Puritan Divinity." In *Transactions of the Colonial Society of Massachusetts, 1933–1937* (1937), reprinted in Perry Miller, *Errand into the Wilderness* (1964). At the time the term *marrow* meant both core or essence and also summary or distillation.
3. G. Walker, *The Manifold Wisdome of God* 39–48 (1641).
4. Perry Miller, "The Halfway Covenant," *New England Quarterly* 6 (1933): 675; and N. Pettit, *The Heart Prepared: Grace and Conversion in Puritan Spiritual Life* (New Haven: Yale University Press, 1966).
5. See Francis Lyall, "Of Metaphors and Analogies: Legal Language and Covenant theology." In *Scottish Journal of Theology* 32, 1–17.
6. Patrick Collinson, *Elizabethan Puritan Movement* (London: J. Cape, 1967), 464–65.

7. See, e.g., anonymous, *The Reformation of Religion by Josiah*, which scholars assume was published in 1590, which as Michael McGiffert writes in "Covenant, Crown and Commons in Elizabethan Puritanism," *Journal of British Studies* 20 (1980): 51, "cast the net of covenant all over England" as something of a "final flicker of the political impulse of Elizabethan Puritanism."

8. McGiffert, "Covenant, Crown and Commons in Elizabethan Puritanism," *Journal of British Studies* 20 (1980): 52. McGiffert may be overly impressed with Puritan moralism and rejection of politics. As Harold Fisch points out, Shakespeare, a contemporary of the Elizabethan Puritans, perceived the truth about Puritanism from its beginning by identifying Puritanism with issues of power in every one of his descriptions of characters which he cast as Puritans. Shylock (perhaps a connection with Jewish "Puritanism"), Malvolio, and Angelo, all of whom are presented as both "a saint or a man of God" who "is also paradoxically a power-seeker." (Harold Fisch, "Shakespeare and the Puritan Dynamic," *Shakespeare Survey*, 81.)

Fisch continues to describe how Shakespeare shows that the Puritans' search for power transforms their godliness and fails, at least until the power demon is exorcised. As Fisch points out, Shakespeare took Puritanism very seriously. He was deeply aware of the moral and religious issues that they represented and did not "dismiss the Puritan system lightly" (Fisch, 83). He saw Puritan as "a mighty force and a revolutionary force" that was "also a serious religion raising profound questions about man's nature and its relationship to God" (Fisch, 83).

Fisch argues that Shakespeare "imaginatively adopts the Puritan outlook and visualizing the world from within the Puritan sensibility" in his plays about them. Fisch, too, leans on William Perkins and his works as his guide to Elizabethan Puritanism. See also Harold Fisch, *Jerusalem and Albion* (New York, 1964), 30–34.

Fisch and others demonstrate that Shakespeare is so faithful to Puritanism when he writes about it that he even follows Ramist logic. Peter Ramus developed the logic adopted by the Puritans and by Reformed Calvinists generally. Cf., Perry Miller, *The New England Mind* (Cambridge, Mass.: Harvard University Press, 1954), and Sister Miriam Joseph, *Shakespeare's Use of the Arts of Language* (New York: Columbia University Press, 1949), 17ff.

Significantly, as Fisch points out, as the way of resolving the major paradoxes of Puritanism involving grace and nature, flesh and spirit, Shakespeare presents the institution of marriage (i.e., a covenantal institute, as Shakespeare himself presents) (Fisch, 89–90)

Marriage for Shakespeare is "of much wider import than that, embracing as it does the whole life of man in his human and divine relationships" (Fisch, 90).

9. William Perkins, *A Golden Chaine* (1591), in Perkins, *Works* 1, 32.

10. Leonard J. Trinterud, ed., *Elizabethan Puritanism* (New York: Oxford University Press, 1971); Patrick Collinson, *The Elizabethan Puritan Movement* (London: J. Cape, 1967); Christina Halbowell Garret, *The Marian Exiles: A Study in the Origins of Elizabethan Puritanism* (Cambridge: Cambridge University Press, 1966); Christopher Hill, *Society and Puritanism in Pre-Revolutionary England* (London: Panther, 1967); Arthur Geoffrey Dickins, *The English Reformation* (University Park, Pa.: Pennsylvania State University Press, 1991); Stephen Brachlow, *The Communion of Saints* (Oxford: Oxford University Press, 1988).

11. William Haller, *Liberty and Reformation in the Puritan Revolution* (New York: Columbia University Press, 1955), 353.

12. John Witte, Jr., "Blessed be the Ties that Bind: Covenant and Community in Puritan Thought," *Emory Law Journal* 36 (1987): 579–601.

13. Perry Miller, "The Marrow of Puritan Divinity." In *Transactions of the Colonial Society of Massachusetts,* in Miller, *Errand into the Wilderness* (New York: Harper and Row, 1964). See also William Ames, *The Marrow of Sacred Divinity* (1623 Latin; 1642 English) and J. Clarke, *The Marrow of Ecclesiastical Historie* (1650).
14. As quoted in Abraham Kuyper, Jr., *Die Vastighaid des Verbonds,* 2nd ed. (1913), 104. Kuyper, the great nineteenth-century Dutch Calvinist theologian and political leader, was perhaps the last great representative of the Calvinist covenant tradition in theology and politics.
15. Witte, "Blessed be the Ties that Bind," *Emory Law Journal* 36, 583.
16. *The Origins of English Puritanism.*
17. As quoted in Michael McGiffert, "William Tyndale's Conception of Covenant," *Journal of Ecclesiastical History* 32, no. 2 (April 1981): 170.
18. G. W. Bernard, *War, Taxation and Rebellion in Early Tudor England* (Brighton: Harvester Press, 1986); Francis Hackett, *Henry the Eighth* (London: The Reprint Society, 1946).
19. Richard Hooker, *Ecclesiastical Polity* I, chap. 10.
20. Harold Fisch, *Jerusalem and Albion* (New York: Schocken Books, 1964); H. Fisch, *Hamlet and the Word: The Covenant Pattern in Shakespeare* (New York: Ungar, 1971); Sigurd Burckhardt, *Shakespeare's Meanings* (Princeton: Princeton University Press, 1968). The covenantal dimension of Shakespeare needs to be more fully explored. In a sense he stands in relation to Puritanism as three centuries later Mark Twain was to stand in relation to American Calvinism: influenced yet skeptical and critical.
21. Milton, *Tenure of Kings and Magistrates* (Cambridge: Cambridge University Press, 1991).
22. Michael McGiffert, "Covenant, Crown and Commons in Elizabethan Puritanism," *Journal of British Studies* XX (1980): 32–52.
23. Nicholas Bownde, *The Doctrine of the Sabbath Plainly Set Forth* (London, 1595). For later books examining English sabbaterianism, see Winton U. Solberg, *Redeem the Time: The Puritan Sabbath in Early America* (Cambridge, Mass.: Harvard University Press, 1977); Patrick Collinson, "The Beginnings of English Sabbaterianism," *Studies in Church History* I (1964): 207–21; Christopher Hill, *Society and Puritanism in Prerevolutionary England,* 2nd ed. (New York: Schocken Books, 1967), especially chap. 5, "The Uses of Sabbaterianism."
24. P. Zagorin, *A History of Political Thought in the English Revolution* (London: Routledge, 1954).
25. Joseph W. Martin, *Religious Radicals in Tudor England* (London: Hambledon Press, 1989).
26. Witte, "Blessed be the Ties that Bind," *Emory Law Journal,* 593–94.
27. Ibid., 594–95.
28. Haller, *Liberty and Reformation in the Puritan Revolution,* 18.
29. Ibid., 18–19.
30. Ibid., 29–31.

13

The Puritans, the Civil War, and Beyond

The Puritan movement climaxed in the parliamentary struggle with Charles I, which precipitated civil war and resulted in the executions of Archbishop Laud (1645) and Charles himself in 1649.[1] As the civil war approached, the Puritans became a party within Parliament and the country. In the course of the actual conflict, they were transformed into an army and, with the defeat of the Royalists, became the governors of a state. At every stage in this transition they sought guidance from covenantal ideas and principles.

The covenantal commitment of the Roundheads in the English civil war was firmly established at the first fast day proclaimed by the Long Parliament on 17 November 1641. The fast was opened by the Reverend Cornelius Burges, citing Jeremiah's prophecy (Jeremiah 50:5), "Let us joyne our selves unto the Lord in an everlasting covenant." He was followed by the Reverend Stephen Marshall, who preached in the afternoon, quoting the words of Azariah to King Asa of Judea (II Chronicles 15:2 and 12) after the king had destroyed the abominations of Rehoboam and overthrown Zerah the Ethiopian, which gives an account of how the Israelites "entred into a covenant to seeke the Lord God of their fathers."

As Haller put it: "Burges and Marshall left no room for doubt as to the relevance of this familiar doctrine to the situation in which members of parliament now found themselves. They were called by the Lord, they were in covenant, to rebuild Zion and overthrow false gods and their priests, assured that the Lord would bring to success the work he had appointed to be done.... The covenant was, moreover, national as well as personal, binding them as Englishmen as well as saints."[2]

The monarchist supporters of the Stuarts understood well that the Puritan revolution was not only religiously grounded, but was an attack on aristocratic values, an effort to elevate what James Howell, a monarchist and the first royal historiographer in England (1594?–1666), defined as "mechanics" in a struggle between "gentlemen" and nonaristocrats. Included among the latter was the rising capitalist class that controlled the municipal corporations, especially London, and the Puritan preachers. In other words, it was their nonaristocratic birth that made the difference. Thus, even at the time, the Puritan revolution was recognized for the greater force that it was, greater in ways that the Puritans themselves did not necessarily seek.[3]

The most comprehensive expression of the governmental covenant was the Solemn League and Covenant that bound the parliaments of England and Scotland into what was intended to become a kind of confederation of the elect, or at least of the polities of the elect. This Solemn League and Covenant, negotiated in 1642 and ratified in 1643, followed on the heels of the Scottish National Covenant of 1638 and was an extension of that effort at Scottish reconstruction. As such it was in the spirit of Scottish Presbyterianism which, despite the common Reformed basis of their respective faiths, differed from English Puritanism politically and sociologically in certain critical ways that vitally affected the outcome of this all-British effort at building a covenant-based polity.

Not only did the two countries start out with different forms of church organization—the Scots had an elaborate national church with a full-blown federal structure, while the English Puritans had built their congregations as "gathered" semiseparated groupings within the framework of the Anglican Church, with no superstructure of their own beyond the local congregation—but there were also major differences in the relationship between church and state. The Scots built an alternate polity through the national kirk to compete with and, indeed, replace the still feudal order of the Scottish kings. Hence, their church was very much involved in public affairs and, indeed, in politics. It was a major national institution in the political arena. The English Puritans had felt no need for an alternate body organized for their religious institutions because they had captured Parliament, which played the same role vis-à-vis the English Crown (recalling that the Crowns of both had the same incumbent), but was a legitimate political institution in its own right. As parliamentarians, the Puritan leaders had some questions about covenanting with what was essentially a church government rather than a parallel parliamentary body.

Nevertheless, the Puritan parliamentarians accepted the proposed covenant, albeit with reservations, and it was ratified by Parliament, but in the last analysis the differences were too great and the covenant did not survive. What did survive was the theory and practice of the "gathered" congregation, the voluntary coming together of consenting adults for religious purposes. Otherwise, then as now, England was not ready for federalism.

In many respects the political high point of Puritan covenantalism came in the Synod of 1643, convened by the English House of Commons and also attended by Scottish commissioners sent to secure the adoption of the Presbyterian form of church government in England as it had been in Scotland under the Solemn League and Covenant. Three factions were represented at that synod, whose 151 original members included 121 ministers from every English and Welsh county, the Channel Islands, the universities, and the City of London; members of the House of Lords; twenty members of Commons; the Scottish commissioners; the independents who wanted the extension of congregationalist church government in England; the Presbyterians, both Scottish and English, who wanted a countrywide church government whose covenant with the state gave it sufficient freedom and protection to act; and the Erastians, who thought that church and state should be united.

The advocates of each of these three positions found the basis for it in the Bible and Reformed Protestant doctrine. Their debates, therefore, set forth almost the entire range of Puritan covenantal political thought except for that of those who were so radical that they did not even fit into the assembly. Several of the Erastians especially, such as Thomas Coleman, John Lightfoot, and John Selden, were enormously knowledgeable in Hebrew learning in the original languages. Coleman was even referred to by the assembly as "rabbi," and Selden was considered the most profound Hebraist of his age.[4]

In the course of the discussion much attention was paid to the nature of the ancient Jewish polity, whose structure, functions, and offices were probed in detail. The proximate outcome of the synod was a parliamentary decree in March 1646 establishing Presbyterianism throughout the land, but, while a few presbyteries were set up in London and some isolated areas, the whole country was not so reorganized, and even those that were established lacked the authority that they needed. Thus, in

May 1648, Parliament passed the Ordinance for the Suppression of Heresy and Blasphemy, in theory moving England toward Erastianism while in fact the independents were taking control of the country. In the end, the Parliament took first a Presbyterian, then an Erastian position, while the people took an independent one, each based on an interpretation of covenantal principles.

Despite the very real differences in doctrine and practice, the civil war came. From a behavioral perspective it can be seen as the result of the fact that King Henry VIII, a century earlier, undertook a pseudo-reformation that did not enable English society to address the burning social questions of the Reformation that manifested themselves through religious reformation throughout Central and Western Europe at that time. When they finally could be put off no longer they exploded with a force far greater than they might have had they been addressed earlier and, instead of unfolding as part of the late medieval world, they were tied in with the opening of the modern epoch and opened the door for the religious-secular battles of modernity.

This is not the place to discuss the Civil War itself with its very dramatic examples of the covenant-bound parliamentary army, the famous Roundheads, an army based on thoughtful religious fervor that informed its political principles and even its military tactics, an army that has come down in history not only for its military successes but for marching to battle singing hymns and following every battle with extensive theological and political discussions in all ranks.[5] The parliamentary forces under Oliver Cromwell were the first example of a modern, ideologically motivated army, a popular army whose members fought for their beliefs rather than because they were professional soldiers. The wars of the Reformation in general, but the English Civil War in particular, were wars based on popular armies, previsioning the format that, after a four-generation hiatus, was to become the modern norm, to continue until the 1960s and the Vietnam war.

The dramatic sight of Cromwell's "Ironsides" marching to battle has stirred the imaginations of generations of young people in the English-speaking world. The great idea behind their special fervor is less well-known. Nevertheless it has become part of the great tradition of the English-speaking peoples. Its spirit is periodically revived with the same sense of Divine covenanted mission and again becomes a great motivating force.

The English Civil War has a special interest for students of civil wars because it did not involve a secession of territory and a conflict between the sessionists and the established government, but a very serious ideological dispute in which the adherents of both ideological positions were scattered around England, Wales, Scotland, and Ireland. Thus, the war was kingdomwide; on a country-by-country basis, true, but without regular lines and with outbreaks by both sides in various parts of the four countries, generally on an ad hoc basis or in response to events in other parts. In this respect, England in particular was torn by the Civil War in all of its parts.

Scotland, although a much smaller country and kingdom in terms of its population and resources, became even more important than it inherently would have been because it was in the hands of one party, the Presbyterians, who were sympathetic toward the Puritan English parliamentarians as fellow Reformed Protestants deserving of support and reinforcement. Indeed, it was the Scots who offered that support and reinforcement in the early summer of 1643 when the war was going badly for the Puritans in England proper. The Scots did so in great part to protect themselves, calculating that a Royalist victory in England could leave King Charles I free to deal with Scotland. Fortunately the Scottish government was in the hands of the Covenanters, as a result of Charles's decision to try to win them over by giving them positions of responsibility. The Scottish government proposed an alliance with the English Puritans through the English Parliament in mid-July and by mid-August the terms of the Solemn League and Covenant had been drafted, including a commitment for the Scots to raise an army of 20,000 men with funds from the English Parliament to support the latter against the "popish and prelatical" faction, which at that point was being blamed by both groups of Reformed Protestants for having seized control of the king, rather than accusing the king himself of treason as was ultimately the case.

The Solemn League and Covenant in its final form was just that. While the English had preferred to confine the alliance to a civil league, its binding dimension was in the form of a religious covenant, as the Scots wanted, and its principal clause was stated in the purpose of the alliance, which was to preserve both countries from "the yoke of prelacy." Neither the specific religious nor political goals of the English Puritans were part of the Scots' long-term plan for them, the British Isles, or humanity. The English wanted to secure parliamentary supremacy and Independency (i.e., congregationalism in the churches); as Presbyterians, the Scots were uninterested in the former and strongly objected to the latter.[6]

While these long-term differences were not only very real but were in the consciousness of both the Covenanters and the Parliamentarians, their short-term need to cooperate prevailed. In a very real sense this was the high point of Scottish influence on Scottish-English relations. The English, badly needing Scottish help, agreed to most of the Scottish demands, merely keeping the door open for Independency, while the Solemn League and Covenant included the decision of the Westminster Assembly of the Covenanters that the religion of the three kingdoms— England and Wales, Scotland, and Ireland—be brought into "the nearest conjunction and uniformity," in the words of Vane. This enabled a sufficient number of Independents to accept the covenant and be faithful to it without giving up their principles.[7] John Seldon's comment in this connection was that oaths were best taken like pills, without chewing.[8]

As the Parliamentary army became stronger and more successful and its generals, capped by Oliver Cromwell, better leaders, the need for Scottish assistance declined and the English Puritans grew stronger. This ultimately lead to a turning of the tables, whereby not only did the English regain the upper hand vis-à-vis Scotland, but Cromwell successfully invaded that country in pursuit of English political-religious goals. In 1643, however, the Scottish leaders were basking in the light of their defeat of the king militarily in 1640 and were even going so far as to talk about invading continental Europe to implant Presbyterianism in Paris and Rome after they finished with England.[9]

In fact, the military situation had changed even before the adoption of the Solemn League and Covenant, although that could not be known at the time. Hence, the break between the two nations was not long in coming. The break was accelerated when the Scottish army did not perform the "miracles" that had been expected of them, while the Scottish military defeat at the hands of Prince Rupert in March 1644 further damaged their reputation. By that time the Scottish army was no longer saving England for the Puritans but was part of an ever more victorious coalition increasingly under the leadership of Cromwell. The actual victories obscured the fact that it was the Scots' intervention that had made possible the further resistance and recouping of the English Puritan armies.

This anomalous situation continued. The Parliamentary forces reorganized as the New Model Army during the winter and early spring of 1644 while the Royalists invaded Scotland and won some victories, causing the Scots to withdraw some of their troops to rescue their own country. By early 1645 the Scots' Presbyterian leaders were so fearful of the rise of English Independency under the Parliamentary regime that some of them began to move toward negotiations with King Charles to reestablish a Scottish-Royalist alliance in what they believed was self-protection. Thus, politics soon replaced religion as the critical factor in determining the moves of all the parties.

Victory: The Political Covenant Diminished

As a party, the Puritans developed a political thought based upon covenant that served them well in raising and governing armies when the war came. Nevertheless, the military experience did bring with it significant changes in the application of the covenant idea. Initially, the Puritan armies followed the radical covenantal ideas of maximum consent at every step down the line and they were unable to develop proper military discipline or command structures. It was then that Oliver Cromwell stepped in to transform the situation, combining forceful Puritan rhetoric with a strong hand, which set limits to covenantal consent. He molded the Puritan army into a winning military machine.

In 1647, the Parliamentary army carried on a series of discussions on the character of the commonwealth. These extraordinary discussions of a people in arms with regard to the future of their government were conducted in a manner generally true to the theoretical premises on which they rested. They were the equivalent of the separatist and Puritan colonists' efforts to establish civil and church government in the New World, only on a grander scale because of the size of the country involved. Initiated by Cromwell, under his guidance, they concluded that men were naturally free but "agreed to come into some form of government that they who were chosen might preserve property."[10] Cromwell himself stated that the king is "king by contract," although he was more conservative in his response to the view that "all government is in the free consent of the governed."

The whole discussion was the closest that the English ever came to reestablishing their polity by political compact, although there are numerous occasions of rulers being empowered in that manner. (Even King James I felt the need to acknowledge the compactual basis of the English monarchy in addressing the English Parliament in 1609.)

> The king binds himself by a double oath to the observation of the fundamental laws of his kingdom. Tacitly, as by being a king, and so bound to protect as well the people as the laws of his kingdom, and expressly by his oath at his coronation; so as every just king, in a settled kingdom, is bound to observe that paction made to his people by his laws, in framing his government agreeable thereunto, according to that paction which God made with Noah after the deluge.... And therefore a king governing in a settled kingdom leaves to be a king and degenerates into a tyrant as soon as he leaves off to rule according to his laws.[11]

Then, at the point of victory, the ascendant Puritans begin to splinter. Two principal parties emerged: the Presbyterians and the Independents. The former emphasized the nationwide federal connections between congregational communities within a common doctrinal framework; the latter emphasized radical congregationalism and doctrinal independence. A deadlock ensued as each side struggled for its constitutional principles. Reflecting the national disgust for the seemingly interminable parliamentary wrangling, Cromwell stepped in, dispersed the Parliament, and made himself dictator in the name of the revolution. His subsequent dictatorship moved far from covenantal principles and aroused hostility toward Puritanism. Two years after Cromwell's death, after his son Richard had failed as his heir, the son of Charles I was invited to return from his Dutch exile (the Calvinist Dutch had sufficient political interest in giving refuge to the Royalists) and assumed the throne as Charles II.

In the last analysis, the Puritan commonwealth, per se, was a failure. While it was successful in enunciating a revolutionary doctrine of covenant, it was unable to take its covenantal ideas a step further and embody them in a proper constitution of government once the revolution was won. Instead it degenerated into dictatorship. In this, too, it set the pattern for so many of the modern ideologically based revolutions, differing primarily (and significantly) in that it did not resort to a reign of terror in the process. Cromwell himself, however autocratic as an Englishman, believed in the basic rights of Englishmen and as a Puritan in the basic principles of federal liberty, that is to say, that all men are bonded by covenant and are made free as long as they live up to its terms. Even as he became more autocratic, these principles had a restraining influence on him. But without proper institutions, Cromwell could neither provide a government that met English expectations of participation and power sharing, nor could he provide for his succession. Hence, in the end a far from Puritanized English public had to turn back to a discredited monarchy and a monarch who himself did the institution no credit.[12]

Liberal Puritanism: John Milton

Perhaps the most potent spokesman for the liberal dimension of Puritanism was John Milton. Influenced by the thrust of the English Civil War, Milton gave the Reformed Protestant covenantalism of the English Puritans a more liberal turn, advocating liberty as the main end of the free commonwealth, especially liberty of thought and speech. His efforts helped build the bridge between the old ideas of the Reformed Protestant commonwealth and the new ones of liberal, republican civil society that were to appear while he lived and become popular shortly after his demise. Milton, like his contemporary Hobbes, was a bridging agent, the first from the commonwealth perspective, the second from that of civil society, in the transformation of the covenanted commonwealth into a constitutional one.[13]

Milton's argument was almost entirely against censorship and he did not particularly concern himself with forms of government or regimes beyond the question of freer speech. He was more of an Arminian than a Calvinist and he, too, like so many of his Puritan or Puritan-influenced peers, looked to the Mosaic polity of the Hebrew Scriptures for model forms of government.

The center of Puritan political thought was in Cambridge, just as the major English royalists were products of Oxford. Cambridge had become a Puritan-dominated institution in the sixteenth century. Located as it was in East Anglia, where the Puritans had their main base of strength, it is not surprising that Cambridge acquired that position. It was to hold it throughout the seventeenth century and even beyond that, with visible echoes of it to be found throughout the nineteenth century and into the twentieth. The great Puritan thinkers and preachers were almost without exception products of Cambridge. From the first, Puritanism was an intellectual faith, one that required a well-educated, not merely educated, ministry, and that relied upon a systematically rigorous theology and politics. In this as in other ways it was a worthy successor to the biblical religion that its adherents embraced.

From Puritanism to Whiggism

A major step in the transition from covenantal to Whig politics was to be found in the championship of what became known as the "good old cause." Coined as a slogan in 1655, the "good old cause" essentially embodied the protection of the rights and liberties of Englishmen by vesting political power in Parliament as the elected assembly of the people. The particular combination of communal and individual rights of Englishmen, which had its origins in Magna Carta, rested on the proposition that power is originally inherent in the people, who retain reserved rights to protect the community from autocratic rule, which rights they vest in their elected assembly.[14] Thus, the slogan and those who rallied around it became the bridge between the covenantal tradition and late seventeenth-century Whiggery.

In the end, Charles II was invited back, committing himself to pardoning the rebels against his father except for the regicides, maintenance of a free parliament with freedom of conscience, and various financial incentives for both his own followers and those who had served in Cromwell's army and were willing to pledge allegiance to the restored king. The final version of these conditions was embodied in the Declaration of Breda in 1660, in essence a pact between king and parliament, even though unilaterally declared. Of course, once back, it was unilaterally enforced or ignored as well.[15]

Under Charles II (1660–85) Puritans were again persecuted, though not as severely as the Scottish Covenanters, as king and parliament legislated policies of Anglican uniformity. Under a restored Anglo-Catholic synthesis embodied in the Act of Uniformity of 1662, the Puritans were pushed out of the established church to become Dissenters and the parents of the later nonconformist churches. Fighting back through the political process, three Puritan (Whig) parliaments were eventually elected in 1679–81; but Charles overwhelmed them. However, when James II (1685–88) sought to resurrect Catholicism in England, both Anglicans (Tories) and Puritans (Whigs) joined in inviting William and Mary to invade England and assume the throne. In this Glorious Revolution, the Dutch army marched on London without opposition; James

II fled, and Parliament approved the Act of Toleration which included dissenters but excluded Catholics and Unitarians.[16]

The Glorious Revolution ended the English Civil War and completed the Puritan revolutionary movement by finding a constitutional compromise with appropriate institutional arrangements suitable to the English genius. In that respect it was a great compromise. The forms of traditional English institutions, including the monarchy, were to be preserved, but their content was sufficiently transformed to reflect the spirit of the revolution. The monarchy was preserved, but only as king-in-parliament, no longer the rule of one with checks and balances from the other estates, but a kind of collective kingship that included both a hereditary and an elective component. This king-in-parliament was bound by a new constitutional settlement including the Act of Toleration and the Bill of Rights of 1689, the first settling the religious conflict initiated by the Reformation and the second providing for the protection of English civil liberties. Since both represented settlements among conflicting parties, both can be said to have had a covenantal dimension, but part of the settlement was ambiguous, just as the new mixed regime was institutionally ambiguous.[17]

After the Glorious Revolution, the Puritans began to recede as an overt political force. Although they were unable to reform civil society entirely in accord with their religious and political teachings, the Puritans succeeded in transforming England into a republic in all but name and in recasting their contemporaries' understanding of civil society in a covenantal-compactual mode that quickly found reinforcement in the writings of Hobbes and Locke, Harrington and Sydney. Many Puritan political ideas were institutionalized in the Whig tradition and the Puritans' drive for parliamentary supremacy eventually succeeded, with the House of Commons becoming the dominant body. Because strong royal and Tory opposition continued for another century, England developed a more mixed constitution that carried many traditionalistic elements, including a tamed monarchy, into modernity.

Whiggism dominated eighteenth-century English politics, beginning with the Act of Union with Scotland in 1707 and continuing until the Napoleonic Wars. The Whigs themselves divided into two groupings: the Court Whigs and the Country Whigs.[18] As their names suggest, the former represented the London establishment whose politics revolved around institutions of king and parliament, while the latter represented the more popular aspects of Whiggism, representing the country squires.

The division essentially meant a reassertion of the organic model of the English polity with the center in the capital and its periphery in the country. Indeed, eighteenth-century political thought sought to reconcile federal and organic theories of the polity by transforming the political compact into an organic multigenerational bond whose compactual character receded into the mists of history. Edmund Burke was the great articulator of this idea in his public philosophy, while Blackstone gave it legal embodiment in his commentaries.[19]

Religious dissent shifted from Puritanism to Methodism, the latter a popular revivalistic movement far removed from the intellectually rich, theologically grounded approach of Puritanism. Whereas Puritan divines were university educated like their Reformed counterparts in Europe (the place of Cambridge in the Puritan revolution was no less than the place of the great Swiss universities in the development of Reformed religion and Calvinism in that country), Methodist ministers were men of the spirit rather than of the book, teachers who reached out to the common folk and whose educational credentials were irrelevant.[20]

In the interim, the Puritans and Puritan covenantalism had crossed the Atlantic to North America. Puritan teachings were already strong among the Anglican ministers in the Jamestown colony in Virginia from its founding in 1607, but it was not until the landing of the Mayflower in 1620 that the beginnings of a covenantal commonwealth in North America were launched. The Mayflower passengers were predominantly Separatists from the radical wing of Puritanism, and the Plymouth colony they founded remained separate from the main Puritan settlement initiated in 1629. Together they created a formidable concentration of followers of covenantal teachings, which by the time of the English Civil War had founded four colonies, each in effect an autonomous Puritan commonwealth. The English Civil War effectively detached them from the mother country for half a generation, strengthening their sense of independence and launching a new phase in the history of covenantal politics.

The Abandonment of Covenant

In the nineteenth century, the eighteenth-century synthesis was transformed into a purely organic understanding of the English people and polity. This was reflected in common speech: Britain and England were rolled up into one conceptually as "England" pure and simple, even by the constitutionalists of the day.[21] Mainstream English thought was strengthened in mid-century by Darwinian theories that transformed the organic view of society from one of harmony to struggle, but reemphasized the organic character of all creation.[22]

Two semicovenantal movements did develop in nineteenth century England. The first was the Chartist movement in the 1830s and 1840s, which called for a charter of social reforms.[23] The second was the imperial federalist movement of the 1880s and 1890s, which sought to transform the British Empire into a federation.[24] Both of those movements drew from the more superficial political principles of political compact with no effort to find their roots in the older covenantal tradition or in its modern Lockean variation. Perhaps that is one of the reasons why neither was successful in achieving its larger goals. Although the Chartist movement, which had greater popular support, did bring about a certain measure of domestic political reform, both movements had more influence overseas in those parts of the empire settled by the British. Australia, in particular, was influenced by both.

The twentieth century replaced the relatively uncomplicated organic world of the Victorian age with new ideologies of socialism, social democracy, and ultimately a revived capitalism. The first two certainly had their roots in those segments of the population that were descended from the old English, Scottish, and Welsh covenanters.[25] Their burning commitment to justice reasserted itself as a commitment to social justice and they marched forward under the banner of these new ideologies to correct the manifold injustices of nineteenth-century Britain. Although they did not particularly seek to do so under the banner of covenant, because so many of them, including their leaders, were drawn from the nonconformist churches, the continuities were visible enough and at times the rhetoric of socialism drew upon the old religion, and not always in secular form either. There were many resemblances between the original Labor party and the old Puritans in political style, if not in substance.

In this case the heirs of nonconformist Protestantism were joined by a significant number of Jews responding to their own traditions of covenant and social justice amalgamated with those of Britain. Jews such as Harold Laski also added significantly to the intellectual component of the struggle. In this sense it can be said that the reform movement in Britain continued to be the heritage of the covenanters even if the covenantal dimension was a matter of heritage rather than an active intellectual force. Today Scotland remains a Labor party bastion as much as it is the bastion of Presbyterianism. Wales has a strong Labor heritage and the relation between Labor and nonconformist England is still pronounced.

What of Margaret Thatcher's new ideology of free enterprise capitalism? With socialism and social democracy it shares a previously un-English commitment to egalitarianism. Its emphasis is on equality of opportunity rather than condition or result. To what extent its sources may have some connection with the Puritan heritage remains to be explored.

Notes

1. Stuart E. Prall, *The Puritan Revolution* (London: Routledge and K. Paul, 1968); John Christopher Hill, *God's Englishman* (London: Weidenfeld and Nicolson, 1970); Maurice Percy Ashley, *Oliver Cromwell and the Puritan Revolution* (New York: Collier Books, 1966); John Christopher Hill, *Puritanism and Revolution* (New York: Schocken Books, 1958).
2. Ibid., 19.
3. Michael Nutkiewicz, "A Rapporteur of the English Civil War: The Courtly Politics of James Howell (1694?–1666)," *Canadian Journal of History* 25 (April 1990): 21–40.
4. Weldon S. Crowley, "Erastianism in the Westminister Assembly," *Church and State* (Winter 1973); and William L. Fisk, "John Selden, Erastian Critic of the English Church," *Church and State* (Autumn 1957).
5. Jacqueline Eales, *Puritans and Roundheads* (Cambridge: Cambridge University Press, 1990); Christopher Hibbert, *Cavaliers and Roundheads* (New York: Scribner, 1993).
6. Robert Baillie, *Letters and Journals of Robert Baillie* 2, 90. See also C. D. Wedgwood, "The Covenanters in the First Civil War," *Scottish Historical Review* 39, no. 127 (April 1960): 1–15.
7. Philip Nye, *The Covenant With a Narrative of the Manner of Taking It* (London, 1643).
8. John Seldon, *Table Talk*, ed. Reynolds (London, 1892), 123.
9. Lord Leven, the commander of the Scottish army, made this claim explicit. See correspondence of Montereul, 2, 550.
10. Sir William Clarke, *The Clarke Papers*, ed. C. H. Firth (New York: Johnson Reprint, 1965) 312.
11. As quoted by Locke in his *Second Treatise on Civil Government*, 200.
12. John Christopher Hill, *Puritanism and Revolution*; John Christopher Hill, *God's Englishman*; Godfrey Davies, *The Restoration of Charles II, 1658–1660* (London: Oxford University Press, 1955); Ronald Hutton, *The Restoration* (Oxford: Clarendon Press, 1985).
13. For a discussion of John Milton's political thought, see Walter Berns, "John Milton." In *History of Political Philosophy*, Leo Strauss and Joseph Cropsey, eds.

(Chicago: Rand McNally, 1963), 397–412. Berns does not make even a single reference to the covenantal basis of Melton's thought but otherwise has an excellent discussion of the thrust of that thought in terms of modern democracy.

14. Barbara Taft, "That Lusty Puss, the Good Old Cause," *History of Political Thought* 5, no. 3 (Winter 1984): 447–468. Taft's article discusses the history of "the old cause" as a mobilizing slogan at the time of Cromwell's protectorate until the Glorious Revolution in 1688–89.

15. Paul H. Hardacre, "The Genesis of the Declaration of Breda, 1657–1660," *Church and State* (Winter 1973): 65–82.

16. Sir Arthur Bryant, *The England of Charles II* (London: Longmans, Green, 1936).

17. Gerald M. Straka, ed., *The Revolution of 1688* (Boston: D. C. Heath, 1963); George Macauley Trevelyan, *The English Revolution 1688–1689* (New York: Oxford University Press, 1965).

18. James Rees Jones, *The First Whigs* (London: Oxford University Press, 1961); B. W. Hill, *The Growth of Parliamentary Parties 1689–1742* (London: Allen and Unwin, 1976); Isaac Kranwick, *Bolingbroke and his Circle: The Politics of Nostalgia in the Age of Walpole* (Cambridge, Mass.: Harvard University Press, 1968); Reed Browning, *Political and Constitutional Ideas of the Court Whigs* (Baton Rouge: Louisiana State University Press, 1982); John Wyan Burrow, *Whigs and Liberals: Continuity and Change in English Political Thought* (Oxford: Clarendon Press, 1988).

19. Edmund Burke, *A Vindication of Natural Society* (Indianapolis: Liberty Classics, 1982); William Blackstone, *Commentaries on the Laws of England* (Oxford: Clarendon Press, 1770).

20. Bernard Semmel, *The Methodist Revolution* (London: Heineman, 1973); John Wesley, *A Plain Account of Christian Perfection* (London: The Epworth Press, 1979); Maldwyn Lloyd Edwards, *John Wesley and the Eighteenth Century* (London: Epworth Press, 1955).

21. Albert Venn Dicey, *Introduction to the Study of the Law of the Constitution* (London: Macmillan, 1959); Sir Henry Buckle, *Introduction to the History of Civilization in England* (London: G. Routledge & Sons, 1904).

22. Greta Jones, *Social Darwinism and English Thought* (Brighton, Sussex: Harvester Press, 1980); Robert C. Barrister, *Social Darwinism* (Philadelphia: Temple University Press, 1979).

23. David Jones, *Chartism and the Chartists* (London: Lane, 1975); Dorothy Thompson, *The Chartists: Popular Politics in the Industrial Revolution* (New York: Pantheon, 1984); Dorothy Thompson, *Outsiders* (London: Verso, 1993).

24. Philip Henry Kerr, Marquis of Lothian, *Studies in Federal Planning* (London: Macmillan, 1943).

25. Francis Elma Gillespie, *Labor and Politics in England 1830–1867* (New York: Ortagon Books, 1966); Henry Pelling, *Origins of the Labor Party* (Oxford: Clarendon, 1966); John H. S. Reid, *The Origins of the British Labour Party* (Minneapolis: University of Minnesota Press, 1955).

14

The Reformation of Covenanted Scotland

In Jerusalem, on the western slopes of the Valley of Gehennom (Gehenna), stands St. Andrew's Church and Hospice, built by the Church of Scotland in 1927 following the British capture of Jerusalem from the Ottoman Turks in World War I. The distinctively Scottish gothic building is noticeable for the flag that flies over it; the flag of Scotland, St. Andrew's cross, undiluted by the symbols of the other countries of Britain, undoubtedly one of the few places in the world where the Scottish flag flies alone.

The rather massive but simple building reflects the spirit of Scotch Presbyterianism. Inside the imageless chapel, whose only religious sign is a modest cross, are plaques and markers commemorating the Scottish connection to Jerusalem and the Holy Land. There is a plaque indicating that the tradition of the church is that of Genevan Reformed Protestantism, testimony to the sources of Scottish religion. There is a marker in memory of the Scottish soldiers who fell in the fight for the Holy Land in World War I, listing the Scottish regiments that took part in the campaign. There is a marker commemorating the request of Robert Bruce that his heart be buried in Jerusalem, and there is a stone from the monastery on the Island of Iona, where Christianity in Scotland began.

The building includes a hospice where travelers, especially academics and clergymen, can find lodging at a very modest price. Services are held in the church weekly and at every appropriate occasion and, above all, there is an English-language school, well known in the Jerusalem area for its quality. Thus, the Scottish connection with Jerusalem takes on concrete form but the connection goes beyond that as the Scottish covenantal tradition is directly derived from that of ancient Israel via the Hebrew Scriptures.

While their covenants were not quite instituted to transcend the state of nature, as was the case in the British North American colonies, the Scottish experience of covenanting also had the virtue of being more than a philosophic statement of the theory of the origins of the polity. The covenants were concrete acts designed to reaffirm the existence of the Scottish nation and to establish the ends for which that nation existed as a community and an organized political entity (in biblical terms both as an *am* and as an *edah*). Thus, they had the substance of reality, which should give them greater weight in the history of human affairs than the more abstract ideas of theologians and philosophers. Both were prominent in Scotland as elsewhere in the late medieval and early modern epochs and both were nourished by the Scottish covenantal reality and fed the Scottish covenantal process.

Scotland is not only a bastion of covenantal religious thinking but it has consistently sought political expressions of covenant as well. Still, left to their own devices, the Scots all too often were politically foolish, misassessing the realities of their situation and committing themselves to the wrong leaders. Hence, their centuries-long war with England, culminating in their support for the Stuarts, whose Scottish ancestry blinded many Scots to their royal commitment to absolutism, led to the loss of Scottish independence. Union with England created economic and social opportunities for the Scots at real political cost. If there is to be a political future for Scotland as a country, it should come within a federal context that provides political expression for its covenant tradition.

Federal Theology and National Revival

In Scotland, on the northern edge of Europe, covenant took a strongly nationalistic turn in addition to that of resistance to tyranny. Indeed, for the Scots, the two were combined because the source of the tyranny was England. The Scots employed covenant to defend themselves against the imposition of religious and governmental practices that were incompatible with their beliefs and interests. In the end, it was the Scottish Presbyterian Church that preserved a separate Scottish political existence.

In Scotland the federal or covenant theology received its fullest and most permanent doctrinal recognition in the Westminster Confession

(1648) of the Presbyterian faith.[1] At the same time, covenant was given strong international expressions by the Scots, who regarded Scotland as the new Israel having the responsibility of spreading Protestantism and enlightening the world. As Samuel Rutherford proclaimed: "though there be new out-casts betwixt Christ and Scotland, I hope that the end of it will be, that Christ and Scotland shall yet weep in one another's arms.... When the Lord shall again take in this land anew.... Now, O Scotland, God be thanked thy name is in the Bible.... Nay more, Scotland was she whom Christ 'made a fair bride to Himself.'"[2]

When covenant ideas were introduced into Scotland during the early part of the sixteenth century, they found receptive soil in an indigenous tradition of public "banding," which had long existed among clans and tribal groupings. Bands, pacts, and oaths were generally formed for purposes of common defense and regional peacemaking. These bands are discussed and many are cited in John Knox's *History of the Reformation of Religion within the Realm of Scotland* (1587, 1644).[3]

In the minds of the Scots, this tradition was easily combined with Reformed notions of covenant, especially in light of the Scots' desire to protect their religious preferences against English intrusions. Furthermore, the biblical idea of covenant served to elevate the practice of banding to a new level of both legitimacy and purpose. We have previously examined the Scottish tradition of banding to show how deeply the idea of such pacts was embedded in Scottish political culture, but Knox was the first to refer to that kind of coming together by the term "covenanting." He himself records the process in his history of the Reformation in Scotland. The first such covenanting was in 1556. In the same period as he was castigating Mary Tudor for theological transgressions, Knox was visiting the Laird of Dun. The gentlemen of the Mearns, as he puts it, "bound themselves...to maintain the true preaching of the Evangel of Jesus Christ." This covenant probably did not assume written form.

Apparently, the first written "godly band" along these lines was made by Protestant lords under the name "Lords of the Congregation," on 3 December 1557 at the urging of John Knox for the purpose of maintaining Presbyterian doctrines and political practices. It included the Earls of Argyll, Glencairn, and Morton, the Lord of Lorne, and John Erskine of Dun, all of whom bound themselves together to do everything within their power to further the cause of Reformed religion.

Subsequent bands were entered into at Perth in May 1559; Edinburgh in July 1559; Stirling in August 1559; Leith in April 1560; Ayr in May 1562; Newcastle in March 1566; Edinburgh in July 1567 and again in May 1568; and Leith in July 1572. Sometimes bands would be "renewed" or "re-subscribed to" after the fashion of covenant renewal in the Bible.[4]

Covenant theology initially became known in the British Isles largely through the writings and sermons of continental theologians. Bullinger's works had been translated into English by 1538, and Bullinger corresponded with theologians in England. The works of Oecolampadius were also known at about this time. During the reign of Edward VI (1537-53), a number of continental theologians carried covenant ideas to England, including Peter Martyr and John Tremellius, who came in 1547, and Martin Bucer and Paul Fagius, who arrived in 1548.

In addition to continental influences, covenant ideas were developed in Scotland by John Knox (1505?-72), Robert Rollock (1555-99), Robert Bruce (sixteenth century) and, later, Samuel Rutherford (1600-61), among many others. Although Bruce was evidently the first to introduce a formal system of federal theology into Scotland in 1589, the idea of covenant had already been current there for about fifty years. Rollock, the first rector of the new University of Edinburgh, had been instrumental in transforming the practice of banding into one of covenanting. His writings, which developed covenant themes, were widely read at home and on the Continent.

John Knox and the Covenant

There is every sign that Knox was the first to articulate and develop the theo-political idea of covenant for Scotland and to undertake to apply that idea in practice as well.[5] Knox began speaking and writing about covenant sometime in 1553-54. Perhaps because of the exigencies of the times, perhaps because he had not yet come to it, Knox, while always concerned with covenant within a political context, at the beginning essentially argued for a theological covenant; that is to say, that God demanded of His human covenant partners that they stamp out idolatry (i.e., Catholicism), and he sought to challenge Mary Tudor for not doing so (1556). Within two years he had moved beyond the theological issue to consider the covenant as a political device, designed to establish regimes, bind rulers and ruled, and offer the possibilities not only for a religiously correct polity, but also for one in which the ruled could call their rulers to account. The progression of his thought should not be examined alone but in the context of actual covenanting in Scotland.

Knox himself not only wrote about the process when he began writing about covenant, but set the idea of a political band in motion by urging the Scottish nobility to come together to act on the basis of the same covenant that God had made with Israel. As Greaves puts it, "by 1558 the Hebrew idea of covenant and the traditional Scottish practice of banding blended in Knox's mind as manifested in his *Appelladion*.[6]

Knox drew his inspiration directly from the Hebrew Scriptures which he cites, and perhaps also from some of the early English Puritans, since William Tyndale had begun thinking of covenant by the mid-1530s from Geneva and Calvin only after he had moved far enough along so that Calvin's thought was reinforcing rather than stimulating. There is every likelihood that he was also influenced by Bullinger, directly or through Tyndale and his colleagues. While the evidence is not so obviously available, there are enough indicators pointing to the direct influence of Bullinger on Tyndale and on Miles Coverdale, who was influenced by Tyndale but who also corresponded with Bullinger and translated two of his works into English.[7] Another possible line of influence for the English Puritans was John Hooper, a disciple of Bullinger.[8]

While Knox acknowledges Calvin with great respect, the concept of covenant that he transmitted remained much closer to the Zurich school and its English Puritan expression than to Calvin, emphasizing the mutual obligations derived from covenant and established by covenant, transposing covenant and its obligations from the religious to the political realm where it found fertile ground in Scottish political culture, up to and including the right of the people to actively resist a tyrannical monarch.[9] If anything, the evidence points to Knox's influence on Calvin, after the former's sojourn in Geneva, in the same direction of the political uses of covenant.[10]

John Knox developed his political views of covenant primarily in response to Mary Tudor's accession to the throne in 1553.[11] The next year, Knox fled into exile on the Continent for five years along with other Protestants, including Christopher Goodman and John Ponet. All three developed covenantal views of civil society and resistance to tyranny; and it is in the work of these Marian exiles that one finds the genesis of Puritanism.

In 1559, Knox returned to Scotland and commenced a successful campaign of religious reformation. At a meeting of the Estates in August 1560, Knox was instrumental in securing a Calvinistic confession of faith for Scottish Protestants. This became the basis for abolishing the authority of the Pope in Scotland along with laws supporting the Catholic Church, and for imposing severe penalties on those who celebrated or attended mass. At the same time, the Scottish Church was organized along federal presbyterian lines with ministers and elders being elected by local congregations. In turn, these local or "particular kirks" were organized into representative provincial associations and then into a nationwide General Assembly of "the whole church convened," or "universal kirk."

Although Knox, as a practitioner rather than scholar, never composed an overall treatise on his political ideas, a general outline can be constructed from his various statements. Basically, Knox construed the people, namely faithful Protestants, as being parties to a covenant with God much like the Israelites of old. Thus, it is easy to see how this idea could be transformed by Scots in their later confrontations with England into a special nationalistic covenant between God and Scotland, the new Israel. This covenant prohibits the people from worshipping in ways contrary to Scripture and requires that they advance and defend the true religion. Since Knox regarded every individual as being a party or signatory to this covenant, he held that each individual was responsible to God for complying with its terms.

Like the Huguenot *Vindiciae*, Knox also appears to have had in mind two covenants pertaining to government. One is a covenant between God, the king and nobles, and the magistrates who represent the people. In seeking biblical support, Knox argued that King Josiah had made a comparable covenant for the people of Israel. This was a particularly appropriate example for Knox because it was a reforming covenant that involved the destruction of idolatrous pagan and monarchical practices that had crept into the religion and politics of Israel (II Kings 23). The second covenant is one between the people and their rulers for which Knox looked to the model of King Asa (I Kings 15:9–24; II Chronicles 15). Consequently, the people possess a right and duty to resist and depose, if necessary, an unjust ruler who violates the covenant with God and/or the people.

The Reformation in Scotland

The Reformation came to Scotland in what is known as the Revolution of 1559–60. In the classic manner of covenantal polities, it began with the equivalent of a declaration of independence in the form of the Scottish Confession of Faith, and then a constitution in the form of the Book of Discipline. The Confession of Faith was first adopted by the Scottish Parliament. Through it Parliament granted the kirk sovereign authority in its sphere, limiting the authority of the state accordingly. It led to the convening of the first General Assembly of the Scottish Church in 1560. The General Assembly adopted the Book of Discipline not only for its own organization, but to organize the nation as a whole.

The Scottish Confession of Faith followed the model of the Swiss Confession, borrowing heavily from it, while the Book of Discipline was a constitution to organize the nation in the true faith according to the principles of the confession. It introduced the idea of congregational election of ministers, a national system of education, and poor relief.

The General Assembly evolved over the next few years. Its synodical base was introduced in 1562 and the position of moderator in 1563. Presbyteries were not added until 1580. J. D. Mackie describes the result in this manner: "Not all men became truly religious. For some religion was a superstition to be disregarded or scorned; for others it was a way to be followed when piety became fashionable; for others it became an insurance against evil punishment, and for others a cloak to conceal an evil life. Yet in the main the Scottish people became not only God-fearing but God-trusting."[12]

The restructuring was completed with the adoption of the second Book of Discipline by the General Assembly in 1581 under the leadership of Melville in consultation with the English Presbyterians. That second constitution explicitly asserted that the kirk derived its power directly from God and that there was a spiritual authority founded upon Scripture and independent of the state.

After Knox, political uses of covenanting became ever more prominent in Scottish struggles against England.[13] A strong nationalist, Presbyterian movement emerged known as the Scottish Covenanters. In 1581,

Scottish leaders signed the King's Confession or National Covenant, which was drafted by John Craig in response to Roman Catholic efforts to regain control of Scotland. This covenant was based on the Confession of 1560 and was renewed in 1590 and 1596.

It must be recalled that the Reformation in Scotland was not an act of state but came in defiance of a highly Catholic monarchy, represented at the time by the highly assertive, romantic, and ultimately tragic figure of Mary, Queen of Scots. Its success is all the more extraordinary for that since in most other parts of Europe success came only after the rulers adopted Protestantism. There seems little doubt that this is what gave the kirk (as the Reformed Church is known in Scotland) and its doctrines such powerful vigor, the Scots their tenacious attitude toward it, and Reformed theology its political as well as intellectual power. As Knox's successor, Andrew Melville, said to King James VI: "There are two kings and two kingdoms in Scotland. There is Christ Jesus the King and his kingdom, the Kirk, whose subject, King James VI, is, and of whose kingdom not a king, nor a lord, nor a head, but a member."[14]

It was Melville who provided the organizational ability to translate Knox's theology into a viable church polity. J. M. Reid describes him as "a man of immense energy, universal learning and vivid intelligence."[15] Melville introduced the Presbyterian system and gave the Presbytery the power of a court to oversee the individual churches, thereby doing away with the need for bishops or royal superintendents. The cornerstone of Melville's system was an educated church membership, sufficiently literate to read the Bible, from whom a leadership, both ordained and lay, could be developed. Ministers were to be trained in the universities, where Reformed doctrine dominated. The result was a system of diffused authority, deeply rooted in an educated and, therefore, self-directed population.

By 1592 the Reformation in Scotland was complete. By its act of that year the Scottish Parliament accepted the second Book of Discipline, authorized the convening of an annual kirk general assembly, and provided for the rest of the Church organization.

The Seventeenth-Century Struggle for Covenant and Independence

Eleven years later, on the death of Elizabeth, James VI of Scotland became also James I of England, inaugurating a century of royal union between Scotland and England. James was committed to royal absolutism. Accordingly, one of his first acts was to initiate an assault on the Scottish kirk for its republican tendencies. In doing so he opened what was to be the main feature of seventeenth-century politics in the British Isles—the struggle between absolutism and covenantalism.

In a series of measures between 1603 and 1616 James managed to reimpose a high degree of royal control over the kirk, principally in the form of introducing hierarchical elements into the Church polity and Anglican elements into the liturgy, forcing back the currents of Reformed Protestantism. Then, in 1616, he overstepped himself and forced an episcopal organization on the kirk, legitimized through his "anti-covenant," the Five Articles of Perth, which he forced upon the Scottish civil and religious leadership. This act provoked strong resistance among the Scots.

When James died in 1625, his son Charles I continued his father's ways. In a sense, James I can be seen as the Solomon of Britain, introducing a new edifice to unite the kingdoms at the expense of traditional English and Scottish liberties, while Charles I was the Rehoboam, who replaced his father's whips with scorpions (cf. I Kings 1:14). Like Rehoboam, he paid the price, losing his kingdom and, in his case, his head as well.

Charles I alienated the Scottish nobility by seeking to recapture ecclesiastical lands that had been expropriated to their advantage. He compounded his problem by trying to impose a version of the English prayerbook upon the Scottish church—as Haller says, "thus at one stroke overriding religious conviction, economic interest, and established legal procedure." Riots broke out in Edinburgh amidst a general demand that the new prayerbook be recalled. When the king refused, the entire Scottish public—nobles, gentry, ministers, and commoners—came together (28 February 1638) to bind themselves by a National Covenant where they promised to defend each other and the "true religion, liberties and laws of the kingdom...against all sorts of persons whatsoever."[16]

Thus, Charles's absolutism in religious and civil matters led in Scotland to the National Covenant of 1638. The sequence of events is clear. Charles neglected Scotland at the beginning and only eight years into his reign, in 1633, came north to be crowned in his original kingdom. There he initiated the repressive acts of 1634 and 1635 that struck at the very foundations of Scottish religious and civil liberties. The Scots acted as "Christians who have renewed the covenant with God." Thus, on Wednesday, 28 February 1638, "that glorious mariage [sic] day of the kingdom with God," the covenant was signed by the nobles and gentlemen in the kirk of Greyfriars in Edinburgh. On 1 March the ministers and representatives of the burgs signed. The general public in the Edinburgh area signed on 2 and 3 March. Then the covenant was circulated throughout the country. By 5 April, signatures had been gathered from every corner of the land, excluding only most of the Highlands and Aberdeen, which remained Roman Catholic and Episcopal, respectively.

This new National Covenant updated and amended the Covenant of 1581. In it, the Scots vowed to die if necessary to protect their civil and religious systems. While not exactly a democratic document in that it recognized classes, the covenant was made to include all Scots: "the noblemen, barons, gentlemen, burgesses, ministers, and commons." They covenanted "before God, His angels and the world." This covenant also assumed a more explicitly constitutional character than the earlier ones. It held, among other things, that Charles I did not possess the authority to mandate such a religious change unilaterally, but that approval was required on the part of "free assemblies" and parliaments.

Once the covenant was signed, the Scots' struggle to preserve their liberties knew no bounds. Political and religious liberties were intertwined. The covenant, originally defensive, became the basis for a thorough reconstitution of the Scottish polity as well as the kirk. The king was forced to recognize the authority of Scottish estates.

The king, recognizing the difficulty he was in, gave his reluctant consent to the convening of a general assembly of the Scottish kirk at Glasgow in November 1638. The general assembly attacked the Scottish bishops as agents of royal authority, at which point the king's commissioner ordered it to dissolve. The response, delivered by assembly moderator Alexander Henderson, acknowledged "the power of Christian kings for convening assemblies, and their power in them, yet that must not derogate from Christ's right, for he has given warrant to convocate assemblies whether magistrates consent or not."[17]

The assembly proceeded to reject the prayerbook, abolish the prelacy, and excommunicate all who refused to bind themselves by the National Covenant. It called for a session of the Scottish Parliament to ratify these acts and, asserting the kirk's authority to convene a general assembly whenever necessary, issued a call for another meeting to be held in Edinburgh the following July.

When Charles tried to fight back, regiments were raised throughout the country. Scottish soldiers of fortune returned from the European war and the first of the covenanters' armies was formed. In 1639–40, there were two military confrontations known as the Bishops' Wars. In each case the king backed down without a fight, realizing that he was outgunned and did not have the requisite backing of the English Parliament.

After his first royal concession, known as the pacification of Berwick (18 June 1639), the General Assembly and the Estates met to introduce more radical constitutional reforms. The king's commissioner (his representative in Scotland) refused to ratify them and prorogued the parliament without its consent. On 2 June 1640, recognizing the king's weakness, the estates reconvened, disregarding a further prorogation. Since no royal commissioner was in attendance, they elected their own president; declared themselves a valid parliament; abolished the clerical estate; ratified all the acts of the last General Assembly, including making the covenant obligatory on all Scots; passed a triennial act; and voted supplies for the strong army that they had raised.

By invoking a fourteenth-century precedent that entrusted the authority of parliament to a single committee uniting the three estates, they in effect established a government responsible to parliament in which the nobility were outnumbered. The Earl of Argyll became their leader; the Presbyterian Church the dominant party. The Scottish government consisted of the standing committee of the Estates and the commission of the General Assembly working together as a single body. Thus, the Scots were the first to make it clear that God required magistrates to be responsible to the people—provided they were God-fearing—and the laws of the realm, and that force could be used to bring magistrates to that position.

Charles made another attempt to regain control in Scotland. His second failure was to further weaken his position in England as well. It involved a Scottish invasion of northern England and was settled on 16 October 1640, also in favor of the Scots. Once again the king was forced to give in. Since Scotland still formally adhered to his rule, the king came back to his native land to try to organize a royalist party in the new parliamentary framework. Not only did he fail, but the Scots now demanded that all senior royal appointments be first approved by parliament. The king retired to England. There his situation went from bad to worse, and within two years the English Civil War had begun.

The Solemn League and Covenant

Both sides appealed to the Scots for support, and in the summer of 1643 the Scottish government decided for the parliamentary side, joining with the English in the Solemn League and Covenant, the treaty of alliance that committed the contracting parties to preserve the Reformed religion throughout the British Isles. The British sought only a "civil league." The Scots insisted on a religious covenant in return for their assistance, and which stipulated that Presbyterianism be introduced into England. As approved by Parliament, the Solemn League and Covenant provided, among other things, for a civil and religious union of Scotland, England, and Ireland under a presbyterian parliamentary system, a further reformation of religion in the union, and the extirpation of Catholicism and prelacy.

This covenant was to have been a prelude for what in the twentieth century would have been called a new "International" linking all the Reformed churches, including those on the continent. The Scots even made concessions, adopting the standards of the Westminster Assembly in place of their own for the sake of religious unity. But while the English government was Presbyterian in sentiment, most of the English Puritans remained congregationalists. Nevertheless, by the end of the summer of 1643 both countries had ratified the Solemn League and Covenant and the Scots began raising an army to go to the relief of England.

Pursuant to the new covenant, the English Parliament ordered the Westminster Assembly of Divines, which had been formed as an advisory body, to frame "a Confession of Faith for the three Kingdoms, according to the Solemn League and Covenant." The Assembly produced a *Confession of Faith,* a *Larger* and *Shorter Catechism,* a *Form of Government,* and a *Directory for Public Worship.* This Westminster Confession (1647–48), which was quickly approved by the Scottish church and parliament, became the basis of modern Presbyterianism and set it firmly in the federalist-covenantal rather than Calvinist-Genevan stream of things. The Confession had a significant impact on the Reformed church movement generally and on other denominations, particularly the seventeenth-century Baptists.[18]

Scottish intervention helped tip the balance in favor of Cromwell's army at Marsten Moor. Their subsequent role in the war was marginal. In the meantime, tensions between the two parliaments grew as the English became less committed to Presbyterianism and, thus, to the covenant. Parliamentary supremacy in the southern country meant that Parliament would not give the Church independence (an anathema, or more precisely, erastianism) to the Scots. While obligated by Parliament to take the covenant, many in Cromwell's army were independents and refused, while many of the English Presbyterians were still committed to maintaining the king on his throne, albeit limited in his powers.

Charles attempted to exploit the widening breach. While he personally would not take the covenant, he initiated discussions on the matter that resulted in his reunion with the Scots in England. The English Parliament and army responded in anger and sought to return the Scottish army to Scotland. The Scots were prepared to return but could not take the king with them as long as he was uncovenanted. Before the Scots left they tried to insure his safety, but in the end he was taken by Cromwell's army.

The Solemn League and Covenant was all but dead. As the Scots perceived that England was not going to fulfill its part of the Solemn League and Covenant, they began to explore renewing their alliance with the king. In the Engagement of December 1647, Charles pledged qualified support for Presbyterianism and the next year the Scottish Estates, where the covenanters were now a minority, sent the army southward in a typically hopeless effort. Cromwell destroyed the Scottish army, captured its general, Alexander Hamilton, and had him beheaded, even though he was a Scottish officer doing his duty as charged by the Scottish Parliament.

Hamilton's defeat restored the covenanters' party to power in Scotland with Cromwell's endorsement. The Engagement was repudiated on 4 January 1649, and the Solemn League and Covenant was renewed. Cromwell used the settlement to clear the way for the execution of the king (against Scottish principles) on 30 January. The Scottish were unreconciled and immediately proclaimed Charles's son as king of Great Britain, France, and Ireland, infuriating Cromwell.

Once again the Scots misassessed the situation. With the army in control in England, they could hardly maintain the Solemn League and Covenant with that country and still have Charles as their king. On the other hand, Charles was no better than his father. He would not accept the covenants. At most, he would agree to maintain Presbyterianism in Scotland. Basically he was trying to hold the Scots while organizing his return to London. He tried to reestablish royalist control in Scotland, though he denied the attempt. After that effort failed, Charles did come to Scotland and sign both covenants, an absurd action for all parties. The king did not believe in them and the covenanters properly did not trust royal rule.

Charles signed the covenants on 23 June 1650. The next month Cromwell invaded Scotland, appealing to the Scottish commitment to Reformed religion. Initially he was blocked by the Scottish army, but a tactical mistake, based on the premise that the English were retreating, gave Cromwell his opportunity. After defeating the Scots in battle, he occupied Edinburgh and the Lowlands, driving a wedge between the hard-line covenanters on one side and the more moderate Presbyterians and royalists on the other.

Argyll placed the crown on Charles's head at Scone on 1 January 1651. The war was resumed with English victories, leading to the capture of the entire committee of the Estates. By 25 February 1652, Charles had lost his last fortress in Scotland and had to flee. Conquered Scotland was forced into union with England, although the appropriate legislation was never fully enacted because of the turbulence in the southern commonwealth throughout the years of Cromwell's rule.

Cromwell sent eight commissioners to rule Scotland. In 1655 they were replaced by a council of state that was maintained by military occupation, generally benevolent in its administration. The Scottish Church continued to function, although the General Assembly was suspended in 1653 for continuing to advocate its independence of the state. In matters of church governance, there was little difference between the Puritans and the Presbyterians, so the moral policies of the covenant were maintained.

Mackie concludes that "in the main, Scotland fared well during the Usurpation."[19] The country was peaceful and prosperous, religion and morality were maintained, the universities supported. The Scottish Presbyterians enjoyed considerable freedom under Cromwell and, in fact, the Covenanters stimulated a series of awakenings in Scotland during this time. The Scots still were pleased when the Union ended as a result of the Restoration. It was perhaps more because of their Presbyterianism

than for any other reason, although heavy taxation, the disgrace of being ruled by a foreign government, and royalist sentiments played their
part as well.

The Restoration and Repression of the Covenanters

Covenant ideas continued to be formally argued in Scotland, at least
through the deposition of James VII (in England James II) in 1688-89,
principally by those who resisted the English conquest under Cromwell.
Their position rested principally on the Scottish national covenants of
1638 and 1643, although in the last analysis they rested on their particular political philosophic or theological logic, for most of them derived
from Scripture. Among the Scottish leadership they were in a progres-
sively smaller minority as the Covenanter revolts failed to dislodge the
English and in the process encouraged the English to deal with Scotland
and the Scots with an ever heavier hand. At first, the Covenanters supported the Stuart monarchy as a Scottish crown standing in opposition
to English rule. In the end Covenanters became anti-Stuart as well as
anti-English. In the process they articulated good seventeenth-century
political theory that men and their households originally lived in a state
of nature and had to covenant with each other to form civil society, that
kings were not like fathers to their people nor even husbands, but were
rather in a fiduciary relationship with them, dependent upon covenants
entered into. Thus, the Scottish Covenanters upheld covenantal political thought well into the days of John Locke.[20]

The restoration of Charles II in 1660 opened a new round of persecution. The new king had three goals: to avoid exile, to become an absolute monarch, and to restore Roman Catholicism as the established
religion throughout Britain. While the first was acceptable to the loyal
Scots, the last two violated every tenet of their political and religious
beliefs. His agents in Scotland proceeded swiftly to implement this program through royal councils, convening Parliament only once in 1661
to enact the legislation necessary to pave the way for absolute monarchical rule and the introduction of episcopal church government.

Charles II repudiated the covenants of 1638 and 1643, declaring them
unlawful oaths. Ministers who refused to abjure the covenants or submit to bishops were persecuted and dismissed from their churches. Many
of these ministers began to preach in fields and secret assemblies and,

by 1665, the Covenanters mounted an armed rebellion that lasted until their defeat in 1679. Because of the barbarous brutality with which the forces of Charles II suppressed the Covenanters, and their equally violent responses, the period of 1665–79 became known in Scotland as "the killing time." As the Covenanter movement waned under this persecution, many sought refuge in the New World. Distressed by their defeat, the more hardened Covenanters signed the Sanquhar Declaration in 1680 under the leadership of Richard Cameron. Becoming known as Cameronians, they separated from the Church of Scotland to become the Reformed Presbyterians, an independent church until it joined with the Free Church in Scotland in 1876. They continued their resistance, rejecting the monarchy and fighting a guerilla war until the last of their ministers was captured and executed in 1688.

In that year both England and Scotland revolted against Charles' successor, James (II in England and VII in Scotland). Upon his proclamation as King of Scots on 10 February 1685, James pointedly did not take the coronation oath to defend the Protestant religion, and in the amnesty that he proclaimed, he excluded all Covenanters. The first Parliament to meet under his reign once more reaffirmed the earlier acts defining the taking of the covenants to be treason and being in the presence of a Covenanters' conventicle punishable by death. The new Earl of Argyll, son of the great leader of the previous generation, led an effort to resist. In an ill-fated invasion of England Argyll was captured and beheaded in June 1685. This triggered a new wave of absolutist repression against Protestants in both countries.

The birth of a son to James in June 1688 made it clear to the English notables that if he were not removed his policies would continue through his heir. They invited William of Orange, a good Dutch Calvinist, and his wife, Mary, to jointly assume the throne. With that mandate in hand, William sent a special address to Scotland offering to rescue the country from James's tyranny. James fled England on 23 December 1688. The Scottish estates were summoned to meet on 14 March 1689 as a convention to decide Scotland's political future. Freed from the disabilities imposed by the previous ruler, the Whigs gained a small majority in the convention and elected a president. On 11 April they issued a declaration that included a radical claim of right reaffirming the covenantal theory of political rule, declaring the throne vacant, and offering the crown to William and Mary. This theory was further spelled out in the Articles of Grievances adopted on 13 April, along with a new coronation oath that included those principles. In neither document was there any mention of the earlier covenant as such. Instead, its theories were presented in secularized form and as such they triumphed when William took the oath before representatives of the three estates. Thus, the Presbyterian party was succeeded by the Whigs as the dominant political force in the land. The latter presented a secularized version of the political views of the Covenanters by holding that the polity was founded by political compact.

The Whig compromise enraged the Jacobite supporters of the Stuarts and the radical Cameronian Covenanters, but it was a compromise that succeeded. (The Cameronians were transformed into a regiment by that name, known colloquially to this day as the Covenanters, who found occasion to take some revenge against their enemies in the Jacobite insurrections of the following years.) In the next several years Presbyterianism was reestablished in fits and starts as William was reluctant to entirely desert the Episcopalians, although the estates in the general assembly pressed hard in that direction.

In general, the years of William's reign were years of political and religious reform. The franchise was enlarged and the famed Education Act of 1696 was enacted. Trade privileges were liberalized. The reestablishment of Presbyterianism brought an end to the religious wars of the Reformation for all intents and purposes.

As one of his last acts before his death in 1702, King William initiated the process of union which, in 1707, united England and Scotland under one parliament. It took five years of difficult negotiations for this to come about against the opposition first of the English and then of the Scots. In the end, neither side felt that they had any choice, considering the problem of succession to the throne in the event of Queen Anne's death and the English struggle with France. The terms of union left Scotland with its own law, judicial system, and established church. Her revolutionary settlement of the relationship between church and state was reaffirmed. The union offered Scotland substantial new opportunities for economic development. The Scottish Estates adjourned on 19 March 1707 and was formally dissolved on 28 April. On 1 May the new Parliament of Great Britain came into existence.

Although the idea of covenant receded from view as an explicit political device after 1680, it had been institutionalized to a great degree in the Westminster Confession and in the school of federal theology that persisted for another century in Scotland.[21] Another lasting influence of the Covenanter movement was the Whig tradition in Britain. It is to the Covenanters that the term *whig* was first applied as an opprobrious epithet ("Whiggamore").[22] After the Glorious Revolution of 1689, the Whig tradition dominated England for the next century (three generations), reshaped into secular form by the public influenced by John Locke. Whig ideas became the bridge between Reformation covenantalism and modern constitutional republicanism.[23]

Notes

1. For a history of the use of the covenant idea for these purposes see S. A. Burrell, "The Covenant Idea as a Revolutionary Symbol in Scotland, 1596-1637, *Church History* 27 (1957): 338-50, and Ian B. Cowan, *The Scottish Covenanters: 1660-1688* (London: Victor Gollancz, 1976), chap. 1, "The Covenants." James B. Torrance, "The Covenant Concept in Scottish Theology and Politics and Its Legacy," inaugural lecture delivered on 20 October 1977 in King's College, University of Aberdeen.

   Torrance suggests that there were three arguments in favor of a covenantal approach in sixteenth- and seventeenth-century Scotland—the historical, the political, and the biblical. He demonstrates how all three were tied together by the major covenant thinkers in Scotland at the time.

   Ian B. Cowan, "The Covenanters," a revision article, *Scottish Historical Review*, no. 47 (April 1968): 35-52. This is a scholarly historical article that attempts to give a balanced account of the latest understanding of the Scottish covenanters, their movement, and covenants, covering the period 1638 to 1690.

   C. V. Wedgewood, "The Covenanters in the First Civil War," *Scottish Historical Review* 39, no. 127 (April 1960): 1-15.
2. S. A. Burrell, "The Apocalyptic Vision of the Early Covenanters," *The Scottish Historical Review* XLIV, no. 135 (April 1964): 16.
3. John Knox, *History of the Reformation of Religion within the Realm of Scotland* (1587, 1644).
4. C. S. Myer, *Elizabeth I and the Religious Settlement of 1559*, in Lewis (1960), 132.
5. See Richard L. Greaves, "John Knox and the Covenant Tradition," *Journal of Ecclesiastical History* 24:1 (January 1973): 23-32.
6. Ibid., 29; *The Political Writings of John Knox*, ed. Marvin A. Breslow (Washington, D.C.: Folger Shakespeare Library, 1985).
7. W. A. Clebsch, *England's Earliest Protestants, 1520-1535* (New Haven: Yale University Press, 1964); L. J. Trinderud, "The Origins of Puritanism," *Church History* 20 (1951); Richard L. Greaves, "The Origins and Early Development of English Covenant Thought," *Historian* 31 (1968): 26-27; J. G. Moler, "The Beginnings of Puritan Covenant Theology," *Journal of Ecclesiastical History* 14 (1963): 50-54.
8. S. Carr, ed., *Early Writings of John Hooper* (Cambridge: Cambridge University Press, 1843), and W. M. S. West, "John Hooper and the Origins of Puritanism," *Baptist Quarterly* (1954): 356-59.

9. J. W. Allan, *A History of Political Thought in the Sixteenth Century,* 2nd ed. (London: Mathuen, 1960), 57–60; C. H. Dodds, *The Political Theory of the Huguenots of the Dispersion* (New York: Columbia University Press, 1947); John Shirley, *Richard Hooker and Contemporary Political Ideas* (London: S.P.C.K., 1949); R. H. Murray, *The Political Consequences of the Reformation* (New York: Russell and Russell, 1960); Christopher Hill, *Intellectual Origins of the English Revolution* (Oxford: Clarendon Press, 1965).

10. Greaves, "John Knox and the Covenant Tradition"; Allan, *A History of Political Thought in the Sixteenth Century*; Calvin, *Institutes* 4, 20–32 and *Commentaries on the Prophet Daniel,* trans. T. Myers (Grand Rapids: Erdmans, 1948), I, 382.

11. Andrew Lang, *John Knox and the Reformation* (London: Longmans, Green, 1905); Jasper Godwin Ridley, *John Knox* (Oxford: Clarendon, 1968).

12. J. D. Mackie, *A History of Scotland* (Middlesex: Penguin Books, rev. ed., 1969), 163.

13. *The Scottish National Covenant in its British Context,* ed. John Morrill (Edinburgh: Edinburgh University Press, 1990); see Burrell, "The Covenant Idea as a Revolutionary Symbol"; and by the same author, "The Apocalyptic Vision of the Early Covenanters," *The Scottish Historical Review* 63, no. 135 (1964).

14. As quoted in J. M. Reid, *Scotland Past and Present* (London: Oxford Unversity Press, 1959), 76.

15. Ibid., 77.

16. *Sourcebook of Scottish History,* 102. On the Scottish National Covenant of 1638, see Morrill, ed., *The Scottish National Covenant.*

17. Mackie, *A History of Scotland.*

18. Jane Lane, *The Reign of King Covenant* (London: Robert Vale, 1956); Henry Thomas Buckle, *On Scotland and the Scotch Intellect* (Chicago: University of Chicago Press, 1970).

19. Mackie, *A History of Scotland,* 229.

20. Ian Michael Smart, "The Political Ideas of the Scottish Covenanters, 1638–88," *History of Political Thought* 1, no. 2 (Summer, June 1980): 167–93.

21. Buckle, *On Scotland*; Reid, *Scotland Past and Present,* chap. 4.

22. *Webster's Third New International Dictionary,* ed., s.v. "Whig," (1) Presbyterian or Covenanter in Scotland in the seventeenth century; (2) One favoring the exclusion in 1679–80 of the Duke of York from the line of succession to the British throne principally because of his Roman Catholicism. Also: of, relating to or constituting one of the two major British political groups from the Roundheads and associated chiefly at first with support of the Hanoverians but later with efforts to limit the royal authority and increase parliamentary power and with preference for Dissenters rather than the established Anglican Church. Whiggamore (from obscure E. dialect from whig—yokel, rustic)—a member of a band composed largely of inhabitants of the Southwestern part of Scotland that in 1548 marched to Edinburgh to oppose the king, Duke of Hamilton, and court party.

23. James Rees Jones, *The First Whigs* (London: Oxford University Press, 1961).

15

Scotland and Covenant after Union: A Case Study

Scotland, like Switzerland and unlike the other examples brought in the foregoing chapters, focused its major covenantal thrust on the achievement of a national covenant that would be both theologically and politically liberating. It persisted in its efforts for a good century and a half. In the end, however, its proximity to England and its own small size compared to its larger neighbor brought about its forced absorption into the emergent United Kingdom of Great Britain. This put an end to the possibility of a full Scottish national covenant with its own comprehensive institutional embodiments. Rather, covenant slowly withdrew to the cultural sphere where, for subsequent centuries until the present day, the covenantal culture, its ideas, and its patterns of behavior has had its influence on the Scots. This chapter focuses on the political impact of those cultural survivals and its implications, to which Scottish unity and distinctiveness were both maintained and undermined.

In the religious sphere, the end of conditions of national unity resulting from the end of the national political covenant opened the door for schisms in the Church as each party or group that had been party to the national covenant on the basis of ideological conviction pursued those convictions to their logical conclusions, leading to the splintering of the Reformed Church, and demonstrating once again that under different conditions the same pride of independent thought that can lead people to come together and covenant with one another can under other conditions lead to schismatic behavior.

From Covenantal Community to Schismatic Kirks

A year after the last James had been driven from the thrones of Britain, the Presbyterian Kirk of Scotland reemerged as a great national institution, largely independent of the state structure, but turned inward to preserve the Covenant and its doctrines in Scotland.[1] In rejecting the expansionist doctrines of the earlier covenants that sought to impose Reformed Protestantism on the other nations of the British Isles, it opened the way to a schism, leading to the emergence of a new church, the Reformed Presbyterians, who held that the National Covenant and the Solemn League and Covenant could never be abandoned because they were covenants between the Scottish people and God. They continue to exist to this day.

Many Scots accepted the union with England of 1707 principally because it guaranteed the independence of the Kirk and its protection from Catholic monarchs. Nevertheless, there were those who feared that putting Scotland under the rule of foreign kings and a foreign parliament not bound by the Scots' covenants would be disastrous. Their fears were confirmed when the British parliament immediately violated the terms of the union that protected the right of the parish representatives to elect their own ministers and by legislation reintroduced patronage (that is to say, the nomination of ministers by local notables, usually landowners).

This led to more schisms in the Kirk, easily enough done under a covenantal system where any dissenting minister or congregation could form a kirk session of their own and any group of ministers could declare themselves a presbytery. There followed a series of secessions, each of which led to further subdivisions. There were divisions into burghers and antiburghers based upon the rejection by the latter of an oath required from burgesses of Scottish towns because to them it implied recognition of the established church. Then came the division between new lichts and auld lichts, because the latter insisted that the civil power had a duty to impose the secessionist orthodoxy on all. Finally, there was a division between lifters and antilifters because the latter forbade ministers to raise communion elements during the consecration service. Then the Relief Church broke away.

Finally, in 1843 there was the Great Disruption when 400 ministers and at least a quarter of a million congregants seceded to establish the Church of Scotland Free in reaction to the British politicians' refusal to allow the kirk to rid itself of patronage. Without any state support and relying entirely on voluntary contributions, the Free Church established itself throughout Scotland. Since every missionary had seceded, it became responsible for the entire missionary work of the Church of Scotland. It was fully organized, with its own assembly, synods, presbyteries, and congregations, introducing a new dynamism into Scottish religion.

A dispute over doctrine between conservatives—those faithful to the original ways—and progressives—those seeking to adapt to the times—brought about the original schism in the Presbyterian Kirk of Scotland. Once unity was shattered, other schisms followed as a matter of course. First of all, it was not only institutionally easy but ideologically justifiable under federalism. While, under the right circumstances, the bonds of covenant may be the bonds of iron, once the sense a covenant is being violated has spread, those bonds fall away.

Subsequent developments were in the direction of reunion, culminating in 1929 when almost all the congregations rejoined a now quite independent National Kirk. Patronage had been abolished by statute in 1874 and the independence of the Church from the civil authorities had been recognized by the Articles Declaratory passed by the General Assembly in 1919 and recognized by act of Parliament in 1921. The actions of 1919 and 1921 essentially constitutionalized Melville's understanding of the two kingdoms. It may fully be said that the British parliament abjured its sovereignty in matters of faith in Scotland.

Universal Education in a Covenantal Community

On the other hand, the twentieth-century church has long since lost control of Scottish education.[2] The educational system's goals were set forth in the *Book of Discipline,* published in 1560, which embodied John Knox's plan for the schools and universities. It remained the constitution of Scottish education until the twentieth century. In typical covenantal fashion, it emphasized elementary schools in every church and secondary schools in every "notable town," "seeing that God hath determined that His Church here on earth shall be taught not by angels but by men." Education was to be for all, with the rich paying their own costs and the poor being supported for at least two years of elementary education and the more talented among them for seven years of secondary. Implementation of this plan began with the universities, which were reorganized by the Reformers and raised from limited provincial institutions to major factors in promoting the covenantal religion and forming a covenanted commonwealth. In Scotland, as in Switzerland and the Netherlands, the alliance between the church and the academy was a vital part of Reformed life. However, the political leadership refused to pay the costs involved. It was not until the 1696 act that local school taxes were imposed and schoolmasters' salaries guaranteed by law.

Until the British reforms of the nineteenth century, the Kirk continued to be responsible for education and social welfare in Scotland, thereby enabling Scots to retain home rule in these critical areas of public activity. While the national system of education had been formally established by an act of the Scottish Estates in 1696, it was not especially protected in the Act of Union. By contrast, the rights of the universities, which were not part of the local parish system, were specifically safeguarded by the Act, perhaps because elementary and secondary education were in the hands of the Church and as such deemed protected.

Scotland became the first country in Europe to establish a common school system open to all. The extraordinary success of the Scottish dominies (teachers) in bringing the people to a high level of literacy in one to three years' time has not only been immortalized in literature, but was reflected in the products of their schools. At the end of the eighteenth century every parish had its school and if education was not compulsory, it was general, with most boys and some girls having at least a year or two of parish school education. Colleges and, in the late eighteenth century, academies did develop in the major towns for secondary education. Management of the schools was left in the hands of the parish ministers and presbyteries under the Act, which remained in force in its original form until 1803 when the British parliament enacted what was, in effect, an amendment to it that doubled teachers' salaries and the minimum size of school buildings.

In the eighteenth century Scottish universities acquired a world reputation. As the loci of the Scottish Enlightenment they were instrumental in secularizing covenantal ideas and applying them to philosophy, politics, and political economy. They were equally important in mathematics, the natural sciences, technological development, and medicine. Since Non-conformists could not be admitted to the Anglican universities of England and Ireland, many of them traveled to Scotland to study, further strengthening the Scottish universities. In addition, because they provided a technological and scientific education, they attracted students who wanted more than the narrowly classical learning of Oxford and Cambridge. Thus, they brought about a new synthesis of the Scottish philosophical, political, and technological traditions.

It was only in the nineteenth century, after the disruption in the Scottish Church and the introduction of state education in England, that the British government began to intervene in Scottish education. The controlling role of the established church was strongly curtailed in the act of 1872, two years after the Education Act of 1870, which established a uniform system of elementary schooling in England and Wales. The Scottish act made education compulsory eight years before that was done for Scotland's neighbors to the south. (By then 80 percent of Scottish children between the ages of six and thirteen were attending schools and it is safe to assume that most of the others had done so sufficiently long enough to learn to read and write.) In 1872, according to Reid, one Scottish child in 140 was attending secondary school, whereas the ratio was one in 249 in Prussia, one in 570 in France, and one in 1300 in England.

The act changed the organization and financing of Scottish schools, substantially increasing the government grants introduced earlier. A Scottish education department was established with responsibility for regulating the entire educational system in Scotland, and elected school boards were introduced in each parish and burgh for both elementary and secondary public schools (in Scotland the term means what it does in the United States). Elementary school fees were abolished and free places were provided for the secondary schools. (Secondary school fees were dropped after 1918.) Universal university education became possible after 1901 when Andrew Carnegie, the American millionaire born and raised in Scotland, established a trust with sufficient funds to pay the university fees of all poor students at Scottish universities. Thus, 300 years after it was proposed, the program of 1560 was almost completely realized.

Unfortunately, in the twentieth century, British intervention turned to standardization. The parish school boards were abolished in 1918 in favor of county boards as in England. For eleven years they were elected, then they too were abolished and responsibility for education was transferred to education committees of the county and city councils. Thus, centralization was introduced into the education system by outside forces against the wishes of the Scots and in the face of the successful operation of the more popularly based system. Centralization of school finance in the hands of the British Treasury continued apace, leaving Scotland with less money for its education system, especially after 1939.

Parliament also imposed English rules for separating academic and vocational education, ending the traditional egalitarianism of Scottish education and virtually killing the tradition of the parish schools. The Scottish education department tried to counter this by establishing comprehensive schools and opening the possibility for most children to pass through the academic track, at least in part. But in the end the egalitarian principles of the covenantal tradition in education have been sacrificed to the hierarchical and elitist traditions of British Toryism in its modern dress.

The Scottish Diaspora Spreads Covenantalism

The ideas and activities of the Scottish Covenanters were also influential in Reformed circles elsewhere in Europe and the New World. The Swiss Reformed churches, especially in Zurich, were very concerned about developments in Scotland and England. When Charles I mobilized against the Scots, the Swiss feared that civil war would damage and retard the Reformed movement in Europe. These events were also watched anxiously by Puritans in the New World, where some 30,000 had fled during the early periods of the Covenanter and Puritan struggles for parliamentary power and religious reformation.

From the accession of Charles II onward, through the Jacobite wars of the mid-eighteenth century, Scottish covenanters moved to the United States in ever-increasing numbers, fleeing English persecution in their native land. Just as the English Puritans introduced covenantalism into New England and the Huguenots did in the South, the Scots became the key force for introducing covenantal ideas and forms of social organization in the Middle colonies. It is true that the Dutch preceded them to New Amsterdam, but their influence was generally confined to the Hudson River Valley, whereas the Scots distributed themselves all over the Middle colonies and then southward into the mountain areas of Virginia and the Carolinas, to become the dominant element of the first American West. Their influence remains strong in those areas to this day.[3]

Princeton University, founded by Scottish theologians, became the center of Presbyterianism in the United States, where federal theology was further developed and where in the mid-eighteenth century the ideas of the Scottish Enlightenment found an American base through which they influenced the founding fathers of the United States.[4] James Madison was but one of the founders educated at Princeton. After graduating, he returned to Princeton for a fifth year to study Hebrew.

When the American Revolution began, many of the Scottish covenanters and their descendants took up arms against the British Crown. Many viewed that war as a continuation of the wars between Scotland and England, which they had lost in the old country but would win in the new.[5] The covenantal character of American civil society gave a certain credibility to that view, which was further enhanced by the prominent role played by Scots and Scottish ideas in its founding.[6]

It is impossible to identify all the strands of influence that were translated from one covenantal society to another. For example, the man responsible for securing the adoption of the basic common school law of the new state of Minnesota in the mid-nineteenth century was Martin McLeod, a Scot who had arrived in what was to become Minnesota from Montreal in 1830 as part of a filibustering expedition and became a fur trader in the Minnesota Territory. Inspired by his own classical education in the common schools of Scotland, he sought a similar system for his adopted state.[7]

In one place at least, Scottish emigres in effect established a new state of their own. That was in Northern Ireland. Throughout the seventeenth century, with English encouragement there was a steady Scottish migration to the Irish province of Ulster. There they came to represent the shock troops of the English occupation of the Emerald Isle and, in turn, built their own way of life based on very conservative expressions of Scottish Presbyterianism.[8]

Needless to say, they were strongly opposed by the Irish, who fought them until decisively defeated at the Battle of the Boyne in 1690, which confirmed the permanence of the Scottish colonization. Until the late nineteenth century, there was no real challenge to what became Scotch-Irish dominion over Ulster. Then, in the late nineteenth century, as the Irish Home Rule movement picked up momentum and became the movement for Irish independence, the Ulster Protestants felt increasingly threatened. Under the terms of the Dominion of Ireland Act of 1921 Ireland was partitioned, with six of the nine counties of Ulster reconstituted as a Protestant-dominated, self-governing entity within the United Kingdom, while the rest of the island became first a self-governing dominion within the British Commonwealth and then an independent state.

This arrangement kept the peace until the 1960s, when the continued tension between Protestants and Catholics led to the eruption of violence whereby the two-thirds of the population that was Protestant was challenged by the Catholic third to give the latter greater equality, and by a new generation of the Irish Republican Army demanding Ulster's reunification with Eire. The civil war in Northern Ireland has now been going on for nearly thirty years; the last place in the world where Catholics and Protestants are battling each other in the name of religion. In the interim, the Ulster Protestants have lost their extensive powers of self-government and have rejected the terms whereby powers would be restored to them, terms that would provide for more substantial representation both for them and for the Catholic minority.

Throughout all of those centuries the Ulster Scots have frequently resorted to covenants to reaffirm their own solidarity and as the constitutional basis for organizing to preserve their claims. On the eve of World War I, they initiated a new national covenant opposing Irish home rule. They did so again in the midst of the present civil war to oppose British government concessions to the Catholics.

The British government's plans for power sharing, whereby the United Kingdom has agreed to share power over policymaking with the Irish Republic on what is formally defined as a consultative basis, while formally retaining full sovereignty over Northern Ireland, is obviously intended to be more than that. It is somewhat ironic that the English-dominated British establishment, with its strong opposition to federal arrangements within the United Kingdom, should be led to testing a new form of *de facto* federal arrangement, resembling condominium, as the result of the stance of a covenanted people.

Other Scottish emigres found new opportunities in the far corners of the British Empire. They formed a major element in the first British settlement of the Cape Colony after it was captured from the Dutch, where they soon came to dominate the local Reformed Church and restructured it and its theology along Scottish Presbyterian lines. Still others became influential in building the Commonwealths of Australia and New Zealand. In many respects they, more than any other covenanted people, helped circulate covenant ideas throughout the world, in the Pacific Islands as much as in central Pennsylvania, thereby fulfilling at least the letter of the mission that they took upon themselves.[9]

Kirk and Chambers: The Twin Pillars of Scottish Autonomy

In 1707, the dual monarchy linking England and Scotland was transformed into a parliamentary union, whereby Scotland gave up its separate and cherished institutions of national government. J. M. Reid claims that "it was chiefly to safeguard the national Church of Scotland that the liquidation of the national State was accepted," leaving Scotland with "a national Church and supra-national State."[10] The independence of the kirk is preserved by the Act of Security, enacted pursuant to the Treaty of Union of 1707, and which every British king or queen must swear to uphold. For years Scots were seen as people who "supped theology with their porridge." This is much less true in the postmodern epoch. Nevertheless, newspapers still carry long letters referring to obscure popes and quoting obscure theologians.

The Church of Scotland has not had a monopoly for two centuries. It remains the state church, albeit free of state control, and the most powerful single institution influencing the country. Scotland remains the only English-speaking country in which a single church is so dominant. Its communicant membership includes more than a third of all Scots and when those who attend church services but have not actually become communicants, known as adherents, are added, over half the population is involved.

The Church remains fully Presbyterian. Each congregation is governed by its kirk session. It includes elders, laymen elected or accepted by the members, presided over by the minister as moderator. Each kirk session sends its minister and one elder to represent it at the Presbytery, of which there are sixty-six in Scotland. They are grouped into twelve Synods that meet twice a year.

The comprehensive governing body of the Church is its General Assembly, which meets annually. Every Scottish kirk session is represented at the General Assembly by its minister and an elder once every four years. The Assembly meets in Edinburgh and has legislative powers in matters of Church governance. It also serves as the Church's highest appellate court.

The British Crown is represented at the assembly by a High Commissioner. Not only is he not a member of the General Assembly by virtue of his office (although some high commissioners are also elders representing a kirk session), but he speaks to the assembly from a place that is technically outside of the assembly hall in order to carefully preserve the boundary between the Crown and the Church. The assembly elects its own moderator for a one-year term. The very term moderator suggests that he is a presiding officer and, in a modest way, a spokesman and representative of the Church, not its head.

The entire Church structure is a classic political matrix to the point where any proposal that would make a serious change in Church law or practice can be "received by the assembly but must be referred to the Presbyteries for final action and is only enacted if two-thirds of the latter accept it." It is this church polity that makes the Church of Scotland distinctive and has given it so prominent a role in Scottish life.

Its present system of government was developed in the seventeenth century and completed before the end of that century. It has hardly changed since. Each cell in the matrix must reach agreement among its members for action to be taken. Extraordinary majorities are required in each arena for critical matters. Normally the system has worked well. When it has occasionally failed it has led to the great crises of modern Scottish history.

The Scottish kirk traces its particular form of government to the monastic origins of Christianity in Scotland, which differed so much from the hierarchical structures that accompanied the establishment of Christianity in other countries. The Church never developed a truly ecclesiastical hierarchy in Scotland. Rather, control over the bishoprics and abbeys and their resources was placed in the hands of the sons of the great families, who rarely took orders or were consecrated in the Church. In a sense the Church became parallel to the clan system and a league of notables. So, for example, when the Reformation came, five illegitimate children of the royal family held six of the great religious houses among them. The Pryor of St. Andrews, James Stewart, actually became the ablest leader of the Protestant nobles.

In Scotland proper, the Presbyterian faith with its federal theology held firm throughout the eighteenth century, even though it was buffeted by the new currents of the Scottish Enlightenment, and only in the nineteenth century did it begin to become undone. In one last effort, a national covenant movement was launched in the 1840s by Thomas Chalmers and others, but the federal theology had run its course. New intellectual currents came to dominate the Scottish scene as they were doing in the rest of the world, based on the scientific discoveries of the nineteenth century. What was left was a covenantal culture deeply rooted in the Scottish population, a culture that continues to be a major dimension of Scottish uniqueness as a nation.

The Westminster Confession formally remains the confession of the Kirk today and is taught as such.[11] In describing it for pedagogic purposes, the Reverend Dr. Sinclair B. Ferguson gives it concisely as "Calvinistic in emphasis, federal in its basic structure, and evangelical in its view of the relationship between God and man."[12] Ferguson further states, "According to the Confession, God's dealings with men are invariably covenantal."[13] He describes God's two covenants with man that establish the framework for the relationship and as a whole emphasizes the centrality of federal theology in the belief system propagated by the Confession.

The other pillar of Scottish nationhood after the Act of Union was the Scottish legal system. Just as the Act left Scotland with its national church, so too did it leave the country with its national law. Scots law has continued to develop without a Scottish legislative body for over 280 years. The system of Scots law took form in the fifteenth century when the Scottish Estates enacted legislation bringing order to a system that, until then, had just grown by custom and accident. In 1532 Scotland's Court of Session was established—the supreme court of civil appeals. Today, it sits in the old parliament house in Edinburgh. Together its two houses with their law-interpreting role constitute the closest thing to a legislative body that Scotland has had since 1707. While there is no appeal out of Scotland in criminal matters, civil matters can be appealed to the British House of Lords. Hence, Scottish civil law has been heavily influenced by acts of the British parliament, while Scottish criminal law remains almost entirely Scottish.

What is sometimes called the common law of Scotland is drawn from Roman law, feudal law, church law, ancient customs, and the acts of the Scots parliament. The president of the Court of Session was still able to declare in 1949 that it was this law rather than British statutes that regulated and defined "all the main rights and duties of the Scottish citizen."[14]

In a curious way, Scottish covenantal society survived after its loss of statehood in a way similar to Jewish covenantal society, that is, through a system of judge-made law. Unlike the Jewish situation, with its single *halakhah* encompassing civil and religious matters, in Scotland two legal systems developed, one civil and one religious, in the spirit of the two kingdoms theory, so much a feature of Scottish Calvinism. Moreover, the means of change in the two systems were the exact reverse of the situation among the Jews. Among the Jews, the religious dimensions of *halakhah* were and are presumably immutable, although they are changed through rabbinical interpretation, while the civil dimensions of *halakhah* can be altered by *takkanot*, ordinances passed by community governing bodies. In Scotland, it is Scottish civil law that has to be changed by judges only since there is no means of legislating, while religious law can be modified by ordinances adopted by the General Assembly of the Kirk.

The foundations for the interpretative approaches to Scots law were actually laid while there still was a Scottish national legislature in the late seventeenth century. The works of jurisprudence that established the lines of its development are still authoritative, the greatest of which is *The Institutions of the Law of Scotland* by Viscount Stair, published in 1681. In his jurisprudence, Stair "fused together the varying strains of material which have gone to make the body of Scots law."[15] Sir Archebald Campbell Black describes Stair's contribution in this way: "The fact that we in Scotland possess a system of law based upon the philosophic method of starting with a right and ending with a vindication is attributable to the genius of Stair."[16]

These seventeenth-century writings provoked a series of eighteenth-century commentaries written after the demise of the Scottish parliament. Men like Don Erskine (1695–1768), David Hume the younger, and George Joseph Bell (1770–1843) who wrote on the criminal and mercantile law, completed the classical foundations of Scots law. Today, the interaction between the Scottish courts; the Faculty of Advocates, including all those who practice at the bar of the supreme courts; and the Law Society of Scotland, to which all solicitors must belong, may have fashioned a legal system that places the rights of the individual before the claims of the state. For example, the Scots legalized divorce three centuries before it became accepted in English law. Legal aid for the poor has been provided for more than five centuries.

One of the most powerfully covenantal features of Scots law was the power to sue the Crown in contract, which had long been legally available and actually was used successfully. Although the right to sue the king in his own court disappeared with the Act of Union, Scots have retained the right to sue the Crown in contract. Moreover, under Scottish law, a Scotsman belongs to himself rather than to the state. Suicide is not a crime and no person may be convicted of any crime without the corroborative evidence of at least two witnesses.

In the postmodern epoch, Scots law has been threatened by absorption into the English system. The great rise in parliamentary legislation and administrative regulation that has characterized the twentieth century has increasingly interfered with the application of Scots law. Not surprisingly, the legislation and regulations reflect English practice. Thus, the Scots are now engaged in a struggle to maintain their own legal system against the administrative state.

Nevertheless, as the Scottish kirk and Scots law have been challenged by the new turns in contemporary society and government, Scotland has reasserted itself through its administrative structure which, in the twentieth century, has given it as close to a separate administrative framework as it has had at any time since 1707. While this is principally a development of the last century, its starting point does lie in the differences between the Scottish and English regimes at the time of the Act of Union. In England, parliament was sovereign. In the government of England, king, Lords, and Commons together represented a concentration of authority unimaginable in Scotland.

Covenant in Contemporary Scotland

The Estates of Scotland, as the Scottish parliament was called, was not sovereign. Rather, it was still based upon a feudal structure in which the rights of the various bodies were constitutionally protected, even against the Crown. Land was the principal basis of feudal organization and the source of rights. This was true even of the towns that were linked through the convention of royal burghs, which became something of a subparliament for municipal affairs. It continued to function after the Union, more like a national chamber of commerce, and still exists. Thus, authority and power in Scotland were divided among at least five bodies: the Crown, the Estates, the law courts, the Kirk, and the burghs. J. M.

Reid suggests that "in these conditions Scotland could not be governed, even after the Union, as England was governed. It had to be 'managed.'"[17]

In the continuing Scottish struggle for at least local self-government since 1707, covenantal principles were both useful and were reinforced by the Scottish situation. One manifestation of this was the emphasis on elections within Scottish institutions, from the congregation to the House of Lords. (The Scottish Lords elect their sixteen representatives to the British House of Lords; they are the only elected members of that body.) Another is through the division of powers among several institutions. Strongly underlying these is a sense of egalitarianism and popular control in the sense of commonwealth, emphasizing the equality of all Scots and their right to a role in their own governance, with the maximum amount of local control and protection of the traditional rights of the Scots.

Scots have had to fight to preserve all of these elements against a constant and recurring tendency on the part of the British parliament, dominated overwhelmingly by the English, to impose English standards and modes of centralization on Scotland, whatever they may be at a particular time. No sooner was union implemented than the English began to violate its terms in constitutional, taxation, and religious matters. In 1713 many thought the union had failed and it came within a hair's breadth of being rescinded in the House of Lords. The successful transition from Queen Anne to George I closed off that possibility but brought discontented Scots to turn again to the Stuarts, leading to the four Jacobite revolts of 1708, 1715, 1719, and 1745. In fact, none had any chance of success. Nor were they supported by most Scots, who saw in the return of the Stuarts royal absolutism and Roman Catholicism, neither of which was acceptable to them. They did serve to further prejudice the English against the Scots and gave the former reasons for further violations of the terms of union. The rebellion of 1745 was sufficiently serious in that it led to severe English reprisals, further limiting Scottish governmental autonomy.

Union came at the very beginning of the historical eighteenth century. In each of the following three centuries, the English have tried to foist a different form of centralization on Scotland. In the eighteenth century it was through control of patronage; in the nineteenth, through the extension of parliamentary legislation to Scotland; and in the twentieth, through administrative centralization.

In each case, the Scots, disadvantaged as they were, have fought back. In the eighteenth century the kirk and the system of justice took the lead in fighting for Scottish home rule. In the nineteenth century, the Scottish system of local government took over from the Church. Elected local school boards were introduced in 1872, partly elected county road trustees in 1878, elected county councils introduced in 1889, and elected parish councils in 1894. Countrywide authorities such as the Scottish Board of Commissioners on Lunacy, the Prison Commissioners, the Scottish Education Department, the Local Government Board for Scotland, and the Scottish Board of Agriculture, the last to be established in 1911, also were established to maintain Scottish self-management.

By the end of the century the Scots came within a hair's breadth of acquiring federal home rule. It was planned to come in the wake of Irish home rule and would have been the first step in transforming the United Kingdom itself into a federal system. World War I put an end to this trend. The Irish rebellion of 1916 and its aftermath led to Irish independence, while the draining impact of World War I all but ended the drive for greater self-rule on the main island.

Then, beginning in 1929, British parliamentary legislation swept away the nineteenth-century structure, again introducing standardization and centralization. Again the Scots tried to devise an answer in the form of "administrative devolution." In the process almost all the employees of the Scottish Office in Whitehall were transferred to Edinburgh and settled in St. Andrews House. In its wake this move brought administrative centralization within Scotland as the Scottish Office's control over local government was extended. Postwar socialism only added to this, substituting state for municipal socialism on a basis in which Scotland was given its own more or less autonomous authorities under the various nationalization acts.

The problem of legislative devolution remained. The British Parliament's Standing Committee for Scotland, established in 1894, was far from sufficient. In 1948 public demands for a Scottish legislature were again put forward. Two national assemblies were convened by the Scottish Nationalist Party: the Scottish Convention and its offshoot, and the General Assembly of the Church of Scotland. Here the covenant idea again came into play. In 1958 John MacCormick, a leader of the Scottish nationalist movement, launched a new Scottish Covenant at Stirling in which the signatories pledged to bind themselves "to act on our belief that the mandate of a majority of Scottish citizens is sufficient authority for setting up an Independent Parliament in Scotland." The response was overwhelming. By 1951 the covenant had more than two million signatures, equal to considerably more than half of the Scottish electorate. While the covenant movement carefully insisted that it was not a political party, it did propose a rather tentative "covenant plan" to give Scotland something like the government and parliament of Ulster but with greater financial control. The National Party wanted dominion status, but most Scots probably would have settled for less.

In the end the English majority did not respond. Some of the movement's leaders got involved in the removal of the Stone of Scone from Westminster Abbey to Scotland in an effort to revive its local role as a national symbol. When the stone was returned to the Abbey, the movement began to lose force. The only practical result was a royal commission appointed by the Conservative government in 1952 with terms of reference that explicitly excluded any recommendation for home rule. The commission recommended some administrative changes, most of which were implemented.

Again, in the 1970s, the Scottish nationalists launched a new national covenant for the same purposes. This time it contributed to forcing a referendum on legislative devolution, but the Conservative party in power in Britain was able to draw the measure so that it alienated most of the strong nationalists, since all it promised was a legislative body that would have fewer powers than the average Scottish municipality. Consequently, the measure failed to win the requisite majority at the polls and the issue again died. Although, like the earlier ones, this covenant failed to achieve the desired goal, it did reaffirm the Scots' sense of covenantally rooted nationalism.

The position of the Church of Scotland during the struggle for a Scottish legislative assembly of the late 1970s illustrates its position in Scotland today.[18] In fact, the Kirk entered the modern campaign for greater Scottish home rule in 1946 when it called for "a greater decentralizing of authority and an increased measure of independence within the sphere of Scottish administration."[19]

When a Scottish national assembly was convened in 1948, the Kirk was represented and pressed for a resolution asking for "devolution of legislative power," and its new proposals, submitted by the Kirk's Church and Nation Committee, were unanimously approved. This helped lead to the launching of a covenant pledging by the Scottish National Assembly, which brought in over a million people as signatories by 1950. The covenant called for the establishment of a Royal Commission on Scottish Devolution.

The Kirk consistently took a stand on behalf of greater devolution. When the Royal Commission produced recommendations calling for no more than the transfer of additional responsibilities of the Secretary of State for Scotland, the Kirk's Church and Nation Committee deplored the Royal Commission's failure to truly respond to "the new upsurge of Scottish patriotism" and to think that a "wee bit of tinkering" would be satisfactory.[20]

It was not until 1960 that the Kirk again considered the issue, reaffirming its earlier stand very publicly and, while taking the prudential course and not recommending a full court press for a legislative assembly, it did continue to be on record as favoring more devolution. It took a strong stand on behalf of Scottish self-government when a new Royal Commission on the Constitution was established in April 1969, invoking, inter alia, the Christian doctrine of stewardship in support of devolution so that the Scots could take charge of their own business, holding that this was something they must do in order to fulfill God's will, since He had entrusted them with certain resources to be used fully and properly for the benefit of all mankind. The Church's general assembly also reaffirmed its concern that Scotland was assimilating into England under the existing system of centralization and that "there could be no Church of Scotland without a living Scotland."[21]

At the same time, it carefully disassociated itself as a church from any devolutionary demands regarding religious organizations, reaffirming that the Acts of Parliament of 1921 and 1925 were sufficient in recognizing the freedom of the Church. Indeed, the Queen had reaffirmed her "determination to uphold the Presbyterian government of the Church of Scotland." What the Church did request was parliamentary modification of those of its laws more appropriate for the Church of England that also applied to the parishes in Scotland so as to enable the Kirk to carry out its functions more effectively.

The situation grew more complex after that and three positions emerged within the general assembly. One saw the establishment of a Scottish parliament as potentially damaging to the Church since a rival Scottish national institution would emerge that might take power and loyalty from the Church general assembly. A second consisted of a group who sought a new federal relationship between Scotland and the United Kingdom. The third sought Scottish independence, either partially or totally. After considerable discussion of the subject, the general assembly opted for devolution as a more realistic option. It differed with the government proposal on a number of specifics such as the system of election to the assembly, its name, and the extent of its powers. When it finally provided for a referendum, but in a manner that would likely assure the defeat of the proposal, the leaders of the Kirk were divided as were other Scots over whether a "yes" vote would represent progress or would close off an issue in a less than satisfactory manner. The Church and Nation Committee did endorse the referendum. Its endorsement was sharply challenged and was in effect suspended so that only some of the churches announced it while others did not.

The referendum failed because although 51.6 percent of those who voted cast affirmative ballots, they constituted only 32.5 percent of the electorate and thus fell below the 40 percent requirement that the British Parliament had imposed. Only 4 percent of the eligible voters voted "no" and 37.1 percent did not vote at all.[22]

The modern epoch was not kind to the Scots. During its first century the Scots were forced to surrender their independence and lost the cream of their manpower in a series of valiant but foolhardy wars with the English. During the second century of the epoch Scotland lost vast numbers of people through emigration as a result of the wars and the impoverishment brought by the industrial revolution that Scots did so much to bring about. The pattern of emigration became so well established that J. M. Reid could say in 1955 that living in Scotland today is a matter of voluntary choice. The last century of the epoch saw the most energetic Scots contributing their services to Britain as a whole, either in London or throughout the Empire, including a string of the most notable British prime ministers—from William Gladstone to Ramsey MacDonald—and many of the major empire builders, while Scotland was increasingly absorbed within a single British system of government, economy, and culture.

Yet, somehow Scotland survived and has even reasserted itself to some extent in the first years of the postmodern epoch. Britain's entry into the European Community may give Scotland a new lease on life as a country and not merely a folkloristic curiosity and a football team. In the new "Europe of regions," one of the products of the Community compact, Scotland stands to reassert itself. In the meantime, it is well to recall that the Scots, like the Jews, have survived by virtue of their covenant but have also engaged in foolish adventures because of the faith it gave them. The problem for them, as for other covenanted peoples, is how to balance that faith with a sense of reality.

Notes

1. On the subsequent history of the Kirk in Scotland, see J. M. Reid, *Scotland Past and Present* (London: Oxford University Press, 1959), chap. 4; J. D. Mackie, *A History of Scotland* (Harmondsworth, Middlesex: Penguin Books, 1969).
2. On education in Scotland, see Reid, *Scotland Past and Present,* chap. 5.
3. Stephen Thernstrom, ed., *The Harvard Encyclopedia of American Ethnic Groups* (Cambridge, Mass: Harvard University Press, 1980).
4. Gary Wills, *Inventing America* (New York: Vantage Press, 1979; also *Under God* (New York: Simon and Schuster, 1990); and James Madison, *The Mind of the Founder,* Marvin Meyers, ed. (Indianapolis: Bobbs-Merrill Co., 1973).
5. *Chronicles of America* (New Haven: Yale University Press, 1919); David Ramsay, *The History of the American Revolution* (Indianapolis: Liberty Classics, 1989).
6. Ibid.; also J. Scott Miyakawa, *Protestants and Pioneers* (Chicago: University of Chicago Press, 1964).
7. *Minnesota History.*
8. Donald Harman Akenson, *God's Peoples: Covenant and Land in South Africa, Israel and Ulster* (Ithaca: Cornell University Press, 1992).
9. T. R. H. Davenport, *South Africa, A Modern History* (Johannesberg: MacMillan, S.A, 1989); Akenson, *God's Peoples*; W. A. de Klerk, *The Puritans in Africa* (Hammondsworth, Middlesex: Penguin Books, 1976). On Australia, see Alan Lindsay McLeod, *The Pattern of Australian Culture* (Ithaca: Cornell University Press, 1963; and Reginald L. Appleyard, *British Emigration to Australia* (London: G. Weidenfeld and Nicolson, 1964). On New Zealand, see *The Oxford History of New Zealand,* ed. W. H. Oliver with B. R. Williams (Oxford: Clarendon Press, 1981).
10. Reid, *Scotland Past and Present,* 68.
11. Alastair T. C. Heron, ed., *The Westminster Confession and the Church Today* (Edinburgh: St. Andrews Press, 1982).
12. Sinclair B. Ferguson, "The Teaching of the Confession." In Ibid., 29.
13. Ibid., 31.
14. Lord Cooper, *The Scottish Legal Tradition,* a Saltire pamphlet, 1949.
15. Reid, *Scotland Past and Present,* 116.
16. From *Sources in Literature of Scots Law,* Stair Society, 1936, as quoted in Ibid., 116.
17. Ibid., 128.
18. J. H. Proctor, "The Church of Scotland and the Struggle for a Scottish Assembly," *Journal of Church and State,* 538, 523–43.
19. Ibid., 524.
20. Ibid., 525.
21. Ibid., 528.
22. Ibid., 540.

Part V

The Survival and Revival of Covenant

16

A Proper Covenantal Commonwealth

Efforts to build covenantally based polities reached their apogee during the Reformation, when repeated attempts were made to reach a new synthesis of liberty, equality, and community informed by the new religious spirit of Reformed Protestant Christianity. Those efforts were part and parcel of Reformed Protestant Christian religious and political thought as well as action. We have touched upon several of these manifestations, but perhaps the most comprehensive theoretical expression of the synthesis was that proposed by the leading political scientist of Reformed Protestantism, Johannes Althusius. Althusius, who lived at the very end of the century of Reformation, on the threshold of the transition to the modern epoch, synthesized the best of Reformation thought as applied to the organization of the body politic in the spirit of covenant, liberty, equality, and community. In a sense, his political thought can serve as a last word on the Reformation synthesis, resting on medieval foundations, yet looking forward to modernity.

The Multifaceted Covenant: The Covenantal Approach to the Problem of Organizations, Constitutions, and Liberty

In his thought Althusius adhered very closely to the system presented in the Bible, which tries to accommodate the individual in the commonwealth without abandoning the fabric of the commonwealth as a collectivity with its own responsibilities. The basis for this effort is threefold: first of all, the idea that every individual is created in the image of God, has a soul, and is holy. Second, that it is the task of the individual and the community, indeed the individual in the community, to strive to be holy by observing not only what are today referred to as prescribed religious rituals, but by doing justice, providing for the poor, maintaining human freedom and dignity, and assuring a basic economic floor for every household.

Third, every individual is morally autonomous and his or her consent is required for all acts, even in response to God's commandments. In biblical terminology, God commands but humans hearken. That is to say, they listen to God's commandment and in essence decide whether or not to observe it. Biblical Hebrew has no word for obey. All human actions require hearkening.

Fourth, humans act together through covenants and covenanting, beginning with the foundation of existence, man's covenant with God, whereby God enters into a partnership with humans for the fulfillment and governance of this world. According to the terms of the constitution that He has set before them, all human organization flows from that original covenant and is ordered by the subsidiary covenants to which the parties must consent and are morally binding under God, who serves as partner, guarantor, or witness. All, of course, are based on consent and the ability of the partners to make autonomous moral commitments.[1]

While we do not know exactly how this biblical system worked in practice in ancient Israel, we can gather some sense of its reality in the way it has shaped the Jewish people, who are noted for their commitment to individual autonomy, liberty, and equality, and for their striving to achieve one or another moral end and the tendency to view public issues in moralistic terms even as they are among the most communal, even tribal, of peoples, tied together through a rich fabric of history and destiny.[2]

The biblical worldview also entered Christianity when that religion emerged out of Judaism, but it did not reach its full flowering until the Protestant Reformation. Reformed Protestants, in particular, not only sought to foster the true faith, but to build the holy commonwealth. The road to modern democracy began with the Protestant Reformation in the sixteenth century, particularly among those exponents of Reformed Protestantism (later rather mistakenly referred to as Calvinism) who developed a theology and politics that set the Western world back on the road to popular self-government, emphasizing liberty and equality. In their efforts they turned to what they referred to as the Old Testament—the Hebrew Bible—for guidance.

There they rediscovered the biblical teaching and sought to adapt it to their Christian commonwealths.[3] We know their principal efforts as milestones in the history of liberty in the Western world, albeit limited or flawed ones—Zwingli's Zurich, Calvin's Geneva, Knox's Scotland, and later Cromwell's England, Winthrop's Massachusetts, Williams's Rhode Island, and Hutchinson's Connecticut. While several of these have been called theocracies, in fact they were so only in the sense that they recognized God's sovereignty as the basis of the commonwealth and tried to use God's law as its foundation. As in ancient Israel, they divided authority and power among magistrates and ministers, civil and ecclesiastical rulers. (In ancient Israel, as in every Jewish polity, the division was threefold, between civil rulers, expounders of the Torah, and priests.) The magistrates were as much responsible for maintaining the moral foundations of the community as the ministers.

However limited these regimes were from the perspective of modern democracy, they did advance the cause of republicanism and strengthened the foundations of what later became democratic republicanism. All were established by covenant. The most important were also federal in the more conventional sense of being federations of polities.

Their great limitations were two: Because they were led by militant reformers during the first flush of the Reformation, most insisted on orthodoxy and expelled or persecuted (and on occasion even executed) those whom they deemed heretics. Nor did they leave room for individualism in the more private ways that we understand to be necessary. Still, those that survived the initial revolutionary period settled down to be bourgeois republics until engulfed by some later revolution or conquest. As such they allowed considerable room for private behavior as long as community norms were publicly honored.

A number of the foregoing figures, particularly Calvin, Knox, and Roger Williams, and to a lesser extent Zwingli and John Winthrop, developed political theories to accompany their work of governing.[4] All, however, were primarily theologians. While they and the other original founders and spokesmen for Reformed Protestantism did much political writing, their writing was either theological or polemic in character. Only at the end of the first century of the Reformation did a political philosopher emerge out of the Reformed tradition who built a systematic political philosophy out of the Reformed experience by synthesizing the political experience of the Holy Roman Empire with the political ideas of covenant theology. That man, Johannes Althusius, presented his political philosophy in a classic work, *Politica Methodice Digesta*, first published in 1603 and revised in final form in 1614. It remained for Althusius, political scientist by his own self-definition, to develop a theory and philosophy of a compound polity that took most of these problems into consideration.

Althusius was born in Westphalia, one of the German states, about 1557. He was educated at the universities of Cologne and Basel, where he received his doctorate in civil and ecclesiastical law in 1586. He then received an appointment to the Reformed Academy of Herborn to teach law. There he spent his academic career, becoming rector in 1597. He published his third and most important book, *Politica Methodice Digesta*, while at Herborn. Althusius wrote as a political scientist, as one who was interested in the theory of the political order, the philosophy behind that theory, and the practical dimension of human behavior that must be addressed and accommodated. Apparently as a result of that book, he was invited to become Syndic of Emden in East Friesland. Known as the "Geneva of the North," Emden had embraced Reformed Protestantism in 1526, one of the first cities in Germany to do so. With the Netherlands just across the border, it was very influential in educating the leaders of Dutch Calvinism and, as a seaport, maintained close connections with the Reformed Protestants of the British Isles. In a way, it was the fulcrum of northern Calvinism during the time of the Dutch revolt against Spain, the rise of Presbyterianism in Scotland, and the Catholic reaction in England. Althusius served Emden as Syndic from 1604 to his death in 1638. He was elected an elder of the church in 1617 and from then on served in both capacities. He published two enlarged editions of the *Politics*, in 1610 and 1614.

While Althusius relied on many classical and contemporary sources as well, his first and foremost source was Scripture, so much so that for him, the others were merely a means to elucidate biblical teaching. Althusius saw in the biblical polity the ideal regime. As he put it: "I more frequently use examples from sacred scripture because it has God or pious men as its author, and because I consider that no polity from the beginning of the world has been more wisely and perfectly constructed than the polity of the Jews. We err, I believe, whenever in similar circumstances we depart from it."[5]

What emerges from the *Politics* is a biblically informed theory of the polity and the society it serves, presented in the systematic fashion of Western political philosophy and adapted to the conditions of Western civilization at the juncture between the end of the medieval and the beginning of the modern epochs. Althusius's *Politics* was the first book to present a comprehensive theory of federal republicanism rooted in a covenantal view of human society derived from, but not dependent on, a theological system. It presented a theory of polity building based on the polity as a compound political association established by its citizens through their primary associations on the basis of consent, rather than a reified state, imposed by a ruler or an elite.

The *Res Publica* of Althusius

Althusius's *Politics* is concerned with ordering and communication, both done through the process of association (*consociatio*)—what he terms symbiotics. Symbiotics is the art and science of association. Every proper association has its own vocation or calling, which is directly or indirectly established by covenant. A proper politics rests on both piety and justice, as reflected in the two tables of the Decalogue, the first of which states the fundamental laws of piety and the second the fundamental laws of justice.

Althusius begins the body of his book by stating:

> Politics is the art of associating (*consociandi*) men for the purpose of establishing, cultivating, and conserving social life among them. Whence it is called "symbiotics." The subject matter of politics is therefore association (*consociatio*), in which the symbiotes (those who live together) pledge themselves each to the other, by explicit or tacit agreement, to mutual communication of whatever is useful and necessary for the harmonious exercise of social life.

> The end of political "symbiotic" man is holy, just, comfortable, and happy symbiosis, a life lacking nothing either necessary or useful.

Symbiotics and communication are the central elements of his system. Communication for Althusius is the sharing of things, services, and right (*jus*, i.e., right as law). Like all covenantal systems it emphasizes relationships first and foremost, which are secured through their embodiment in proper institutions.

Althusius emphasized that the greatest safeguards for liberty were to be found in the structuring of the body politic into five permanent associations: two private—the family and the collegium—and three public—the city, the province, and the commonwealth. It was through those permanent structures that individuals were able to function, to be represented, and to preserve their liberties. The private sphere was real and was protected not by abstract principle alone but by the constitutional authority and political power of the family and the collegium as private institutions. The individual for Althusius (as for the Bible) was a reality because every individual was created in God's image with his or her own soul. But individuals did not stand naked in the face of powerful public institutions, rather, they were protected by being located within families and collegia.

Nor was that deemed sufficient. The public sphere, too, was divided into three arenas—the city, the province, and the commonwealth—each with its own structure that gave each its authority and empowered each to play its role. At first glance this seems to be a variant of the medieval corporatist model and, indeed, some have argued that Althusius was only a modified late medieval corporatist.[6] A better case can be made, however, that Althusius developed a different model based on political and social covenants.

There are two kinds of associations—simple and private, and mixed and public. Among the former are the family and the collegium. The family is a natural association that takes the form of a comprehensive union, while the collegium is a limited civil association. There are two kinds of families, based on conjugal and kinship relations. A collegium is any private association in which "three or more men of the same trade, training, or profession are united for the purpose of holding in common such things they jointly profess as duty, way of life or craft." Secular collegia are those composed of magistrates and judges or people engaged in common agricultural, industrial, or commercial pursuits. An ecclesiastical collegium is composed of clergymen, philosophers, or teachers.

Among the mixed and public associations are the city, the province, and the commonwealth, each of which has a civil and an ecclesiastical dimension. While each is autonomous in its own sphere, the commonwealth is the most comprehensive and, as such, is the universal association. There are two forms of universal association—the *res publica* or commonwealth, and the *regnum* or realm, with the former preferred. Althusius as a political scientist emphasizes that he deals with the reality of political life; not only with the "ought," as do jurists, but with the "is," hence his recognition that there are *regna* as well as *res publica*.

In his twofold division, Althusius implicitly recognizes the two dimensions of what he refers to as symbiotics presented in the Bible, namely kinship and consent. As a natural private association, Althusius sees the family as a permanent union of its members, "with the same boundaries as life itself." The collegium, on the other hand, as a civil private association, is more voluntary and "need not last as long as the lifetime of man," even though "a certain necessity can be said to have brought it into existence." In these associations there is a balance between necessity and volition.

However natural the family may be, it is based upon marriage, a tacit or expressed agreement among its members ordering the manner of its communication or sharing of things, services, and rights. However strong its roots in kinship, the continued existence of the family is essentially a confirmation of this tacit or expressed agreement. Althusius realistically recognizes that some families do not continue to exist.

"The collegium is the primary civil association. It is a body organized by assembled persons according to their own pleasure and will to serve a common utility and necessity in human life."[7] There can be all kinds of collegia with all kinds of purposes. Althusius brings lengthy examples from the histories of Israel, Egypt, and ancient Rome.

Althusius holds that it is in the nature of a collegium that its members "agree among themselves by common consent on a manner of ruling and obeying for the utility both of the whole body and of its individuals."[8] The essence of the collegium for Althusius consists of "men united by their own consent."[9] Essential to the voluntary character of the collegium is the fact that it is transitory and can be discontinued by being "disbanded honorably and in good faith by the mutual agreement of those who have come together, however much it may have been necessary and useful for social life on another occasion."[10] Since the collegium is outside the family, it is a civil association, albeit a private one. Unlike Bodin, who defines all activities outside of the home as the activities of citizenship, Althusius distinguishes membership in the collegium from citizenship, referring to members as "colleagues, associates, or even brothers."[11]

Althusius insists upon a minimum of three people to form a collegium, so as to overcome dissension. Althusius cites many biblical examples of collegia, in this case more particularly in the New Testament than in the Old, no doubt because Christianity organized itself on a voluntary basis within an existing civil society, while the Israelites developed as a single comprehensive people or commonwealth.[12] Upon this Scriptural base, Althusius builds his discussion of the collegium on Roman law.[13] Colleagues are equals unless they organize themselves otherwise. Decision making is by majority rule and decisions pertain "jointly and wholly to the colleagues as a united group, but not in matters separately affecting individual colleagues outside the corporate fellowship."[14] Althusius even requires a quorum of two-thirds of all members to make decisions. "In matters common to all, one by one, or pertaining to colleagues as individuals...even one person is able to object."[15] "The reason is that in this case what is common to everyone is also my private concern."[16] The president, rector, or director of the collegium is elected by the colleagues. He is "superior to the individual colleague but inferior to the united colleagues...whose pleasure he must serve."[17]

Althusius continues: "Communication among the colleagues is the activity by which an individual helps his colleague, and so upholds the plan of social life set forth in covenant agreements. These covenants and laws (*pacta et leges*) of the colleagues are described in their corporate books.... Such communication pertains to (1) things, (2) services, (3) right and (4) mutual benevolence" communicated by the collegium.[18]

Because the idea of the collegium at first glance resembles guilds common to the medieval city, many assume that it is merely a restatement of medieval corporatism. This is not the case. Althusius's reform is to emphasize the voluntary, transient, and limited nature of the collegium as distinct from the feudal corporate structure of the guild.

In the case of the collegium, Althusius adds communication of something beyond things, services, and rights—namely, mutual benevolence, parallel to the biblical concept of *hesed* (covenant love) or *re'ut* (neighborliness). Althusius defines mutual benevolence as "that affection and love of individuals toward their colleagues because of which they harmoniously will and 'nil' on behalf of the common utility."[19] He understands that this kind of brotherly love is necessary for the collegium as a moral community of colleagues. For Althusius, as for all proper covenantal thinkers, covenants are not enough. There must also be a covenantal dynamic, as symbolized by *hesed* and *re'ut*, which is "nourished, sustained, and conserved by public banquets, entertainments, and love feasts."[20]

Since the collegium develops from a natural need, it is not completely voluntary and presumably would not be disbanded unless alternate means existed to meet the needs for which it arose in the first place. While it comes into existence through an act of will and covenant, it is this relationship to necessity that makes it more than merely a matter of individual choice. Althusius emphasizes that all five of the associations he describes are rooted in necessity, although their existence, form, and means of communication are determined through acts of will and covenant.

Unlike public associations where individual participation is essentially indirect, in the collegium the colleagues can participate directly. Still, they need a leader to administer the affairs of the collegium. That leader is "bound by the purposes for which the collegium exists, and by the laws defined through its corporative processes."[21]

Public associations are directly constituted by families and collegia, not individuals, with families and collegia constituting cities, cities constituting provinces, and provinces commonwealths. What is critical here is that while public association also exists out of necessity, a public association cannot come into existence or continue to exist without the private associations that constitute it. Again, for Althusius this is a matter of reality and not only of right.

There is also another distinction between private and public associations. Public associations are territorial, that is to say, they have jurisdiction over specific territory, while private associations are not. Thus the two forms of associations together cover the two principal options for human organization. Private civil associations, in particular, offer means to modify or supplement the territoriality of public associations. Althusius's Latin term for association, *consociatio,* has been revived in our times as consociationalism to describe institutionalized political power sharing on a nonterritorial basis (i.e., a kind of nonterritorial federalism). Further than that distinction however, the same general principles of communication and rule apply equally to both forms of association. This is a major departure from medieval Roman law, in which public associations were essentially hierarchical and administrative, that is to say, they served an imperial power pyramid. Althusius makes public associations symbiotic (i.e., covenantal, of the same general genus as private associations). Basing both on the same sources of legitimacy and modes of operation is a major federal element in Althusian thought.

There are two forms of public association—particular and universal. In the full-fledged commonwealth, the city and the province are particular forms of association while the *res publica* or *regnum* is universal. Sovereignty, which Althusius clearly vests in the people (see below), is vested in the people of the universal public association which, in a sense, is what distinguishes it as universal. In that sense, the question of the locus of popular sovereignty determines what is universal and what is particular rather than the other way around. Althusius recognizes that citystates like Venice are universal associations since they have commonwealth status. In a sense this unstated reversal is part of a further inconsistency in the status of provinces. The realistic political scientist looking at the Holy Roman Empire of Althusius's time had to take note of its formally feudal structure, whereby princes, dukes, counts, or other nobility who ruled provinces were at least nominally subsidiary to the Holy Roman Emperor, the Supreme Magistrate, rather than chosen by the citizenry, thus partly compromising the symbiotic foundations of provincial rule.

All three public associations are governed through a system of separation of powers, with a Senate or similar body representing the people through representatives from their private associations and a chief executive who presides over the communication of things, services, and rights. The task of the Senate is to establish, defend, and, if necessary, modify the fundamental laws of the public association. Under certain circumstances it may even remove the chief executive.

Critical in the rule of every public association are the ecclesiastical, civil, and private associations—what we today refer to as mediating institutions that provide the basis for representation in the public associations. Ecclesiastical associations are not only concerned with piety in the traditional sense, but also with public education in both religion and the liberal arts.

Constitutional Design or the Rules of Order

Althusius emphasizes that one of the principal rights of a commonwealth is the communication of rights by the citizens among themselves. The basis for this communication of rights is embodied in the *jus commune,* here the common right, fundamental law or constitution of an association. Althusius uses the term *jus commune* in two senses: as referring to God's divine constitution, the unchanging moral law binding upon all people and their associations (on this larger constitutional meaning see chapters 21 and 22); and also more narrowly to refer to the constitutional foundations of particular associations.

Voluntary associations may establish their own statutes in the frame-work of public law and in harmony with their *jus commune,* which is customarily written in the association's records. The constitution is best established by the common consent of the colleagues or citizens but (in an allowance for late medieval reality) it may be granted to them as a special privilege by a superior magistrate. Althusius does not distinguish between covenants and constitutions, treating every constitution as a covenant and using the terms almost interchange-ably, as in his discussion of the "covenant or constitution by which the supreme magistrate is constituted by the Ephors with the consent of the associated bodies."[22]

Althusius discusses the more comprehensive *jus commune* in his chap-ters on political prudence. The constitutional ordering of rules, then, is an act of political prudence:

> The rule of living, obeying, and administering is the will of God alone, which is the way of life, and the law of things to be done and to be omitted. It is necessary that the magistrate rule, appoint, and examine all the business of his administration with this law as a touchstone and measure, unless he wishes to rule the ship of state as an unreliable vessel at sea, and to wander about and move at random. Thus administration and government of a commonwealth is nothing other than the ex-ecution of law. Therefore, this law alone prescribes not only the order of adminis-tering for the magistrate, but also the rule of living for all subjects.[23]

> Law in the general sense is a precept for doing those things that pertain to living a pious, holy, just, and suitable life. That is to say, it pertains to the duties that are to be performed toward God and one's neighbor, and to the love of God and one's neighbor.... laws or rights in human society are as fences, walls, guards, or bound-aries of our life, guiding us along the appointed way for achieving wisdom, happi-ness, and peace in human society.[24]

Basing his discussion on biblical sources (particularly Romans I:19 and II:14f), Althusius sees the *jus commune* as "naturally implanted by God in all men."[25] At that level, "this *jus commune* is set forth for all men nothing other than the general theory and practice of love, both for God and for one's neighbor."[26] Althusius soon moves beyond that be-cause he notes that this law is "not inscribed equally on the hearts of all. The knowledge of it is communicated more abundantly to some and more sparingly to others."[27]

The next step is the writing down of this constitutional law in the Decalogue. Its first table deals with love of God and piety; and the sec-ond, love of man and civil or political life. Althusius refers to the Ten

Commandments as "mandates and precepts," but indicates that in the Bible they are referred to as "judgements, statutes, and witnesses." His analysis of each of the commandments sets forth what he understands to be the general constitution of all humanity. As he says, "the Decalogue has been prescribed for all people to the extent that it agrees with and explains the common law of nature for all peoples."[28]

> Proper law (*lex propria*) is the law that is drawn up and established by the magistrate on the basis of common law (*lex communis*) [Althusius uses *jus* and *lex* interchangeably in this particular discussion] and according to the nature, utility, condition and other special circumstances of his country. It indicates the peculiar way, means, and manner by which this natural equity among men can be upheld, observed, and cultivated in any given commonwealth.[29] *Lex propria* has two parts: that which is in agreement with the *jus commune* (*convenientia*), and that which is different from it (*discrepantia*).

He then turns to focus more explicitly on Jewish proper law, which is divided into ceremonial law and forensic or civil law, the first designed to aid in the observance of the first table of the Decalogue and the second designed to make possible the maintenance of the second. With regard to the ceremonial law, he follows the Orthodox Christian view. It leads to Christ and should now be viewed through the teachings of Jesus. With regard to the civil law, however, "it follows that the magistrate is obligated in the administration of the commonwealth to the proper law of Moses so far as moral equity or common law are expressed therein."[30] At the same time the proper law of Moses, which is not so directed, should not be compulsory in a Christian commonwealth.

Every institution in the commonwealth needs to have its rules established by consent of its citizens or members and written down. In other words, they must be in covenantal form and in harmony with God's original covenant with ancient Israel as embodied in the Decalogue. As a covenant, the constitution is a reciprocal contract, binding all parties to it whether equals or unequals, that is to say, rulers and ruled, and granting powers as determined by the body of the association. Such a covenant/constitution is designed to prevent any exercise of absolute power within the association. Althusius makes it clear that "power...is established for the utility of those who are ruled, not of those who rule, and the utility of the people...does not in the least require unlimited power."[31] Althusius is very strong on the point that "absolute power is wicked and prohibitive...even almighty God is said not to be able to do what is evil and contrary to His nature."[32]

This brief, structurally oriented description of Althusius's system does not do it justice. Critical to understanding how this structure is to work is Althusius's emphasis on communication as the sharing of things, services, and right. Institutions exist as means to order and foster communication or sharing in a situation where consent is the foundation of the commonwealth. Althusius is resolutely opposed to tyranny, in part because it is unjust and in part because he sees it as ineffective.

As a result of his emphasis on covenant and communication, Althusius has essentially rejected the reified state and with it, statism. His idea of vesting sovereignty in the people through their associations counters the argument of Jean Bodin that there must be a single point in which sovereignty is concentrated; in Althusius's time, the monarch and, later, the reified state. In this Althusius is a precursor of the solution devised by the founders of the United States to resolve the problem of sovereignty by vesting it in the people.[33] The American founders had an easier time of it because of the more homogeneous character of the people to whom they addressed their solution. In the more complex and heterogeneous society of the German Holy Roman Empire, the Althusian idea of vesting sovereignty in the people through their associations offered a role to both soften the impact of the "state" and to preserve the diverse primordial and civil ties that characterize European society.

In all this Althusius has provided a proper application of the biblical model. For the Bible, only God is ultimately sovereign. Politically, however, sovereignty is vested in the people, who possess operational sovereignty within the framework of God's constitution. For the Bible, that constitution is the Torah; for Althusius, it is the Decalogue. Thus, the two expressions of sovereignty come together in a constitutional document that, barring direct Heavenly intervention, becomes the actual source of authority, which can be modified by the people within the limits imposed by the laws of piety and justice represented by the two tables of the Decalogue. This constitutional document and the network of associations, symbiotic relationships, and communication of things, services, and right/law are in a sense the best protection against tyranny and for what we would today call human rights.

What of the matter of rights? For both the Bible and Althusius, the question of rights is derived essentially from the question of justice and the human obligation provided by God to act justly. Politics is symbiotics in communication. It provides the framework and the means to act justly and to do justice. Thus the fundamental associations of political community—public and private, civil and natural—are media for doing justice.

Beyond that, each form of association forms a particular kind of moral community within which justice is to be achieved and right or rights protected in a different way. One of the principal lessons of Althusius's teaching for us today is that humans are organized in different moral communities, and right or rights with regard to each must be treated in a manner appropriate to it.

The modern worldview, by emphasizing the individual standing naked against civil society as represented by government, has increasingly come to emphasize the legal enforcement of legally defined rights. Originally applied to government alone, this approach to rights has been extended to other forms of civil associations and even more recently to natural associations, public and private, because of that oversimple and limited perception of the political relationship underlying civil society, what constitutes rights, and how they are to be enforced.

In a just society, there must be an appropriate conceptualization of right and rights for relationships within each different kind of moral community with appropriate means of enforcement. In ancient and medieval society, much justice was promised without sufficient means of enforcement. Modern political thought successfully attacked that problem by providing means of enforcement but, in the process, rejected a more complex view of what constitutes justice or right, a view based upon an understanding of the different forms of association in which humans are involved, recognizing the fact that all such associations established on the basis of covenant include the dimensions of justice and right and establish or systematize relationships upon which appropriate theories of rights and rights enforcement can be based.

While Althusius does not directly concern himself with what we today define as the problem of individual rights, as in the Bible, individuals are recognized in his system by their uniqueness, godliness, and individual moral responsibility. Government, for Althusius as for the Bible, is concerned primarily with justice, though the question is left open as to how much it is concerned with holiness or morality. If we can summarize biblical and Althusian thought on the matter, public associations must give due recognition to piety, holiness, and morality, but should go easy on efforts to do more than be exhortative in those spheres. In other words, they should make clear what the standards are but should limit their role as God's policemen. Liberty is protected by the rejection of the reified state and statism, and the emphasis in its place on the compound of associations, the separation of powers, and on right procedures.

Trained in theology and jurisprudence, Althusius became a political scientist and, indeed, makes a strong argument that politics is the equal of the first two disciplines. In his Preface to the first edition, Althusius goes into a long discussion of the relationship between political science, theology, and jurisprudence, and the separation between them, summarizing the task of the political scientist as follows:

> A political scientist properly teaches what are the sources of sovereignty and enquires to determine what may be essential for the constituting of a commonwealth. The jurist, on the other hand, properly treats of the right (*jus* or law) that arises at certain times from these sources of sovereignty in the contract entered into between the people and the prince. Both therefore discuss the rights of sovereignty, the political scientist concerning the fact of them and the jurist concerning the right of them.

While couched in the language of the sixteenth century, the distinction is not foreign to us. In the Preface to the Third Edition, Althusius elaborates on this by elaborating on the relationship between political science and theology through his emphasis on the role of the Decalogue.

Polity and Political Economy

Althusius's polity is one that is built from the beginning on a political economy, since so many of the civil private associations that he has in mind are basically occupational in character. Nevertheless, he does separate politics and economics.[34]

> So therefore economics and politics differ greatly as the subject and end. The subject of the former is the good of the family; its end is the acquisition of whatever is necessary for food and clothing. The subject of the latter, namely politics, is pious and just symbiosis; its end is the governing and preserving of association and symbiotic life.

In posing this definition it should be noted that Althusius deliberately rejects the notion that economics is exclusively private and politics exclusively public. At least with regard to politics, it is also private. The linkage of the two is to be found in the fact that symbiotic communication or sharing involves things or goods, services and rights, or lawful structures.[35]

Throughout each of the five arenas of association, the civil private association is usually an economic association of one kind or another that nevertheless requires political order within it as well so as to be part of the political order of the three public associations. In the relationship between the public associations and the economy, a city has responsibility both for regulating economic life and for providing the public infrastructure necessary for economic life.[36] The province has the responsibility for the support of commercial activity and the care of the public good of the province,[37] and also for the education and training of "merchants, farmers, and workmen who are skilled, industrious and distinguished."[38]

The commonwealth, following the fifth commandment, is charged with the responsibility of protecting the system's goods, their use, and ownership.[39] Althusius understands this as involving not only a citizen's goods, but also his safety and good name, all of which are viewed as property not to be stolen.[40] The commonwealth is also charged with the regulation of commerce and contracts, and is responsible for providing an adequate system of coinage.[41] In this respect, the commonwealth is charged with overseeing the means necessary for procuring advantages for social life.[42]

A Summing Up

1. The foundations of Althusius's political philosophy are covenantal through and through. *Pactum* is the only basis for legitimate political organization. More than that, Althusius develops a covenantal-federal basis that is comprehensive. Not only is the universal association constructed as a federation of communities, but politics as such is federal through and through, based as it is on union and communication (in the sense of sharing), as expressed in the idea that its members are symbiotes.

Althusius's dual emphasis on federalism as a relationship and on sharing as the basis of federal relationships has turned out to be a basic axiom of federalism. While there can be different forms of a federal relationship and sharing can be expressed in different ways, federalism remains essentially a relationship and sharing its guiding principle. The polity, then, is a symbiotic association based upon symbiosis and constituted by symbiotes.

2. Althusius deals with the problem of sovereignty, then becoming the critical juridical problem for modern state building, by vesting it in the people as a whole. On the one hand this is what makes the good polity a *res publica* or commonwealth. On the other, it also makes it possible to be a *consociatio consociationum*, a *universitas* composed of *collegia,* since the people can delegate the exercise of sovereign power to different bodies as they please (according to their sovereign will).

The problem of indivisible sovereignty raised by Jean Bodin became the rock upon which premodern federalism foundered. The modern state system was based on the principle of indivisible sovereignty, which in an age of increasingly monolithic and energetic states, became a *sine qua non* for political existence. Thus the medieval world of states based on shared sovereignty had to give way. It was not until the American founders invented modern federalism that a practical solution to this problem was found, enabling the development of modern federation as a form of government. Althusius provided the theoretical basis for dealing with the sovereignty question over 175 years earlier (no doubt unbeknownst to them) and gave it the necessary philosophic grounding.

Althusius further understands political sovereignty as the constituent power. This is at once a narrower, more republican definition of sovereignty, whose plenary character is harnessed as the power to constitute government—a power that is vested in the organic body of the commonwealth (i.e., the people). Moreover, once the people act, the sovereignty is located in the *jus regni,* the fundamental right/law of the realm or the constitution.

This Althusian concept has important implications in contemporary international law, which is grappling with the problem of how to mitigate the effects of the principle of absolute and undivided sovereignty inherited from modern jurisprudence in an increasingly interdependent world. Even where the principle is not challenged, the practical exercise of absolute sovereignty is no longer possible. There are an increasing number of situations in which even the principle cannot be applied as it was. One way out in such cases has been to vest sovereignty in the constitutional document itself, that is to say, in what Althusius would refer to as the *jus regni*. Vesting sovereignty in a constitutional document is entirely consonant with a covenantal federalism.

3. Althusius serves as a bridge between the biblical foundations of Western civilization and modern political ideas and institutions. As such

he translates the biblical political tradition into useful modern forms. In this he must be contrasted with Spinoza, who a few years later in his *Theological Political Tractate* makes the case for a new modern political science by presumably demonstrating that biblical political ideas applied only to ancient Israel and ceased to be relevant once the Jews lost their state (unless and until the Jews were restored). Althusius confronts the same problems of modern politics without jettisoning or denying the biblical foundations. In part this rendered him less useful during the modern epoch, when his unbending Calvinist emphasis on the necessary links between religion, state, and society in the form of twinned civil and ecclesiastical jurisdictions fell afoul of the development of the modern secular state.

The Althusian version of the Calvinist model of the religiously homogeneous polity is not likely to be revived in the postmodern epoch. Nevertheless, we are beginning to recover an old understanding that no civil society can exist without some basis in transcendent norms, which obligate and bind the citizens and establish the necessary basis for trust and communication. The connection between the Decalogue and *jus* as both law and right, while hardly original to Althusius, may offer possibilities for renewed development in our times. Althusius adopts a conventional understanding of the two tables of the Decalogue of his time, namely, that the first table addresses itself to piety and the second to justice, both of which are necessary foundations for civil society.

4. Very important in this connection is Althusius's development of the concept of *jus regni,* which he derives explicitly from the biblical *mishpat hamelukhah* (law of the kingdom), enunciated in I Samuel 10, to serve as constitution of the universal association, at one and the same time establishing the constitution as a civil rather than a religious document, yet one that has its source in or at least is in harmony with divine and natural law.[43] While contemporary political scientists emphasize the secular character of modern constitutionalism, examination of most contemporary constitutions reveals that they reflect the same combination of claims, namely, linkage to transcendent law, more often divine than natural, yet human artifacts that are civil in character. While in recent years we have made considerable advances in developing an understanding of constitutional design, in doing so we have neglected this linkage and its implications for right law that Althusius calls to our attention.

5. While Althusius was clearly a product of his times and the ideal state of his design is one that reflects the class and reference group structure of sixteenth-century German society, it is significant that Althusius leaves open the possibility for democracy as we know it, including female participation in public life and office holding, and a more classless and egalitarian basis for participation generally. Since I do not have a sufficient command of the Latin text to properly explore the issue, I cannot say whether Althusius has an esoteric as well as an exoteric teaching, but this suggests that there may be a hidden dimension to be explored in the *Politics* and Althusian thought generally. Nor is the federal aspect insignificant here. Althusius suggests different forms and extents of participation in the different arenas of government as one possible way to extend participation in public life to groups heretofore disenfranchised in the world that he knew.

6. Althusius recognizes the modern distinction between public and private realms, yet also preserves the connection between them. In this respect he, like the moderns who were to follow him, breaks with classic notions of the all-embracing *polis* to recognize the legitimacy of a sphere of private activity that exists constitutionally by right, thereby preventing totalitarianism. Yet he recognizes the connection between the simple and private dissociations of family and collegium and the mixed and public associations of city, province, and commonwealth. Indeed, the relationship between private and public spheres and associations is a major concern of his, as it is increasingly to those of us who must reckon with the realities of the postmodern epoch in which everything is tied into everything else, like it or not.

One of the advantages of the modern epoch was that it was possible to more sharply separate the public and private spheres because the modern epoch was one in which increased distance between them was possible. Since this is no longer the case, the new commonwealth requires more Althusian communication; that is to say, as everything impinges upon everything else, more sharing is necessary. Althusius's emphasis on the existence of both natural and civil associations in the private sphere reflects his emphasis on what we would call the natural right of association. The family is a natural association based on two relationships: conjugal and kinship. Since the nuclear family is a conjugal relationship, even it is covenantal. The *collegium* or civil association in both its secular and ecclesiastical forms is covenantal.

Mixed and public associations are equally covenantal: the city is a covenantal republic formed of a union of *collegia,* the province a covenantal union of cities, and the commonwealth a covenantal union of provinces (this is so even though Althusius talks of the rights of the province as an arm of the commonwealth and not simply a union of cities). Covenants for Althusius are the ways in which symbiotes can initiate and maintain associations. They are products of both necessity and volition.

7. Althusius's definition of politics as the effective ordering of communication (of things, services, and rights) offers us a starting point for understanding political phenomena that speaks to contemporary political science. This leads us to the second half of Althusian thought: that dealing with statesmanship, prudence, and administration. It would be possible to say that the second half of Althusian teaching is general to all of politics and not specifically to federalism, except that this would do violence to the first half of Althusian teaching, which sees all politics as federal politics in the broadest sense.

It should be clear that Althusius directly addresses the issues that surround the relationship between collective organization and individual liberty and the role of rules or constitutions in constituting and constraining collective organizations and constraining and protecting individual liberty. First of all, in the manner of contemporary public choice theorists, Althusius reduces the distinctions between private and public associations to those of function and scope rather than essence (essentially following the biblical view of the matter). For Althusius, following the biblical model, the constituting rules governing collective organizations and the relations among them are embodied in covenants, which also serve to ground liberty in the rules themselves. Covenants are made among the symbiotes to initiate and maintain all associations. Universal association is further served by the *jus regni* as its constitution. The *jus regni* is explicitly derived from the biblical *mishpat hamelukhah* and, indeed, is a translation of that term. For Althusius, as for the Bible, the *jus regni* is the civil constitutional law derived from the Decalogue.

Althusius published the last edition of his *Politics* in 1614, just on the eve of the philosophic revolution of the seventeenth century. Ironically, his contribution was ignored, if not forgotten, for the next three hundred years; considered only by Otto von Gierke in the nineteenth century, as part of Gierke's effort to revive medieval forms for the development of a modern German political thought and a few other German thinkers.[44] Althusius was rediscovered by Carl Friedrich, who published a complete Latin edition of the *Politics* in 1932 with an extensive (if, in my opinion, a somewhat misleading) introduction.[45] Frederick Carney prepared his masterfully digested translation of the *Politics* in English nearly thirty years later.[46] His was and remains the first translation of the *Politics* in any vernacular language.

Althusius was ignored because his philosophy was bounded by the same biblical principles of polity building that informed Reformed Protestantism and that were rejected by modern statist political thought. In many respects, he was the theoretical godfather of modern federalism but was never recognized as such because of what were deemed archaic elements in the form of his thought. It is doubly ironic, then, that precisely for those reasons that led him to be rejected by the moderns he becomes useful to us in the postmodern epoch.

Modern political philosophy is based upon a revolution in the theory of natural right, which was deemed to be rooted in the natural psychology of humanity and methodological individualism. It is rooted in the liberal principle that the individual is the only atom from which to begin the construction or analysis of civil society. While early modern thought recognized and emphasized that all society is civil society, organized politically from its foundations (in contradistinction to nineteenth-century views of the subjects that sought the "automatic society" that existed independently of political organization), it also emphasizes that civil society's governmental dimension should be limited; indeed, as limited as possible.

We postmoderns understand the truth and vital importance of that revolutionary modern idea. But we also understand that while it may be the truth, it is not necessarily the whole truth. We may better understand that, while individual liberty is essential for us all, so, too are the institutions of family and community so that the public institutions of civil society will rest on the proper foundations; not only in the way that they are constituted but in terms of the private dimension in which they serve to function as they are intended to function. The character of the *res publica* (or commonwealth) depends on the character of the public it serves; and just as there can be no *res publica* without a public, so does the character of the *res publica* rest upon the kind of public within it.

Notes

1. On the federal dimension of the biblical worldview, one of the best available sources is Martin Buber, *Kingship of God* (New York: Harper and Row, 1967). This writer has treated the subject in "Government in Biblical Israel," *Tradition* (Spring-Summer, 1973) and in "Covenant as the Basis of the Jewish Political Tradition," *Jewish Journal of Sociology* (June, 1978). See also Daniel J. Elazar, *Kinship and Consent: The Jewish Political Tradition and its Contemporary Uses* (Lanham, Md.: University Press of America and Jerusalem Center for Public Affairs, 1983); Daniel J. Elazar and Stuart A. Cohen, *The Jewish Polity* (Bloomington: Indiana University Press, 1984); Daniel J. Elazar and John Kincaid, eds. *Covenant, Polity, and Constitutionalism* (Lanham, Md.: University Press of America and the Center for the Study of Federalism, 1984).

2. On Jews and politics, see: Daniel J. Elazar, *People and Polity* (Detroit: Wayne State University Press, 1989), especially chap. 1; "Kinship and Consent in the Jewish Community: Patterns of Continuity in Jewish Communal Life," *Tradition* 14, no. 4 (Fall 1974): 63-79; and "Covenant as the Basis of the Jewish Political Tradition," *Jewish Journal of Sociology* (1978).

3. On the biblical roots of Reformed Protestantism, see: Daniel J. Elazar and John C. Kincaid, *The Covenant Connection: Federal Theology and the Origins of Modern Politics* (Center for the Study of Federalism, forthcoming); Perry Miller, *The New England Mind* (Cambridge, Mass: Harvard University Press, 1967); R. H. Murray, *The Political Consequences of the Reformation* (New York: Russell and Russell, 1960).

4. See, for example, John Calvin, *Institutes of the Christian Religion* 2 vols., trans. Henry Beveridge (London: J. Clarke, 1953); Robert McCune Kingdon, ed., *Calvin and Calvinism: Sources of Democracy?* (Lexington, Mass.: Heath, 1970); George Laird Hunt, ed., *Calvinism and the Political Order*. Essays prepared for the Woodrow Wilson Lectureship of the National Presbyterian Center (Philadelphia, Pa.: Westminster Press, 1965); John Knox, *The History of the Reformation of Religion in Scotland*, Introduction and Notes by William McGavin (Glasgow: Blackie, Fullarton, 1831); Roger Williams, *Experiments of Spiritual Life* (London, 1652; repr. Providence, S. S. Rider, 1863); Perry Miller, *Roger Williams; His Contribution to the American Tradition* (New York: Atheneum, 1970); Edmund Sears Morgan, *Roger Williams; the Church and the State* (New York: Harcourt, Brace & World, 1967); John Winthrop, *Winthrop's Journal "History of New England" 1630-1649*, ed. James Kendall Hosmer (New York: Barnes & Noble, 1953); Darret Bruce Rutman, *John Winthrop's Decision for America* (Philadelphia: J. B. Lippincott, 1975); and his other work *Winthrop's Boston; Portrait of a Puritan Town, 1630-1649* (Chapel Hill: University of North Carolina Press, 1965). On Ulrich Zwingli, see Rupert Eric Davies, *The Problem of Authority in the Continental Reformers; A Study in Luther, Zwingli and Calvin* (London: Epworth Press, 1946).

5. Althusius, Preface to the 3rd ed. In *The Politics of Johannes Althusius*, abridged and trans. Frederick S. Carney (Boston: Beacon Press, 1964), 10.

6. Cf. Patrick Reilly, "Three 17th Century German Theorists of Federalism: Althusius, Hugo and Leibniz." In a special issue of *Publius: The Journal of Federalism*, ed. David L. Schaefer, vol. 5, no. 3 (Summer 1976).

7. Carney, trans., *The Politics of Johannes Althusius*, 28.

8. Ibid.

9. *Dicaelogicae* I, 8.
10. Carney, trans., *The Politics of Johannes Althusius,* 28.
11. Ibid., 29.
12. Examples of this association can be seen in Acts 6:2f.; 12:12; 13:15, 27; 15:21; 28:23, 30f.; Matthew 4; 6:2; 10:24; 13; Exodus 29:42; Numbers 10:10.
13. Carney, trans., *The Politics of Johannes Althusius,* 29, nt. 3.
14. Ibid., 32.
15. Ibid.
16. Ibid.
17. Ibid., 29.
18. Ibid., 29-32.
19. Ibid., 32.
20. Ibid.
21. Ibid., xxii.
22. Ibid., 118.
23. Ibid., 134.
24. Ibid.
25. Ibid.
26. Ibid., 135.
27. Ibid.
28. Ibid., 139.
29. Ibid.
30. Ibid., 143.
31. Ibid., 117.
32. Ibid.
33. Cf. Donald Lutz and Jack D. Warden, *A Covenanted People: The Religious Traditions and the Origins of American Constitutionalism* (Providence: John Carter Brown Library, 1987). See also Daniel J. Elazar, *The American Constitutional Tradition* (Lincoln and London: University of Nebraska Press, 1987).
34. Carney, trans., *The Politics in Johannes Althusius,* 26-27.
35. Ibid., 14 *passim.*
36. Ibid., 42-43.
37. Ibid., 48.
38. Ibid., 56.
39. Ibid., 76.
40. Ibid., 75.
41. Ibid., 79-80.
42. Ibid., 170 *passim.*
43. On *mishpat hamlukhah,* see "King, Kinship: The Covenant of Monarchy," *Encyclopaedia Judaica* 10 (Jerusalem: Keter, 1972): 1019; see also Daniel J. Elazar and Stuart A. Cohen, *The Jewish Polity: Jewish Political Organization from Biblical Times to the Present* (Bloomington, Ind.: Indiana University Press, 1985), Part I, Epoch IV.
44. Otto von Gierke, *Johannes Althusius und die Entwicklund der naturrechtlichen Staatstheorem,* published in translation as *The Development of Political Theory* in 1939, and *Political Theories of the Middle Ages,* trans. with an Introduction F. W. Maitland (Cambridge, England: The University Press, 1900: reprinted 1968).
45. Carl J. Friederick, ed., *The Politica Methodice Digesta of Johannes Althusius* (Cambridge, Mass: Harvard University Press, 1932).
46. Carney, *The Politics of Johannes Althusius.*

7

Conclusion: Covenantal Space
in a Hierarchical World

The alliance between the Catholic Church and the Roman Empire that led to the triumph of Christianity in the fourth century C.E. more or less guaranteed that hierarchy would be the dominant mode of political organization in what came to be known as Christendom. The feudal age that followed was built on the hierarchical model that emerged out of the ruins of the Roman Empire and the triumph of the Roman Catholic Church. Hence, feudalism may have emerged as a functional response to the disorder that accompanied the decline of the empire, offering new means of protection for local populations facing anarchy and its deleterious consequences. But it was a hierarchy modified by oaths and pacts that reflected the practical weaknesses of those at the top of the pyramid to acquire power equivalent to their authority. These oath and pact arrangements left the feudal order in a somewhat ambiguous position, which helped keep covenantal ideas from being extinguished altogether.

The Church, which adopted the imperial system of hierarchy, not only endorsed but championed ever more hierarchical arrangements, fostering them wherever it could and associating the very spread of Christianity with the introduction or strengthening of hierarchical rule. Popes, cardinals, and bishops found it easier to live with emperors, princes, and counts than in a more egalitarian system. The end result well nigh eliminated liberty as well as equality, not only establishing the most rigid class system that Europe has ever known, but reducing freedom, both individual and communal, to a minimum.

Even so, true covenant ideas and practices somehow survived in the interstices of this hierarchical order or in spaces beyond its reach, or among populations not fully assimilated within it. Those survivals of covenant were in due course to influence medieval constitutionalism and finally to be instrumental in the breakdown of the medieval order through the Protestant Reformation.

We have seen how oath and pact societies survived beyond the boundaries of medieval Christendom, specifically in the Scandinavian north and in the British Isles. Strictly speaking, those societies were not covenantal. They belonged to an earlier precovenantal sociopolitical order that relied upon oaths and pacts to bind individuals and communities and provide for their governance. All were ultimately absorbed into Christian Europe through religious conversion, which brought with it social reorganization, emphasizing standard hierarchical arrangements. It was only where pagans or barely Christianized semipagans managed to flee beyond the reach of the Church, as in Iceland, that the pre-Christian oath and pact systems survived more or less intact until conquered by prince and church.

In some places a certain covenantal space was made available through an institution of the Church itself—the monastery. After all, Christianity did have a covenantal dimension even before it had a hierarchical one. As Catholicism became dominant in the West, there were those freer spirits who wanted to preserve a space for the covenanted community within the new Church framework. Initially, the monasteries, which were complete, permanent, and self-perpetuating bisexual communities that did not practice celibacy and encouraged family life, represented serious competition for Rome and its hierarchy. In time they were to be subdued and transformed into the austere, celibate institutions that we know today, but in the early Middle Ages they offered a way for certain oath and pact societies to become covenantal ones after Christianization. This was the case in Scotland and to some extent in the other Celtic borderlands of the British Isles.

These monasteries also played a role in carving covenantal space in the heart of Europe. The Irish-originated monks of St. Gallen helped transmit a more covenantal Christianity to those liberty-loving people who fled to the Swiss mountains and valleys to escape feudalism, and from there carved free covenantal space in the course of hundreds of years of warfare. For those people and others like them in other mountainous or coastal borderlands regions in Europe, the desire for liberty and equality went hand in hand and made covenantal organization a "natural" for them. So it was for the Helvetians and Rhateians of today's

Switzerland and with the Frisians and Nederlanders in today's Netherlands, as well as with little pockets in places like Andorra and San Marino. In each case the seekers of liberty and equality found ways to use covenantal devices to successfully manipulate their environment to achieve their ends.

A third form of covenantal space was carved within the interstices of the feudal system itself. Feudalism, after all, was not simply hierarchical. It consisted of a hierarchy of pacts and oaths. In some cases, in Aragon for example, the pacts and oaths considerably softened and even weakened the hierarchical element in the feudal system. In essence those arrangements were the functional equivalents in the civil polity of the monastic system in the religious.

Finally, at the same time that this mixed system produced medieval constitutional theories, it also produced the free or imperially chartered cities within the Holy Roman Empire, themselves unions of guilds that became spearheads in the growth of liberty through municipal institutions of self-government.

In truth, Western civilization is a combination of organic, hierarchical, and covenantal elements. During the Middle Ages the hierarchical element was by far the dominant one, but this did not mean that organic or covenantal elements totally disappeared, just as in the modern epoch the covenantal element was to become far more pronounced and in many cases even dominant without the hierarchical or organic elements disappearing.

The Sources of Covenant: Culture, Frontier, Borderlands

How, then, did the covenantal element survive and, equally important, how did it become strengthened over time to reemerge as so decisive a force in the Reformation? Three factors in particular were influential: (1) there appear to be certain peoples or cultural groupings that were more disposed to be covenantal or accept the covenantal modes; (2) confrontation with a land or sea frontier whose challenges or requisites for survival were greater equalization through pacts to establish agreed-upon systems of governance, with status and rewards given on the basis of achievement; and (3) prolonged contact between peoples and groups in borderlands regions where the differences between them would either lead to war or had to be harmonized by agreement.

The history of the survival of covenant in medieval Europe has the advantage of highlighting these three dimensions in an environment otherwise hostile to the covenantal tradition, allowing covenantal traditions to survive or covenantal patterns of behavior to emerge only where absolutely necessary as a result of culture or conditions. In the previous chapters we noted that the South Germans (Alemannians), Celts, Scandinavians, and Jews seemed to have a particular predilection for covenantal arrangements. This is not a suggestion of racial or ethnic determinism. What conditions lost in history generated that predisposition among those groups we do not know, but it must be more than coincidence that covenantal polities appear and reappear where those groups are concentrated.

Culture, however, is not enough. It must be reinforced by experience. The frontier, both as a wilderness that challenged human initiative and as a source of opportunity, was a major source of such experiences. For the Swiss that meant confrontation with the difficulties of living in the mountains and high mountain valleys; for the Norse it meant coping with the sea; for the Scots, survival on difficult soil in a difficult climate; for the Jews it meant coping with constant persecution, expulsions, and forced migrations, leading to the need to found new communities time and again. Each of these was a kind of frontier experience in the sense that it required a particular group of humans to cope with the wild or to rebuild themselves through the settlement of new territories. In no case were these frontiers to be conquered once and for all. Rather, they were permanent conditions of struggle that constantly upset old balances and required new ones to be established. Thus such static frontiers were for certain purposes more like borderlands except that, in all but the case of the Jews, the struggle was with nature rather than with other humans.

The most critical factor in the generation of covenantal ideas and behavior seems to have been the actual borderlands experience. In various parts of Europe, there were regions where different peoples came into contact and were forced to find a *modus vivendi* for common survival. Where those peoples had covenantal predispositions they turned in that direction for appropriate ideas, institutions, and procedures. As it happened, the great borderlands of Western Europe, running from Switzerland up the Rhine River Valley to the North Sea and across Britain, which had once marked the outer limits of the Roman Empire, were settled and populated by such groups who, when left alone to pursue their own bent, turned to covenantal arrangements to work out means of living together or, if necessary, defending themselves from one another.

Borderlands provided an environment that necessitated adaptation. In too many cases, however, borderlands contacts have led to perpetual conflict rather than institutional arrangements for conflict resolution. Thus, something special must be brought to a borderlands situation, at the very least a cultural predisposition toward covenantal arrangements as means for achieving appropriate conflict resolution and a predisposition on the part of those involved to accept and nurture that idea.

This was the situation that prevailed in the Rhine River valley and adjacent territories, the borderlands between Roman and Germanic Western Europe. Between the days of the Roman withdrawal and the Reformation this borderlands area continued to exist under a political-social order that reflected its borderlands character. We can find this distinctly in Carolingian times, when the empire of Charlemagne stretched from the Pyrenees and the Spanish marshes on the southwest to the eastern part of Germany on the east, from below Rome to Denmark, roughly the territory of the original European Community before its expansion through the accession of Great Britain and the Scandinavian countries, Spain, Greece, and eastern Germany.

In 843 that empire was divided into three parts by the Treaty of Verdun: the West Frankish kingdom granted to Charles the Bald, the first king of France; an East Frankish kingdom set aside for his brother, Louis the German, who could be described as the first king of Germany; and an area in between for a third brother, Lothar, who inherited the imperial crown of his father and the lands lying between France and Germany known as the Middle Frankish kingdom. That kingdom was renamed after Lothar, Lotharii Regnum, or Lotharingia, which became Lothringen in German, Lorrain in French. The Middle Frankish kingdom consisted of the three Benelux nations of today, the provinces of Lorrain, Alsace, Burgundy and Provence in France; Frisia, the whole west bank of the Rhine, and the eastern part of the Cologne area in Germany; Switzerland and the northern half of Italy—the heartland of federalist Europe then and now.

In 875 Lothar's son died childless so the middle territories were divided between the other two kingdoms, but since what had been the heartland of the middle kingdom were borderlands for the other two, neither France nor Germany were able to establish clear-cut rule over them. For a thousand years, throughout the Middle Ages and for some of them up to the eighteenth century, these lands were essentially self-governing, in some cases republics of farmers as in Switzerland, in others cities and counties controlled by burghers as in the Netherlands and along the Rhine, or city republics as in northern Italy. A few became formally independent. Others were nominally subject to feudal lords but were essentially self-governing.

Modern capitalism, as well as modern federalism, originated in this area, which stretched from Amsterdam to Siena. Over the years, various confederal arrangements emerged in the region as leagues or confederations. It was in this territory that sophisticated political theories were developed to justify republicanism, federalism, and capitalism. One sign of the borderlands character of this region was to be found in the fact that the confederations that emerged were multilingual and in some cases their member states were as well.

The political culture that developed out of all of this promoted noncentralization and even a great deal of localism. Moreover, this tradition was anchored in interpretations of Roman civil law that developed in the various polities within the region, different from English common law but also pointed toward constitutional order and a systematic legal system that could give rise in time to democratic republicanism. As Paul Belien, who has written about this phenomenon in connection with the formation of the European Union, has stated: "Thus federalism was born. It is almost a synonym of constitutionally guaranteed limited government, both at the local and at the highest federal level."[1]

Despite Belien's use of the terminology of "levels," his point is to make an argument that subsidiarity is not just for hierarchies but that its real meaning is federalist. "Power is delegated to the lowest possible level which can guarantee a decent civil order—and the lowest possible level of all is often the individual citizen."

Belien traces the beginnings of capitalism to the Netherlands, with the arrival of the Dutch in the New World to their colonization of the New Netherlands (now New York) along the Hudson River. He claims that federalist ideas also took root in these Dutch Reformed territories and discusses how those ideas came to be embodied in the U.S. constitution.

The Protestant Reformation brought about a fuller flowering of the federalist elements in what was once the Middle Frankish realm, but the climax of the modern epoch in the French Revolution and the Napoleonic Empire brought centralized statism to the fore within the region, most prominently in France and Prussia, each of which subdued their parts of the Rhine Valley. Only Switzerland fully returned to its own constitutional order after the Napoleonic Wars. The Netherlands and Belgium found a way to walk between the raindrops, creating what were centralized nation-states for external purposes but maintaining great decentralization through their respective provinces within them.

This dual tradition of federalism and capitalism survived 150 years of centralization to reemerge in part as the thrust for the European community. Belien states: "It is no coincidence either that virtually all the founding fathers of the EEC were people from the old middle Frankish kingdom. This applies even to Robert Schuman and Konrad Adenauer. Schuman was a Luxembourgian by birth who as a young man had settled in the neighboring region of Lorrain/Lothringen.... Adenauer regarded himself first and foremost as a Rhinelander—so much so that he once toyed with the separatist idea of establishing an autonomous Rhine-republic, independent of Germany." Belien continues: "The EEC did not start out as a combined initiative of France and Germany...it started out as a middle-Frankish venture. It wanted to check both French and German national ambitions as well as all tendencies toward state absolutism."

The Concretization of Covenantal Behavior: The Biblical Idea and the Limits of Barbarism

The history of every oath or pact society discussed in the previous pages tests the limits of barbarism when confronted by a civilization with a strong mobilizing set of beliefs. Those societies may have developed their tribal or social forms out of an oath and pact tradition but, when push came to shove, those forms were unable to stand up to the ideological onslaught of Christianity, with its concomitant political and social demands on behalf of a reordering of the polity and the society along hierarchical lines. Who today actively remembers the Norse oath societies or the Alemannian pacts? Whatever cultural traces they have left—and here we have suggested that they are not insignificant—they themselves have been forgotten even by their descendants, except for those who study the details of Scandinavian or Swiss history. Indeed, what is remembered about the Norsemen is precisely the least covenantal aspects of their behavior.

It took the combination of cultural tendencies and historical opportunities with a great and galvanizing idea to leave a concrete and conscious mark on world history and affairs. In the case of covenant, that idea was the biblical idea. Where it came into play, the impact of the covenantal tradition was much greater, reaching its climax in the Reformation, the greatest synthesis between the biblical idea and more mundane cultural and historical factors in the postbiblical history of the West. The Reformation shook the world to its very foundations, almost as much as did the original monotheistic revolution of biblical times. We are still living in its shadow and its influence, which became so powerful in the early modern age of revolutions, has not faded to this day.

It was the biblical idea that raised covenanting and its consequences from customary or conventional behavior to the ideologically right way of doing things, which linked the two powerful forces of religion and politics, uniting religious and political ideas to powerfully influence behavior in both spheres. It was the power of the biblical covenant idea that made Reformed Protestantism more of a world movement than Lutheranism or other manifestations of the religious Reformation.

The Uses of Covenant: Preserving and Fostering Liberty and Equality

Whatever its other uses, covenant was critical to the fostering and preservation of liberty and equality, whether of individuals, of groups, of territories, or of peoples, making it possible to establish relations among them by combining self-rule and shared rule, whereby each individual or entity preserves his or its integrity within a larger relationship. We have seen that this was true to a greater or lesser extent in every case discussed in this volume. In the best cases, liberty and equality were built into the collective expectations of the elements involved. Even where they were not, the end result was to enhance liberty and equality. Thus the nobles of Aragon and the barons of England acted to protect their liberties, yet, by extension, they also protected those of the other estates in both countries. Similarly, the citizens of the Swiss mountain republics preserved theirs by the enhancement of the liberty of their polities through their confederation against Hapsburg domination and the Netherlands provinces attained independence from Spain by banding together in their fight for local liberty. Even in the first two cases there was a measure of equality to be preserved and fostered.

Moreover, it was in the nature of the covenantal worldview that once equality was found for some, equality had to be found for others, if not for all. During the early and high Middle Ages the search for liberty or equality was partly deflected by the hierarchical canons of medieval thought and expectations. Later the same quest was influenced by the religious expectations of the Reformation. But in any case, both dimensions were always there.

What is characteristic of the covenantal approach as distinct from other kinds of pacts is the covenantal emphasis on the achievement of true liberty and equality within the framework of community while at the same time insisting that true community can only be a community that fosters liberty and equality. Throughout the period under consideration here, these issues were prominently raised in connection with the covenantal manifestations that we have noted. The Middle Ages, indeed, were a period when community was a principal theme, a goal to be pursued even at the expense of liberty and equality. During that period the covenantal answer was to insist that liberty and equality were major dimensions of the good community, just as in the modern and postmodern epochs, which have emphasized individual liberty and equality, the task before covenantal thinking has been to find a way to retain or adapt the possibilities for community within the framework of individualistic liberal democracy.

The political ideal of Western Europe was the Christian commonwealth. That ideal reached its apotheosis as a covenanted commonwealth in the years between 1517 and 1676 in those lands where the Reformed Protestant version of the Reformation held sway. The polity that was the Reformed Protestant commonwealth was founded or refounded by covenant or, more accurately, by a network of political, social, and religious covenants that bound its inhabitants together as neighbors and as citizens, animated by a common vision that the commonwealth was to serve. That vision, primarily religious, meant that the polity had to be secure for one religious community. Often no others were tolerated within it, but even where they were, they were tolerated on a limited basis since, by definition, they could not share the common religious vision that animated the commonwealth and whose fulfillment was its goal.

Like other Christian commonwealths, the Reformed Protestant commonwealth aimed at achieving solidarity and community as a primary political goal. Its policies were normative and its leaders and citizens expected them to be followed by all inhabitants. Any internal divisions were divisions that had somewhat different views of the common vision. Hence they were more camps than separate communities, divisions within the whole body politic rather than fragments of it.

The polity was conceived to be an educator, one of whose primary tasks was to educate the public within it as to the truth and the right path. Following that truth and right path was the basis for the solidarity sought through the common vision.

This polity made many contributions to the growth of liberty and equality in the West but its expectations of solidarity and common vision led it to reach its limits as the world became more pluralistic because of the opportunities that developed to do so. In the end, commonwealth was replaced by civil society, looser, more secular, less demanding, more individualistic, and governmentally neutral in matters deemed to be of private concern. Civil society was the modern answer to the perceived limitations of commonwealth. Developed as an idea in the seventeenth century, from the middle of that century onward, it was pushed forward to replace the commonwealth in the minds of the leaders of the people and did so. The ideas of covenant and the covenantal tradition, so central to the Reformed Protestant commonwealth, had to adapt themselves to the new thrusts of modernity. In this their way was eased by the fathers of the idea of civil society, who drew heavily on covenantal ideas and traditions to explain and justify their new invention. Their thought gave birth to the ideas and traditions of constitutionalism that connected covenant to the new realities, but that is another story.

Note

1. Paul Belien, "[T]hat Limited Government Works Best," *Wall Street Journal (Europe)* (9 June 1994): 6.

Excursis: Covenant versus Hierarchy
in Islam and Asia

In the West, covenant has been a dynamic founding principle. It may even be said that it is the West's most distinctive principle of religion and politics. One of the best demonstrations of this is to be found in the difficulties covenant ideas have had in Islam and their virtual essential absence from the lands and peoples east of the Fertile Crescent.

Islam: An Abortive Beginning

As the second great religion to emerge from Judaism, it is not surprising that Islam also has a covenantal dimension, albeit a very small and limited one. Islamic reliance on covenant (*mitha', 'ahd*) was particularly strong in its founding period when Muhammad, if not his successors, needed to mobilize consent to the new faith. Even Muhammad used it only as a compromise with the realities of ethnicity and kinship in his world, mobilizing covenant ideas only when the kinship of the Arabs was not enough to extend the scope of their consent to his new faith. Hence, it is not surprising that the covenant idea lost importance once those formative generations had passed.

Islamic covenantal doctrine emphasizes the covenants that Allah made with His earlier prophets—Noah, Abraham, Moses, and Jesus—before His Last and greatest Covenant with Muhammad. In each case, God sent a prophet with a revelation designed to establish a religion through a new covenant and the prophet was charged to witness it faithfully. Some 700 references to covenant themes appear in the Koran and the Islamic community is defined by many Muslim theologians as being constituted by those who have accepted Muhammad's Last Covenant with God. The principal terms of that covenant include: obedience to Allah's commands, particularly prayer; paying the *zakat* (a charitable head tax); belief in the messengers of Allah; fearing God alone; refraining from theft, adultery, murder, and false witness; showing kindness to parents; and striving in the cause of God ("Al-Jihad fi Sabil Allah" in the Koran) to spread Allah's will over the world.

Some have claimed that this doctrine was derived from actual covenantal acts creating the community of Islam during that religion's formative period. Through those acts, Muslims formally proclaimed their acceptance of Muhammad's message and swore oaths of loyalty to the new faith, accepting the basic obligations of Islam.

However, only Muhammad employed covenanting for political purposes, principally the covenant of Medina initiated by Muhammad after his flight from Mecca, while he was still weak. Ideas of civil covenanting and social contracting were later explored by such distinguished Islamic political philosophers as Alfarabi, whose works, among others, were read or known by European thinkers who contributed to the renaissance of political and social thought in the early modern era.[1] For the Muslims, however, they remained in the realm of ideas, insignificant ones at that.

The idea of covenant adapted from the Bible was compatible, to a degree, with indigenous Arab tribal traditions of contractual oath taking, which may date back to the very first periods of oaths and acts in the ancient Near East. Those oaths, which established associations and prevented blood feuds, involved pacts of collective responsibility and mutual accountability in which the group acquired rights *in rem* over its members.[2] However, most of these pacts appear to have been narrow in scope, more like treaties, and quite Hobbesian. A blood revenge "is the beginning of the most horrible condition the tribesmen can imagine." As one Bedouin explained to an observer: "Killing spreads like fire from one tribe to another. It can be the end of the world."[3]

Although this tradition of oath taking among tribes continues into the present in some areas, the importance of covenant as a theological and political concept declined sharply as Islam became more institutionalized after Muhammad and integrated with large-scale, often imperial, civil systems. The character of later Islamic political life, like that of medieval Christianity, became less covenantal and more feudal, to the point where covenant effectively disappeared.

The Problematics of Covenant in Islamic Political Thought

Islamic political thought begins with the premise that men are born free, that liberty is the natural condition of mankind, and that Muslims, those who accept Islam, submit (Islam means submission) to the will of God as conveyed by His greatest prophet, Muhammad, and written in the Koran. Thus, as in Judaism, men surrender some of their liberty to live under law.

The necessity to live in society requires the abridgement of man's original state of liberty. Leonna summarizes the Islamic position: "Islamic jurists have reached a two-fold conclusion: 1) liberty finds its limit in its very nature, because liberty unlimited would mean self-destruction—and that limit or boundary is in the legal norm or Law. 2) No limit is arbitrary because it is determined by its utility or the greatest good of the individual or of society. Utility, which is the foundation of law, traces also its boundary and extent."[4] Islamic jurisprudence is then "knowledge of the practical rules of religion," or as Ibn Khaldun put it, "the knowledge of the rules of God which concern the actions of persons who own themselves bound to obey the Law respecting what is required, forbidden, recommended, disapproved, or merely permitted."[5] This jurisprudence is known as *fiqh*, which together with the Sunna, the Koran, and the Traditions of the Prophet, builds the *shari'a* (the straight path).

To the greatest extent possible, that law is to be derived from the Koran and Muhammad's teachings, but interpretation of the law is required to apply it to society. In principle, Islamic law provides all that is necessary for the perfect society, but in practice the bare bones of the law have to be searched for that comprehensive scheme. This is the task of the *'ulama,* the interpreters of the law, and the result is embodied in the *shari'a,* the Islamic equivalent of the Jewish *halakhah.*

In the generations following the death of Muhammad, two principal sects and a number of smaller ones emerged within Islam, the Sunni and the Shi'i. Within Sunni Islam, the dominant sect, four schools of interpretation developed, each with its own sphere of influence. All these Sunni groups shared the same methodology, namely that the *shari'a* was to be built up through consensus, in this case the consensus of its legitimate interpreters.

This consensus is known as the *'ijma.* A decision regarding the *shari'a* determined by *'ijma* is binding and precedent setting. In practice over the years, the accumulating of *'ijma* decisions has drastically limited room for further decision making, leading to the official closing of the Gates of Ijtihad after the tenth century.

Parallel to this was the tribal system of the Arabs. Arab tribes were led by the *sayyid,* the chieftain of a tribe or agglomeration of tribes who held office through a combination of noble lineage and personal prestige. The *sayyid* came from one of the notable families but attained his office because of his leadership qualities, including his ability to conciliate the members of the tribe; formally he had no power of enforcement. He ruled by consensus building and his rule did not impinge upon the essential equality that prevailed among the members of the tribe. He had to be immediately accessible to his constituents. On the other hand, he was bound only by tribal custom and otherwise was free to decide all matters on a personal basis if he could muster support for his decisions.

All of this could have formed the basis for a covenantal approach. However, after a glimmer in the days of Muhammad, the first *caliphs* rejected the *sayyid* system in practice even if they claimed to maintain it in theory. In short order, all that was left was the dimension of personal rule without the restraints of face-to-face governance that maintained the *sayyid* as a consensual leader of equals. The Umayyad dynasty (661–750) is identified with this effort, but when the Umayyads gave way to the Abbasids, who gained the caliphate with the support of the Yaman Arab tribal bloc on a Shi'ite platform, kingship in the Eastern manner was introduced following Persian models.[6]

Instead, the realities of the preexisting political culture inherited from the imperial systems that the Arab conquerors replaced won out, no doubt aided by the fact that Muhammad himself was a single source of authority, unlike Moses who, even when he was God's prime minister, had to share authority with Aaron the priest, the elders of the tribes, and the people.

Muhammad himself determined that there would be no distinction between the temporal and the spiritual, not only in law but in leadership. After the death of Muhammad, who left no instructions regarding a successor, the *umma* was in a state of confusion. Out of the many different splinter groups that formed, each with its own beliefs regarding the identity and manner of selection of the ruler, two main streams emerged, which later crystallized into the *Sunna* and *Shi'ah*. The legitimate head of an Islamic state, according to the Sunnis, was the *caliph,* literally a replacement or substitute of the prophet in both spheres. Technically under such a system, there was no politics, only administration of the community of Allah, in other words a perfect hierarchical model.

Thus within the framework of Islamic law, hierarchy became the prevailing system of government. Oriental despotism was combined with the theocratic power granted to the representative of Allah. All pretense of choosing the ruler by consensus, as was the case with the *sayyid* and the tribe, was abandoned. Kingship became hereditary. Since the Abbasids were to rule the empire for the next five centuries, their way became the Islamic way.

The result was an immense gap between Islamic political theory and the actual practice of government and politics. The caliph is also known as the *imam*. In Sunni theory the imamate is an elective office that every Muslim male of good moral character, from the tribe of Quraish, possessing the knowledge and the judgement requisite to discern the qualities required in an imam, is qualified as an elector. The catch is that the only Muslims able to participate are those near the seat of the caliphate. Nor is there a clear rule as to how many must actually participate in the election. Apparently a minimum of five is satisfactory; others argue that three is sufficient and there is even a position that a single elector can designate the next *imam* if it is the right person. In other words, appointment and election were merged.

During the generations when the Islamic empire was at its height, the role of the *caliph* and his central administration varied. At times he and his ministers were able to maintain a more centralized imperial system and at other times the empire became a loosely linked group of provinces with local rulers asserting their authority. In a sense this paralleled the cyclical process of Bedouin tribal government, but like tribal government, the question of centralized or noncentralized government or confederation was based on the realities of the balance of power within the empire and was never constitutionalized. Within each province, of course, there was a replica of the caliphate, the provincial governor ruling as autocratically as his real or nominal master.

So centralized was the Islamic state in practice that while under Islamic law a *Qadi* or judge must be appointed in every community, in practice many of the early caliphs or provincial governors took the responsibilities of the *Qadi* for themselves along with the responsibilities of civil and religious rule for a complete centralization of the three great

functions of government. Even where separate judgeships were be-
stowed, the judges were so subordinate to the rulers that they rarely
were in a position to resist the ruler's will if and when asserted.
Grunebaum calls the result "theocratic authoritarianism," which led in
time to widespread bribery and corruption and an absolute destruction
of any sense of civic responsibility.

This decay began as early as the ninth century and by the middle of
the tenth century was complete. Having no covenant, there was no constitution; having no constitution, there was no way to distinguish between tyranny and legitimate rule, even if the tyrant had seized power
rather than ascending to the throne legally. By the eleventh century Islamic political theorists began to accommodate their theories to the new
reality, accepting bad government as better than no government at all.
What resulted was, in Grunebaum's words, "utter hopelessness and resignation" in matters political. Ibn Jima, the Qadi of Damascus, put it in
the following words at the beginning of the fourteenth century: "The
sovereign has a right to govern until another and stronger one shall oust
him from power and rule in his stead. The latter will rule by the same
title and will have to be acknowledged on the same grounds; for a government, however objectionable, is better than none at all; and between
two evils we must choose the lesser."[7]

Although the tribal oaths and pacts and *shari'a* became increasingly
incompatible, the Bedouin tribes have continued to maintain their ways
to this day. For example, in the law of the tribes of the Yemen there is
the key principle of *hilf* or *tahaluf,* an alliance based on mutual oath.[8] In
the Bani Murad tribe, *hilf* is described as a matter of "deep feelings,"
and anyone who violates the alliance or the oath will be ostracized by
the entire tribe. A partner to a *hilf* is called a *halif.* To be a *halif* is to be
allied with the other partners "like a kinsman," gaining protection and
sharing in collective responsibility with one's allies, including the allied tribes. It is a sacred duty to protect a *halif* except when he commits
major crimes or treason.

Thus the tribal system combines ties of actual kinship and *tahaluf* or
alliance, which creates artificial kinship. Since protection is the central
idea in the moral world of the tribesman, the extension of the obligation
of protection from the primary group to embrace *halif* (an ally), and for
that matter clients (*gar*), becomes the principle of *tahaluf* and provides
what Obermayer describes as "a political bond between men who can-

not otherwise justify it on the basis of common blood, kinship." Obermayer continues: "This tribal principle was perceived by the Prophet himself as the hallmark of the tribal man and one which it is said that he opposed: 'There is no *ḥilf* in Islam.'"⁹

In the Yemen this system carried beyond individual tribes or tribal confederations to the countrywide arena, with each *imam* gaining office through the traditional procedure of *Shiʾi zaidi* succession. To become *imam* the religious and tribal notables had to swear an oath of allegiance (the *baiʾa*). This could occur only after the candidate, who must be a descendant of the Prophet's daughter Fatima, had proved himself on the battlefield as a *mujahid,* that is to say, a successful conductor of a *jihad,* and by demonstrating his intellectual capacity to reason before a board of *ʾulama.* This system continued to function through the succession of Yahya, the sixty-fifth Imam, in 1904.

This is an oath that is more reminiscent of feudalism than of covenantalism since once chosen from the royal family, the *imam* organizes the polity on a strictly hierarchical basis in the Islamic manner.¹⁰ Yahya, who ruled until 1948, went further than the traditional hierarchical pattern through an attempt to build a modern state with a strong standing army and bureaucracy, an extensive system of taxation, and an ideology justifying his efforts, doing so precisely because his predecessors had only a tenuous control over the country that rested upon tribal loyalty. This transformation, which has been characteristic of other newly emergent Arab states, was modified by the *imam's* maintenance of the patriarchal style of being personally available for judging and much "hands-on" contact with his subjects, but in fact it was the new hierarchy of statism fit relatively comfortably within the traditionally hierarchical forms of Muslim rule.

In Egypt's western desert, a covenant of blood responsibility is the equivalent compact of mutual accountability.¹¹ It is known as the *ʾaqila* (plural *ʾawaqil*). It is a compact of mutual accountability whose adherents share equally in the responsibility to pay blood money and as required to support a fellow member in litigation. It is formed by oath (*yamin*). These *ʾawaqil* have become well defined and quite explicit over the years and serve as the basis for establishing relationships with other groups. Once again there is some combination of kinship and consent since the groups related through compact are usually but not always related through some immediate ancestor. The formal agreements themselves are referred to as *ittifaq al-'awaqil,* or the agreement of the leaders. These contractual political relationships are spread throughout the western desert and Cyrenaica where all the Bedouin tribes are linked through one loosely connected political system.[12]

Politics and power in this Bedouin society are determined by the interplay of kinship ties and covenantal bodies. The office of *aqila* is the channel through which formal litigation is conducted. There is also a channel for arbitration through the *rajal khair* (good man) and there is a certain competition for power between the *aqila* and the *rajal khair,* although at times the *aqila* can go to the *rajal khair* along with the litigating parties to secure binding arbitration.

The importance of this kind of oath is that someone accused of thievery or some other serious crime can swear that he did not commit the crime, and if he is backed by his *aqila,* who will swear accordingly, he is considered innocent. At least in modern times this has enabled guilty parties to go free, leading to a challenge to the system by some of the more forward-looking leaders.

Since these are pre-Islamic, they are covenants only in the sense that at one time the old gods were witnesses to them. Today they are better described as compacts or even contracts involving a minimum of Divine intervention, only that having to do with swearing a false oath.

The formal procedures for oath taking to settle disputes presumably are designed to overcome this by requiring different numbers of supporters to swear the oath along with the accused. Thus in the case of homicide or wounding, fifty supporters are required to swear. Only twenty-five are required in cases involving the rightful ownership of land or a water well. In cases of conflicting claims over a camel, only five are needed to swear and even fewer for smaller animals (e.g., sheep). The swearing of the oath always takes place at a sacred place, often at the tomb of a holy man or at the mosque in the nearest town. As Obermayer puts it, "The oath is all at the same time a show, a show-up, and a show-down." The oath is always sworn on Friday from a standard text that must be recited from memory. An oath taker who forgets the text or faulters in repeating it is considered to have failed in the oath taking (i.e., that God has caused him to fail the test). Part of the oath includes a curse, for false swearing. Oath taking is regulated by the *rawabit* or *'ittifaq,* the first translated as "bonds" and the second as "covenant," which explicitly established the obligations of oath taking. These covenants serve as "the written moral charters which bind together smaller kinship groupings into larger lineage alliances."[13]

The political demands based upon kinship and alliance, that is to say, 'asabiyya and tahaluf, probably were connected with tawaghit, swearing before the traditional gods. Classic Islam understands that as taghut, namely, the worship of false idols. Hence Islam strove to replace tribalism with the principle of the umma and the shari'a but tribal peoples continued to view the two as being in harmony regardless of orthodox Islamic doctrine.

Obermayer suggests that Islam placed the shari'a in opposition to the taghut more on political than religious grounds, that is to say, claiming that the taghut interfered with the development of an Islamic umma by maintaining tribalism rather than by fostering idolatry. Hence it was possible to harmonize customary law (man') with the shari'a where tribalism continued to exist without falling into idolatry per se. At the very least, however, the Muslim ulama believe that mu'ahi, which are certain forms of compacts that are made in secret and may involve actually mixing blood, are to be considered taghut in the sense of unlawful idolatry.

Only in the twentieth century, after Islamic theologians were exposed to Western theology, most of these by living in the West, has the covenant idea been revived within a segment of Islamic thought. Today there are a number of Islamic theologians and scholars who search the religion's classic texts for indications of covenant, which they are bringing into a more substantial theological position.

Even more to the point, covenant is acquiring a new political significance in Islam as efforts to reform the polities and economies of the Islamic world are phrased in covenantal terms, often as an effort to reassert the rule of Islamic principles in Muslim lands to the exclusion of foreign ideologies. Perhaps the most prominent public examples of this are al mithaq (the covenant), the ideological statement issued in the name of the Egyptian revolution by Gamal Abdel Nasser in 1962, which proclaimed the principles of Nasserism to the Arab world, and the covenant of the Palestine Liberation Organization adopted in 1964. Both seek to present modern visions of the relationship between Islam and the sociopolitical or the economic order.[14] Neither are covenants in the sense that the term has been used in this volume, but both use the term to give weight to the documents.

Similarly, a full-page ad appeared in the *International Herald Tribune* of Thursday, 19 June 1986 under the title "In the name of Allah the Beneficent, the Merciful, Dar Tadine Al Umma Limited, Covenant and Call to Ummat Al Islam, from the Honorary Founders of Dar Tadine Al Umma, a pan-Islamic group of economic enterprises and financial institutions for mining gold and silver, organized on Islamic principles, to provide a proper Islamic fiscal base for the Muslim states."

Unfortunately, the revival of covenant as a political instrument in contemporary Islam is mostly reflected in its dark side in such documents as the Palestinian National Covenant dedicated to the destruction of the State of Israel, adopted in 1964, and the Covenant of Hamas, the Islamic resistance movement, adopted in August 1988 to provide a fundamentalist reinforcement of the extreme anti-Israel position. Unlike the Palestinian National Covenant, which at least tries to separate Israel and the Jews, albeit artificially, the Hamas covenant is openly anti-Jewish, referring to the Jews as "the accursed of Allah." In other words, covenantalism in contemporary Islam seems to be going the way of similar phenomenon in Nazi Germany and Afrikaner nationalist South Africa, to be used as a device to morally legitimize the destruction or repression of one's enemies rather than as a means to morally elevate one's own community.

What is characteristic of Islamic "covenants" is that they are not true covenants at all, but hierarchical documents handed down by the ruler at the top of the political pyramid as a kind of beneficence to the ruled below him on the pyramid. Perhaps they are referred to as covenants because they represent beneficence rather than brute displays of force and as such demand some kind of response from the recipients.[15]

"Covenants" with "Peoples of the Book"

There was one other way in which Islam applied the idea of covenant; there, too, in an ambivalent, half-way manner, and that was in relation to non-Muslim ethno-religious communities that fell under Islamic rule without accepting the new faith. The first conquests of the new religion were complete; that is to say, the Arab peoples either accepted Islam or were exterminated by the newly faithful. However, once the victorious Islamic armies left the desert and began to conquer the areas of older civilization in the Fertile Crescent, they could neither convert all of the inhabitants, nor could they exterminate them, either because there were too many or they were necessary for the maintenance of commerce and the economy.

Accommodating to necessity, the eighth-century Caliph Umar II, the only pious Muslim among the Ummayads, resolved the problem by essentially limiting the Prophet's injunction not to take Jews or Christians as friends, by designating them "peoples of the Book," that is to say, other religions that are based on Scripture. On that basis, he entered into a protective treaty or covenant with them, through which they renounced certain rights in order to gain protection and the right to practice their religion and customs. This is the so-called "covenant of 'Umar." In fact, there was no single covenant, but rather many individual covenants with local communities as the conquest progressed, which together established an arrangement that held until modernization.

The "people of the Book" are referred to as *dhimmi,* each individual referred to as a *dhimma.* The covenant or protective treaty is not generous since Jews and Christians must pay tribute out of hand and accept "humiliation," must protect and assist Muslims who come to them, and must conduct their prayers in a quiet and inoffensive manner. They were forbidden to build any new churches or synagogues or even to repair old ones. Christians were forbidden to show crosses on their churches and there could be no praying by *dhimmi* in a Muslim quarter. They had to dress differently and could not prevent any of their members or families from converting to Islam if they so chose. Their houses had to be lower than Muslim houses and they could not ride horses lest they rise above Muslims. They were not allowed to possess weapons (specific Jewish communities from time to time won the great privilege of exemption from this clause as a result of services rendered). In general they had to show their submissiveness to their Muslim hosts.[16]

Formally, Jewish and Christian communities requested these covenants. In fact they had no choice. On the other hand, their formal restrictions often were bent more liberally in practice to the extent that in any particular country, "the people of the Book" were needed for government service, as physicians, or for commerce. The advantage of these treaties to the minorities was that they were able to maintain their autonomy as ethno-religious communities. Von Grunebaum describes them as "having more or less the status of crown colonies in our day."[17]

Covenant in Islam: An Assessment

The question may be posed as to what extent is covenant a serious tradition in Islam and to what extent is it simply a practical means of dealing with non-Muslims located in polities under Islamic rule who must be dealt with in some way? The answer to this question is not at all clear. On one hand, Islam sprung from Arab tribal society, a society that had a certain contractual dimension in the sense that the Bedouin tribes were essentially confederations of clans. On the other hand, after Islam became institutionalized, rule became very hierarchical. Even in the first case, the clan confederations were justified by the Bedouin themselves through the invention of putative common ancestors. Thus a tribal confederation could be known as *bani Yusuf* or *bani Ya'qub*, with the idea that the clans had Yusuf or Ya'qub or whoever as a common ancestor, hence the ties between them. By the same token the hierarchical Islamic government was formally and to no small extent practically bound by Islamic law. For Muslims the ideal commonwealth was that which had existed during the ten years of Muhammad's prophecy and in the thirty years following until his successors had completed the first stage of Islamic institutionalization. Under the Ummayads, the first dynasty of Islamic rulers, the old tribal system intersected with the new Islamic imperial polity that was to become the caliphate. It was possible that in that period there was some synthesis between the rather casual system of tribal confederations masquerading as extended families and the more structured political system. If there was, there is no significant echo of it in subsequent Islamic literature. Instead, the Islamic imperial polity, following the hierarchical tendencies implicit in the Islamic view of law and society, became a very rigid hierarchy based upon the principle that the world is Allah's garden, that Allah both rules and governs His garden, but delegates the powers of administering it to his caliph who redelegates them to subordinate officials, that the caliph to maintain the garden requires taxes, that the people must obey the caliph in return for the privilege of living in the garden and pay the taxes to him so that he may maintain it. All that remained of the older political organization was what survived in the Bedouin tribes living at the peripheries of the Islamic empires but retaining a special status, at least in the minds of the Arabs, as the desert folk who lived as Muhammad had lived.

It seems that the peoples among whom Islam took root were simply not open to covenantal ideas, having had no previous relevant tradition, while Islam itself had too ambiguous a covenantal dimension to become the transformatory instrument in this respect that it was with respect to monotheism. Covenant remained at most a minor chord in Islamic thought, but no more.

Among the Arabs of today, the Bedouin heritage is most reflected in the combination of fragmentation and striving for national unity that has been characteristic of the Arab nation in modern times. One Islamic scholar has referred to the Arabs as by nature a federal nation, preserving their separate countries (*watani*) while striving for the unification of the *umma al'Arabi*, the Arab nation. Be that as it may, many attempts at actually establishing and maintaining federal regimes in the Arab world have come to naught, whether internal federations such as that of Libya after its liberation from Italian colonial rule after World War II or efforts at federation or union of existing Arab states such as the United Arab Republic or various North African efforts. Most have been foreign impositions by colonial powers either during their rule or as they departed, or the whim of one powerful local leader seeking to extend his rule beyond his own country.

The one successful exception is the United Arab Emirates, a federation of seven sheikhdoms along the Persian Gulf. What characterizes the UAE as a polity is that it has translated Bedouin confederal principles into the modern world. Its political ends are limited, its powers are divided among the seven sheikhs, and its overarching structure is minimal. The success of the UAE seems to suggest that there is a strain in Arab political culture that can sustain federal arrangements provided that they are in tune with that political culture that apparently rests upon older Bedouin notions of pact and oath to some degree.

Covenant in Baha'i: An Extension of the Islamic Worldview

The birth in mid-nineteenth century Persia of Baha'i, an Islamic heresy with the same universalist aspirations but in a less militant way, offered another opportunity for covenant ideas to surface in the Islamic culture area. The Baha'i faith was strongly influenced by nineteenth-century notions of a world order. Its principal prophet, Baha'u'llah, emphasized that the unity of the human race required the establishment of a world commonwealth to unite all nations, races, creeds, and classes. Expected to be a permanent federal union of states, it was to have a world legislature, a world executive, international peace-keeping force, and a world tribunal.

The Baha'i belief that Jesus has returned in the manifestation of Baha'u'llah leads them to believe that the Kingdom of God will be established gradually on earth though humanitarian pursuits and that God has given man that task. Baha'i doctrine sees the Kingdom as coming in three stages: the first, a period of social breakdown and widespread suffering; the second, known as the "lesser peace," will involve the restoration of social order and the cessation of war, essentially a political peace described by the Baha'i prophet 'Abdu'l-Baha as the sovereigns of the world concluding a binding treaty and establishing the great covenant:

> All the forces of humanity must be mobilized to ensure the stability and permanence of this Most Great Covenant. In this all-embracing Pact, the limits and frontiers of each and every nation should be clearly fixed, the principles underlying the relations of governments towards one another definitely laid down, and all international agreements and obligations ascertained.... The fundamental principle underlying this solemn Pact should be so fixed that if any government later violate one of its provisions, all the governments on earth should arise to reduce it to utter submission, nay the human race as a whole should resolve, with every power at its disposal, to destroy that government.[18]

A third and final stage, the "most great peace," will coincide with the emergence of the Baha'i world order, when all acknowledge the faith of Baha'u'llah. The administrative order of the Baha'i faith is organized as the embryonic form of this future world order. Its institutions and laws, according to Bahai leader Shoghi Effendi, "are destined to be a pattern for future society, a supreme instrument for the establishment of the Most Great Peace, and the one agency for the unification of the world, the proclamation of the reign of righteousness and justice upon the earth."[19]

"Then will the Everlasting Covenant be fulfilled in its completeness. Then will the promise enshrined in all the Books of God be redeemed and all the prophecies uttered by the Prophets of old come to pass and the vision of seers and poets be realized."[20] This is known as the special covenant of Baha'u'llah.

There is much in the foregoing description that reflects the Bedouin approach to peace pacts among families and tribes writ large, but with the added dimension of religious reinforcement absent in classical Islam, which, as we have seen, essentially opposed the old tribal order as resting on idolatrous foundations. The Baha'i religion has remained a small faith on the world scene, intensely persecuted in its Iranian homeland. In the West it has attracted a handful of adherents, who have found in it a kind of post-Christian universalism that does not contradict their Christian principles in the new faith. It can fairly be said that Baha'i has no real presence in Asia or the Islamic world. Its world headquarters are in Haifa, Israel, a covenantal faith returned to the homeland of covenant, remaining as close as possible to its original environment but forced to seek the protection of the heirs of the original covenant.

Asia East of the Fertile Crescent: A Continent without Covenant

East of the lands of the Semites there is no serious evidence of covenantal thinking and even oath societies are subordinated to Asian imperialism, the normal way of governance then and now on that vast continent. Asia, like Africa, follows the hierarchical model of polity building, beginning with the vitally important role of conquest in political organization. At the most, the conquest is mitigated by the prior existence of kinship groups, which are recognized by each succeeding conqueror as entitled to preserve their own ethnocultural integrities. Indeed, Asian imperialism is softened by this common recognition of the permanence of peoples, a permanence that transcends states or empires. The products of conquest come and go. Peoples or ethnic groups seem to survive forever. What is missing in that constellation is covenant, which is why Oriental despotism has become the best descriptor of politics and society on that continent.

Covenant ideas are of central importance only in the religions stemming from the biblical tradition. It is true that other religions have provisions for oaths in which gods are invoked to guarantee promises, but those are essentially private or limited oaths and do not constitute a covenantal tradition, only the primordial reality of people having to make pacts with one another in order to act together. At the same time, early Iranian religion did have Mithra as a god of covenant, a god reflected in Hindu religion as Mitra-Varuna, a term that means "friend" in old Persian. Originating as a minor figure in Zoroastrian religion, in the fifth century B.C.E. he became the chief Persian god.

Mitra-Varuna was far less significant in Hindu religion. In the Hindu system Mitra is the god of light, the meaning of his name in Sanskrit. In

Zoroastrianism he plays the same role, but is also the guardian of oaths and the protector of the righteous in both this world and the next. As the arch-foe of the powers of evil and darkness, Mithra became the god of battles. As it acquired its more universal form, it emphasized the mysteries absorbed from Babylonian cults. The equality of all worshippers and the vigorous positive morality that characterizes Mithraism throughout its history may attest to some covenantal basis.

Mithraism soon spread into Mesopotamia and Armenia and then into the Roman Empire, to become a worldwide religion. By the second century of the Common Era, it was one of the great religions of the Roman Empire, far more widespread than Christianity. By that time, if not earlier, it was a mystery faith, although it had rigorous ethics emphasizing covenant loyalty. Baptism, and a sacred banquet, may have had covenantal associations in Mithraism.

Practically speaking, the closest examples of covenantal polities were the tribal federations or confederations in the foothills of the Himalayas. Significantly, Gautama Buddha (c. 563–483 B.C.E.) found his inspiration in those hill tribes and they are the only peoples in the Indian subcontinent who took his message en masse. To the best of this writer's knowledge, the covenantal federal character of those tribes and its moral-religious implications has never been studied. Hence very little can be said about the phenomenon, other than to note it is a possible byroad of covenantalism.

Basically, India was a subcontinent of empires, albeit often very decentralized ones. Even those invading groups such as the Bactrian tribes and the Greeks who initiated their presence in India in some other way, through tribal regimes or city-states, were soon either swallowed up or transformed by the Indian tendency to imperialism, tempered by lack of roads.

The closest the Chinese have ever come to constitutionalized power sharing is through feudalism in situations where kings had strong vassals and had to share powers with them. The emergence of the Chinese state between 1500 and 1000 B.C.E. occurred within this kind of feudal framework, under the Shang Dynasty. It continued between 1000 and 770 B.C.E. with the Western Chou Dynasty, after which the feudal lords became almost completely independent. From 770 to 256 B.C.E., under the Eastern Chou Dynasty the kings were essentially figureheads, with the country divided into local principalities in which

Biographies to read

Abraham	Kuyper
Ulrich	Zwingli
John	Calvin
John	Knox
Heinrich	Bullinger
	Bede